D1266102

The Watchful State

The Watchful State

Security Police and Opposition in Russia 1906–1917

WITHDRAWN

Jonathan W. Daly

NORTHERN ILLINOIS UNIVERSITY PRESS | DEKALB

© 2004 by Northern Illinois University Press

Published by the Northern Illinois University Press, DeKalb, Illinois   60115

Manufactured in the United States using acid-free paper

All Rights Reserved

Design by Julia Fauci

Library of Congress Cataloging-in-Publication Data

Daly, Jonathan W.

The watchful state : security police and opposition in Russia, 1906–1917 /
Jonathan W. Daly.— 1st ed.

    p.   cm.

Includes bibliographical references and index.

ISBN 0-87580-331-8 (hardbound : alk. paper)

1. Secret service—Russia. 2. Police—Russia. 3. Internal security—Russia. I. Title.

HV8224.D32 2004

363.28'3'094709041—dc22

2004004279

For my parents

CONTENTS

LIST OF FIGURES

- The Russian poet Aleksandr Blok concluded from his study of police files in 1917 that the security police were Russia's "only properly functioning institution." Police reports throughout 1916, he wrote, "give a good characterization of the public moods; they are full of alarm, but the dying regime could not hear their loud voice any more."[1] It would be hard to encapsulate better the key issues I address in this book: the efficiency and effectiveness of Russia's security police, and their role during the constitutional period.

The security police were undoubtedly efficient, despite relatively modest funding, an inadequate number of security policemen given the huge population and territory, and often incompetent, or at least poorly trained, middle- and even upper-level officials. Even the least adept security policemen managed to keep under their watchful eye a large proportion of radical political activists, while the handful of dedicated, experienced, skillful security officers consistently thwarted revolutionary plots and laid snares for conspirators. All of the security police institutions gathered masses of data, and specialized officials in St. Petersburg carefully and intelligently analyzed the data to prepare detailed political surveys, timely warnings, and operational directives. One could well marvel at the system's efficiency.

Yet was it effective? Throughout most of the constitutional period the revolutionary underground suffered continuous assault and organizational disruption at the hands of the police. We can never know how many times Russia narrowly escaped political breakdown thanks to the thwarting of a political assassination, a troop mutiny, or an act of mass protest. Yet after their arrest and their exile or imprisonment, revolutionary activists repeatedly managed to escape and begin their work anew. I. V. Stalin, who himself fled captivity five times, marveled "at the toothless way the tsarist regime struggled with its 'gravediggers.'"[2] Such dedicated revolutionaries, joined by those whom the police were leaving at liberty while gathering evidence against them and by the quiet ones who avoided police detection altogether, continued to carry out their propaganda work, steadily and assiduously undermining the government's legitimacy.

The greatest threat to the imperial government ultimately may have come from popular discontent and the organized educated public, in the face of whose massive expansion Russia's tiny security police force stood like a pitiful scarecrow in a vast field. The security police apparatus was neither intended to nor equipped to enforce political conformity or to suppress mass unrest. Since large-scale political activism nearly toppled the imperial government in 1905 and actually did so in 1917, one could argue that Russia needed a radically different security apparatus during the constitutional era, a more aggressive, better-funded force with a broader mandate to disrupt the potentially subversive endeavors of liberal and moderate activists. Although some senior officials, and probably the emperor himself, would have favored such a course, most of Russian senior officialdom advocated strengthening the rule of law, expanding civil rights or at least respecting existing rights, and continuing down the path of Europeanization on which Russia had embarked in the time of Peter the Great.

For these reasons and others, Russia's security police were restricted to matching wits with genuinely subversive conspirators who wreaked violence and incited mass constituencies to unrest and rebellion and to watching and reporting on, with increasing concern, the broader public alienation from the government. When during the World War a few bold security officers sought permission to arrest liberal political figures—some of whom took posts in the Provisional Government following the collapse of the monarchy—they met with rebuke. Still, although the security police rarely harassed liberal and moderate activists during the constitutional era, the regular administration often did so, sometimes with abandon, especially in the provinces. Moreover, both elements of the repressive apparatus continuously worked together and through each other. They formed, to a large extent, a political security system with one primary goal: to maintain the political status quo and to thwart social and political elements seeking to undermine it. For this reason, repression applied by broader officialdom receives significant attention in these pages, to illustrate more clearly the highly specific, generally efficient actions of Russia's security police.

It was impossible before the opening of the Russian archives in 1989 to undertake a serious study of the pre-1917 security police. Happily, despite the destruction of some police records, including a large proportion of the regular criminal files, most of Russia's pre-1917 police records remained intact, unlike those in the United Kingdom and imperial Germany.[3] Since the fall of Communism in Russia, three monographs illuminating the history of the last decades of Russia's security police have appeared, but each addresses only discrete topics, and none tells its story in a comprehensive, chronological fashion.[4] The present study aims to fill this important historiographical gap by carrying forward in time the comprehensive treatment of the Russian security police provided in my first book, *Autocracy under Siege*. The introduction of the present volume provides an overview of that earlier study for readers unfamiliar with it.

Autocracy under Siege tells the story of the rise and development of fanatical conspirators and mass opposition movements in Russia, of the government's failure to cope with them, and of the government's near collapse in 1905. The present monograph chronicles major reforms of the security police apparatus, its crushing of the revolutionary opposition, and its coming to terms with the expansion of civil society. The government during most of the constitutional period was no longer under siege, having mastered the political opposition, or so it seemed, through repression and the making of concessions. It might have appeared in early 1914 that the political security system would preserve the political establishment against all possible assaults, but two and one-half years of wrenching warfare and the attendant social pressures overwhelmed both police and administration, and the old political order was swept away in February 1917. The new government quickly dismantled the entire political security system, laying itself open to massive political subversion.

▪ ▪ ▪

For carefully reading part or all of my manuscript and offering invaluable advice and criticism, I am grateful to John Bushnell, Philip Devenish, Gregory Freeze, Marc Raeff, Richard Robbins, Leonid Trofimov, Sofia Villafuerte, and William Wagner. My thanks also to Stephen Wiberley and the library staff at the University of Illinois at Chicago, the staff at the Slavic Reference Service at the University of Illinois at Urbana-Champaign, Ronald M. Bulatoff of the Hoover Institution Archives, Molly Molloy of the Hoover Institution Library, and Zinaida Ivanovna Peregudova of the State Archive of the Russian Federation for expert bibliographical and archival assistance, and to Vladimir Marinich for kindly sharing with me his knowledge and artifacts relating to his grandfather, I. K. Globachev.

Several of my research trips to Moscow were made possible by grants from the International Research and Exchanges Board (IREX), with funds provided by the National Endowment for the Humanities and the United States Information Agency. Additional research in Moscow was generously funded by the Campus Research Board and the Office of the Vice-Chancellor for Research of the University of Illinois at Chicago. I am especially thankful to the Harry Frank Guggenheim Foundation for supporting this book's beginnings and to the Institute for the Humanities of the University of Illinois at Chicago for enabling me to devote half a year to completing this book. None of these organizations is responsible for the views expressed.

■ ■ ■

Unless otherwise indicated, all dates appear in Old Style. The Julian calendar, in use in Russia until February 1918, lagged behind the Gregorian calendar by twelve days in the nineteenth century and thirteen days in the twentieth. Russian words and most names have been transliterated according to Library of Congress conventions minus the diacritical marks.

The Watchful State

INTRODUCTION

■ Russia's first modern police force, made up of the Third Section and its Gendarme Corps, was created in 1826 in response to the Decembrist Uprising of the year before. Nicholas I deployed them to conduct surveillance over high society, the masses, and his own bureaucracy. The Third Section was not at first an unpopular institution, but repression spurred by the wave of European revolutions in 1848 gave it an unsavory, fearful reputation. When it failed to avert an attempt on Alexander II's life in 1866, when it stumbled upon S. G. Nechaev's terrorist conspiracy in 1871, when thousands of youths fanned out into the countryside to propagandize the peasant masses in the early 1870s, and when systematic political terrorism broke out later in the decade, the government essayed diverse measures to reassert its mastery of the political scene. In 1866 a bureau for security policing was created in St. Petersburg to deploy specialized agents and to foil terrorist plots. A year later the Gendarme Corps was reorganized and expanded. In 1871 gendarmes gained the power to conduct investigations into state-crime cases. On this basis alleged criminals could receive administrative punishments, including administrative exile; this marked a partial return to pre-reform arbitrary justice. Finally, in 1880 a second security bureau was established, in Moscow, and the Third Section was abolished and replaced by an integrated police agency, the Police Department of the Interior Ministry. Russia no longer had an autonomous security policing institution.

Despite all these changes, the security service remained ill-suited to combating the rising tide of revolutionary activism. By the late 1870s, the Russian government faced a tightly organized, highly disciplined band of almost religiously devoted crusaders with whom the public tended to sympathize.

It is not surprising, then, that the government, in a manner not unlike its counterpart in Berlin in the same era, empowered administrative officials to detain, fine, and impose a range of other punishments without judicial oversight. The most notorious empowering legislation was the security law of 14 August 1881, adopted in the wake of the assassination of Alexander II. Popular legends and scholarly arguments to the contrary, this law actually systematized the existing emergency legislation and *curtailed* administrative power. It certainly did not innovate: its most weighty provision, administrative exile for a period of up to five years, had already been formally instituted in 1871.[1] Officials disagreed about the effectiveness of administrative exile. In 1903, P. I. Kutaisov, the governor general of eastern Siberia, complained to Interior Minister V. K. Plehve that it merely "spreads revolutionary ideas all over Russia." I. F. Koshko, another senior provincial official, found that exile to remote rural areas acted like a "cold shower" on revolutionary activists who had great trouble getting peasants to listen to them.[2] There is no doubt, however, that the practice alienated the educated public.

Several other measures enabled the police to crush the budding opposition in the 1880s. A secret directive of 5 June 1882 expanded and systematized "perlustration," that is, the interception of personal correspondence. This strategy henceforth targeted far broader segments of the population than did the work of the relatively small security police force. Also, a security bureau was established in Paris in 1884 to keep track of Russia's revolutionary émigrés. The simultaneous tightening of censorship probably struck a weightier blow against opposition movements, since radical literature was their lifeblood, although the policy undoubtedly alienated public opinion. By 1886 L. A. Tikhomirov, one of the People's Will's most talented propagandists, could write that: "I have finally become convinced that revolutionary Russia, as a serious, creative force does not exist. . . . Revolutionaries are active and will remain active, but this is an eddy on the surface of the sea, not a storm."[3] In 1888 the emperor pardoned Tikhomirov and twelve other former revolutionaries.

Many observers have described the Russian polity as a police state. V. M. Gessen argued, for example, that the relations of the state with individuals in Russia were "defined by categories of authority not by categories of law." Therefore Russia was a police state, not a *Rechtstaat,* or a law-governed state. Howard Payne characterized France in the 1850s and 1860s as a police state because the government could impose and enforce decrees without judicial review;[4] that characterization applied largely to Russia as well before 1906. Thereafter no executive act could become law for more than six months without legislative sanction. Even before 1906, however, the Senate occasionally overturned or circumscribed imperial decrees and executive orders.

Thus, one might call the Russian Empire a *Justizstaat,* since the courts could adjudicate any aspects of social and political life but did not impose clearly defined legal restraints on the whole bureaucracy.[5] The emperor's subjects were unable to limit the bureaucracy in any systematic way, that is, to demand that it adhere to the principle of the rule of law. As D. N. Shipov lamented, the "masses had no sense of the rule of law and complex problems of political life, because of a lack of education and unfavorable economic and legal conditions."[6] In general, government in Russia before

1905 was highly arbitrary because it was subject to few mechanisms of public control. Yet to a significant extent beginning in 1906, public opinion, expressed through the State Duma, the zemstvos and town dumas, a vibrant press, institutions of higher learning, the bar, the independent judiciary, and a variety of voluntary associations, exerted more and more pressure on the bureaucracy and the monarch.

The bureaucracy, furthermore, was divided against itself. At its apex stood the "autocratic" emperor, whose power was limited by the bureaucracy. Nicolas II viewed initiatives by his ministers as attempts to curtail his own power, so he tried to play them against each other, which may explain why in 1905 he approved as education minister I. I. Tolstoi, who admitted to being "a resolute opponent of the existing government order," while simultaneously appointing as interior minister P. N. Durnovo, who believed that "the Russian people expected political power to be unlimited, indeed terrifying." Yet as Tolstoi noted in regard to Nicholas II, "Even if you were very smart, it was impossible to know as much as the ministers, so they could influence you. . . . No constitution could have restrained the monarch to the extent that officialdom in fact did." Or as Truman Cross argues, the bureaucracy became "a cumbrance on autocratic will simply because more people had to make and apply more decisions." There were several occasions when Nicholas's extreme impulses were checked by willful senior officials. For example, in 1905 S. Iu. Witte and Justice Minister S. S. Manukhin rebuffed his suggestion that "illegal measures" be used to "save Russia."[7]

Other factors limiting the government's efficiency and increasing its propensity to exercise arbitrary administrative rule were Russia's relative poverty and its immense size and diversity. It was by far the poorest great power in terms of its economic output per capita and especially in proportion to its overall territory. The regular police force expanded significantly in the 1860s and in the 1904–1908 period; its budget increased from twenty-three million rubles in 1902 to sixty-one million in 1910 (or 165 percent—more than the military budget rose in the same years). Yet given the huge and multifarious administrative and welfare burden borne by the regular police and because of a massive rise in population, criminality, and activity among opposition groups and organizations, Russia remained significantly underpoliced.[8]

In general, the Russian Empire was the most undergoverned great power of its time. Comprising dozens of nationalities and ethnic groups, its largely illiterate population dispersed broadly over eleven time zones and linked by relatively sparse lines of communication, imperial Russia employed over one hundred times fewer policemen per unit of population than France. Russia's borderlands, unlike anything in western or central Europe for their otherness, were its least controlled, most violent regions. There one found the greatest anti-Russian and prorevolutionary sympathies. Finland, as a semiautonomous imperial possession, served as a staging ground for revolutionary and terrorist activism. On the empire's periphery the government applied a disproportionate share of political repression and harsh judicial and administrative punishments.

Overall, the Russian government in this period was not a well-oiled machine for oppressing political opposition movements but rather a traditional absolutist monarchy with many layers of institutions and authority that regularly offset and voided each other. Individual ministers often fought among themselves, for example, over whether the state should favor industrial development, with its attendant social dislocations, or social stability and public tranquility, and over the extent to which judicial authorities should limit administrative power.[9] Many officials, especially military officers, were apparently almost entirely apolitical. A. V. Kolchak told the Cheka, the early Bolshevik secret police, in 1920 that his point of view "was that of a serving officer" who did not concern himself with politics. "I considered the monarch an existing fact, neither criticizing nor considering the issue of changing it. As a military man I considered my duty to fulfill my oath and that was the whole of my relationship to the monarchy."[10]

There was a prejudice within officialdom and at court against the police apparatus as a whole. Of all the ministries, Interior was the least represented at court, and the emperor was "not pleased to give court titles to officials in police service," as one such official was told.[11] Yet senior and even middle-level officials were often highly talented and well educated. Indeed, there was a large gulf between the bureaucratic elites in every branch of the service and the untrained officials and the underfinanced and underinstitutionalized infrastructure they oversaw. This gulf also undermined the service's cohesion and effectiveness.

One typically did not rise to a senior or even a middling position in the Russian bureaucracy without patronage: "The whole system seems to have depended on it," according to the son and biographer of A. V. Krivoshein, a powerful official in the last decade of the monarchy. There are many stories of regimental comrades ascending through the ranks together. Especially striking is I. I. Tolstoi's remark that all the influential courtiers in Nicholas's last years had served as horse guards.[12] Security policemen often owed their advancement to the influence of prosecutors and, to a lesser extent, to other officials, such as governors. Some very talented men reached high positions, but so did mediocre men. The majority of security policemen in late imperial Russia were undistinguished figures. Add to this the tensions between the apolitical timeservers and the staunchly dedicated fighters against sedition, as well as the high turnover of personnel within the bureaucracy of the Police Department, and one realizes what an accomplishment it was to maintain an efficient security service in Russia.

Nearly all Russia's security policemen were gendarme officers, but only a small proportion of gendarmes were security policemen. There were 6,708 gendarmes in 1880; 9,243 in 1895; and 12,369 in 1907. Over 80 percent were noncommissioned officers, of whom only about one-quarter conducted regular surveillance over the population, chiefly in the countryside at the district *(uezd)* level. Roughly 60 percent of gendarmes were, for all practical purposes, regular policemen preserving order on railroad lines. Only 521 gendarmes were officers in 1880; the number rose to 693 in 1895 and 903 in 1907. Of these, about half worked in various nonpolitical capacities, including on the railroads. The other half were based in the provincial and district gendarme stations. At the turn of the century, perhaps 200 to 300 of these, including roughly 150 special surveillance personnel, directly and regularly acted as security policemen.

Most gendarme officers were landless Russian Orthodox gentrymen. Ambitious young men from gentry families who could not aspire to enter the elite guard units often wished to serve in the Gendarme Corps, which seemed more prestigious than the regular military service. Candidates underwent a three-to-six-month preparatory course in law, history, administrative regulations, and some operational procedures. Few gendarme officers aspired to match wits with revolutionary activists. In the words of A. P. Martynov, himself a gentryman, the Russian gentry strongly believed that "it was unbecoming for them to engage in 'business' or 'trade' or anything that requires continuous, uninterrupted, painstaking, and difficult work. One could hardly expect an officer of the Gendarme Corps, a nobleman by origin and an officer of the Russian army by profession, to undertake the 'dirty work' of the security police."[13]

Provincial gendarme officers engaged in security policing usually derived intelligence from the interrogation of suspects under investigation and from unsolicited denunciations. The latter rarely yielded fruitful results, and as the revolutionaries grew more secretive and tight-lipped, gendarme investigations became less valuable. Already in the early 1880s, however, G. P. Sudeikin had begun to develop sophisticated methods for infiltrating the revolutionary underground, most importantly by deploying secret informants. Those policemen who followed in his footsteps—chiefly out of the call of duty, a love of adventure, and a desire for power—came to be known as security officers or *okhranniki*. In many cases their honor-conscious, militaristic fellow gendarmes all but disowned them.

Neither these nor other security policemen had a clearly articulated vision of Russian politics and society—indeed, they even seemed averse to ideology and political philosophy. Yet their actions and scattered official writings make their outlook fairly clear. Certainly they were skeptical that democratic principles and institutions were appropriate for Russia: the interests of the state—"state" *(gosudarstvo)* in Russian is a cognate of "sovereign" *(gosudar')*—transcended those of any class, group, or individual. The officers' primary duty was to protect the monarch and the state.[14]

All regular policemen, including the specialized criminal detectives, were obligated to assist the security police with conducting surveillance of the population, making arrests, and other concrete tasks. For example, they verified the internal passports of all people entering Russia's major cities, helped assess the "political reliability" of people applying for civil service jobs or university admission,[15] and monitored public lectures and meetings. The mostly incorruptible security police could not always count on the probity and devotion to duty of the regular police, who at least occasionally turned a blind eye to revolutionary activities in exchange for material favors. Given the small number of security policemen, however, their support was essential. Following massive strikes in 1896, the security bureaus in Moscow and St. Petersburg began to employ forty to fifty regular police inspectors *(nadzirateli)* to coordinate their work with the regular police.

Among the most committed, talented, energetic security officers was S. V. Zubatov. After a few years of radical activism in high school, he reportedly grew disillusioned with his former comrades, and in 1885 he volunteered to inform on them. Four years later, his cover blown, he accepted permanent employment at the Moscow security bureau. Zubatov evolved into a staunch monarchist who argued zealously against revolutionary violence and believed that only the imperial government could carry out the social reforms needed to avert an explosion of mass discontent. In 1894 Zubatov was appointed director of the security bureau in Moscow, which for the next eight years served as the "quasi-official central investigatory agency of the Police Department."[16]

The main reasons for Zubatov's success in combating revolutionary activists were his understanding of their mentality and methods from the inside and his cultivation and development of Sudeikin's methods of police detection, namely, the training and deployment of specialized agents of surveillance. By means of "external surveillance" *(naruzhnoe nabliudenie)*, plainclothes police agents called surveillants *(filëry)* observed suspects without entering into contact with them. "Internal surveillance" *(vnutrennee nabliudenie)* was conducted by police informants, or "secret employees" *(sekretnye sotrudniki)*, who reported on radical organizations from within.

Surveillants were trained to recognize known revolutionary activists, to distinguish tiny differences in physiognomy, and to observe a wide range of apparently trivial phenomena. They noted in journals masses of detail about the movements, relations, and actions of their targets. Since surveillants always worked in pairs, and because around the turn of the century the Moscow security bureau employed only about fifty of them, on any given day they could keep watch over no more than two or three dozen people. Some they watched for weeks on end; others for only a few days. The tens of thousands of surveillants' journals housed in the police archives provided some of the raw material for a sophisticated system of domestic intelligence. In order to expand Moscow's reach during a period when other security police institutions were relatively underdeveloped, in 1894 the Police Department funded the establishment in Moscow of a mobile unit of experienced surveillants *(Letuchii otriad filёrov)*.

Zubatov wreaked havoc in the revolutionary milieux, largely thanks to his methods for recruiting and directing secret informants, who were few in number but powerful in effect. Zubatov was a master at interrogating and winning over radical activists by appealing to their idealism. The "monarchist idea, properly understood," he argued, "can provide everything that the country needs including the unleashing of social forces and all without bloodshed."[17] He also sought to flabbergast them with his intimate knowledge of the activities, members, and relationships of their underground circles and political organizations.

Case officers, Zubatov believed, needed to show their informants who was boss, but also to win their complete trust. An officer should treat each informant "as a beloved woman with whom you have entered into illicit relations. Look after her like the apple of your eye. One careless move and you will dishonor her."[18] The key thing was to avoid an informant's unmasking. Therefore, case officers met with them infrequently and only in secret *(konspirativnye)* apartments, and informants rarely submitted written reports or any other documentation in their own hand. As a former radical and denizen of the political underground, Zubatov steadfastly championed *konspiratsiia:* stealth and strict adherence to complex rules of secrecy. It was a way of life, an integral feature of the outlook and methods of operation of security police and revolutionaries alike.

Informants served from diverse motives, usually in some knotty association with one another. Zubatov himself wanted to show local officialdom that he was no longer a radical, to get back at his former colleagues, and to combat the radicalism he had lately espoused. Others craved adventure, fell under the spell of their case officers, or dreaded punishment. A few informants were extremely idealistic. None disdained the material benefits— money, travel, and occasionally assistance with finding employment or entering university. Most informants were relatively well educated. The majority was either Great Russian or Jewish. The more successful ones were clever, resourceful, and very capable of flattery, dissimulation, and the feigning of honesty and loyalty.

There were several kinds of informants. *Shtuchniki* usually stood on the periphery of target organizations and sporadically received modest payments of five or so rubles for individual, generally minor reports. Salaried informants earned from ten to two hundred rubles monthly (rarely more) for regular reports. After the turn of the century, Zubatov employed some forty to fifty such informants in Moscow. They reported on those radical groups and individuals deemed most dangerous at any given time. Once the Socialist-Revolutionaries commenced their campaign of political murder beginning in 1901, the lion's share of informants focused on them.

There were also a few "central" informants *(tsentral'naia agentura)*, or rather two distinct types of informants, both referred to as central informants. One type stood within or close to the revolutionary parties' decision-making bodies. These informants were highly valuable, of course, but also faced constant danger and posed risks for the police: reaching the leadership circles in a revolutionary party required participating actively in its illegal work. Another type of central informant, perhaps better termed a remote informant, was guided by senior officials in St. Petersburg but operated in other cities. Zubatov opposed the use of central informants of both types because he feared granting them too much liberty and letting them slip away from strict control. The rise of highly centralized terrorist organizations, however, made the deployment of central agents irresistible.

Both revolutionary and liberal activists loathed informants as traitors to the sacred oppositional cause. Admitted E. G. Broitman, "revolutionaries look at informants like animals that must be shot like dogs." Even the Octobrist A. I. Guchkov likened them to "swarming worms" "feeding on the live organism of the people . . . who made . . . from our slow death the justification of their life."[19] Whether they provoked anyone into criminal activity or not, the public invariably called them *provokatory*.

Zubatov brought enormous inventiveness to the security police. He taught that security policemen should never arrest people immediately after suspicion fell upon them but should wait to accumulate sufficient incriminating evidence to permit building up a solid case against them. When arrests occurred, moreover, he always left at liberty a few members of each group or circle in order to provide cover for any informants in their ranks and to keep the security police force's channels of information open.

His most surprising innovation concerned the labor movement, which expanded dramatically in the second half of the 1890s and began to flex its muscles in those years through a serious of big strikes. Zubatov was willing to fight tooth and nail against the revolutionary underground not only to preserve the monarchy but also because he believed their designs would harm more than help the laboring masses and because he perceived a more effective way of promoting their interests. From countless hours of discussion with workers and worker-intellectuals, Zubatov found them almost solely concerned with economic improvements. Who could satisfy these concerns better than an autocratic but benevolent monarch? In 1899 Zubatov used an informant to launch a monthly journal of Revisionist (antirevolutionary) thought, *Nachalo*, to draw moderate labor leaders away from the radicals. Despite initial success, the journal was soon closed down by the censors for printing "seditious" articles. The next year Zubatov's patrons in the government supported his proposal to organize Russia's factory workers into an organic estate by tending to their economic, cultural, and political needs and aspirations. Within a year he had set up government-sponsored worker associations in Moscow and a few other cities.

In 1902 Zubatov impressed—and perhaps frightened—senior officials by organizing a giant procession of workers in Moscow to commemorate Alexander II's abolition of serfdom. Even more frightened of Zubatov's influence among the workers were the Social Democrats. Their newspaper, *Iskra,* published thirty-eight reports denouncing Zubatovism between 1901 and 1903, stating in one case that it was "more terrible to us than is police brutality."[20]

In 1898 the Police Department created a separate office dedicated to coordinating the ever-expanding struggle of the security police against their conspiratorial adversaries. The new office, the Special Section, developed into the nerve center of the security police system. Its highly efficient, professional, and well-educated staff coordinated the search for political criminals; processed information furnished by the entire surveillance apparatus; and prepared detailed reports on opposition groups, on social classes and disorders, and, for the emperor himself, on the state of the empire. Clerks of the Special Section compiled a vast collection of illegal political imprints, comprising five thousand titles in 1901, and drafted fantastically complex schematic diagrams displaying the relationships among political suspects. Their purpose was to comprehend as thoroughly as possible the revolutionary organizations and the networks of their members.

Russia's revolutionary opposition were a fanatical brotherhood endowed by society with an aura of honor and purity. As F. A. Stepun, the religious philosopher, noted, "all Russian families, even the tsar's, always had a more or less radical relative, a personal, household *[sobstvennyi domashnyi]* revolutionary." Osip Mandel'shtam, one of Russia's greatest poets, was

> intellectually attracted to Social Democrats, but nothing rivaled the Socialist-Revolutionaries and their deeds in terms of heroism. . . . The boys of 1905 went to revolution with the same sensation with which little Nikolai Rostov joined the Hussars. It was a question of infatuation and honor. Neither one thought he could live without the warmth of the glory of their age. Neither one could imagine life without valor. *War and Peace* went on; the glory simply migrated. After all, glory was not and could not be with the Semenovskii Colonel [G. A.] Min or with the generals of the Imperial Suite, in lacquered boots that looked like bottles. Glory was with the Central Committee, with the Combat Organization."[21]

Most committed revolutionaries were wildly devoted to their cause and to Russia. N. V. Chaikovskii, a member of the People's Will, lived for over twenty years in England. During the Revolution of 1905 he entered Russia illegally and in late 1907 was arrested and imprisoned in the Peter-Paul Fortress, where he told another inmate: "sitting inside these four walls I feel myself more linked with real life, more involved, than passing a meaningless existence in free England with a consciousness of my uselessness. . . . Foreign people are good only in superficial encounters, only as an aside."

Similarly V. M. Zenzinov spent 1908 in Paris. "This was the harshest of all my revolutionary years. Even Siberian exile is not as bad. I dreamed only of my homeland, of being of service to her." Arrested in Moscow in 1910, he was sent to an isolated village in distant Iakutsk. His relatives implored the governor to send him to a better place. The governor would have been willing had Zenzinov agreed to ask for the favor himself, but Zenzinov refused. As A. L. Parvus later claimed, "clemency for us was an insult. We were not the criminals; it was they who held us in prison."[22] Revolutionary activists expected, even fatalistically awaited, arrest followed by exile or imprisonment, which proved to the world their readiness to sacrifice self in the service of their cause.

Even so, most revolutionaries were unwilling to throw themselves into the arms of the police. As their efforts to forge a mass movement laid their secretive core organizations more open to police detection, the leading activists developed complex rules of *konspiratsiia*. Some techniques were almost childishly simple, but effective, like meeting in brothels, at weddings, in forests, and on riverboats.[23] Others were sophisticated, including the creation of internal security services; use of false passports, secret codes, and aliases; isolation of party members; and disciplined behavior under interrogation. Although Social Democrats theorized more about *konspiratsiia* than their revolutionary counterparts did, the Socialist-Revolutionary terrorists were more tightly knit. The fear the latter group struck in the hearts of officialdom drove it to spare no expense in penetrating their ranks. In both cases, over time interrogations yielded less and less intelligence.

Some observers have claimed that the Russian government incited radicals to terrorism by applying arbitrary, humiliating repressive measures to them. O. V. Budnitskii also believes that the government was responsible for the rise of a doggedly active terrorist movement in Russia, but not because of repression. Instead, he argues that officialdom attributed to terrorists "too much significance, helped them to rise in their own eyes and the eyes of the public."[24] One can certainly argue that the violence of the government fed on the violence of the revolutionaries and vice versa, but to single one side out as more deserving of blame seems pointless: if fear of and anger about repression shaped the views and attitudes of the revolutionaries, then fear of terror must have shaped the views and attitudes of the officials. What is perhaps most surprising is that so few members of the educated public supported the government's efforts to crush the terrorist wave that gripped the country.

As mass movements arose and terrorists began to assassinate officials in 1901 and 1902, police officials laid the groundwork for a major reform of the security police apparatus. In early summer 1902, Zubatov was named Special Section director, and he presided over the gradual creation of a network of security bureaus in twenty important provincial cities, including Vilna, Kiev, Odessa, Saratov, Tiflis, Nizhnii Novgorod, Rostov-na-Donu,

Tomsk, and Irkutsk. In those twenty cities younger, carefully selected security officers displaced the older, higher-ranked provincial gendarme officers as the counterrevolutionary vanguard in their jurisdictions. It is not surprising that the senior officers resented their juniors, who now enjoyed greater de facto authority and could hope for more rapid promotion, largely because they were more capable of deploying specialized agents and gathering domestic intelligence. Each bureau received special resources to this end, including one to two experienced surveillants from the Mobile Surveillance Brigade. One police official described the first year of the bureaus' functioning as "the most brilliant year in the history of political investigation."[25]

Zubatov remained at the helm of the renovated security system for just under one year, however. While he devoted himself to overseeing the system, his labor programs lost momentum and then slipped out of control. The Odessa general strike of summer 1903, which spread across the Black Sea littoral and in which Zubatovites took part, frightened Interior Minister V. K. Plehve, who dismissed Zubatov, to the relief of many conservative officials. Probably they had sensed what F. I. Dan later admitted: "more than a few tens of thousands of workers, now loyal members of the Social Democratic Party, attended the school of Zubatovism, which aroused them more or less to conscious life."[26]

The political security system declined and sedition and political opposition increased after Zubatov's dismissal. The Special Section was overwhelmed with the flood of information pouring in from the new security bureaus. The directors of the two major bureaus inside Russia lacked Zubatov's charisma and ability. The new director of the Paris security bureau, L. A. Rataev, was also relatively incompetent; certainly he was no match for the cunning E. F. Azef, the Police Department's star informant, whom he was supposed to supervise. Azef was especially dangerous now because the arrest in early 1903 of the terrorist mastermind G. A. Gershuni permitted Azef to take his place at the head of the Socialist-Revolutionary combat organization. Azef now had the capacity not only to foil the revolutionaries' plots, but also to further them.

Plehve had apparently supported Azef's advancement because he hoped to avoid the fate of his predecessor, who had died at the hands of terrorists in 1902. At the same time, Plehve alienated the liberal opposition by arbitrarily harassing its leading members and organizations. Yet because the bureaucracy was divided against itself and to a large extent respected legality and the rule of law, these activists could often wriggle free from Plehve's snares by flattering powerful officials or by appealing to their legal consciousness. Plehve also turned several ethnic minorities in the borderlands against the government by imposing on them harsh policies of Russification and central control.

There were a few countervailing tendencies within the apparatus of repression. A new criminal code, adopted in spring 1903, expanded the range of state crimes and therefore opened the possibility of more court adjudication

of political infractions. A decree of June 1904 abolished the practice of imposing administrative punishments by imperial order, and many contemporary
observers anticipated the disappearance of all administrative punishments
from Russia's repressive arsenal. In the meantime, the level of repression
and punishment failed to keep up with the rising tide of unrest and sedition, leaving many officials feeling disoriented and listless.

On 15 July 1904, Plehve died from the impact of a terrorist's bomb. Society reacted with equanimity, in some cases even joy. The new interior minister, the moderate prince P. D. Sviatopolk-Mirskii, set about mending
fences with the educated public. Radical and liberal activists, perceiving his
overtures as a sign of weakness, accelerated their efforts at political organization. The administration mostly just watched their feverish activities un-
fold. The emperor's 12 December 1904 promise to curtail administrative arbitrariness, coupled with reversals in the war with Japan, further sapped
officialdom's resolve and emboldened the opposition.

The spark that ignited revolution was Bloody Sunday, 9 January 1905,
when troops gunned down over one hundred peacefully marching workers
in St. Petersburg. The opposition movement swelled, massive strikes and
agrarian unrest periodically gripped the country, terrorists struck with increasing frequency, rebelliousness gripped the soldiery, and the Russian
military suffered one defeat after another. The government seemed to lose
its nerve. True, in February a tough gendarme officer, A. V. Gerasimov, took
the helm of the security bureau in St. Petersburg; P. I. Rachkovskii, a talented and experienced security policeman, created a new command center
(politicheskaia chast') within the Police Department; and the security police
managed to arrest several revolutionary leaders. Yet in many parts of the
borderlands order broke down almost completely. Attacks against officials
increased in frequency, and many local officials turned a blind eye to opposition and revolutionary activism.

By early fall most elements of the opposition, including students, industrial workers, liberal professionals, and revolutionary activists, coalesced. In
October a general strike nearly paralyzed Russia. On the 17th, Nicholas issued his October Manifesto promising a constitutional order. Many administrative officials, flummoxed, sat on their hands. The countryside burst
into violence. Massive pogroms swept the Pale of Settlement and other
places inhabited by Jews. Nascent right-wing organizations clashed with
their leftist counterparts. Troops and sailors mutinied. A Soviet of workers'
deputies in St. Petersburg declared itself the legitimate government. Revolutionary activists sabotaged lines of transportation and communication.[27]
Senior officials might have imposed a state of extraordinary security in numerous regions of the country. They did not. Chaos gripped Russia.

Then in early December, although a general strike failed in St. Petersburg, armed rebellion broke out in Moscow, testing the government's resolve and marking the turning point toward the restoration of order. In the

middle of the month Colonel G. A. Min arrived with the Semenov Guards Regiment and ordered to fire without mercy on armed insurgents. Around the same time, Nicholas gave orders to begin the first punitive expeditions to restore order on rail lines and in especially rebellious provinces. The government had been hanging by a thread, and only loyal soldiers from guard and cavalry units—the sole reliable ones left in European Russia—preserved it from collapse.[28]

In the face of massive popular discontent, with huge street demonstrations, giant strikes, daily political violence, and the radicalization of political elites, the role of the security police necessarily was diminished. Security officers could match wits with their revolutionary-conspirator counterparts, but they were all but impotent against mass movements in schools, factories, streets, and villages.

Even so, the political security system of which the security officers formed an integral part was far from impotent, especially once the government began to reassert its authority. In the public mind, moreover, that system enjoyed a pernicious omnipotence. In the late 1890s, I. P. Belokonskii was arbitrarily removed as chief statistician for the Kursk zemstvo. P. A. Geiden, the moderate president of the Free Economic Society, remarked philosophically to him that the poet F. I. Tiutchev had advised against seeking to understand Russia with the mind. When Belokonskii reminded Geiden that "the poet counseled believing in Russia, not in the Police Department," Geiden retorted, "Of course you will agree that Russia is the Police Department." His interlocutor agreed.[29] It was essential that educated elites in the constitutional era cease to believe such things, but old prejudices die hard. P. N. Miliukov believed the government had purposely stirred radicals in Moscow to armed rebellion in December 1905 so as to justify massacring them. V. A. Maklakov was sure that the Semenov Regiment had proceeded to Kolomna, southeast of Moscow, and had shot people singled out by officials at the Moscow security bureau.[30]

In reality, Russia's security system was far less diabolical and far less robust than Maklakov imagined. Still, once the political order grew more stable and as civil society luxuriated in the interrevolutionary years, the importance of a sophisticated security police would increase. Their main task would be to single out and suppress violent and other extremist political actors whose actions might threaten the existence of the constitutional order. How and to what extent the security police accomplished this task and whether it alienated the broader society while it did so is the subject of this volume.

CHAPTER ONE

POLICING THE

CONSTITUTIONAL

ORDER IN 1906

■ The end of 1905 and beginning of 1906 witnessed massive social disorder. The specter of *Pugachevshchina*, the massive peasant rebellion of 1773–1774, haunted the countryside, and the major revolutionary parties sought to prepare new armed uprisings. To this end, Social Democrats in Moscow set up a "military technical bureau" and in January and February distributed some 365,000 handbills and brochures. "We all were sure," wrote one activist, "that . . . we would overcome the tsarist scum *[svoloch']* and with it the whole hated capitalist system." Political terrorists worked feverishly. In January leading Socialist-Revolutionaries—E. F. Azef, B. V. Savinkov, G. A. Gershuni—reconstituted the party's combat organization and undertook large-scale operations to kill senior government officials.[1] The details of bomb making, according to A. I. Spiridovich, a security police official, "became so widespread that practically any child could produce one and blow up his nanny."[2] In the words of V. P. Obninskii, a left-wing Kadet: "There were days when several major incidents of terrorism were accompanied by virtually dozens of lesser attacks and assassinations against the lower ranks of the administration, not counting threats received in the mail by almost every police official." Obninskii admitted that harsh repression was inevitable.[3]

REPRESSION BEFORE REFORM

Interior Minister P. N. Durnovo, the driving force behind the government's counterrevolutionary offensive, was the man of the hour. Nicholas greatly esteemed him, along with the hard-line justice minister M. G. Akimov, who was Durnovo's brother-in-law. "The rest of the ministers," Nicholas wrote on 12 January, "are people without importance." The best he could say about S. Iu. Witte, the prime minister, was that he had finally understood that "against terror it is necessary to answer with terror."[4]

Born in 1845 to a landless old noble family, Petr Nikolaevich Durnovo had served from 1858 to 1870 as an officer at sea, where he completely missed the era of Great Reforms. He was a prosecutor in the 1870s and headed the Police Department from 1884 until 1893, when he was named senator. I. I. Tkhorzhevskii, a well-connected middle-level official, called him "most intelligent, most lively, most independent";[5] G. O. Raukh, a senior military officer, recalled that he spoke "briefly, clearly, and concretely";[6] and Dominic Lieven describes Durnovo as "a man of great intelligence and strongly defined views." Though not opposed to democracy in principle, Durnovo believed that the vast majority of Russians, including most of the educated elite, were far from prepared to govern themselves. He was deeply pessimistic about human nature in general and acutely aware of the immense threats to the existing political order in Russia.[7]

Much stronger men rose to key positions in the police apparatus during this period. Anatolii Anatol'evich Reinbot, an intelligent, energetic administrator, was named Moscow city governor. He immediately proceeded to reorganize and reinvigorate the regular police forces. He fired nearly all of the one thousand policemen hastily appointed in December, named new police chiefs *(politsmeistery)* and captains *(pristavy)*, and issued orders to repress disorderly public gatherings. By fall, V. F. Dzhunkovskii, Moscow's provincial governor, informed the interior ministry that the supplementary police forces, re-hired and better trained thanks to a new program instituted by Reinbot, were able to maintain order without recourse to military reinforcements.[8] Reinbot's firmness helped stiffen the spine of Moscow's security police.

Their new director, Evgenii Konstantinovich Klimovich, appointed on 23 January 1906, was, according to Dzhunkovskii, "an outstanding administrator thanks to his mental faculties. A real expert in domestic intelligence gathering." A Byelorussian by origin, Klimovich was of "medium height and sturdy build, with a large forehead, a pale face of the Lithuanian-Polish type, and a sparse little mustache." Appointed director of the security bureau in Vilna in January 1904, Klimovich so impressed his superiors that a report of 1904 predicted he would become one of the most serious *okhranniki*. His recipe for success was twofold, according to A. P. Martynov. He spent all his days and nights in the security bureau and expected the same of his subordinates, and he launched assault after assault on the revolutionary underground, often without regard for his informants. His feverish activity paid off in terms of his career. He progressed from lieutenant colonel to colonel at breakneck speed—in one and a half years counting from late December 1905.[9]

Security policing in the northern capital remained in the able hands of Aleksandr Vasil'evich Gerasimov. Born in 1861, he was "tall, solidly built, with a slightly Tatar-style face, a small pointed beard, and . . . a well-fitted suit." A. P. Martynov, who met him in summer 1906, came away with a bit of advice from Gerasimov ("one only needs to keep one's wits about him")

Evgenii Konstantinovich Klimovich, chief of Moscow security bureau (1906–1907), director of the Special Section (1908–1909), and director of the Police Department (1916).

and the impression that he had a brilliant mind. Gerasimov had spent the previous year building up discipline among the security bureau's personnel and recruiting informants throughout the revolutionary milieux. Following standard procedure, the informants were grouped according to target party and directed by case officers assigned to them. In order to protect their identities, they met their directors only in safe apartments scattered throughout the city. Gerasimov himself met with those few informants closest to the center of revolutionary parties.[10]

At the very start of the new year a court security force *(Dvortsovaia okhrana)* was instituted to coordinate measures for the protection of the imperial family. It was not that the emperor and his family had previously enjoyed no physical protection. The palace commandant, D. F. Trepov, disposed of four separate guard units, largely ceremonial forces dating from the nineteenth century. And to transport the emperor there were two identical light blue trains that always traveled one behind the other to confuse potential assailants. Yet no politically sophisticated command center that was alert to terrorist threats guided their actions, and in general, according to A. I. Spiridovich, the protection of the emperor's physical security "was organized in a naive and infantile manner."[11]

It probably would have made the most sense to combine all the security forces into one entity and then to coordinate its operations from within the Police Department. Trepov refused to subordinate his office to other agencies in any way, however, and the commanders of the existing security forces were loath to relinquish their own power. So Trepov created an entirely new office and named Aleksandr Ivanovich Spiridovich as its director.

A staunch monarchist and an accomplished security officer trained by S. V. Zubatov himself, Spiridovich accepted the position as the fulfillment of a fanciful dream. He conferred first with Trepov in his grand, mahogany-paneled office in Tsarskoe Selo, in the building where Pushkin had once attended the Alexander Lycée; then with special agent of the interior ministry Petr Ivanovich Rachkovskii; and finally with other officials at the Police Department. They all seemed to Spiridovich uninformed and inordinately fearful about terrorist plots and revolutionary threats. After the meeting he consulted with the eminently calm Gerasimov, who appeared to be "aware of everything" and claimed that there was no immediate danger of terrorist attacks.[12] Spiridovich would work especially closely with Gerasimov.

The new force had an annual budget of some two hundred thousand rubles. It deployed no informants. Assisted by four gendarme officers, Spiridovich supervised 275 former noncommissioned officers of St. Petersburg guard regiments whose two chief tasks were to physically protect the emperor and members of his family and to be continuously watchful in and around the places they frequented. Many of the force's agents were trained specifically to recognize known terrorists. A contingent of these surveillants always traveled with the emperor and his family both inside the empire and abroad. Spiridovich apparently won the fondness of Nicholas, who soon granted him permission to photograph him and his family at will.[13]

The work of a resolute interior minister in St. Petersburg and of competent police officials in the two imperial capitals was essential to containing and repressing unrest and disorder. Two other requisites were forthcoming: more funds and support from the highest levels of government. From 6 to 17 January 1906 the Council of Ministers repeatedly discussed the dangers of popular rebelliousness and proposed means for its suppression. Nicholas, who insisted on receiving weekly reports detailing every major instance of political violence, staunchly favored harsh repression. The government allocated roughly eighteen million rubles in 1906 to hire thirty thousand more policemen—an increase of one-third. Moscow's contingent alone rose from 2,335 in 1904 to 4,843 in 1907. According to available statistics for 1913–1914, Moscow had a higher ratio of police to population (1:270) than St. Petersburg (1:343), Berlin (1:325), or Vienna (1:442). (Rural Russia remained underpoliced: the whole province outside Moscow city had only 101 trained policemen in late 1906.)[14] The wages of most categories of policemen increased by roughly one-quarter, and the total budget devoted to their upkeep rose from twenty-seven million rubles in 1904 to nearly fifty-one million rubles in 1907. To all these figures must be added the 2.5 million rubles distributed to policemen as compensation for the hardship they had incurred during the popular unrest of 1905–1907.[15]

Besides increasing their number and pay, senior police officials sought repeatedly to strengthen the resolve of policemen in the field. Between February and July 1906 the Police Department sent them no fewer than fifteen orders to prepare to avert renewed revolutionary activism. On 21 January Durnovo sent governors precise and detailed instructions on restricting public meetings. They should allow only moderates to convene them, should authorize only as many meetings as they had police to disperse, and should prohibit military personnel and high school students from attending. On 7 February the Council of Ministers forbade troops to shoot in the air or to use blanks when repressing social unrest, actions that allegedly would only embolden rebellious crowds. On 13 February the Council of Ministers criminalized the distribution of false information about the actions of the government and its officials. In late February, the Police Department ordered increased security at government institutions and the "most decisive measures" to discover and to arrest persons trying to foment disorder.[16]

Senior government officials feared no social crisis so much as agrarian unrest, which had caused forty-seven million rubles' damage in late 1905, and anti-Jewish violence, which also typically resulted in massive destruction of private property. On 6 January 1906 the Council of Ministers recommended that troops be used only as a last resort to restore order in the countryside but that once summoned they should act mercilessly: "arrive, punish, depart." (This part of the proposal became law on 7 February.) On 3 February Nicholas approved proposals for both harsh repression of peasant unrest and reforms to improve peasant livelihoods. Nine days later Durnovo directed governors to root out political agitation among peasants. On 12 March Nicholas approved a plan to divide the provinces into four groups in order to concentrate military forces in those provinces experiencing the highest levels of unrest.[17]

By early April nearly all governors reckoned they had enough troops and police forces, including rural guards (strazhniki), who numbered nearly sixty thousand in the empire as a whole, to maintain order in their jurisdictions. I. I. Tolstoi, education minister and a staunch advocate of the expansion of Jewish rights, wrote that the Council of Ministers was "almost constantly concerned with the dangers of anti-Jewish pogroms" in late 1905 and spring 1906. Thus on 24 February the Council of Ministers asked the interior minister to instruct all governors and governors-general that "their responsibility to take measures to prevent cases of mass violence against Jews was every bit as binding as their obligation to thwart other breaches of public safety and tranquility and to preserve the inviolability of the person and property of private individuals." In practice, however, some middle- and lower-level officials disregarded, sanctioned, or even encouraged anti-Jewish violence, and when they were caught, they often received lenient punishments.[18]

The government officials given the broadest latitude in the effort to pacify the country were the commanders of the so-called punitive expeditions (karatel'nye ekspeditsii), which crushed rebellions along major rail lines and in Ukraine, the Caucasus, and the Baltic region. All told, the expeditions may have left as many as 1,369 corpses in their wake.[19] Yet Nicholas praised the commanders' efforts. In 1911, he ordered the justice ministry to drop a civil case of 150 counts of wrongful death lodged against N. K. Riman, who had crushed unrest on the Moscow-Kazan railroad. "If all military commanders had acted as Riman," opined the emperor, "then Russia would not have experienced its hard and shameful trial of six years ago."[20]

States of emergency enhanced the powers of much of administrative officialdom. By February 1906, Russia's normal laws had been suspended in thirty entire provinces and parts of thirty more; reinforced security had been imposed in seventeen full provinces; martial law was in force in the Kingdom of Poland and in seven Baltic, Caucasian, and central Asian provinces; and extraordinary security had been imposed in Ekaterinoslav, Kaluga, Moscow, Minsk, Ufa, and Chernigov provinces, as well as along portions of twenty-seven railroad lines.[21]

The security police were vigilant. They foiled most of the Socialist-Revolutionaries' terrorist plans in Moscow throughout December 1905, arrested members of the Social Democrats' combat organization in Riga on 2 January 1906, and launched waves of arrests in St. Petersburg in early January.[22] Gerasimov arrested associates of *Novaia zhizn'*, a Social Democratic newspaper, and participants in a meeting of the regional and St. Petersburg Social Democratic committees on 7 and 11 February. The police seized a large cache of inflammatory literature in Saratov in mid-February. March was an especially busy month. Security police sources indicated throughout March that revolutionary activists were laying the groundwork for a general strike and an armed uprising.[23] In the meantime Socialist-Revolutionaries killed informant N. Iu. Tatarov (22 March) and the organizer of the Bloody Sunday demonstration, Father Grigorii Gapon (28 March), because of his suspected collaboration with the police. Just before his death Tatarov had provided information enabling the arrest of several Socialist-Revolutionary leaders (16–17 March) and had revealed plans to kill Grand Duke Vladimir Aleksandrovich and a number of senior government officials.[24]

Gerasimov detained agitators in mid- and late March. Klimovich arrested activists of the printers union and seized weapons from them; apprehended members of the Social Democratic combat organization, nabbing bombs and explosives; shut down a Bolshevik explosives laboratory; and arrested revolutionary agitators infiltrating military units. A private letter intercepted by censors on 21 March complained that Moscow was "full of surveillants" and that frequent police raids were making life in the underground unbearable.[25]

In mid-April 1906 one of the security police force's most talented and well-placed informants, a sort of prodigal son, returned to the fold and became an even more effective antirevolutionary actor. Gerasimov's surveillants in St. Petersburg had been straining every nerve to protect government officials, in particular P. N. Durnovo, from Socialist-Revolutionary terrorists. On 15 April surveillants noticed three Socialist-Revolutionaries lying in wait for Durnovo. The three reported to a fourth, whom one surveillant identified as "Filippovskii." Five or six years before, the surveillant had learned his name and face and that he had been a valuable informant in Moscow for S. V. Zubatov. Filippovskii had been espied by E. P. Mednikov, Zubatov's right-hand man, in the fashionable Filippov Bakery on Tverskaia Street in Moscow; hence his nickname. Because none of Gerasimov's men knew his real name, they brought him in for questioning. For two days he denied being an informant. On the third day he demanded to see his case officer, Rachkovskii.[26]

The detainee, it turned out, was E. F. Azef—the security police force's most highly placed informant. At its first congress, in January, the Socialist-Revolutionary Party had elected Azef to the five-member central committee and reappointed him head of the combat organization. As such he had been supervising several plots to assassinate senior officials. He had betrayed none of the plots but had disrupted all of them—except the effort to murder hard-line governor-general of Moscow, F. V. Dubasov, who survived by something like a miracle.[27] Now Azef accused Rachkovskii of negligent supervision and of failing to pay him in full. Azef swore at him and sputtered, "Gapon is hanging from a ceiling near Finland." This was the authorities' first news of Gapon's demise. Sympathetic to Azef's plight, Gerasimov agreed to give him five thousand rubles in back pay, plus money for incidental expenses. Azef became Gerasimov's "best agent" and helped him to undermine the Socialist-Revolutionary terrorist movement.[28]

The combined repressive forces of the punitive expeditions, the security police, and the administrative officials, who were spread throughout the Russian Empire, struck very broadly. Between October 1905 and March 1906, they arrested at least 14,200 people, including over 7,000 in January alone.[29] Yet the government avoided a wholesale descent into administrative despotism. In early January Durnovo rejected S. E. Kryzhanovskii's proposal that entire villages be subjected to administrative exile if the majority had participated in a rebellion. In the same vein, the Council of Ministers argued on 20 January that once rebels had been handed over to civil authorities, they must never be yielded up to military personnel. Troops could shoot rebels in order to restore order but not when they no longer posed a threat to public tranquility. Nicholas agreed completely with this opinion. Indeed, when the temporary governor-general of Kurland Province released five peasant rebels from prison and had them executed on 30 January, the Council of Ministers asked the interior ministry to prosecute him.[30]

Thus, although the government granted senior provincial officials broad latitude for action, and some meted out excessive punishments on their own authority, they did so at their own risk. And not all senior administrative officials in the field resorted to merciless repression in response to unrest. As early as 7 January 1906, Dubasov had recommended to Nicholas that rebels be tried not in military but in civilian courts, which were less likely to commit procedural errors and which enjoyed greater authority in the public eye. Most important, the civilian courts corresponded to the principles of the new constitutional order established by the October Manifesto.[31]

Two weeks later, Nicholas himself upheld a State Council minority that opposed a proposal to subject to military trial persons accused of violently attacking government officials, since in such cases the military courts would usually hand down death sentences. The minority argued, first, that the proposal ran counter to Russian legal traditions and that it would have instituted a provision unknown in any European legal system and would have stood "in complete contradiction with the intention of establishing in Russia the rule of law." Second, they noted that the revolutionary movement was already subsiding and that its continued suppression did not require such drastic measures. Third, they contended that it would be unwise to invest every local official with the power to transfer criminals to military courts. Fourth, they argued, most of the Russian public opposed capital punishment. Finally, Russian and European criminological studies had demonstrated that it is not the severity, but the inevitability of punishment that deters crime.[32]

Numerous senior officials expressed concern about the suspension and nonenforcement of ordinary laws and about administrative arbitrariness in general. For example, a Police Department directive of 14 February enjoined gendarmes and local police officials to inform detainees of the reasons for their detainment and to obtain a statement from them within twenty-four hours of their arrest.[33] On 17 February the Council of Ministers admitted that because so many people were being examined by the ad hoc committee on administrative punishments as possible candidates for administrative exile, those eventually deemed innocent often had to wait a long time before their release. "This is having a very bad effect on the mood of society," according to the majority opinion on this question, "and gives rise to criticism of local authorities." The members of the council agreed that it was impossible to avoid mistakes, given the high volume of arrests, but they proposed to speed up the processing of cases by creating a second ad hoc committee.[34] Although in most cases the committees acted as a rubber stamp, there were some successful appeals for clemency. For example, a cable from the father of V. I. Kobylianskii pleading that a sentence of exile would ruin his son's career persuaded committee members to drop the case.[35]

Russia's senior officials were, in any event, concerned to circumscribe the abuse of power that exceptional legislation invited as Russia embarked on major constitutional changes. The anxiety of many officials must have been enormous. Strikes continued to break out across Russia, as did peasant and student unrest, and the major revolutionary organizations carried on their preparations for armed struggle.[36] Social Democrats and Socialist-Revolutionaries agitated vigorously among the armed forces throughout

1906, maintaining as many as fifty organizations within the military with the sole purpose of preparing the ground for an armed insurrection.[37] Police officials were alarmed because as potential instruments of both repression and revolution Russia's soldiers represented a double-edged sword. Yet military commanders resisted cooperating with the security police, and the number of informants within military units was apparently small.[38]

Terrorist acts took place with intense frequency throughout the year. On or just before 8 March twenty revolutionaries robbed a bank in Moscow and stole 875,000 rubles, and on 25 March a bomb blast killed P. A. Sleptsov, the governor of Tver Province.[39] Still, many people were eager to participate in legal forums, including trade unions, the legal press, and the new legislature. Doubtless, many who opposed the government found constructive work very appealing after months of social chaos. Others, especially some leaders of the major revolutionary parties, sought to use the new freedom to undermine the government.

THE CONSTITUTIONALIST ORDER

The Fundamental Laws, promulgated on 23 April, codified the civil liberties promised by the October Manifesto and created a bicameral legislature. The constitutionalists D. N. Shipov, I. V. Gessen, and V. A. Maklakov admitted that the Fundamental Laws created a constitutional order in Russia and limited the power of the monarch; but they believed that the laws did not go far enough. Most grievously, they did not fulfill the emperor's promise to guarantee the inviolability of the person; nor did they empower the legislature to overrule declarations of states of emergency, an omission that Shipov called "outrageous." A commission did review the security law of 1881, and it concluded on 23 April that the law "must be rescinded but not before new laws are issued." A new commission was then created to draft a new emergency law. In any event, the Fundamental Laws could have turned out far worse from the point of view of constitutionalism. For example, Witte and other senior officials had unsuccessfully sought to include a provision for removing uncooperative judges and had even tried to add a coup d'etat clause to make possible the abolition of the Duma and State Council.[40]

The press was now far freer than ever before in Russia, and a torrent of antigovernment publications had begun gushing forth in late fall 1905. They portrayed the police, especially the gendarmes, as incompetent and brutal. Stunned by the brazen tone of the opposition press, senior officials adopted both defensive and offensive policies. They increased subsidies to the progovernment press and created two semiofficial newspapers, *Rossiiskoe gosudarstvo* (February–May) and *Rossiia* (beginning in June). On 26 April and 3 May 1906 the government issued new temporary rules on censorship.

Although these were far more liberal than the previous legislation, for months the press had operated with almost complete freedom, so the new rules appeared relatively restrictive. Preliminary censorship was abolished (except in the case of articles concerning religion, the Orthodox Church, the military, or the emperor's court), but copies of most publications had to be presented to censorship bureaus called committees on press affairs one to seven days before distribution. The censors could temporarily block the distribution of a particular publication, but only a court decision could result in the destruction of one or could require the closing of a periodical or the fining or detaining of a publisher or editor. A court could reach such a decision only if it was demonstrated that a given publication contained "untrue information," incitement of social groups to mutual antagonism, approval of criminal acts, or other legally defined criminal content. Administrative officials were obligated to authorize the creation of new periodical publications within two weeks, so long as specific information on the editors and publishers was provided.[41]

Most opposition publishers employed a wide variety of ruses to evade repression, such as issuing several different booklets inside the same innocent-looking cover; indicating that a print run *(tirazh)* was much lower than it actually was; printing the text and cover in two different printers' shops; using different covers for the same text; displaying phony places of publication or names of nonexistent publishers; changing the names of periodical publications—sometimes a dozen or more times; and hiring indigents to pose as "responsible editors" and thus serve the jail sentence if the police came to make arrests. Under these relatively favorable conditions, periodicals from across the political spectrum proliferated over the next two years. The number of Bolshevik periodical publications expanded to sixty in 1906 and eighty-seven in early 1907, and the growth of the press effectively overwhelmed the censorship apparatus. While the number of book and pamphlet titles rose from 8,699 in 1895 to 23,852 in 1908, and the number of periodicals from 980 in 1898 to 2,391 in 1910, the staffs and budgets of the committees on press affairs remained inadequate: the committees employed forty-four people in 1882 and forty-six in 1917.[42]

On 4 March 1906 the government issued temporary rules on voluntary societies and trade unions, making it easier to register them. The purpose was partly to regulate organizations that had already sprung up and partly to create conditions under which industrial workers could, according to Witte, abandon the revolutionary leaders and "embark on a purely economic struggle." Previously, in the absence of any general law, the governors had decided whether to approve or to ban public organizations, a process on which the security police had exerted considerable influence. Officialdom frowned on empire-wide organizations, and previously only academic and philanthropic societies enjoying the protection of the emperor or his family had been immune from administrative meddling. In a word, the regulation of public organizations had been completely arbitrary.[43]

Russia had not had a formal ban on worker associations, but these had been virtually nonexistent before the mid-1890s. On the other hand, non-labor voluntary associations had existed legally for well over a century—by 1897 there were already some four hundred in St. Petersburg alone. The new procedures were much more lenient and predictable: local boards subordinate to the governors and hence to the interior ministry were to approve or reject applications to establish a public society or trade union. Notarized statutes clearly defined the goals and activities of each public society. Any deviation from them gave administrative officials the right to disband the group, though any legally constituted society that adhered to its charter could not be arbitrarily shut down.[44]

The number of trade unions increased from some 220 in 1899 to approximately 600 in December 1906 and 900 six months later. The number would have been higher had it not been for administrative delays in approving union statutes. For example, the powerful St. Petersburg–based Union of Metalworkers, one of the few unions to merit its own rubric in the Police Department filing system, existed for over one year in a semilegal status as officials deferred approval on the basis of a variety of legal technicalities.[45]

Administrative and police authorities correctly believed that radicals pervaded the trade unions.[46] On 18 May 1906 police officials in Moscow, warning that the city's five thousand Social Democrats and two thousand Socialist-Revolutionaries were seeking to organize trade unions and to set up a branch of the extralegal Council of Unemployed Workers, asked permission to send back to their villages those unemployed workers who took part in illegal meetings or violated public order. They were not overreacting. The Socialist-Revolutionary S. D. Mstislavskii described a "militant worker union" *(boevoi rabochii soiuz)* that received funding from the Council of Unemployed Workers in St. Petersburg. Its main goal, or at least that of the leaders, was an armed uprising; its day-to-day activities included armed assaults and street fighting with rightists. On 3 April 1906, for example, a band of inebriated members surrounded the house of a rightist, blockaded its front entrance, and set it afire. They prevented the fire squad from approaching, and the building burned down, though apparently no one was killed.[47]

The security police, while keeping a careful watch over worker organizations, usually bided their time and avoided premature arrests. In the case of the All-Russian Railroad Union, which also had its own Police Department rubric and a leadership dominated by Socialist-Revolutionaries, the police patiently worked to identify the union leaders with the strongest ties to the Socialist-Revolutionaries. Only in March and May 1907 did they arrest a few key leaders of the union and seize the group's underground press.[48] The broader administration's approach to trade unionism was more heavy-handed. Although a law of 2 December 1905 had legalized nonviolent strikes, state officials often intervened and sometimes prevented them from occurring, especially beginning in fall 1906. In spring 1907, for example, city governor Reinbot warned two unions that if they persisted in their "unreasonable economic demands," he would be forced to close them down and expel their leaders from Moscow.[49]

Public associations, like trade unions, had to be registered and approved by the police. Private assemblies could meet without police supervision, but police officers had the right to attend every session of every public meeting, and they continuously strove to prevent speakers at public meetings of professionals from straying from their approved agenda. The police had their work cut out for them, since orators learned to speak in Aesopian language. According to Menshevik P. A. Garvi, although the phrase "constituent assembly" was forbidden in public meetings, "all Russia came to know the expression that it seems was first used in a meeting in Kiev, 'long live you know what [znamo shche].'"[50]

The most politically significant element of the constitutional order was the bicameral legislature: the Duma, or lower chamber, and the State Council, or upper chamber. Most Russians were animated by a sort of parliamentary fever as elections took place almost continuously from January until late April. Throughout, administrative repression was heavy. It fell mostly on the Kadets because the Socialist-Revolutionaries and Social Democrats had decided to boycott the elections and the Octobrists were a legal political association. Kadet activists in the two imperial capitals campaigned with little restriction, albeit under the watchful eye of the police. In most provinces, however, the Kadets, whose party had never acquired legal status, often faced harassment by local administrative authorities, including arrest and temporary banishment. Even so, they managed to publish as many as fifty newspapers in twenty-nine provinces.[51] One might have expected the party, as a highly influential illegal association, to be a prime target of the security police, but the latter were too preoccupied with the revolutionary parties to pay much attention to it. Here is a prime example of the division of repressive labor between the vast administrative apparatus— the governors and the police—and its specialized security police, who focused almost exclusively on genuine subversives.

The whole of April on the eve of the first Duma witnessed intense revolutionary agitation, including a general strike in Warsaw at mid-month. On 19 April Durnovo instructed governors to take the most decisive measures to prevent and suppress disorders. Numerous arrests and further preparations for repression ensued.[52] Boris Viktorovich Savinkov and other terrorist leaders were planning to assassinate Durnovo and Moscow governor-general F. V. Dubasov. They discovered that Durnovo had adopted a secretive method often used by revolutionaries but rarely by ministers—avoiding routine.[53] Perhaps it was in this way that Durnovo ducked the bullets and bombs planned for him. Dubasov was nearly as lucky: on 23 April a Socialist-Revolutionary terrorist, B. U. Vnorovskii, killed his aide-de-camp but only wounded him. (Dubasov urged clemency for his assailant, saying, "It's ungodly to kill such irresponsible youths.")[54] According to Police Department data, which a recent historian has judged incomplete, from February to May 1906 terrorists killed or gravely wounded 1,421 people, mostly lower-level government officials. The vast majority of these crimes were apparently committed by local, largely autonomous combat units of the major revolutionary parties.[55] The Socialist-Revolutionary Party officially suspended its terrorist campaign to coincide with the opening of the Duma on 27 April, though some members of the combat organization, "uninformed" of the policy, continued to commit acts of terrorism, especially in Sevastopol and the Volga region.[56]

On 27 April, just before the Duma was to convene, Nicholas dismissed Witte and Durnovo and chose new ministers. For the position of prime minister, he selected the aged but utterly loyal Ivan Logginovich Goremykin, who had served as interior minister from 1895 to 1899. The public recoiled at the appointment, and Goremykin himself referred to "the incredible nonsense" of governing the country "in a time of revolutionary upheaval through a parody of west European parliamentarism." Goremykin relied heavily on P. I. Rachkovskii, then a special agent of the interior ministry, trusting him enough to invite him to live in his apartment in the interior ministry building on the Fontanka Embankment.[57]

Nicholas chose the dynamic, youthful Petr Arkad'evich Stolypin as interior minister. Stolypin had drawn the attention of officials in St. Petersburg by dealing creatively but forcefully with popular unrest when he was governor of Saratov Province. His leadership has received mixed reviews from scholars. One historian has concluded that although Stolypin urged local officials to respect individual rights and most of all "to respect the letter of the law," he "never made a clear distinction between those who were, as a party, dedicated to a legal change in the existing order and those who would overthrow it by violence." More recently, Abraham Ascher has argued that Stolypin wanted to cooperate with the opposition "but only if they did his bidding," largely because he "never understood the true meaning of compromise."[58] Spiridovich and Gerasimov, however, had nothing but praise for Stolypin as the man responsible for the security police. Gerasimov called his years of collaboration with him "the best time of my life." According to Spiridovich, Stolypin was one of very few interior ministers who understood the "immense value" of security police reports, whose single most important source of information was informants—and he was the last interior minister to understand this. To most other senior officials, by contrast, the reports were "merely literature."[59]

Stolypin picked as his assistant for police affairs not a tough administrator like himself, but the man who had served as prosecutor in Saratov from 1901 to 1906. Born into a family of merchants in St. Petersburg in 1857, Aleksandr Aleksandrovich Makarov graduated from St. Petersburg University in law and had served in the judiciary since 1878. Ever since the Police Department's creation, its key principle had been to appoint only judicial officials to senior posts, and Makarov's experience corresponded to this principle. One of his major tasks was to oversee a complete reform of the police system, though not of security policing, which Stolypin actively and personally supervised; indeed, Makarov apparently was not particularly interested in the latter aspect of his office.[60]

Nicholas selected another prosecutor, Ivan Grigor'evich Shcheglovitov, as justice minister. Shcheglovitov later claimed that he had greeted the October Manifesto with joy but had then grown disillusioned. A taciturn man, he chose his words carefully and earned the respect even of his opponents for his intelligence, broad education, tactical flexibility, and subtle understanding of the bureaucratic machine. He became one of the most conservative, long-serving, and influential members of the government.[61]

The Kadets won 34 percent of the seats in the Duma, by far the largest share. The party's leaders believed that their victory gave them a popular mandate to challenge the executive's political hegemony, a fight many of them thought they would win. Confrontation over legislation ensued. The government proposed modest reforms, including the privatization of communal land (what became Stolypin's land reform). The Kadets demanded an amnesty of political prisoners, the abolition of capital punishment, the confiscation of some private land, and ministerial responsibility to the Duma. The government not only categorically rejected these desiderata but sent very little legislation to the Duma. What could the Duma, in which the Kadets did not even have a majority, do in return? "On one side," lamented the prominent Kadet M. M. Vinaver, "was a giant bureaucracy; on the other side only five hundred people."[62]

That "giant bureaucracy," moreover, was not taking any chances. One of Gerasimov's officers, G. P. Bertgol'dt, created a special bureau to maintain surveillance over Duma members. With a direct telephone line to the Winter Palace, it sent daily reports to senior police officials, and even to the emperor on occasion. According to Iain Lauchlan, the government was seeking not so much to control the activities of the majority of Duma deputies but to avert any minority's close cooperation with revolutionary activists.[63]

The Duma continuously challenged the government's authority and legitimacy. Its members were in a unique position: they could say nearly anything they wanted, and nearly all they said could be quoted in the press. Moreover, a deputy could engage in seditious activities outside the Duma but could be arrested only with the permission of the Duma.[64] The legislative body's main tool for challenging the government was that of interpellation *(zapros):* it had the right to demand a legal justification of the actions of a given department or official. The First Duma interpellated the government prodigiously, lodging three hundred challenges to the Interior Ministry alone. Most times the deputies alleged abuse of power by policemen and other administrative officials in the form of improper arrests or mistreatment of prisoners. Over one-quarter of the interpellations concerned administrative exile or banishment of specific individuals, which, it was argued, the October Manifesto's promise of civil liberties had rendered unlawful.[65] It was a sore point for many liberals and centrists that the government rejected their vehement demands for amnesty for political detainees, especially administrative exiles. The interior ministry's willingness to allow administrative exiles who were in poor health to petition to spend their period of exile abroad could not allay the deputies' disappointment.[66]

Some interpellations did not challenge the lawfulness of government actions but were merely statements of disapproval, as on 5 May, when the Duma questioned the government's application of the death penalty. This was a terrible bone of contention between the government and the Duma: the government could legally execute those who violently attacked the emperor or rose up against the state, but public opinion staunchly opposed the practice. On 1 June, four hundred public activists submitted a petition to the Duma urging Nicholas to declare a moratorium on executions. Later, eighteen thousand more signatures were added. And as one critic of the government argued in the pages of *Pravo:* "Trying to suppress political crimes with capital punishment is like pouring fuel oil on a fire." Only changing the political system, starting with the abolition of capital punishment, would put an end to political crime, the critic asserted. The highly respected Kadet jurist and former military prosecutor V. D. Kuz'min-Karavaev argued further that "to trample upon *[popirat']* the law cruelly and inhumanely, for the state, is a hundred times more criminal than for the revolution."[67]

When Justice Minister I. G. Shcheglovitov conceded before the Duma on 15 June that the death penalty should not be applied to regular criminals—which was allowed in places that were under a state of emergency—but then asserted that it would be imprudent to abolish the penalty altogether, he was shouted down until he left the rostrum. The very next day, the chief military prosecutor, V. P. Pavlov, who had applied the death penalty in political cases, was driven from the Duma hall in a similar manner. "Even the quietest Kadets were furious," according to Vinaver, "banging on their benches, just seeing Pavlov." On 19 June the Duma unanimously approved a bill abolishing capital punishment altogether. The State Council began to discuss the bill on 27 June, and great conflict ensued among its members.[68]

The biggest political scandal in the First Duma directly involving the security system was the so-called Kommisarov affair. In January 1906 several Jews told A. A. Lopukhin, former director of the Police Department, that pogroms were being prepared. Under suspicion was M. S. Kommisarov, a gendarme officer and assistant to Rachkovskii who apparently operated the press in the Police Department to print anti-Jewish leaflets under Rachkovskii's direction. Lopukhin reported on the operation to Witte, who questioned Kommisarov. The latter admitted his culpability to both Witte and Lopukhin. Witte made Kommisarov swear to terminate the operation but pleaded his case before the emperor, who was indulgently disposed toward Kommisarov both for his valuable counterintelligence work during the Russo-Japanese War and for his rightist connections. The case was dropped, presumably on the emperor's orders.[69]

Iain Lauchlan has intriguingly argued that Lopukhin and Witte had hoped to use the whole affair, which may have been a setup, to ensnare and bring down Rachkovskii and Durnovo. This contention is bolstered by rumors that I. F. Manasevich-Manuilov, a shadowy agent of the interior ministry, had denounced the secret-press operation to Lopukhin in order to damage Rachkovskii. Although Manuilov himself denied that allegation, he certainly had reason to feel enmity toward Rachkovskii, who had precipitated Manuilov's dismissal from the interior ministry in summer 1905.[70]

On 8 June 1906, on the floor of the Duma, Prince S. D. Urusov denounced the government and Kommisarov for printing incendiary leaflets on a Police Department press. From October through December 1905 Urusov, as deputy interior minister, had helped to crush the revolution, principally by overseeing the system of administrative exile. In January, however, his brother-in-law Lopukhin had denounced Kommisarov to him, which apparently caused Urusov to resign his government position in disgust over Kommisarov. The prince then successfully ran as a Kadet from Kaluga Province in the elections for the First Duma. In his speech before that body, Urusov conceded that the central government did not orchestrate pogroms. Yet, he alleged, some governors and lesser local officials approved of antirevolutionary disorders and mandated their prevention only for appearance's sake, which "naturally" led to "complete chaos, complete disorder, complete disorganization, and the demoralization of the authorities." Urusov believed that a tiny clique of "dark forces" under the direction of Trepov was behind the secretive Kommisarov affair. Urusov's allegations, which Stolypin did not deny in his response to the Duma interpellation related to the affair, "utterly discredited the government," according to I. V. Gessen.[71]

The scandal reflected badly on the imperial Russian government, but Spiridovich was surely right that only in the chaos of late 1905 could someone have gotten away with printing incendiary leaflets within the Police Department. Certainly no similar case has ever come to light. In May, Stolypin dismissed Rachkovskii, who retired, then died in 1911. Also in May, Kommisarov was transferred to the St. Petersburg security bureau. Later that year he was decorated as a member of the order of St. Vladimir, fourth degree, an honorific award, pretty much on the same schedule as other ambitious, successful gendarme officers. Lopukhin, on the other hand, lost his six-thousand-ruble yearly pension. He found work in a bank after the bar refused to permit him to practice law, presumably because he had been director of the Police Department.[72]

Years later, V. P. Obninskii furnished a strikingly excellent example of the difficulties faced by senior officials who tried to rein in provincial senior and middle-level officials involved in, or turning a blind eye to, right-wing violence. In early 1906, as chairman of the provincial zemstvo board, he complained to Durnovo about the behavior of officials in Kaluga during a recent pogrom. Durnovo listened attentively, then read to his interlocutor a report from the Kaluga gendarme station, which repeated Obninskii's allegations almost perfectly. "Not without implicit irony," wrote Obninskii, "Durnovo said that he was glad that the report of the chairman of the provincial zemstvo board mirrored that of the provincial gendarme station." Obninskii admitted to having been "stunned" by the accuracy of the gendarme report. Durnovo promised to investigate the case and to punish strictly the wrongdoers. Indeed, that day a telegram was sent dismissing the police captain who had organized the pogrom. Durnovo soon also asked A. A. Ofrosimov, the governor, to retire, "to take care of his health." Ofrosimov had connections at court, however, which enabled him to retain his post. The police captain who had organized the pogrom, it turned out, had merely been transferred, and soon Durnovo himself was dismissed.[73]

The day after his meeting with Durnovo, Obninskii spoke with War Minister A. F. Rediger, who promised to look into the actions of the local military commander, Mezentsev. Rediger lamented to Obninskii that he and other senior military officers were "paralyzed because grand dukes are at the head of various units of army." Nevertheless, Mezentsev was removed.[74]

On 13 June Stolypin appointed Maksimilian Ivanovich Trusevich, a vigorous and intelligent jurist of Polish noble origin, to replace E. I. Vuich as Police Department director. Born in 1863, Trusevich had attended the prestigious Imperial School of Jurisprudence in St. Petersburg and had served since 1903 as assistant prosecutor of the St. Petersburg judicial tribunal. He later asserted that part of his new job would be to "clean out" the Police Department; perhaps he was making reference to the Kommisarov affair. He also sought to increase his control over the Russian Empire's police apparatus, as when, soon after his appointment, he began to regulate the numerous private police forces that had been established in factories and on estates in the wake of the revolution.[75]

Martynov described Trusevich as "tall, slim, very elegant, and with a clever, penetrating, even slightly sarcastic look," a "typical European gentleman" who possessed a "grand-imperial" approach to administration, as a result of which he appointed non-Russians to high positions. Professional assessments of Trusevich were varied. Martynov, who had worked with him on political crime cases in St. Petersburg, wrote that he always immediately grasped the essence of his cases and gave the gendarme officers working with him precise directions for dealing with them. Gerasimov, by contrast, considered Trusevich arrogant and "weak in security policing." P. G. Kurlov, a senior police official, called Trusevich "smart and talented, but also arrogant and convinced that only he understood police affairs, which was injurious to the Department," though he added that Trusevich entrusted the supervision of security policing to highly competent subordinates. S. P. Beletskii, who would later be a senior police official, did not like Trusevich personally. Nevertheless, he considered him an "extremely effective" director of the Police Department. Spiridovich wrote that he was "frenetic . . . highly independent, wanted to control the whole security system." At the time of his appointment, he was "wild over a beautiful brunette, desirous of adventure."[76]

STATE OF SIEGE

Stolypin reported to the Council of Ministers on 29 May that the social situation in Russia had never before been "so threatening as now, for sedition, unrest, and criminal attacks against the existing state order and the security of official and private persons and their property have spread across the entire territory of the empire." That same day he instructed governors to suppress sedition "without hesitation in cooperation with military authorities."[77] The incidence of political terrorism had remained high. From 27 April to 9 July terrorists had killed 177 people, attempted to assassinate 52 officials and 88 private individuals, and perpetrated 189 attacks on official institutions and 93 attacks on commercial and apartment buildings. Government statistics compiled in August showed that attacks on government officials remained largely steady whether the Duma was in session or not. Most sensationally, on 29 June a sailor mortally wounded Vice Admiral G. P. Chukhnin in Sevastopol, and among promenaders in a Peterhof park a Socialist-Revolutionary killed former Moscow governor-general A. A. Kozlov, having mistaken him for D. F. Trepov. "Thank God; I killed Trepov," he exclaimed. (Trepov died of natural causes that September.) In response, numerous conservative voices began to call for the dissolution of the Duma, and in this context Nicholas let it be known to the Kadet leaders that he would not allow them to form a new government despite earlier assurances.[78]

The government prepared to confront massive unrest. On 10 June Interior Minister Stolypin warned all governors to prepare for a strike of railroad workers and urged them to take the most decisive measures to prevent its outbreak.[79] Then he convoked city and provincial governors in Petersburg in order to coordinate such measures. In early July gendarme and security chiefs were ordered to place secret documents in a safe place, to hire private couriers to be prepared in the event of a telegraph strike, to work assiduously to keep agitators away from military personnel, and immediately to raid suspected caches of explosives. Governors were ordered to protect government buildings as well as the railroads, banks, and other properties. Recourse to military force was authorized to halt disorder, but only if the troops could be relied upon. Above all, the governors were to cooperate fully with gendarme and security chiefs.[80]

On 9 July Stolypin ordered the imposition of a state of extraordinary security in St. Petersburg. Police surrounded the Taurida Palace, and the legislature was dissolved.[81] Two days later, Stolypin ordered administrative officials to effect a "rapid, firm, and undeviating" reestablishment of order by every legal means. He cautioned, however, that the struggle must be waged "not against society, but against the enemies of society," and therefore that "indiscriminate repression cannot be approved."[82]

In a coup de théâtre, to use Foreign Minister A. P. Izvol'skii's phrase, Nicholas replaced Goremykin with Stolypin, who immediately declared that "if the state does not retaliate against evil deeds, then the very meaning of the state is lost." Stolypin also proposed reforming the police system and completely reworking all emergency legislation, made further overtures to moderate opposition figures, and promised that "all the reforms required by the spirit of liberalism will be realized as soon as the ground for this has been prepared." Yet few liberals took such assertions seriously. The philosopher E. N. Trubetskoi, formerly a Kadet, warned Nicholas by letter that the dissolution would provoke a "last and final explosion that will overthrow the existing order and destroy Russian culture." The more radical Kadet deputies joined leftist deputies in issuing what came to be known as the Vyborg Manifesto, urging the people to refuse to pay taxes; their Menshevik counterparts called for a general strike. Neither appeal provoked an immediate popular response.[83]

Yet all was not calm. A moderately high number of strikes took place in July, and agrarian disorders reached massive proportions, apparently in response to the government's rejection of radical agrarian reform. Most threatening, unrest in military units gathered strength across Russia in May and June and burst into mass mutinies from 17 to 20 July in naval bases at Sveaborg, Kronstadt, and Reval (now Tallinn). Socialist-Revolutionaries and Social Democrats hoped to use the mutinies to spark a general uprising throughout the Baltic fleet. Although the security police had reported on the discontent among the sailors and on revolutionaries' efforts to exploit it, on 17 July 1906 the Special Section accused them of failing energetically to root out and to arrest propagandists who were active in military units. In the first clashes with loyal troops, the rebellion melted, though "red guards" continued to fight until 21 July. Many contemporaries must have thought, with K. D. Nabokov, the brother of the Kadet leader, that "the Russian tsar is no more worshiped by his army." For the rest of the year Nicholas lavished on his military a careful attention he would never have considered paying to the police forces.[84]

Repeatedly throughout the summer, the security police launched raids against suspected revolutionary activists and made arrests. On 30 June the Moscow district organization of the Social Democrats was struck; on 7 July it was the turn of several middle-level Bolsheviks, including P. N. Krasikov and E. D. Stasova; the Social Democratic military organization in Moscow fell under police fire on 18 and 23 July; and on 23 July Gerasimov raided the Social Democratic St. Petersburg committee. Yet, as Klimovich warned Trusevich, revolutionary activists often quickly replaced their operatives in Moscow by ferrying exiles back from Siberia using their "revolutionary red cross." Railroad workers, who enjoyed unlimited free travel on the steel rails, were an important element in this work, he wrote.[85]

Time and again terrorists struck at officialdom. The liberal lawyers' weekly *Pravo* listed 233 violent attacks against government officials from 4 June to 20 August 1906, an average of 19.4 instances per week. Many of the attacks affected more than one person and most resulted in death.[86] With the dissolution of the Duma, the Socialist-Revolutionary leadership officially resumed their campaign of terror, with Stolypin as their primary target. Any hard-line senior official—even in retirement—could become a target for terrorism. On 11 July in St. Petersburg a bomb exploded near the retired chief procurator of the Holy Synod, K. P. Pobedonostsev, but did not harm him. Two days later the Police Department urged governors to permit security bureau chiefs to report to them only in cases of "absolute necessity" and only in civilian clothes. On 12 August terrorists dressed as gendarmes blew to pieces part of Stolypin's official summer residence on Apteka Island outside St. Petersburg in the delta of the Neva River. The bomb killed twenty-seven people and wounded sixty more, including Stolypin's daughter. To ensure the Prime Minister's security, Nicholas invited him to move into the heavily fortified Elagin Palace farther out toward the mouth of the Neva in summer and into the Winter Palace the rest of the year.

Around 18 August, the Socialist-Revolutionary terrorist Tatiana Leont'eva murdered a French citizen, Charles Muller, in the Swiss town of Interlaken, having mistaken him for P. N. Durnovo. Having been warned of an impending attack, the former interior minister, who was on vacation, had only just departed from town. War Minister A. F. Rediger was happy to live in an apartment above the publisher of the Kadet daily *Rech'*, which "provided a certain guarantee against attacks."[87]

Officials lived in constant fear. I. F. Koshko recalled how in Samara, where he was vice-governor, Governor I. L. Blok was in a particularly gloomy mood on a day soon after the proclamation of the Vyborg Manifesto. "You risk your life," he lamented, "your nerves are frazzled to exhaustion, in order to maintain calm, so that people can live normally, and what do you encounter everywhere? . . . Glances full of hatred, as if you were some kind of monster, drinking human blood." He then departed. Koshko

Wreckage caused by a bomb detonated at Stolypin's summer residence in August 1906 by members of the Socialist-Revolutionary Maximalist organization.

and another official sat down to dinner. Twenty minutes later a servant screamed, ran into the room, and exclaimed, "just now the governor's head has been blown off by a bomb." The scene of the crime was a gruesome sight, with splatterings of human remains up the sides of nearby houses. A crowd formed and some yelled, "It's all the fault of Yids. We have to beat them up." Koshko immediately and successfully took measures to avert an anti-Jewish pogrom.[88]

Koshko himself was, not surprisingly, afraid of terrorist attacks. He would dress up in his uniform and walk deliberately out in public, saying to himself "This time I'll walk 'this far,' then next time 'this far.'" Each time, having made it back without incident, he felt much safer and more relieved. In late July 1906, on the other side of the Volga, some two hundred miles to the south in Saratov, A. P. Martynov arrived to take charge of the security bureau. His predecessor, N. D. Fedorov, was harried and glad to be leaving the city. He could not wait to depart for a calmer life in St. Petersburg. In his haste, he neglected to brief Martynov on security police matters. Three weeks later Fedorov was killed in a bomb attack meant for Stolypin.[89]

Woe befell police informants whose true identity was discovered by their party "comrades." V. I. Lenin, defending the Latvian Social Democratic Party's publication of lists of informants in summer or early fall 1906, argued that "killing them is the duty of any honest [chestnyi] person. Those who help the police are enemies of the revolution and deserve to be executed, and their property should be subject to confiscation." This became the modus operandi of the early Bolshevik state. Numerous informants were indeed killed in this period, including three who worked for the Warsaw security bureau. One of the terrorists who systematically assassinated informants and police officials in Warsaw, a revolutionary acting under the pseudonym "Tsygan," or Gypsy, confessed after his capture to having killed nineteen policemen and police agents. He had always acted alone, he insisted after his capture, and he had attended the funeral of each of his victims.[90]

The Socialist-Revolutionaries' terrorist organization was disrupted by Azef under the guidance of Gerasimov in St. Petersburg. Yet the Socialist-Revolutionary Maximalists, who had split off in fall 1905 to carry out political terror independently, were not under Azef's watchful eye; nor were several other maverick organizations and perhaps hundreds of armed squads *(boevye druzhiny)*, which committed most of the acts of terrorism associated with the Socialist-Revolutionaries. The Maximalists' plan to send suicide bombers into the State Council on 11 July was cancelled only because the council unexpectedly recessed that day. In summer and fall 1906 the police seized, solely from Maximalists, some ten thousand rounds of ammunition and some two hundred pounds of dynamite.[91]

Scholars are divided over whom the police's key informant among the Maximalists served more loyally—the police or his party comrades. Arrested and recruited by the police in June, S. Ia. Ryss was highly educated, with a doctorate in philosophy and minor works in that discipline to his credit. P. Berlin, a friend from high school, described him as "impulsive, unbalanced, exalted, easily captivating others, easily captivated by others." It seems certain that Ryss provided valuable information to the security police, yet his service lasted only a few months, and in late fall he disappeared and joined the terrorists again (he was arrested and executed by sentence of a military court in 1908).[92]

Social Democrats also took part in the killings, as did anarchists and a welter of other unaffiliated terrorists, including some whose violence shaded off into ordinary criminality. In the atmosphere of revolutionary social unrest, respectable public figures like P. N. Miliukov were willing to condone cruel violence on the part of the established revolutionary parties, and the parties seem to have been ready to turn a blind eye to senseless brutality perpetrated by a variety of criminals and psychologically unbalanced terrorists.[93]

Terrorists, especially those active in St. Petersburg, generally used Finland as the base for their operations. As B. V. Savinkov later recalled, the question of extraditing revolutionaries to Russia never came up in Finnish government circles. "If this issue had been raised," he wrote, "we would have been informed about it and would have had time to escape," thanks to sympathizers in all of Finnish government and even in its police institutions. Indeed, according to St. Petersburg city governor V. A. Dediulin, the police chief of Vyborg, Finland, once urged Socialist-Revolutionary delegates staying at various hotels there to depart for Imatra, Finland, in order to avoid an imminent police raid. Bolshevik activists made use of contacts within the Finnish administration to facilitate the shipment of weapons and explosives into Russia. Finnish law was on their side: unlike Russian law, it did not forbid the importation of firearms. "We have lots of intelligence," wrote one official, "but we are helpless to stop the shipments." The leniency of Finnish laws in this respect was not surprising. In Finnish parliament elections in 1907, Social Democrats captured eighty of two hundred seats, the highest proportion anywhere in Europe.[94]

Part of the funding for weapons acquisition and other terrorist ventures came from armed robberies, or so-called expropriations. In October 1906 Maximalists made off with a half-million rubles from the state bank in St. Petersburg. In other cases, the robbers made off with paltry sums, as when, in mid-September, a well-dressed but armed young man demanded twenty-five rubles from a clerk in a watch shop in Moscow, then tendered him a receipt certifying that the money would go to support an unspecified "revolutionary committee." As Baron P. N. Vrangel' remarked several years later, "Now even the most modest little shops were not robbed but 'expropriated' in noble fashion."[95]

Party leaders found it hard to stop party members from keeping expropriated money and from carrying out unauthorized expropriations, but the Bolsheviks must have been pleased at Eliso Lomidze's fervent desire to steal two to three hundred thousand rubles and to hand them over to Lenin. (Once, when the loot disappeared, Lomidze tortured two peasants all night, demanding they tell him where it was. Finally, he admitted they did not know. He felt badly.) In exasperation, Mstislavskii quit one combat unit *(boevoi rabochii soiuz)* that had "degenerated into private expropriation groups." In Latvia the established Social Democrats considered an allied combat organization "a robber gang."[96]

Such units pullulated. Although comprehensive statistics are unavailable and one cannot easily distinguish political from nonpolitical crime—and indeed both the government and the revolutionaries had their own reasons for exaggerating the level of political criminality—the incidence of politically motivated armed robbery must have been prodigious. In both 1906 and 1907 there were probably many hundreds of expropriations netting millions of rubles in proceeds. In October and November alone 160 state liquor stores were robbed in St. Petersburg.[97] Excepting the Mensheviks, all the main revolutionary organizations, or at least a fraction of each, undertook such operations. It was such a lucrative method of fund-raising that, according to Police Department sources, as late as mid-December the Socialist-Revolutionary central committee was beginning to form ten-to-fifteen-person squads to rob more banks.[98]

For three years beginning in 1905 Russia saw a massive increase in the gravest regular crimes and in property crime. The increase was most noticeable in central Russia and in the Baltic, Volga, and southern steppe regions. The yearly number of murder investigations throughout the Russian Empire rose from roughly 17,000 at the turn of the century to 22,000 in 1904; then it shot up to over 30,000 during the next four years, peaking at 36,500 in 1906. Throughout the revolutionary period regular criminality blended with violent political dissidence to engender something like what I. V. Gessen referred to as "a general pogrom, a sophomoric, but bloody universal bedlam [smaz']."[99]

An element in the bedlam, though a relatively minor one, was the activity of violent right-wing activists. After hundreds of anti-Jewish pogroms in late fall 1905 and ten more in January and February 1906, no such events occurred until mid-June, when one major and a few minor pogroms broke out in Grodno Province. In Russia proper, violent altercations between rightists and leftists took place in the major cities though, according to Donald Rawson, "it was an uneven battle," with the rightists suffering comparatively greater losses. Rightist militants also attacked intellectuals and liberal activists. Miliukov, for example, personally received threats of violence and an actual beating. It seems that on 18 July 1906 in Terioki, thirty miles northeast of St. Petersburg, the combat organization of the Union of Russian People murdered economist M. Ia. Gertsenshtein, a Jewish convert to Christianity, a founder of the Kadet Party, and one of that party's rightward leaning deputies in the First Duma. An alleged organizer of the murder, A. V. Polovnev, claimed that Gerasimov later summoned him to the security bureau in St. Petersburg and asked him whether he had indeed taken part in the murder. When Polovnev replied in the negative, Gerasimov supposedly told him to "sit tight and everything will blow over." Polovnev took this to mean that Gerasimov was fully in the know.[100]

As in the case of anti-Jewish pogroms, it is hard to figure out just how many government officials were in the know. It would seem an exaggeration to assert, with S. A. Stepanov, that right-wing terrorism "took place only where local administrative authorities allowed it,"[101] since right-wing terrorists were presumably able to avoid police detection just like their left-wing counterparts. Still, it does seem that some—perhaps even many—individual middle-level officials turned a blind eye to right-wing violence aimed at specific people, something that cannot be said about left-wing violence.

In his memoirs, Gerasimov alleged that the St. Petersburg city governor, V. F. von der Launits, staunchly supported the Union of Russian People, including those members involved with Gertsenshtein's murder. And Reinbot in Moscow, in testimony before the Provisional Government's investigating commission in 1917, alleged that Klimovich had also been involved in some way in that crime. These recriminations probably reveal more about mutual animosity between security officers and the regular police authorities than about any links between right-wing terrorists and the security police. The only official documentary evidence available shows that soon after the murder of Gertsenshtein the Moscow security bureau and the Special Section thoroughly investigated extortionist threats against Gertsenshtein's widow and provided her with protection from the nebulous organization making the threats, "Office of People's Vengeance" *(kontora narodnoi raspravy)*. Like pogromists, however, right-wing terrorists presumably expected to receive official succor. For example, a few low-level officials helped Gertsenshtein's assassins evade police detection until 1909, and when they were finally brought to trial in late 1909, Nicholas pardoned two of them.[102]

Iain Lauchlan has suggested, quite persuasively, that officials supported right-wing terrorists not because the officials were fighting against society but because they were trying to work with right-wing elements in society. After all, the Union of Russian People enjoyed a broader popular base of support than did the Kadet Party, which itself seemed to condone political terrorism. Russia was engaged in a quasi civil war in which even otherwise reasonable people reluctantly and temporarily felt a need to support extremist political elements in their battle to preserve Russia or to reorder it along radically opposed lines. Not surprisingly, few specialized security officers were willing to lend succor to right-wing advocates of violence,[103] even though only left-wing violence appeared to threaten the established political order.

The day after the attempt on Stolypin, a terrorist named Z. V. Konopliannikova killed General G. A. Min, the suppressor of the Moscow armed uprising, as he sat awaiting a train in Novyi Peterhof. The terrorist, who had been living in Luisino on the other side of the railroad tracks, pulled the trigger four times in plain sight of her victim's wife and children. Nicholas felt himself in the terrorists' crosshairs, and well he might have. "Back in 1905–1906," wrote A. F. Kerenskii, "I wanted to be a terrorist and kill the tsar. I was a Socialist-Revolutionary back then and a decent young man. Any decent young man would wish the same thing."[104] Spiridovich urged a tightening of security around the imperial residences. Nicholas and his family moved onto their yacht off the coast in the Gulf of Finland, and its location, which changed every few days, was kept secret. A naval unit guarded them night and day. Nicholas wrote to his mother on 30 August that the "nasty anarchists . . . have come to Peterhof hunting for me. You can imagine my feelings, dear Mother, not to be able to ride a horse or to drive out from my gates to wherever, and this is in my own home in Peterhof."[105]

GOVERNMENT RESPONSES

During the first nine months of the year, troops were called out to suppress disorder 2,330 times, and in 158 cases they had to use force of arms. War Minister Rediger feared that these extraneous duties would diminish the battle readiness of military personnel and perhaps even weaken their loyalty to the government. Stolypin, by contrast, considered the civilian deployment of troops for crowd control and other police duties imperative for maintaining domestic tranquility. The policeman won the debate: in spring 1906 all military training exercises were cancelled for the year to maintain the troops' availability for domestic repression.[106]

The incidence of police repression, which had hovered around five hundred people searched or arrested each month from April through June, suddenly shot up to nearly 3,600 in July 1906, presumably because of the dissolution of the Duma.[107] The regular courts tried 3,395 political defendants in 1906 and found 68 percent of them, or 2,315, guilty. Although a large proportion of the crimes for which they were sentenced were insignificant (at least a third had made insulting reference to the emperor and were sentenced to a brief term in jail), the large increase in cases overwhelmed the criminal justice and administrative punishment systems. On 14 July 1906 the justice ministry ordered prosecutors to deal with these cases more expeditiously by "disregarding circumstances of a secondary nature." Then directives of 31 July and 8 August enjoined gendarme chiefs to curtail most of their investigations *(doznaniia)* into political crimes by either freeing or proposing to administratively exile the accused. Finally, in a directive of 28 July railroad gendarmes were empowered to conduct *doznaniia* in their own jurisdictions, since the gendarme stations were overwhelmed with work.[108]

In mid-1906, the Senate reinterpreted article 129 of the criminal code, which forbade social groups from inciting animosity against one another; the reinterpretation made it easier to prosecute radical publications. The previous interpretation had required the government to prove that the distributor of the publications in question intended to incite animosity. Henceforth it was enough that the defendant understood the nature of the publications themselves. By fall the courts were inundated with new cases.[109]

The regular courts were, however, often frail vessels for the realization of the government's repressive designs. Many of Russia's most brilliant and eloquent defense attorneys were more than willing to defend revolutionary activists in court. Even in major trials the prosecutors were often far less competent than their opponents. Furthermore, some judges were favorably disposed toward members of the revolutionary opposition. The Bolshevik V. D. Bonch-Bruevich referred to an "implicit animosity" that he sensed between antirevolutionary judges like N. S. Krasheninnikov, the chairman of the St. Petersburg judicial tribunal, and his assistant, the more liberal A. I. Ruadze.[110]

The brilliant jurist and defense lawyer O. O. Gruzenberg defended V. M. Gessen, who was tried in late spring 1906 for having published in *Pravo* the St. Petersburg Soviet's early December 1905 call for a general political strike and massive civil disobedience. Gruzenberg arranged to postpone the trial until rumors of the imminent establishment of a Kadet government were at their height. The president of the St. Petersburg judicial tribunal, I. K. Maksimovich, who believed in the Kadets' rising star, found Gessen not guilty.[111]

In the fall, Gruzenberg defended Trotsky in the trial of the leaders of the St. Petersburg Soviet. Gruzenberg argued that the Soviet had not been just a group of revolutionaries but in fact had enjoyed popular support and had protected citizens against pogroms. Three of seven judges voted to exonerate Trotsky; the remainder sentenced him and thirteen others to exile in Siberia. Trotsky escaped en route to Siberia in early 1907.[112]

Also in fall 1906 the Moscow judicial tribunal found most of the alleged leaders of the December armed uprising innocent. Governor Dzhunkovskii complained to Stolypin that the judges and judicial investigators in the Moscow judicial tribunal were too liberal. At a retrial later in the month, the defendants screamed and comported themselves as in a street demonstration, and the court still exculpated more than half of them, though nine received sentences of hard labor ranging from four to twelve years in length.[113]

In the large number of localities governed under emergency laws, the majority of political crimes, and all the more serious ones, were tried in the military courts.[114] These courts' streamlined procedural rules required military judges to adjudicate their cases rapidly, but the rules maintained several important elements of due process, and the military judges were not all hard-liners. According to William Fuller, they often disappointed "repression-minded bureaucrats," and a large number of military judges deeply resented being asked to play a repressive role. It was apparently for this reason that one-sixth of all military judges quit in 1906.[115]

A Soviet historian calculated from official government figures that military judges exonerated from 22 to 44 percent of defendants in state-crime cases between 1905 and 1909. Sentences were especially mild in those jurisdictions where military commanders were least likely to overturn death sentences. Overall, the military judges meted out harsh sentences to only about 40 percent of those found guilty of political crimes. The military courts tried 4,683 people in 1906 (up from 408 in 1905) in cases concerning state crimes, grave regular crimes, and some military crimes. In 1906 military judges, the only officials who could issue death sentences, condemned to death 182 civilians (17 for political crimes) and 65 soldiers. Military judges also condemned 229 people to *katorga*, or hard labor, and 512 people to exile for political crimes.[116]

By August the government was seeking a harsher method for crushing sedition. On 14 August, two days after the explosion on Apteka Island, Nicholas wrote to Stolypin that only the use of military field courts could restore calm. On 19 August, using Article 87, which empowered the emperor to issue temporary decrees when the legislature was not in session, the government gave governors-general in places under extraordinary security or martial law the power to transfer to military field courts persons whose guilt of grave, violent attacks against state officials or institutions was so "self-evident" as not to require investigation. A directive of 9 October explained that in most cases this would mean catching the culprits in flagrante delicto. The field courts were obliged to pass judgment in no more than two days and to carry out the sentence thus rendered within one day. The courts applied capital punishment in all but 145 of the total 1,247 cases from late August to 20 April 1907. A portion of the expenses occasioned by the courts' activity was covered by secret Police Department funds.[117]

In order to justify his policy to a skeptical public, on 24 August Stolypin issued a statement in the official daily, *Rossiia*, detailing both the threats to state security and public tranquility and the government's plan for the restoration of order and further reform. The field courts, he wrote, "were only a means and not an end." The government would use all the strength of the state to restore order based upon the rule of law and, "properly understood, true freedom." Reforms would include measures to limit administrative arbitrariness. For the moment, however, arbitrariness and repression were the order of the day.[118]

On 26 August, Nicholas told War Minister Rediger to order military commanders to apply the law on military field courts in all its harshness and not to trouble him with appeals for clemency. The next day Nicholas wrote his mother that he felt a "turning point toward order. Of course, there will still be individual acts of anarchists, but this existed before, and they will not accomplish anything." The field courts, he added, were "painful but necessary and already are having the needed effect."[119]

The only prominent moderate public figure who agreed with this assessment was the Octobrist leader A. I. Guchkov. In an article in the conservative newspaper *Novoe vremia* he argued that since the country was in a state of civil war, extreme repressive measures were unavoidable. The liberal intelligentsia was outraged by this assertion. Guchkov's comrade D. N. Shipov quit the party in protest. A few senior officials also condemned the policy, for two main reasons. Rediger resented his ministry being saddled with yet more responsibility for political repression, though he admitted that the guards and the cavalry alone saved the government from collapse. V. F. Dzhunkovskii, by contrast, complained that the field courts gave too much discretionary authority to individual military officers. In October V. A. Maklakov, a leading Kadet, brought before the Duma an official report that conceded as much.[120]

By far the largest number of political activists were punished administratively. In 1906 administrative officials exiled 8,701 people to European and Siberian Russia and banished another 1,828 from the empire's major cities. The total number, 10,529, had shot up from 1,609 in 1905 and would climb farther before falling again in 1909.[121] K. D. Kafafov, a judge in the Moscow judicial tribunal, considered administrative punishments the weakest link in the police system. First, their broad use stemmed from the frequent inability of the police and gendarmes to gather sufficient incriminating evidence to permit prosecutors to win political-crime cases in the courts, and second, it sometimes resulted in the exile of "harmless blabberers" while failing to take dangerous revolutionaries out of circulation. In a word, the practice was arbitrary. Senator A. M. Kuz'minskii, who had inspected the police institutions in Baku, Tiflis, and Odessa in 1905, had reached similar conclusions.[122] Several directives in the second half of 1906 urged gendarme and security chiefs to observe strict legal procedure even when resorting to administrative measures. For example, on 8 September gendarmes and governors were chided for occasionally subjecting people to administrative exile on flimsy grounds.[123]

Punishments were harshest and most frequent on the empire's southern and western periphery, where disorder and unrest attained their highest level. Of 629 executions imposed by the military field courts from 31 August 1906 through January 1907, only 83 took place in European Russia, including 28 in the south and 17 in Kronstadt. Similarly, most of the 3,382 executions sanctioned by the military district courts from 1906 to 1913 were carried out in the borderlands, and even there quite unevenly. On 24 November 1906 a military commander in Vladikavkaz warned that if any Russian was killed or the slightest resistance to government authority was made, "guilty" villages (auly) would be razed by artillery.[124]

In Poland the number of death sentences during the period from 1905 to 1908 never fell below one-seventh of the total number of such sentences for the whole empire.[125] G. A. Skalon, the governor-general of Poland, reported to Stolypin in mid-1906 that death sentences no longer intimidated anyone in Poland. He therefore recommended that the government either increase their number drastically or stop issuing them.[126] Moreover, ten thousand people in Poland were exiled or banished administratively between 1905 and 1908, which was about one-third the total for the empire.[127] When P. P. Zavarzin arrived in Warsaw in September 1906 to take charge of the security bureau, he found the entire administration demoralized. His predecessor had desperately telegraphed to Trusevich, "all of Poland is rising up; no way to fight it." The security bureau had become so unpopular, according to Zavarzin, that all employees with "another means of subsistence have fled." The gendarme station was in disarray. A large number of police had been killed, and authority had simply broken down. It is not surprising, then, that some officials in Poland, when not cowed into inaction, grossly exceeded their authority. M. E. Bakai, an employee of the security bureau, wrote that Skalon had had political prisoners tortured, though he admitted the practice had stopped after the press got wind of it. L. P. Men'shchikov, who was sent to inspect the security bureau in summer and fall 1906, found evidence of the "most desperate abuse of power."[128]

All over the empire, determined revolutionaries managed to evade police detection or to abscond from places of confinement. In early 1906 V. L. Burtsev lived for two months in St. Petersburg without a passport. Then a police official issued him a passport without verifying the personal information Burtsev had given him—except that he was unwilling to trust Burtsev on the issue of his marital status. "One never knows," the policeman said, and he wrote, "claimed to be single." Apparently, the policeman's premodern outlook prevented him from imagining that anyone would lie about his whole identity.[129]

Also in early 1906, in Dvinsk, a Social Democrat named M. I. Frumkin, who had fled a court investigation in Mogilev, was arrested as a suspicious person by officers of the local gendarme station. His romantic partner, Z. G. Bogoliubova, knew she had to liberate him before the gendarmes received word from Mogilev. She made a visiting card in the name of Trusevich with an inscription on the back saying that she was his niece, then she returned to Dvinsk and told the gendarme chief that Frumkin was her fiancé. "He is a Jew," she admitted, "but a very good, loyal one." The gendarme officer was courteous and kind, but he told her apologetically that he could not release Frumkin without receiving word from Mogilev. She then harassed the officer, accusing him of formalism and the like. Finally he relented, saying "I don't want to seem like a heartless formalist; we gendarmes also have human feelings. . . . I will immediately release him and hope that neither you nor your bridegroom will abuse my help." Frumkin returned to St. Petersburg, took an engineering degree, and then emigrated to Germany. Bogoliubova lived illegally in St. Petersburg until 1914, when she was arrested.[130]

Those revolutionaries who landed in prison or exile often found the conditions of confinement less harsh than one might imagine. In 1906 "prisons were clubs," wrote M. A. Spiridonova. Even at the hard-labor prison in Nerchinsk in eastern Siberia she found that political prisoners enjoyed "complete freedom" *(polnoe privol'e)*. Upon her arrival in July, over one hundred prisoners with red banners, singing revolutionary songs, greeted her. The prisoners could leave the prison to pick mushrooms, and some families with children lived outside the prison walls, in houses. The guards entered the prison only for roll call.[131]

Of course, much depended on the attitudes of local authorities, but in 1906 nearly all prison authorities appear to have been lenient. A worker-revolutionary who had spent time in prisons in both Sevastopol and Smolensk in 1906, I. Genkin, found conditions for political prisoners "quite decent." He also noted that if "the repression had been harsher, we would not have rioted or been so disobedient." In summer 1906 Governor I. F. Koshko of Samara cabled Stolypin to report that the local prison inspector sympathized with revolutionary activists. Soon thereafter, a verbatim excerpt from this telegram appeared in a local revolutionary newspaper. Even the notorious Shlissel'burg Fortress had had a relatively mild regime, but it was shut down in mid-1906. G. A. Gershuni, the Socialist-Revolutionary terrorist mastermind, recalled how, after the fortress closed, he was conveyed to Moscow by a dozen gendarme noncommissioned officers, who all saluted and bowed to him, saying "don't remember us badly" *(ne pominaite likhom)*. I. K. Mikhailov, a Social Democratic worker who tried to escape from the regular police in early 1906, was taken into a basement and beaten until he yelled, "Beat me, beat me; they beat the Lord God." He found that this generally caused violent, angry policemen to relent.[132]

Mikhailov was not the only political detainee who attempted to escape in 1906. The famous trial lawyer, O. O. Gruzenberg, claimed with considerable justification that anyone could escape from exile. Ia. M. Sverdlov found that "so many people ran away the guards were not even punished for escapes," and local officials also turned a blind eye. Of course, administrative officials were sometimes punished for failing to thwart the escape of political prisoners. In August gendarmes were transporting prisoners in a second-class wagon instead of a jail car, and the prisoners got away by crashing headfirst through a window. The gendarmes were tried by a court-martial.[133] Yet it seems likely that their prosecution was the exception rather than the rule.

All told, over three thousand prisoners—both regular and political—escaped in 1906 (or some 1,500 per 48,000 prisoners, compared to 5 per 48,000 prisoners in Prussia.)[134] The number of those who escaped from exile must have been much greater. The Council of Ministers discussed ways to prevent escapes twice in late August and early September. The justice ministry proposed applying light handcuffs to certain, limited categories of prisoners. Most ministers opposed this proposal, fearing it would inflame public opinion. The fact that such devices were currently in use in western Europe, however, was a point in their favor for most ministers. The case was cited of one Belentsov, who was extradited from Switzerland to Russia in handcuffs. When he arrived in Russia, the handcuffs were removed, and he escaped. The council agreed, finally, to adopt the proposal as a temporary measure by means of Article 87 of the Fundamental Laws. Still it would remain difficult to prevent the escape of experienced members of the revolutionary underground. According to P. P. Zavarzin, such escapes were usually well organized by a small number of revolutionary activists. Only with advance notice from informants—and this was quite rare—could the authorities hope to frustrate them.[135]

Much of the overall public considered Stolypin to be a butcher—they referred to a noose as a "Stolypin necktie"—or at the very least they considered him unduly authoritarian. Shipov characterized Stolypin's entire approach to governance as the cultivation of a "cult of the strong and the maintenance of bureaucratic absolutism." Yet Stolypin believed himself a bulwark of moderation. "A more liberal government than mine is unthinkable," he told Russian-American journalist P. A. Tverskoi in December 1906, "whereas the possibility of the opposite direction is essentially unlimited."[136] Moreover Stolypin saw myriad dangers to the established order. On 15 September he issued to governors comprehensive instructions for confronting unrest. In the countryside, police and gendarmes should arrest and exile propagandists, and disorders should be suppressed with the greatest decisiveness. Stolypin demanded "absolutely loyal support" from rightist organizations and rejected "any pursuits that involve internecine conflict, terrorist undertakings, or the like." Governors were advised to abet security police efforts to insinuate informants into military units, assiduously to confiscate guns from criminals, and to organize voluntary associations for the preservation of order. Stolypin conceded that revolutionary agitation among the educated segments of the population had taken on immense proportions.[137] It seemed imperative, therefore, to enhance the security police force's capacity for surveillance. The government undertook a few steps in this direction in summer and fall before embarking on major reforms in early 1907.

In July 1906, Trusevich named a new Special Section chief to replace N. A. Makarov, who had retired in February in the wake of the Kommisarov affair. Aleksei Tikhonovich Vasil'ev had grown up and studied law in Kiev, where his parents owned three houses. A. P. Martynov described him as a "wonderful person of rare cordiality and simplicity, very gifted, clever, broadly educated, and with a variety of interests." He was also "quite inclined to laziness," greatly enjoying lunches and dinners at which he was always the wittiest joke teller. As a prosecutor in Kiev and St. Petersburg, Vasil'ev had maintained excellent relations with gendarme and security officers, whom he had helped to build effective political cases.[138]

Vasil'ev reorganized the Special Section, enlarging its purview. He divided it into two units *(chasti)*, designated A and B. Unit A remained the command center for security policing, while Unit B was broken into five geographical regions and concentrated on surveillance over broad segments of the population, including industrial workers, public activists, peasants, students, railroad workers, and telegraphists. It was also concerned with diverse forms of unrest, strikes, and other mass phenomena. One employee of Unit B, erstwhile informant N. E. Pankrat'ev, prepared weekly reports for the interior minister and the emperor and supervised the drafting of relational charts of people under surveillance. The Special Section's filing system was also reconfigured. From that point on, each record *(delo)* number corresponded to a specific topic, such as worker disorders, revolutionary propaganda, or nationalist movements. Many such records were broken down into subsections *(chasti)* according to province. The vast majority of records, however, were still devoted to specific individuals.[139]

The Police Department possessed voluminous data, enough to fill several offices at 16 Fontanka Embankment. In order to systematize this material, Trusevich ordered the creation of a central registration bureau ("Registratsionnyi otdel s Tsentral'nym spravochnym apparatom") that combined the diverse card catalogues of the entire Police Department. Once this was in place, it was possible to determine within three to four minutes whether information existed on a given person.[140]

Several minor reforms of the security police force's "external," or plainclothes, surveillant capability occurred during the summer. The department's twenty-man Mobile Surveillance Brigade had been abolished in April in the interest of saving money, and its director, E. P. Mednikov, who had suffered a nervous breakdown, had retired on 20 May 1906. Yet it soon became apparent that the Police Department would still need to send surveillants on regular missions into the provinces. Therefore, later in May a central surveillance unit was recreated and was informally attached to Gerasimov's security bureau. In order to help surveillants recognize revolutionaries, Trusevich ordered that they be supplied with pocket-sized photographic albums of major activists, though in the provinces gendarme officers received only a few dozen such photographs per year in 1906 and 1907. In late summer and fall Trusevich solicited detailed recommendations from security officers, then supervised the drafting of new directives on external surveillance. Finally, Trusevich sought to improve surveillants' service status. They were not permanent civil servants and therefore lacked such privileges as the right to a state pension. On 16 November 1906, Trusevich proposed to enroll a large portion of all surveillants as regular, uniformed policemen in Moscow and a few other cities while the Police Department would continue to pay their wages. As if by magic, they were transformed into bona fide civil servants.[141]

Police officials sought to inspire gendarme officers to self-sacrifice and combat readiness. On 6 October the temporary commander of the Gendarme Corps, S. S. Savvich, wrote: "These are times of war, and by the nature of our service we stand at the front lines of the battlefield, where one must be ever ready to react to the most unexpected designs of the enemy and with the most vigorous and decisive measures to nip them in the bud." In reality, most gendarme officers must have been confused. They were military men, and many of them possessed revolvers, but they generally did not carry them. They probably grasped that the best way for them to struggle against the enemies of the government, beyond investigating state crimes, was to deploy secret informants. Yet few gendarme officers disposed of competent informants. The Moscow gendarme station had thirteen informants, and only one of them was highly effective. Code-name "Doktor," he had been transferred from the Moscow security bureau and earned two hundred rubles per month, almost half the entire informant budget. In 1906 the Kiev gendarme station chief complained that although Kiev Province was the most populous in the empire, he had to maintain his entire informant network on 250 rubles monthly.[142]

When A. P. Martynov arrived in Saratov, he found that his predecessor had only one good informant, who was away at the time. By November, Martynov had managed to recruit thirteen new informants at a total cost of 590 rubles per month, an amount that increased by fifty rubles in late November. But Martynov was an exceptional provincial gendarme officer, "a fanatic of duty" who worked "Sundays and holidays, all day and part of the night."[143] Few provincial gendarme officers shared Martynov's enthusi-

The Police Department building at 16 Fontanka Embankment; photo taken in the early 1900s.

asm for combating revolutionary activism, largely because they saw themselves as military men and had a deeply ingrained sense of dignity and honor. One might say that they loved their uniforms and other external signs of service too much to be willing to trade them for inconspicuous civilian garments.[144]

All told, only a handful of talented security officers and their highly placed informants, nearly all of them based in the imperial capitals, were truly on the front lines of that fight. Yet in spite of their small number, they enjoyed remarkable success. Information provided by S. Ia. Ryss, for example, enabled the police to crush the Maximalists in the fall. These operations had been hindered by the fact that many of the Maximalists abided in Finland. After some initial hesitation, however, N. N. Gerard, the governor-general of Finland, had acceded to Stolypin's entreaties and authorized the police in Finland to undertake numerous arrests in November 1906. Arrests in St. Petersburg and Odessa also ensued, and by the end of the year the Maximalists' combat organization practically ceased to exist.[145]

Thanks to Klimovich's informant, V. P. Kulagin, on 20 September the Moscow security bureau carried out major arrests of members of the Socialist-Revolutionary combat organization in Moscow. In September Z. F. Zhuchenko, a star informant operating among the Socialist-Revolutionaries, returned to Moscow after a bitter struggle between Klimovich and A. M. Garting, the Paris security bureau chief, who wanted to keep her in Paris. In November she became secretary of the regional committee of the Socialist-Revolutionary Party and immediately facilitated the arrest of the members of the party's newly created combat squad *(boevaia druzhina)*. Finally, unnamed informants enabled the police in Moscow, Kiev, and St. Petersburg to launch mass arrests against Social Democrats from October to December.[146]

Recruiting informants in the military was a ticklish matter. Sometime in late spring or early summer, Stolypin apparently persuaded Nicholas to soften his opposition to the policy. Stolypin's directive of 15 September formally advocated the recruitment of informants in military units; even earlier informal directives had apparently encouraged this policy. Indeed, by fall 1906 the security police had managed to establish surveillance over about half of all Social Democratic military organizations, which operated within the Russian military, including some twenty-three Bolshevik organizations. Police intelligence indicated in late November that revolutionary activists were planning to bombard new military recruits with antigovernment propaganda. Orders were issued throughout the police system to take measures to keep the agitators away from the recruits. November and December then saw major arrests among members of the Social Democratic military organization in St. Petersburg. In mid-March 1907 Rediger proposed to Stolypin a coordination of efforts toward interdicting revolutionary propaganda in the military.[147]

The security police force's ability to combat revolutionary activism was circumscribed by the bounds of the repressive infrastructure, which by fall 1906 was stretched to the limit. With ordinary and political offenses blending together in a paroxysm of criminality, regular and security police had to cooperate with each other more than ever. The number of political offenders under regular police surveillance *(nadzor politsii)* had risen from under one thousand on 1 January 1906 to six thousand on 1 September. In some cases, the security police undertook preliminary investigations of crimes only to discover that they exhibited no political features, as when, in mid-November, the Moscow security bureau probed a sensational murder case and then transferred it to regular police officials. But in many more instances, the results of preliminary investigations flowed the other way. On 14 December, therefore, the Moscow security bureau issued detailed directions to precinct captains reiterating that all policemen were required by law to try to uncover and to prevent political crimes, but only under the supervision of the security police.[148]

Yet the security police could not always count on the full support of the regular police, who sometimes resented taking on expanded burdens. Just the added crowd control and the greater volume of search-and-arrest operations were already placing the uniformed police under immense pressure.

Moreover, street policemen *(gorodovye)* were poorly paid, and at least some must have sympathized with the revolutionary agitators. V. P. Obninskii recalled that *gorodovye* and soldiers of the *okhrana* of the emperor's court would gather together in the courtyard of the Taurida Palace when the Duma was first in session, eagerly reading radical newspapers. Also, unlike the security police, the regular police in Russia were notorious bribe takers. According to Bonch-Bruevich, revolutionary activists continuously had to give money, alcohol, and other items to lower-level administrative officials, including regular policemen, to avoid being denounced by them to the security police. By contrast, security policemen and even the relatively poorly paid surveillants were apparently such loyal servants of the tsar that revolutionary activists could rarely bribe them to turn a blind eye to illegal activity.[149]

■ ■ ■

The turbulent year 1906 ended with a divisive election campaign for the Second Duma and a campaign of terror against government officials. On 2 December terrorists attempted to kill Admiral F. V. Dubasov. On 9 December in the city of Tver a Socialist-Revolutionary schoolboy named S. N. Il'inskii murdered State Council member A. P. Ignat'ev. On 21 December E. P. Kudriavtsev, a Socialist-Revolutionary, fatally shot V. F. von der Launits, the city governor of St. Petersburg, then turned his miniature pistol on himself. On the eve of the assassination, Gerasimov had warned Launits that his life was in danger. Prudently, Launits had acquired a bulletproof vest, but, trusting in right-wing activists for protection, he had foolishly begun to walk about more freely. (Kudriavtsev, killed by shots fired by armed guards as well as those of his own hand, was identified only later by Azef; neither his name nor his party's was mentioned at the time, to protect Azef's identity.) V. P. Pavlov, the chief military prosecutor, knew terrorists were gunning for him, so he practically never left the military court building in St. Petersburg. He even took his strolls in its courtyard. Unfortunately for him, a few employees were revolutionary sympathizers. They told former sailor Nikolai Egorov, a Socialist-Revolutionary who had helped lead the mid-July rebellion in Kronstadt, when Pavlov would take his walk. Egorov entered the building on 27 December dressed as a courier and shot him dead.[150]

Few constitutionalist activists could bring themselves to condemn revolutionary terrorism publicly, much less to support political repression. Guchkov considered this refusal a proof of their unsuitability for assuming state responsibilities in a time of crisis. He was outraged when P. A. Geiden, a conservative Octobrist and former government official in the provinces, declared that if he were interior minister and received word of an outbreak of violence between been Armenians and Azerbaijanis, he would rather resign than impose martial law.[151] It seems hard to disagree with Guchkov's argument that Stolypin's willingness to resort to harsh repression was an essential attribute of a statesman in a time of crisis. The true test of Stolypin as a statesman, however, was whether he could preside over the suppression of revolutionaries while protecting civil rights, nurturing the development of civil society, and winning the support of the public. The violent revolutionary opposition had to be defeated without an expansion of administrative arbitrariness and without recourse to grossly violent means. One of the government's most important tasks, therefore, was to develop a security police force capable of singling out violent political activists without implicating everyone else.

CHAPTER TWO

REVOLUTION'S END

■ Toward the end of 1906, police officials began planning major reforms in the security system. In 1902 S. V. Zubatov had created a network of security bureaus whose main purpose was to bypass the provincial gendarme officers, who were deemed irremediably incompetent fighters in the struggle against sedition. Then in the intervening four years the revolutionary movements had expanded enormously, penetrating to the farthest corners of provincial Russia, and a revolution had shaken the country. Maksimilian Ivanovich Trusevich therefore created a network of regional bureaus that corresponded roughly to the revolutionary parties' territorial configuration and were directed by young, dynamic security officers. He also renovated security police methods and operations and improved training and oversight. Meanwhile, in the first half of 1907, society continued to enjoy broad latitude for oppositional activity and government repression was only modest. But when an increase in tensions between government and society developed, manifested especially in conflicts centered on the Second Duma, the administration dissolved that body, changed its electoral law, and launched a crackdown on public activism. The security police devastated the revolutionary underground, and the government appeared triumphant.

SECURITY POLICE REFORMS

In a report of 13 September 1906, N. S. Uranov, a gendarme officer attached to the Special Section, advocated reorganizing the security system. Since "the enemy is united," he argued, the Police Department needed to consolidate its counterrevolutionary forces. As gendarme chief in Tver in 1903, Uranov had successfully reorganized his station and had totally undermined the Social Democratic operations in the province. His main proposals now were that the government create some eighty investigative offices *(rozysknye punkty)* at the provincial gendarme stations, at a cost of seven hundred thousand rubles annually, and that it place province gendarme officers in charge of the security system.[1]

Uranov was touching here on one of the most ticklish questions debated among police officials: Should the more highly ranked gendarme officers answer to the more professionally sophisticated security officers, or the other way around? Relations between A. P. Martynov and D. S. Pomerantsev were illustrative of the acuteness of the problem. Appointed to head the security bureau in Saratov in August 1906, Martynov had immediately set about organizing a counterrevolutionary crusade. Pomerantsev, the local gendarme chief, resented being upstaged by the lower-ranked Martynov, whom he denounced to senior police officials. After investigating the matter, Trusevich ordered Pomerantsev to cooperate fully with Martynov. Pomerantsev, who had got wind of Uranov's report, then complained to A. T. Vasil'ev that "in four years the security bureau has never informed me about revolutionary activity in the province." Provincial gendarme officers were unsatisfactory security policemen, he conceded, but only for want of decent training. "They need to be drawn into security policing," he argued, and this could be done if the security bureaus were brought under the control of gendarme station chiefs.[2] Trusevich approved of instituting a rigorous and more extensive training program for the few hundred provincial gendarme officers, but he considered the younger *okhranniki* like Martynov the most effective security policemen and the best fitted to train the others.

So where and how would the training take place? Since, according to Police Department sources, revolutionary activists had chosen as the centers of their operations "places where local gendarme and police authorities have displayed more or less continuous ineptitude or negligence, as well as places of geographical importance, such as Minsk, Saratov, Poltava, Riga, Warsaw, Belostok, etc.," Trusevich proposed to create regional security bureaus corresponding in part to the network of the Socialist-Revolutionary Party, with due consideration to the major centers of Social Democratic operations. An experienced but young and dynamic gendarme officer at the helm of each regional bureau would bear the responsibility for training local gendarmes and security officers and for coordinating their operations.[3]

In December 1906 and January 1907 senior police officials created eight regional security bureaus entirely within European Russia, each comprising from four to twelve provinces and centering on St. Petersburg, Moscow, Samara, Kiev, Odessa, Khar'kov, Vilna, and Riga. The first five bureaus corresponded closely to the Socialist-Revolutionary Party's regional committees. For example, all but the first three of the Moscow bureau's twelve provinces (Arkhangel'sk, Vologda, Kazan, Vladimir, Kostroma, Moscow, Nizhegorod, Orel, Riazan, Tver, Tula, and Iaroslavl) fell within the Socialist-Revolutionary Party's central region. Each regional bureau was headed by the local security bureau chief, though the Volga bureau, which was soon moved to Saratov, a more important revolutionary center than Samara, was temporarily headed by the local gendarme chief. Numerous, often temporary investigative offices were also created at gendarme stations to beef up their capacity for security policing.[4]

Maintaining the regional as well as the ordinary security bureaus, of which there were between twenty-four and twenty-seven in 1907, cost 1,268,934 rubles, up from one million rubles in 1904—a 27 percent increase, but far less than a program like Uranov's would have cost. These numbers excluded the salaries for gendarme officers, the cost of office space, and other expenses borne by diverse government departments. Nevertheless, it is surprising that despite the massive growth of the revolutionary opposition, the near collapse of the government in late 1905, and the continued high incidence of revolutionary terrorism (in the last two weeks of January alone, terrorists killed twenty and wounded forty-seven officials), the interior ministry did not manage to boost spending on security policing more substantially. After all, in 1906 it had increased spending on regular police forces by 22 million rubles, that is, by 73 percent over the 1905 budget of 30 million (out of a total interior ministry budget of 109 million rubles in 1905 and 131 million rubles in 1906).[5] Presumably the Duma was willing to vote for increased funding for the regular but not for the security police. Yet the interior ministry might have increased the latter's funding before the Duma first convened in April 1906. Why it did not remains a mystery.

Trusevich placed greater responsibility on youthful, dynamic security officers just as Zubatov had done. For example, of the twelve gendarme chiefs in the Moscow region in 1909 four were generals and the rest were majors. The regional bureau chief, Evgenii Konstantinovich Klimovich, was a mere lieutenant colonel. So was M. F. von Koten, who succeeded him on 4 April 1907. Von Koten rose to the rank of colonel only in late 1909, after more than two years of instructing several major generals.[6]

Klimovich and Mikhail Fridrikhovich von Koten had attended both the Polotskii Cadet Corps and the Pavlovskoe Military School, where they forged a rock-solid bond of friendship, according to Martynov. Von Koten went on to graduate in the top third of his class from the Nikolaevskaia Military Academy of the General Staff in St. Petersburg, making him the only important security officer with a higher education. Perhaps that was why K. D. Kafafov recalled that von Koten was one of a tiny number of very educated, cultivated gendarme officers who were accepted "everywhere in society." The city governor of Moscow called von Koten "a brilliant administrator" who inspired in his employees a devotion to their work and a "corporatist spirit." Aleksandr Ivanovich Spiridovich called him "intelligent and capable" but thought he "used risky methods." An informant described him as "hard to talk with, coarse, a teller of off-color jokes, full of canine loyalty to the autocracy."[7]

Another informant, Arsenii Bel'skii, an active Socialist-Revolutionary, found von Koten "intelligent, firm *[stoikii]*, immeasurably stronger than" Bel'skii himself. Von Koten knew intimate details about Bel'skii's underground contacts and activities. He even ran through a list of the informant's friends, noting who were Socialist-Revolutionaries and who were not. But what really scared Bel'skii was when "von Koten described his trip to Finland where he met with Gershuni and cited their conversation almost verbatim." Deploying arguments once used by Zubatov, von Koten then assured Bel'skii that he only wanted help in "saving hotheads from the consequences of terror. . . . We would not fight against the Socialist-Revolutionaries if they did not engage in terror." He then offered him four thousand rubles a year, and Bel'skii was hooked.[8]

The senior provincial officials' resentment of the upstart security officers must have been palpable. In late December 1906, for example, both City Governor Anatolii Anatol'evich Reinbot and Governor-General S. K. Gershel'man had voiced their opposition to giving Klimovich so much power. In order to allay the inevitable anxieties of the older gendarme chiefs, Trusevich appealed to them personally to lay aside questions of rank and to work harmoniously together. "Each government official who is devoted to the throne and the fatherland," he wrote, "*must forget the privileges redounding to him by his position on the Table of Ranks in those circumstances when the vital interests of Russia demand that he accept directions . . . from individuals who, albeit lower in rank, possess special expertise.*" Petr Arkad'evich Stolypin extended to the governors a similar appeal, which was doubtless drafted by Trusevich.[9]

Simultaneously, the Police Department warned the regional security chiefs that the role of their bureaus was defined as advisory, not supervisory. The regional security chiefs, with their greater experience and expertise in conducting domestic intelligence, were supposed to help train the provincial gendarme chiefs in security policing but not to boss them around. Yet since security policing was supposed to be an extremely important task of all provincial gendarme officers, the experts in this realm automatically wielded power over their trainees. A clear authority relationship, even an attitude of condescension, was implied in the Special Section's request to von Koten that he "explain to the chief of the railroad gendarme station in Tver what informants are and how one uses them." Worse still, the regional chiefs could order provincial gendarme and security chiefs in their jurisdictions to carry out arrests. As a revolutionary publication wryly commented, those security policemen without competent and well-connected informants, "like the old insignificant appanage prince, come under the authority of their more fortunate neighbor, who begins to reign and rule over their territory."[10]

The Special Section relied heavily on the regional bureaus for information gathering and operations management. Directives issued in the second half of April and early May 1907 requested data on informants and urged the regional chiefs to engage with the Special Section in a sophisticated and critical exchange of documentary materials, including perlustrated letters, informant reports, and accounts of revolutionary activities. Paperwork flooded into the regional bureaus and thence on to 16 Fontanka Embankment, The regional chiefs were also expected to send officers regularly to the security police institutions in their jurisdictions, both to report on their work and to teach local officials how to recruit and manage secret informants.[11]

In summer 1907 the regional security bureaus began to supervise the recruitment and use of informants by railroad gendarme officers, most of whom considered security police work beneath them and avoided it assiduously, which naturally increased tensions within the security service. This supervision was accomplished by way of both correspondence and direct inspections. Senior police officials sought to increase security on the railroad lines for three principal reasons. First, railroad worker strikes, including the October 1905 general strike, had played a prominent role in the disorder of the previous two years. Second, the incidence of robbery on railroad lines had lately increased. And third, police sources indicated that terrorists planned to use "Kaiser torpedoes," automobiles loaded with explosive devices that could run on railroad tracks without a driver.[12]

Despite persistent problems in provincial Russia, including inadequate funding of gendarme stations and security bureaus, the regional bureaus seem to have largely fulfilled the expectations of police officials. An issue of the Socialist-Revolutionary journal *Znamia truda* (Banner of Labor) reported in late 1907, for example, that the party organization in the Volga region had been devastated, in part because "in the Volga region the gendarmes have a regional organization of policing [sysk] that conforms to the party region." Over the next two years seven more regional security bureaus were created, based in Turkestan, the Caucasus, Perm, Sevastopol, Irkutsk, Poland, and Tomsk; the first five corresponded to regions in the Socialist-Revolutionary Party's network.[13]

The other major element in Trusevich's reform of security policing in the provinces was the further improvement of plainclothes surveillance capacity. The directive on regional security bureaus obligated all provincial security and gendarme chiefs to transform a large proportion of their gendarme noncommissioned officers (NCOs) into surveillants. Beginning in summer 1907, funding became available for civilian clothes and disguises. Yet the habit makes not the monk, as the French say: provincial gendarme officers often had no idea how to deploy surveillants. In October, for example, police officials had to remind provincial chiefs never to outfit surveillants in uniforms and never to use informants to carry out the work of surveillants. This misuse of informants in the provinces may have stemmed from the perennial difficulty in very small towns, where everyone knew everyone else, of keeping the identity of surveillants confidential.[14]

In early fall 1907 Trusevich undertook the task of reforming the training of surveillants. Between September 1907 and December 1908, hundreds of new recruits, many of them gendarme NCOs, were attached to the Moscow city governor's office to receive instruction from officers of the security bureau. To assist with this training program, the Special Section compiled stories of successful surveillants and prepared an instruction on the use of disguises. In March 1908 Vasil'ev urged the regular deployment of surveillants to all industrialized and unstable rural areas. Yet the dispatching of surveillants into the countryside did not always bear fruit. Several of von Koten's surveillants who were dressed as booksellers had little success among the peasants, many of whom were uninterested in the religious and moralistic books they purveyed. Von Koten went so far as to admit that many peasants felt caught between the revolutionaries and the police.[15]

Around the same time, A. I. Spiridovich inaugurated courses for the surveillants who protected the emperor. They learned Russian and European history, geography, and the history of the revolutionary movements. To help them better familiarize themselves with the major terrorist organizations, he created "a museum of terrorism" complete with photographs, maps, charts, and models of bombs. The surveillants also underwent more rigorous physical training than they had previously, including sessions on shooting a pistol, riding a bicycle, and skiing. They were also taught table manners. Finally, some were sent to the security bureau in St. Petersburg for additional practical training.[16]

At the start of 1907, Trusevich appointed two seasoned security officers, A. M. Eremin and V. A. Beklemishev, to transform the Special Section into an operations command center. They and other Special Section officials began to specialize in the study of specific political parties, especially those of the Socialist-Revolutionaries and the Social Democrats. The Special Section was split into four subdivisions, or *otdeleniia,* thus replacing Unit A and Unit B, which had been created in 1906. The first subdivision oversaw the entire security police system and developed and applied modern policing techniques, such as photography, code breaking, and records management. The second, headed by Eremin, studied the Socialist-Revolutionaries and various peasant groupings allied with them, as well as the Maximalists, the Anarchists, and other terrorist organizations. The third focused on Social Democratic organizations and the Jewish revolutionary parties. The fourth, under Beklemishev, watched the railroad and postal-telegraph workers' unions, as well as most nationalist parties.[17]

Previously, by contrast, the Special Section had directed its attention largely to individual people and to specific manifestations of oppositional and revolutionary activity. Now that surveillance over a wide variety of legal public organizations, including trade unions, voluntary associations, and the press, had been transferred to the fourth division of the Police Department, the Special Section was in charge of surveillance only over revolutionary parties and organizations, including some trade unions permeated by revolutionary activists. This change suggests that Trusevich and Vasil'ev understood the distinction, fundamental for the security police, between revolutionary and nonrevolutionary opposition movements and organizations.[18]

The fourth division served as an organ of paternalistic surveillance, while the Special Section developed into a specialized security police agency. In January 1908, for example, the fourth division requested that governors furnish monthly reports containing precise information on every imaginable social group, occurrence, or theme. The required information included reports on, among other things, peasant and workers' groups; professional unions; the political reliability of civil servants; demonstrations, strikes, and armed resistance to troops; terrorist acts, political killings, and attacks on officials and private citizens; expropriations; the orientation of the local press; and the mood within military units, institutions of local self-government, political parties, and schools and institutions of higher learning. Tellingly, the main focus of the directive's surveillance categories remained "the mood of the population," just as in the earliest days of the Third Section.[19]

The Special Section, by contrast, soon acquired a much more sophisticated classification system. Building on Vasil'ev's reform of the previous year, now every major organization dominated or influenced by revolutionary activists was assigned a number that has remained to this day its archival designation in the records of the Special Section in Moscow. *Delo* (record) 5 refers to the Social Democratic Party, *delo* 9 to the Socialist-Revolutionary Party, *delo* 12 to the Anarchist Party, and so on. These records were further subdivided by province, with *chast'* (part) 46 referring to Moscow and *chast'* 57 to St. Petersburg. This work was facilitated by the consolidation, at the end of 1907, of all the Police Department's card catalogs into one central alphabetical reference comprising some eight hundred thousand cards relating to employees, suspects, and criminals mentioned in Fontanka's filing system.[20]

In order to enhance the Police Department's usefulness as an information clearinghouse, in November 1907 gendarme and security officers were ordered to send three copies of all antigovernment publications entering their possession to Fontanka, and in 1909 the Paris security bureau was ordered to furnish Social Democratic and Socialist-Revolutionary newspapers in German, French, and English also to Fontanka. Such publications had previously trickled in to the Police Department's library; now the collection grew rapidly, reaching 41,956 titles, some quite rare, by 1917. Sometime in 1908 a new librarian, N. E. Pankrat'ev, the erstwhile informant, took over from an incompetent, half-literate clerk. Thereafter the library became more use-oriented.[21]

Special Section experts worked to increase security police effectiveness in the field. For one thing, they undertook to inspect security bureaus and gendarme stations, in 1907 visiting the security bureaus in Nizhnii Novgorod and Kiev and the gendarme stations in Voronezh, Vologda, Iaroslavl, and Vladimir. Inspectors found much to criticize. Security policemen had too few informants at their disposal, they often directed them without skill, and they received inadequate cooperation from the regular police. The inspection tours continued over the next several years. Four important organizational and operational directives were also issued in 1907. One reinforced the autonomy and authority of the security bureaus vis-à-vis the gendarmes and regular police in matters of domestic intelligence gathering. Two defined and systematized the methods for guiding surveillants. The last one set forth the security police force's wisdom on guiding secret informants. One important new rule prescribed keeping the true identity of informants utterly secret. Rendering void all previous directives and instructions on these spheres of activity, the last directive placed the use of secret informants squarely at the center of security policing.[22]

Senior police officials were apparently serious about keeping informants on a tighter leash and rooting out provocateurs. Thus, Trusevich and Vasil'ev banned outright the employment of erstwhile informants within the Police Department. This change marked the end of an era during which important police officials could begin their careers as informants, as S. V. Zubatov, P. I. Rachkovskii, and L. P. Men'shchikov had done. The heyday of talented nonbureaucrats was passing, and the security police were growing more professionalized. In May Trusevich prohibited informants from taking an active part in illegal party work without the express permission of their case officers. Police officials also regularly distributed lists of informants who had allegedly engaged in provocation. Security policemen were supposed to watch out for these people and avoid hiring them.[23]

Some provocation may nevertheless have been unavoidable. As S. E. Vissarionov remarked, how could security officers forbid it but encourage active work in the revolutionary milieu? If an informant passed on seditious literature, received weapons for safekeeping, or even chatted enthusiastically about revolutionary operations—was he a provocateur? Perhaps so, especially if his actions directly led to a crime that otherwise would not have taken place. Yet P. G. Kurlov argued perceptively that by underscoring the superiority of security officers over provincial gendarme officers Trusevich's reforms had tempted the provincial officers to overlook or even to encourage provocation.[24]

POLICING THE CONSTITUTIONAL ORDER

From December 1906 into February 1907 the government strove to ensure the return of a conservative majority to the Second Duma. It subsidized conservative political organizations, like the Union of Russian People and the Octobrists and progovernment newspapers, especially in the provinces, but also pitted rightists against each other, by fostering discord within the Union of Russian People and by subsidizing competing rightist organizations. It also used *Rossiia* and "other well-disposed organs" to publish articles refuting criticism of the government. Police and other administrative officials also pressured those opposed to the regime, especially revolutionaries. Between 25 and 28 January 1907, for example, the security police arrested over two hundred Social Democrats in Moscow. Unregistered moderate leftist parties, like the Kadets, suffered frequent administrative harassment, including the closing of their information bureaus and the dispersal of their public gatherings.[25]

Not all officials persecuted political activists. The Special Section pointed to "a significant number" of governors and city police chiefs who had hesitated to suppress antigovernment agitation during the electoral campaign, motivated in part by a "desire to fall in line with the current tendencies." One reason for the vacillation of local officials surely was the conflicting signals they received from their superiors. On 9 January 1907, for example, the Moscow city governor dutifully ordered district police captains to prohibit all public gatherings of Kadets. Yet earlier directives had authorized private individuals known to be Kadets to organize public meetings, only requiring that police officials monitor them. And, more generally, on 29 January 1907 the Police Department reported to local police that "one of the most important objectives of the government" toward the realization of the principles of the October Manifesto was the protection of the inviolability of the person.[26]

What were local officials to make of all this? Was repression or the inviolability of the person the order of the day? A directive of 24 February suggests that Stolypin had a middle course in mind. Governors should avoid both "wavering" and abusing their power or "inserting passions into their work." They should root out "attempts at crime in all its forms," banning "illegal meetings, revolutionary ideas in print, and the creation of underground organizations," even if doing so might be unpopular. Finally they should strive to achieve complete awareness *(osvedomlennost')* about all antigovernment groups and activists.[27] This was a tall order, one complicated by the tactics of leftist electoral campaigners, who veiled subversive utterances in Aesopian language and often saved their most objectionable statements for a conference's end.

The Second Duma had 222 socialists, twice as many as the first. On 24 February 1907 Stolypin demanded the decisive suppression of revolutionary agitation, "without regard for criticism in the leftist press or . . . the Duma." The Duma members' immunity from prosecution engendered a "dangerous" situation, he wrote. Taking the governors into his confidence, Stolypin revealed that the government was planning to load the Duma with legislation in order to compel it to engage in "constructive work."

Meanwhile, police officials were urged to establish thorough surveillance over Duma members and to report instances of participation in revolutionary agitation to the prosecutor's office. Most important in the new constitutional era, governors were also instructed to make sure their police forces distinguished between isolated individuals displaying political "unreliability," on the one hand, and attempts to organize mass demonstrations, terrorist acts, expropriations, and agitation among the armed forces, on the other.[28] Emphasizing the distinction was an element in Stolypin's strategy of seeking to split the liberal constitutionalists from the revolutionaries.

Stolypin also sought to meet some of the demands of the liberal opposition. Thus, on 6 March 1907 he presented to the Duma a bill on reforming the police system and another one on the inviolability of the person. Drawing heavily on western European legislation, the latter would have prohibited, except during war or major civil unrest, the arrest or search of persons or their property without special authorization. Almost none of Stolypin's proposals to limit police and administrative authority became law, however, mostly because the Duma thought they did not go far enough. So, if I. I. Petrunkevich, a leading Kadet, was right to argue that Stolypin's policies did far more to enhance the power of the interior ministry than that of society, the Duma deserved some of the blame. Still, F. A. Golovin, a moderate Kadet and the chairman of the Second Duma, felt that Stolypin considered the parliament a subordinate institution. For example, on 26 March he barred from entering the Duma's premises anyone except the deputies themselves—even experts invited to testify on this or that matter under consideration. Golovin protested in vain; Stolypin, who bore responsibility for preserving the institution's security, stood firm.[29]

The Duma repeatedly clashed with the government on issues relating to the government's alleged abuse of power. Liberal and leftist deputies argued vehemently for the abolition of both capital punishment and the military field courts. V. A. Maklakov argued, to huge applause, that the government was "undermining what is protecting us all. If you crush the revolution by these means, . . . [there] will remain not a law-bound state but only wild people returned to savagery, only chaos and state disintegration." Stolypin countered that in extraordinary circumstances, the demands of state must be higher than the law. "When a house is burning," he said, "you break in." Privately, in conversation with A. I. Shingarev, a Kadet deputy, Stolypin characterized rebellious peasants as "mad beasts who can be restrained only by terror [uzhas]. If they are released, they will slay everyone—me, you, and anyone who wears a suit." Then Stolypin showed him a chart indicating the incidence of terrorism by opponents of the state. "Terrorism is continuing and growing," he exclaimed. "I am responsible for this; you do not have the right to demand from me the abolition of capital punishment."[30]

Rightists and conservatives in the Duma shrewdly argued that the Duma should vote to condemn revolutionary terrorism, which the field courts had been created to eradicate, *before* voting to abolish the field courts. The Kadets were flummoxed. Though several Kadets advocated issuing a formal condemnation of terrorism, the leadership used various procedural means to postpone the consideration of it. The Duma failed to pass bills abolishing the field courts, and the field courts fell into abeyance on 20 April 1907. They also failed to abolish capital punishment, or to make it a crime to praise criminal acts.[31]

The Second Duma issued thirty-five hotly debated interpellations, most of which concerned alleged police brutality, violations of civil liberties, and repression of political activity. The interpellation that held the public's interest more than any other concerned the "Riga Museum of Horrors." It was brought before the Duma on 10 April 1907 by the widely respected Kadet deputy, O. Ia. Pergament, who described a system of brutal treatment of political prisoners that had begun in Riga and then had allegedly spread throughout the Baltic region. Local police officials, prison guards, and gendarme officers, according to Pergament, systematically tortured their prisoners. The Duma discussed the allegations during two subsequent meetings, on 13 April and 17 May, and heard explanations from the justice and interior ministries before voting for a mild rebuke of the government. Little evidence of a conclusive nature was ever brought forward by contemporaries—or has been uncovered by historians—on the basis of which a sound judgment of the accusations can be made.[32] Still, it seems likely they were largely accurate.

Accusations from the rostrum of the Duma concerning official abuse of power were echoed throughout 1907 and 1908 in a continuous flow of publications, including memoirs, journalistic works, and scholarly analyses. Former Police Department director A. A. Lopukhin's scathing critique, in the form of written recollections of his service, had an especially big impact given his former official position, as did the magisterial study of emergency legislation in Russia by V. M. Gessen, an esteemed Kadet jurist. Gessen argued that the security law of 1881, which, he said, was evidence of the government's "principled lawlessness," had helped to trigger the 1905 revolution by undermining the prestige of the government and deepening the resentment of the population. Senior police officials did not entirely reject these criticisms. For example, a directive issued on 30 April and reiterated on 27 June warned security policemen to propose the use of administrative exile more selectively. Yet in August the government reaffirmed that the security law would remain in force, provoking fits of indignation in the liberal and leftist press.[33]

It was nevertheless relatively easy for official Russia to justify continued recourse to broad repressive powers, given the still high level of social disorder. Although the extent of agrarian and industrial unrest was modest until April and May, political terrorism repeatedly struck at government officials and private individuals. Partisan warfare became a way of life in the major cities. Manuals on street-fighting tactics were hawked openly in Moscow, Social Democratic and Socialist-Revolutionary activists imported huge numbers of weapons into Russia, and the Bolsheviks set up a school for terrorism in February 1907 in Kuokkala, Finland. In 1907 alone, according to the Police Department, 1,231 officials were killed and 1,312 wounded, an increase of 38 percent in each case over the comparable figures for 1906. M. I. Leonov has counted 3,487 terrorist acts in 1907, most against lower-ranked officials. Senior officials felt vulnerable too. War Minister A. F. Rediger received warnings from the security police in mid-1907, but plots against him were foiled. Major life insurance companies in Russia, France, Germany, and England refused to insure his life, even for an upfront lump-sum payment of the entire projected series of premiums.[34]

The emperor was still not considered safe. He returned to St. Petersburg only in August 1907 to dedicate a memorial to the victims of Apteka Island. In early 1907 Socialist-Revolutionary terrorists plotted to kill Nicholas in Peterhof, but a Cossack in the imperial entourage who was enlisted to implement the plan, Nikolai Ratimov, told Spiridovich about it and helped Aleksandr Vasil'evich Gerasimov gather incriminating evidence that led to the arrest of twenty-eight suspected conspirators. Eighteen of the conspirators were tried in a military court on 7–15 August. Government prosecutors argued that the defendants were closely associated with the Socialist-Revolutionary Party and even with several Socialist-Revolutionary deputies in the Duma, who because of their legal immunity avoided prosecution entirely. Renowned liberal defense attorneys, including V. A. Maklakov and A. S. Zarudnyi, cited the Socialist-Revolutionary Party's central committee's categorical denial of involvement. In a closed court session held in the St. Petersburg security bureau at 20 Moika Quay, however, Gerasimov rejected this denial. He refused to name the source of his information—it was Azef—yet his testimony proved decisive. At one point, according to Spiridovich, Maklakov threw his briefcase on a table in frustration and stormed out. The court sentenced three defendants to death and seven others to hard labor and exile; six were exonerated. Gerasimov was promoted to major general (after two years as colonel instead of the usual ten). After 1917 a number of Socialist-Revolutionaries admitted their party's complicity in the affair.[35]

Only a small part of the terrorist violence was the work of right-wing activists, it seems, despite Abraham Ascher's suggestion that in the first months of 1907 "the extremists on the right were perpetrating more acts of terror than those on the left." In fact, Ascher is able to cite only five instances of right-wing violence, only one resulting in death. There was also in 1907 one anti-Jewish pogrom that he does not mention, which killed one Jew and wounded over a dozen in Elizavetgrad, Kherson Province. An act of vengeance, it followed the murder on 25 February of a local leader of the Union of Russian People, but when assassins killed another member of the union, no additional anti-Jewish violence ensued. The Russian right was largely on the defensive. In an 11 April 1907 open letter to Stolypin, the right-wing activist P. F. Bulatsel' warned that leaders of the Union of Russian People were "being killed one by one. . . . This cannot go on forever. The storm is already coming. . . . The wave of death will change its course." It never did, but Stolypin urged governors to try to stop the attacks against the rightist parties.[36] In any event, the number of victims of right-wing attacks does not come close to the over one thousand officials killed by what were presumably almost entirely left-wing assailants.

There were a few more cases of right-wing violence in 1907. Early that year the leaders of the Union of Russian People singled out forty-three public activists, several but not all of them Jewish, as targets for murder. Some, including I. V. and V. M Gessen, P. N. Miliukov, and O. O. Gruzenberg, received death threats. I. V. Dukel'skii, an assistant to Gerasimov, independently warned Gruzenberg that attacks against him and Miliukov might occur. He offered them protection, but they pointedly declined it, presumably from distaste for the security police.[37]

Rightists killed one man on their hit list and attempted to kill a prominent official. V. D. Fedorov, a worker, and A. E. Kazantsev, formerly a Socialist-Revolutionary but now a member of an obscure right-wing organization, were apparently involved in two attempts to assassinate S. Iu. Witte. In January 1907, two bombs were found in chimneys on the roof of Witte's house. In late May, D. N. Shipov warned Witte not to attend a State Council meeting, en route to which an attempt was supposed to be made on his life. On 14 March 1907 in broad daylight in central Moscow rightists gunned down one person on the hit list, G. B. Iollos, a prominent Kadet, a doctor of law, and an editor of *Russkie vedomosti*. His alleged assailant, the same Fedorov, testified to the St. Petersburg judicial tribunal that Kazantsev had incited him to kill Iollos, whom he had denounced as a traitor to the Socialist-Revolutionary Maximalists.[38] In other words, Fedorov had thought he was serving the revolutionary cause by killing Iollos. Revolutionary terror remained at the center of political life; counterrevolutionary terror was peripheral.

St. Petersburg security bureau head Gerasimov and Moscow city governor Reinbot alleged that the Moscow security bureau was directly involved in these conspiracies. Gerasimov called the Moscow bureau "the center of the combat operations of the Union of Russian People" and asserted that Kazantsev had been in the bureau's employ. Gerasimov failed to mention, though, that his own assistant, M. S. Kommisarov, had intimate ties to E. K. Klimovich and the Union of Russian People. Gerasimov also claimed that when he inspected the bomb discovered in Witte's chimney, he "quickly saw that it was not the work of the revolutionaries." It is unclear why Gerasimov drew this conclusion. After all, with all their experience with munitions, revolutionaries should have known how to make various kinds of bombs.[39]

I. F. Manasevich-Manuilov, not a very reliable witness, claimed that Reinbot had told him that Klimovich had been directly involved in the assassination of Iollos. Klimovich, who was very much afraid of the revolutionary terrorist movements, allegedly had told Reinbot that "terrorism has to be combated with terrorism." In his own testimony, Reinbot recalled only that he had been troubled by the fact that Klimovich had given a false passport to a certain Bogdanov, an aide to A. A. Buksgevden, a noted rightist and an assistant to Moscow governor-general S. K. Gershel'man. These shadowy figures also had ties to semiofficial security forces, which further complicates the picture. In Moscow Buksgevden apparently headed one such force, of which Kazantsev supposedly was a member. In April 1907 a Moscow judicial investigator determined that there was also a fully autonomous security organization headed by the controller of the Ministry of the Imperial Household, D. R. Gofshtetter, who employed five or six people, sometimes armed, to guard important officials.[40]

Fedorov apparently killed Kazantsev, then fled abroad, where, at the end of May 1907, he allegedly tried several times to kill radical émigré V. L. Burtsev. Witte came to believe that the government, and Stolypin in particular, had been mixed up with the attempts on his life. Iain Lauchlan, noting that conspiracy theorizing infected the entire Russian body politic, conceded that the security police naturally had ties to right-wing terror, but they also "had connections to the trade union movement, the Duma, the free press, revolutionary terror, freemasonry, etc., etc." Ultimately, the guilty parties are "concealed by the plethora, not the paucity, of incriminating evidence."[41]

Nicholas was leaning toward dissolving the Second Duma, but the Special Section warned that this step could lead to an armed uprising organized by revolutionary activists and involving the sabotage of railroad bridges and other strategic targets. To be prepared in the event that Nicholas did move to dissolve the Duma, the security police in the imperial capitals launched a massive attack against revolutionary activists during the second half of April. On 14 April 1907, thanks to information provided by Azef, Gerasimov's bureau arrested twenty-eight members of the Socialist-Revolutionary combat organization. The police also prevented the party's central bureau of trade unions in St. Petersburg from holding normal meetings for over six weeks beginning in mid-April. In late April, Klimovich, still security chief in Moscow, undertook a wave of arrests that totally disorganized the Social Democratic Moscow regional (oblastnoi) committee. He also managed to seize one of the largest and most sophisticated underground presses then functioning in the empire.[42]

Assiduous, widespread police repression in April reduced the incidence of May Day strikes and demonstrations throughout the empire compared to the previous year. Yet as a whole the month of May witnessed the second highest incidence of strikes and the highest number of cases of agrarian unrest in 1907. Fearing further disorder, P. G. Kurlov, whom Stolypin was grooming to head the police system, advocated the dissolution of the Duma and the arrest of all leftist deputies. Toward the end of May, the hard-line N. V. Kleigel's, a governor-general in Ukraine, urged Nicholas to adopt a more repressive policy.[43]

While Kurlov, Kleigel's, and many others clamored for shutting down the Second Duma, the pretext for its dissolution was provided by revolutionaries. Revolutionary agitators had failed to win converts within military units. Therefore, sometime in early 1907, the Social Democratic Party's central committee decided that the Duma could be a "means to tear troops away from the government." The party's St. Petersburg military organization arranged in early May for radical soldiers to deliver to the assembled Social Democratic Duma faction a statement of the soldiers' intention to support the Duma should it be dissolved. After the soldiers left, the security police burst in. They could not search the Duma deputies or the apartment because of their immunity, but an informant, E. N. Shornikova-Iudkevich, gave the police a copy of the statement, which she had typed herself. The next day, the police arrested alleged associates of the Social Democratic military organization and seized 108 pounds of supposedly incriminating documents. On May 7 the Duma interpellated the ministers of Interior and Justice, who defended their subordinates' actions. Three days later Trusevich ordered governors to shut down trade unions affiliated with the Social Democratic Party and to prosecute their leaders. On 1 June Stolypin demanded the Duma's permission to investigate fifty-five deputies and to arrest fifteen more. The Duma set up a commission to investigate the matter, but it would not have the chance to complete its work.[44]

On 3 June guards were posted around the Taurida Palace and along nearby streets to prevent the escape of the Social Democratic deputies. Declaring that the Duma had, among many other things, "worked to increase sedition and promote the disintegration of the state . . . and declined to condemn murder and violence," Nicholas announced the body's dissolution. Police established surveillance over the headquarters of opposition factions and the apartments of their members and detained most of the Social Democratic deputies. Their trials took place several months later, and seventeen defendants were sentenced to four or five years of hard labor. The criminal charges, while not wholly unwarranted, were meant to justify dissolving the Duma and altering the electoral law.[45] Although these actions apparently provoked no immediate popular response, social unrest remained vigorous for several months. The Socialist-Revolutionaries and Social Democrats repeatedly attempted to launch an armed uprising. Three troop mutinies with revolutionary support occurred in Kiev (5 June), Sevastopol (September), and Vladivostok (October). In June terrorists killed fifty-four and wounded forty-seven officials, and on 12 June Bolshevik robbers made off with 250,000 rubles from the Tiflis State Bank.[46] Political larceny of this magnitude could underwrite extensive revolutionary activities.

A NEW WAVE OF REPRESSION

The period following the so-called 3 June coup d'état saw increased repression but only a gradual, limited expansion of administrative prerogatives. On the night of 2–3 June, the governors of several major provinces and cities issued binding orders, with almost identical wording, forbidding the publication of materials liable to arouse antigovernment sentiments or to cause anxiety about misfortunes, government directives, or other events. Although in Moscow and other places in a state of extraordinary security people who disobeyed the order could face a three-thousand-ruble fine or three months in prison, the punishments were rarely so Draconian. On 4 June Moscow governor-general F. V. Dubasov forbade insulting or assaulting policemen, and the city governor immediately began to enforce the rule. The enforcement resulted in ten arrests and the imposition of a few minor fines (three to fifty rubles) and jail sentences (four to thirty days). On 5 June Stolypin ordered administrative and police authorities to preserve order at any cost.[47]

The police launched large-scale arrest campaigns all over the empire in June. Gerasimov and von Koten conducted several operations against the Social Democrats, including their combat organization, arresting dozens of activists and crushing their underground structure in the imperial capitals. The security police raided Social Democratic organizations throughout the Russian Empire 194 times in 1907 and 108 times in 1908. The Menshevik underground disintegrated completely. Most of the Social Democratic military organizations were liquidated, and by the end of 1908 the Bolsheviks did not have a single soldiers' newspaper. Overall, the Social Democratic ranks plummeted from a high of over 150,000 in May 1907 to no more than 10,000 in 1910 (including 1,000 in Ukraine and 506 in St. Petersburg). A few centers of activity remained for a time within the Russian Empire, especially in Finland, but by late 1907 nearly all the party's leaders had fled abroad, mostly to Switzerland. In spring 1908 Social Democratic leaflets bewailed the "dark and deep night of reaction."[48]

The police also subjected Socialist-Revolutionary Party members and organizations to countless arrests. The party's membership fell precipitously and its organizational network was devastated. Its terrorist arm languished: party terrorists failed to kill a single senior government official after a semi-autonomous combat unit killed V. P. Pavlov in December 1906. At the same time, the Maximalists' autonomous terrorist groups declined in number from some 68 in 1907, to 42 in 1908, and 10 in 1910, while the party's antiterrorist wing, the Popular Socialist Party, remained "a network of small intellectual circles, not a real party."[49] The continuing terrorist violence was therefore the work of autonomous groups and individuals.

The methods the security police used to achieve these successes were sophisticated. They insinuated informants into whatever places revolutionary activists were found: into jails and prisons, into high schools (because "propaganda in that milieu always enjoys success and takes deep root"), into the military, and into the countryside—a ticklish business when peasants viewed every outsider as a potential spy and where it was necessary to know the local customs. Informants were directed very carefully. On 4 October 1907 A. T. Vasil'ev ordered security chiefs to detain extremist party members temporarily on the eve of party conferences, to use informants to argue for moderation at these conferences, to recruit new informants, and to employ this time of flux to move them upward in the parties. In early 1907, Gerasimov used a winsome student couple to infiltrate a terrorist ring operating out of a hotel near Imatra Falls in southeastern Finland. The agents endeared themselves to the terrorists by singing, dancing, talking about student life, and parodying professors of the University of St. Petersburg. In July 1908 Trusevich shifted tactics, arguing that informants should "express more and more radical views" in order to gain better access to the terrorist underground.[50]

Informants turned up in unexpected places and did unexpected things. An informant of Moscow security chief von Koten managed in December 1907 to place at the chief's disposal, for one night, the archive of the all-Russian railroad union of the Socialist-Revolutionary Party. That organization was exposed and crushed by the police in early 1908. Iu. O. Serova, code name Ulianov, helped the police arrest such Social Democratic luminaries as G. E. Zinov'ev and L. B. Kamenev in late April 1908. Soviet historian P. Kudelli claimed that Serova married the Social Democratic deputy of the Duma V. M. Serov purely in the line of police duty. Even if this allegation is false, it captures well the revolutionaries' belief in the diabolic nature of informants who made the security police seem almost omniscient. For example, Azef told the security police that a Socialist-Revolutionary Party conference would take place in Tamerfors (Tampere), Finland, in mid-February 1907, whereas well-informed participants like O. S. Minor learned of it at the very last minute. The Maximalist G. A. Nestroev could well grumble that whenever three comrades gathered together, one was a police informant. There were never anywhere close to that many informants in the revolutionary milieu, but they were devastating however few in number. No wonder that in November 1908 Klimovich ordered security policemen to assist their more valuable informants, once exposed, to reestablish themselves in society, by providing them with severance pay, for example.[51]

The business of recruiting informants required cleverness. Many revolutionary activists were highly vulnerable to police blandishments, in part because of their lifestyle. I. V. Narskii has argued persuasively that the milieu of revolutionary activists was highly permeable to police informants because radical activists rotated regularly under the impact of police repression, rejected conventional moral norms, were not financially secure, and had to live illegally.[52]

One student, excluded from the University of St. Petersburg for political activism and fed up with his radical comrades, turned to the security bureau. P. S. Statkovskii, "with a cunning smile on a wrinkled face," advised the student against applying for clemency, saying "your comrades will turn away from you, the newspapers will laugh at you, the professors will despise you." Still, said Statkovskii encouragingly, "I can speak to my supervisor, and you can be admitted conditionally. Let's meet at the zoo. I always try to help those who sincerely try to break with the revolutionary underground."[53]

The young man, enticed, thought to himself, "if they ask me to inform, I'll refuse to cooperate." But they slowly reeled him in. He agreed to write a personal letter asking for help from the police, which the latter could use to blackmail him by threatening to show it to his party comrades. But what did he care? He had no intention of returning to the revolutionary camp. Statkovskii then asked for help in "saving the innocent." He promised the young man, "We are not asking you to betray anyone. We'll just ask you about various people, and you tell us if they are innocent." He then handed him the coveted certificate of reliability, which would permit him to reenter the university.[54]

They soon met in a cafe on the Nevskii Prospekt. Statkovskii arrived with an attractive blond man whom he introduced as "I. V. Fedorov." Apparently "Fedorov" was one-time informant I. V. Dobroskok. Notes of the meeting indicate that he was impressive: "intelligent, knew literature, very polite, gentle." Dobroskok asked the new young informant for information on student activism, adding "Oh, by the way, here's the money—just for cabs, no receipts needed." Gradually Dubroskok and von Koten, whom the informant soon met, asked him to report on his fellow students without providing last names. Eventually they asked for full names—and much more. At one point they dropped a bombshell: a bit of knowledge about the informant's personal life that very few people knew. He was cornered. "Sometimes I wanted to kill them," he declared.[55]

Efforts to extend and improve the informant network ran into the predictable obstacles of incompetence and inadequate funding in provincial Russia. Numerous provincial gendarme stations could afford to maintain neither secret apartments nor informants, according to reports from the Moscow region in late 1907. The Moscow gendarme station's fifteen modestly paid informants—only four earned forty or more rubles per month—constituted the sole important provincial informant network in the central region in 1908, aside from that of von Koten's security bureau. In March 1908, however, without increasing the funding for hiring informants, Vasil'ev urged provincial gendarme chiefs to recruit informants in trouble spots, to use conspiratorial methods when meeting with them, to recruit auxiliary agents in rural shops and government offices, and carefully to record information supplied by both kinds of agents.[56]

It is unlikely that large numbers of provincial gendarme chiefs leaped at the chance to undertake this kind of work. Quite a few of them, like K. A. Rybal'chenko, an assistant to the chief of the Kostroma security bureau, considered informants "scoundrels" with whom a gentleman should refuse "even to speak." He and others like him were more likely to rely on denunciations received anonymously, a mainstay of security police operations in the early and middle nineteenth century. As late as March 1908 Trusevich admonished governors and security policemen to abandon such methods, which tended merely to arouse public hostility against representatives of government authority.[57] Yet without extra funding, how were provincial gendarme chiefs to recruit more informants? Unlike their successors under the Bolsheviks, they could not terrorize people into spying.

The government pressured the military district courts, which were flooded with cases, to crack down on political defendants. A law of 27 June made it technically possible to prosecute, try, and sentence a defendant, then to apply the sentence, all within four days. This law also authorized reading the depositions of witnesses who failed to show up "for whatever reasons"; it was no longer required that their testimony be presented in person at the trial. The Soviet historian N. N. Polianskii suggests that the purpose of this clause was to permit informants and surveillants to make depositions so they could contribute their testimony to the trial without revealing their identity. The law was probably meant as well to encourage testimony by witnesses afraid of terrorist reprisals. Stolypin also sought to increase the conviction rate in military courts, repeatedly goading War Minister Rediger and individual military judges into applying the harshest punishments possible to defendants convicted of attacking the person or property of private individuals or government officials. He categorically rejected the argument put forth by General M. A. Gazenkampf, an assistant to Grand Duke Nikolai Nikolaevich, who was commander of the St. Petersburg military district, that apolitical robbers deserved more indulgence than those motivated by political fanaticism. The revolutionary movement, argued Stolypin, had lately been directly involved with ordinary robbery and looting.[58]

The incidence of government repression peaked from mid-1907 through 1908. From 1906 to 1912 the Senate and the judicial tribunals tried 5,052 people annually for state crimes, or a total of roughly 35,000. Most stood accused of rebellion *(bunt)*, agitation *(smuta)*, belonging to illegal organizations, or distributing seditious imprints. Roughly 70 percent were found guilty; of these over 75 percent (or 18,600) were sentenced to short terms in prison or jail. Put another way, only 17.5 percent (or 6,189) of those tried received moderate to harsh sentences.[59]

Of course, even short prison terms could be painful in this era of increased repression. Though in some prisons the inmates enjoyed freedom of movement and access to newspapers and food from the outside, in others the walls dripped with humidity like "the inside of a samovar," paint on floors stuck to naked bodies, and prisoners slept almost heaped on each other. Indeed, the number of prisoners shot up from 88,520 in January 1906 to 122,008 a year later in space planned for 101,000, leading to a higher rate of mortality. In 1911 the rate hit fifty per one thousand inmates, twice that in French prisons. When P. G. Kurlov replaced Chief of Prisons A. M. Maksimovskii, who was assassinated in late 1907, he stiffened prison discipline, reducing the annual number of escapes from 2,730 in 1907 to 1,371 in 1908.[60]

From 1907 to July 1914, the district military courts, which issued most of the harshest sentences (including all death sentences), convicted 21,351 civilian defendants for activities linked to civil unrest, 7,016 of them in 1908 alone. Of that total, 2,468 (or 11.6%) were sentenced to death and 5,828 (or 27.6%) were sentenced to *katorga*, or hard labor. Only a small proportion of these convicts were executed on sentences issued by the district military courts for crimes against the state: between 1905 and 1912 only 214 people (or 0.09 percent) were. Finally, in 1906–1909 administrative officials exiled 32,891 people, 22,530 of them (68.5%) for "revolutionary activity" and 4,203 (12.7%) for agrarian unrest. Because of frequent escapes, however, the authorities could never account for more than 18,563 administrative exiles at any one time.[61]

There were several reasons beyond police repression for the weakening of the revolutionary parties. The Bolshevik V. D. Bonch-Bruevich blamed "the corroding influence of the seeming freedom, of which we had a few breaths after the revolution of 1905." Having tasted this freedom, many party activists no longer wished to return to the underground. Also, acrimonious disputes among Social Democratic Party leaders abroad alienated rank-and-file activists back in Russia, contributing to party disaffection and decline. The decreased recruitment and weakened finances of which police reports took note were both a cause and a consequence of the parties' debility.[62] One also presumes the operation of a "snowball effect": the broader population's declining involvement in revolutionary activity, partly in view of the apparent might of the state and partly because of political weariness, must have demoralized the revolutionary activists, depressed recruitment, and diminished the success of party fund-raising.

The revolutionary movement was losing some of its luster. Perhaps the crowning token of antirevolutionary sentiment in Russia was embodied in works of fiction, like A. I. Kuprin's "Morskaia bolezn'" (Sea Sickness), published in early 1908. Elena Travlina, a young revolutionary, is raped several times aboard a steamer. When she confesses to her husband, a Social Democrat of short stature with a paunch and a white, broad-brimmed hat like "all Social Democrats wore," he grows cold to her. In despair, she laments that he had turned out no different from other men. He was "a tiny, suspicious proprietor of love, untrusting, full of humiliating jealousy." Gorky was outraged at the negative depiction of these Social Democrats, and his camp broke with Kuprin. N. I. Iordanskii, then a Menshevik, called the story "disgusting, obnoxious," and he railed against "writers like Kuprin" for "moving to the right, cursing 1905, and falling on their knees before impertinent representatives of the autocratic government."[63] As the pure goddess of revolution began to show her clay feet, the triumph of the regime seemed assured.

Although the revolutionary parties ceased to function as empire-wide organizations in late 1907, there continued to exist a grassroots level revolutionary movement made up of many smaller organizations, unions, societies, and the like, many of which cooperated closely despite their nominal party affiliations.[64] They often intersected or even coalesced with legal vehicles for political expression, especially the Duma, and also the press and trade unions and other voluntary associations, which kept on growing even though they were subjected to increasing levels of police regulation.

The Third Duma first convened on 1 November 1907, and it completed its five-year term in June 1912. Extensive meddling by the authorities—together with the new franchise law—aided in the election of, out of 442 deputies, 147 rightists and 154 Octobrists. They cooperated tolerably well for two years, but they were no pliant tool of the government. For example, the government did not dare to ask the Duma to approve an increase in the size of the Police Department's middle-level staff, largely because the institution had been created outside the normal legislative process back in 1880, and any discussion of staffing levels would invite unwanted scrutiny of personnel and other matters—such as the fact that some money for the police was provided from a secret discretionary fund. The Ignat'ev Commission's new emergency law was never brought to the floor. Likewise, in 1909 the Duma rejected Stolypin's bill on the inviolability of the person, which would have limited the security police force's right of search and detention but not in places declared to be in a state of emergency—which covered a large proportion of the population at the time.[65]

The Duma also interpellated the government on a wide variety of policing matters. Some were rather trivial. One interpellation in January 1908 decried as "provocation" an incident in which the security police in Vilna allowed contrabandists to transport illegal literature across the Russian border so they would be able to arrest the recipients. In another case, in February 1908 a Social Democratic deputy, G. E. Belousov, urged the Duma to refuse to approve the budget of the Postal-Telegraph Administration because of its alleged involvement with perlustration, which the Fundamental Laws forbade. When its director appeared before the Duma and categorically denied such involvement, the budget was approved, even though nearly everyone knew that perlustration was happening.[66]

Police analysts also read extensively in the periodical press and cut out and filed articles of a "tendentious" or "suspicious" nature. The purpose of this work was primarily to help senior police officials to understand better the public mood, but it also permitted them to monitor, and occasionally to refute, allegations about government policies and officials.[67] Although the mainstream press remained vibrant, repression targeting liberal and radical outlets was extensive. The courts ordered the suspension of dozens of publications, the fining of dozens of publishers and editors, and the confiscation of hundreds of books and issues of periodicals.

In 1908 alone, 73 mostly trade union and other leftist periodical publications were temporarily shut down, 42 of them in St. Petersburg and Moscow, and in the period from 1907 to 1910 some 1,200 different books were seized, compared to only 46 in 1905–1906. The total number of discrete "books and brochures" confiscated from 1907 to 1910 was nearly four thousand, though between 1907 and 1912 only fourteen plays were prohibited. Similarly, the sum of the fines the administration levied against newspapers rose from 15,525 rubles against 16 newspapers in 1906, to 65,000 rubles against 148 papers in 1907, and 82,200 rubles against 120 papers in 1908. Shcheglovitov admitted that the administrative punishments against the press angered the public, but he argued that without them the press would get completely out of hand. Government repression crushed the revolutionary press. Between spring 1907 and the end of 1910 neither the Social Democrats nor the Socialist-Revolutionaries managed to publish a newspaper legally in the Russian Empire. It seems that during this period revolutionary activists resorted more and more to the use of illegal presses, despite fierce police repression.[68]

The growth of the trade union movement posed another challenge to both the government and its security police. By early June 1907 some eight hundred trade unions had been registered, and over one hundred more were operating illegally. While the number of strikes fell from some 7,000 in 1906 to 3,500 in 1907, the proportion of strikes that were political apparently rose from 58 percent in 1906 to 72 percent in 1907. Revolutionary activists sought to use the unions as recruiting grounds and as front organizations for antigovernment agitation.[69]

Intelligence reports indicated that Social Democrats dominated eighteen and Socialist-Revolutionaries nine of the thirty-four main trade unions in St. Petersburg. The government repeatedly brought suits against the unions, arguing that the 1906 temporary rules should be interpreted more strictly and that unions should be prohibited from holding public meetings and putting on concerts and other entertainment events. In the second half of 1907 city and provincial governors closed 159 unions and denied registration to 169, citing their the support of strikes, holding of illegal meetings, and possession of illegal publications. Overall, from 1906 to 1910 the government closed 497 unions and refused to register 604 more, and the total number of legal unions fell from 904 in July 1907 to 720 in December 1910. Union membership plummeted from 300,000 in 1907 to 35,000 in 1910, in part because of economic hardship and disillusionment with union leaders. Yet key police officials were loath to close more trade unions, since this would make it harder to keep worker-activists under surveillance and would tend to radicalize the workers. Historically speaking, wrote one official, "trade unions in Europe had ceased to fight against governments as soon as the latter stopped persecuting them."[70]

Voluntary associations retained considerable room to maneuver, even in the post–3 June period. According to Joseph Bradley, these associations "aspired to create" common democratic liberties in late imperial Russia, a goal they attempted mightily to achieve. Perhaps the most significant example of voluntary associations' efforts to strengthen civil society was the plethora of empire-wide congresses held to discuss professional concerns, public policy issues, economic matters, and so on. True, governors refused to approve the status of many associations, including organizations aimed at overturning existing laws or inciting people to disobey them, such as the League for the Struggle against Capital Punishment, and nearly all political parties, though in practice many parties still led an abundantly rich semilegal existence.[71]

Though they often sent policemen to attend them, governors seldom forbade associations from holding public meetings, since the organizers were usually clever about framing the topics of discussion. The level and frequency of police interference in public political meetings varied over space and time, often depending on the character and vigor of local officials. Sometimes their vigor was in doubt: a directive of fall 1908 reminded governors that police officers should shut down public assemblies whenever participants called for the overthrow of the existing order. A. A. Kizevetter divided police observers into university graduates who "felt good about cutting off a speaker" and simpletons who were unsure of themselves and feared ridicule should they interrupt political speakers without good reason. Kizevetter recalled one old police captain who had approached him saying, "Please, professor, if I have to stop you, do not make fun of me." Perhaps ridicule was inevitable. One policeman allegedly stopped Andrei Belyi in the midst of a lecture on ancient Egypt when he mentioned Ramses II. "Please do not mention that name," he entreated. "Perhaps it is a veiled reference to Nicholas II."[72] Ironically, it may well have been.

The most numerous voluntary associations in Russia, the cooperative organizations, deserve special mention because the government saw them as both suspicious and necessary. In March 1908 Stolypin authorized the convocation of an empire-wide congress of cooperative organizations in Moscow, because he recognized that the cooperative movement was "intended to help develop the economy and to assist the working masses [rabochie massy]." At the same time, however, police intelligence indicated that leftist activists, especially Social Democrats, were trying to infiltrate the cooperative movement and to use it toward their own ends. Therefore, von Koten arrested eleven activists associated with the cooperatives on the eve of the congress, but he had to release all but one for lack of incriminating evidence.[73]

The city governor shut down the congress before it was completed because V. A. Posse, an anarchist-communist, delivered a speech on how to conduct illegal party work. In an apparently unusual decision, von Koten asked N. N. Zhedenov, the publisher of the right-wing newspaper *Groza*, to draft a report on Posse and his consumer cooperative *Trudovoi soiuz*, presumably because the security police had no informants within that branch of the cooperative movement. On 27 November 1909 the government shut down Posse's cooperative for good. Even so, the movement remained extremely vibrant. The number of cooperatives changed in almost exactly inverse proportion to that of the trade unions: from 605 in 1907 to 816 in 1910, with a total membership of 375,000 in 1908.[74] The security police had no hope of keeping them all under surveillance.

FURTHER POLICE REFORMS

To help him carry out further reforms, Trusevich selected two highly competent officials for key posts. On 12 January 1908 he named as his assistant for security police affairs the dynamic and intelligent Sergei Evlampievich Vissarionov. The new assistant had graduated in law from Moscow University in 1889 and, beginning in the late 1890s, had served as an assistant prosecutor in Vologda, Nizhnii Novgorod, and Moscow, then had been prosecutor for two years in Iaroslavl. In Moscow he had worked closely with Klimovich and von Koten, and he was deeply knowledgeable about the revolutionary underground. Aleksandr Blok described him as thin and pale with curly "black hair, a huge forehead. . . . Very little grey, save in his beard and a bit in his hair." When listening "he fiercely knits his brow. Then immediately his face smooths out and he talks in a business-like tone but a bit anemically. . . . He's smart, but somehow childlike." Vissarionov's father was Jewish, but he himself was staunchly Russian Orthodox. He went to church regularly and crossed himself before and after meals and when passing before churches. He worked with the Special Section staff to provide both concrete and theoretical guidance to the security police forces in the field and over the next five years undertook several inspection tours of gendarme stations and security bureaus throughout the empire.[75]

On 22 June 1908 Trusevich selected E. K. Klimovich, who the year before had been appointed deputy city governor of Moscow, as the first gendarme officer to head the Special Section. It is not surprising, given his firsthand experience in matching wits with revolutionary activists, that Klimovich's main contribution was to center the work of the Special Section on a careful analysis of the programs and activities of the revolutionary parties. He oversaw the preparation of surveys of all the major revolutionary parties and urged gendarme officers to read up on the revolutionary party programs.[76]

To tighten control over police personnel at all levels and to provide a setting for the investigation of complaints against policemen and institutions, in March 1908 Trusevich created a separate department, the *Inspektorskii otdel*.[77] Then on 2–4 April 1908 he convened a conference of regional security chiefs and their assistants to discuss security police methods, ongoing operations, approaches to various social groups and layers of the population, and strategies for combating revolutionary activism. They agreed that it was necessary for their informants to try to win promotion into positions of authority within the various revolutionary organizations, especially terrorist groups, but Trusevich urged that they vigilantly watch out for signs of provocation. He also informed everyone at the conference that laws expanding civil rights and restricting administrative powers would soon go into effect. They had to prepare for this day, largely by developing ever more sophisticated informant networks in order to avoid importuning people unduly.[78]

Information sharing was the order of the day. In March 1908 Klimovich, then still in Moscow, advocated closer cooperation between the security and regular police because, he argued, political and regular crime had become more and more intertwined. In May 1908 Stolypin recommended that gendarme and security officers meet together at the regular conferences of rural police chiefs. "Personal contacts are essential," he concluded, "and formality in the business of security policing is inadmissible." Then in December the Police Department hosted a conference of provincial gendarme chiefs. Simultaneously, the regional chiefs stepped up their efforts to coordinate and to improve the work of the security police in their jurisdictions. In the second half of 1908 von Koten distributed within the central security region an instruction on directing informants intended to supplement the general instruction that was prepared by Klimovich and A. M. Eremin and sent to regional security chiefs on 10 February 1907.[79]

Von Koten, following a recommendation made at the April conference, summoned the security and gendarme chiefs in his region for talks in January 1909. On the agenda was an analysis of the revolutionary movements in Russia and the Moscow region, as well as technical advice on the training and deployment of surveillants and the recruitment and guidance of secret informants. It is not clear that these efforts increased the competency or even the enthusiasm of provincial gendarme authorities: in November 1908 Klimovich was still complaining that some gendarme chiefs failed to read the revolutionary programs and operational directives supplied to them by the Police Department.[80] Perhaps the security police were simply imitating the public mania for conferences.

Trusevich also attended to combating regular crime more decisively. Hooliganism plagued town and country and worried both the government and the public. Ordinary crime seems to have been on the rise throughout the empire, especially in the borderlands. The prosecutor of the Odessa district court, for example, reported that crime cases had increased from approximately 1,000 to 1,200 annually in preceding years to 3,087 in 1906 and then declined only slightly in 1907. The proportion of unsolved cases remained well over 70 percent, while sophisticated, audacious, and grave crimes multiplied in number.[81]

In June 1907 Trusevich traveled to various European countries to acquaint himself with their police institutions. In late 1907 he launched a weekly newspaper, *Vestnik politsii* (Police Herald), to help train the criminal detective police in the use of modern police techniques, to encourage the sharing of methods and ideas about regular policing, and to increase police officers' self-discipline, self-restraint, respect for the law, and sense of dignity, all in order to increase respect for the police and the government among the public. In March 1908 Trusevich created an eighth division of the Police Department that would coordinate regular criminal detection, promote the use of modern police technology, and maintain relations with European police forces. In early spring 1908, he created a special school to train regular policemen to use photography and anthropometry and, "in a spirit of conformity with the law, to achieve the highest success." A law of 6 July 1908, duly adopted by legislative process, created criminal detective bureaus *(Sysknye otdeleniia)* in eighty-nine cities and towns across the empire with a yearly budget of 130,000 rubles for 1908 and 913,500 thereafter (compared to 1.3 million rubles for the network of security bureaus). The new criminal detective bureaus were modeled on the network of security bureaus both in structure, though on a smaller scale, and to some extent in method. They were, moreover, obligated to render assistance to the security bureaus whenever necessary.[82]

Meanwhile, the Makarov Commission, charged in fall 1906 with reforming the entire police apparatus, proposed some radical reforms. One subcommission, chaired by V. E. Frisch, who had carefully studied the police institutions in France, Italy, Austria, Germany, and Spain, advocated unifying all of the various police institutions—the gendarmes, the security police, the regular police, the rural guards, and even private security services—into one single police corps whose personnel, called "guardsmen" *(strazhniki)*, would number 150,000. The war ministry would train them and pay their salary; the interior ministry would supervise their work. The guardsmen would restrict themselves to law enforcement, leaving the investigation of crimes to judicial authorities. These proposals were rejected almost in their entirety, both in the interest of frugality and because subordinating the police force to the war ministry seemed inadvisable.[83]

Another subcommission, concerned with reforming the security police system and headed by Trusevich, proposed to abolish the gendarme stations, to transfer their personnel to the provincial and city governors' staffs, and to appoint the former gendarme chiefs as assistant governors for policing. The governors staunchly supported this plan; the Police Department's opposition killed it. The subcommission also proposed that the law define the rights and duties of the security bureaus, which hitherto had operated solely on the basis of secret instructions and directives. This proposal also failed.[84] It seems unlikely that such a law could have passed the Duma.

■ ■ ■

The government seemed triumphant. The commander of the Moscow military district reported in early 1908 that "Everywhere revolutionary newspapers bitterly complain about the intensification of the 'reaction' and about the indifference of the population to the activity of revolutionaries." In April Socialist-Revolutionary leaders in Paris founded a new journal, *Revoliutsionnaia mysl'* (Revolutionary Thought) in order to come to terms with the crisis in the movement. The first issue declared, "The autocracy has reestablished itself." May Day demonstrations, assemblies, and strikes were far less prominent in 1908 than the year before. A failed attempt against the life of A. A. Reinbot, the Moscow city governor, in October 1907 was the last major terrorist attack in Russia until late 1909.[85]

Much discontent was simply driven underground. A cache of private letters intercepted by the police in 1908 reveals profound disappointment with the government among educated, politically moderate elites. D. N. Shipov wrote apocalyptically to his daughter: "The sooner the revolutionary catastrophe comes the better. . . . The government is pushing people into the abyss. . . . We have freedoms in principle, but they are abused, denied piecemeal; now there are more areas for *proizvol* [abuse of power]. . . . Stolypin's policies can lead only to . . . a horrible revolution." Similarly, Leo Tolstoy published his famous "I Cannot Be Silent" in May 1908, calling revolutionary terrorists the government's "disciples" and "creations."[86]

Revolutionary terror striking low-level officials was still intense along the Russian Empire's western and southern borders, especially in Poland and the Caucasus. A. M. Eremin, who had left the Special Section in January 1908 to head the regional security bureau in Tiflis, reported in April that security policing had collapsed, an assertion confirmed by the viceroy, I. I. Vorontsov-Dashkov. During the first four months of 1908 in Tiflis alone, political terrorists killed twelve and wounded eight police officials. Out in the province, the gendarmes conducted almost no surveillance of revolutionaries or terrorists. Eremin urged temporarily restricting civil rights in the region in order to strengthen the security police. He proposed to bar natives from police service, to search all suspicious people during unrest, to ban all lectures and readings not in Russian, and to close all leftist newspapers.[87] It seems that his recommendations were not implemented, probably because of opposition from Vorontsov-Dashkov, who favored a softer line.

The security police brilliantly foiled plot after plot conceived by the major revolutionary parties across the Russian Empire, but these efforts had a dark underside. The Socialist-Revolutionaries planned to kill the entire right wing of the State Council, Justice Minister I. G. Shcheglovitov, Grand Duke Nikolai Nikolaevich, and the emperor himself. These plans apparently included a projected airplane attack (the party spent thousands of rubles on designing the aircraft, but its designer ultimately sold his plans to the German military) and three sailors who were ready to shoot the emperor on two separate ships, one at Reval on 27 May 1908, the other at Kronstadt on 24 September 1908. At the center of the security police force's defensive effort stood A. V. Gerasimov, and behind him, Azef. Gerasimov trusted Azef utterly, though he checked and rechecked his assertions. Yet Azef omitted mention of the plot at Kronstadt, and only blind luck saved Nicholas, when the sailors could not bring themselves to shoot their sovereign. The security police force was not aware of this near failure. Spiridovich later wrote, "We had no idea how close we were to the abyss."[88]

CHAPTER THREE

WATERSHED:

THE AZEF AFFAIR

■ In early 1909 Stolypin met with his first major setback as prime minister: the emperor's veto of the naval staff bill. In March and April rumors of Stolypin's imminent resignation circulated widely. Around this time Nicholas may have entertained a proposal to transform the Duma into a consultative body. In March seven prominent authors, some of them former Marxists, published a collection of articles titled *Vekhi* (Signposts), condemning mindless devotion to the ideal of revolution and blaming Russia's failure to establish a fully constitutional order on the extremism of the major political parties and organizations. The collection quickly went through five editions and provoked an intense debate about the nature of Russia, the role of its intellectuals, and its chances for peaceful reform and progress. Recently an historian has called the *Vekhi* debate the dominant event of 1909.[1] Doubtless the second most important topic of public debate, and by far the most significant for the security police, was the unmasking of Azef as a police informant in January. This revelation exploded like a bombshell in the public consciousness and severely undermined the self-confidence of both conspiratorial revolutionaries and security policemen.

STOLYPIN'S NEW SENIOR POLICE OFFICIALS

Stolypin began the new year with a shake-up of the police apparatus and a decided move to the right politically. On 1 January 1909 he appointed as deputy interior minister for police affairs P. G. Kurlov, whom he had been grooming since summer 1906. Pavel Grigor'evich Kurlov was born in 1860 into a landowning gentry family in Kursk Province. His father and uncle had served in the military. As he later wrote, he "grew up with strong faith in God and loyalty to the sovereign, which only grew in strength over the course of my career." Absolute monarchy, he wrote, was "clearly the only form of government that conforms to the needs of the Russian people."[2]

After graduating from the Military Academy of Law in 1889, Kurlov devoted fourteen years to military and civil prosecution work. According to A. I. Spiridovich, he was "intelligent, capable, vigorous, resolute, and deeply attached to the police and the gendarmerie." K. D. Kafafov and A. P. Martynov considered him highly talented but also somewhat unsavory. Appointed governor of Minsk in 1905, he was forced to leave office in January 1906 amid allegations of improper actions during the suppression of revolutionary disorder. The charges were dropped, however, perhaps because of pressure from the court: the empress herself apparently told Stolypin that she would not cease to fear for the emperor's life "until Kurlov shall stand at the head of the security police." Yet the public despised him. The left Octobrist S. I. Shidlovskii waxed indignant at Kurlov's appointment. Stolypin could only reply: "You know what our police is like; it must be held in an iron fist. Kurlov has that kind of fist."[3]

Kurlov received the title Commander of the Gendarme Corps, supposedly in order to facilitate the unification of the Corps with the Police Department, and his annual salary was raised to fifteen thousand rubles. Nicholas also made him a major general and most exceptionally gave him a court title, *shtalmeister,* as a separate post *(dolzhnost'),* even though military officers could not legally hold court titles. This was an artifice Nicholas used only four times in the last decade of his reign. Formally Kurlov's main responsibilities would be to oversee the Police Department and the Department of Religious Affairs of Non-Orthodox Religions. (A second deputy interior minister, S. E. Kryzhanovskii, oversaw the other branches of the ministry.) In actuality, Kurlov's most important task was to ensure the emperor's security during his official travels within Russia, beginning with the July bicentennial celebration of Peter the Great's victory in Poltava. Kurlov's second most important task was to reform the security police system. Most important, he improved the program of gendarme officer training and expanded the periodic systematic inspection of the security police institutions in the field. Finally, Kurlov began to implement Trusevich's plan to create a network of counterespionage bureaus within the Russian Empire.[4]

Kurlov's appointment was attended by a typical flurry of promotions and demotions. His predecessor, A. A. Makarov, became the secretary of the State Council. The director of the Police Department, M. I. Trusevich, was "kicked upstairs" into the Senate. Kurlov disliked Trusevich and apparently made a point of humiliating him from January until his retirement on 9 March, a slight Trusevich would repay. The man Kurlov favored to head the Police Department was Nil Petrovich Zuev, a rather timid and indolent, though honest and intelligent, official whom colleagues had sardonically dubbed "Crocodile Petrovich." Since 1903 Zuev had managed legal and financial matters as vice-director of the Police Department. Martynov called him a "typical Petersburg civil-servant-bureaucrat . . . who knew all about

Stepan Petrovich Beletskii, director of
the Police Department (1912–1914)
and deputy interior minister
(1915–1916).

the intrigues and gossip of the service . . . but was unsuited to oversee security policing"; Spiridovich suggests that he was "uninterested in it." Kurlov
admitted that he had chosen Zuev for three reasons: early in his career he
had prosecuted political crimes, he knew accounting (Trusevich had left a
budget deficit), and he was utterly loyal to Kurlov. As one police official
later wrote, Zuev became Kurlov's creature.[5]

Zuev's vice-director for legislative affairs, appointed in July, was Stepan
Petrovich Beletskii, who subsequently became an extremely important police official. Born into a middle-class merchant family in Chernigov
Province in 1872, Beletskii was "of medium height and thickset, with a
square head, a large face framed by a beard, and hair parted on the side."
He received his law degree from Kiev University in 1894. He served in diverse administrative positions and had a reputation for hard work and
meticulous records management. Stolypin met Beletskii during a stint as
gentry marshal in Kovno around the turn of the century.[6]

In early 1907 Beletskii became vice-governor of Samara Province. A. N.
Naumov, then a conservative public activist in Samara, remembered him as

"a very subservient, unpleasant personality, but a very resourceful worker, able to sort out even the most complicated situations and who spent his nights working to figure out complicated questions. He was amazingly aware of details in the lives of provincial elites." V. P. Nikol'skii, aide-decamp of the commander of the Moscow military directorate, described Beletskii as "cunning, ingratiating *(vkradchivyi)*, with a charming manner. . . . He had a sharp mind, capable of grasping quickly the most complex issues, an immense capacity for work." N. P. Kharlamov, a vice-director of the Police Department also appointed in mid-1909, found Beletskii very accessible and simple in his ways, indeed always very nice, even excessively sweet, with everybody.[7]

Kurlov's links to court circles also helped facilitate the rise of Grigorii Rasputin. Gerasimov claims that V. A. Dediulin, the court commandant, had not long before ordered him to maintain surveillance over Rasputin, whereas now, in early 1909, the cunning peasant had become a regular visitor at court. With Kurlov's promotion in particular, according to Gerasimov, "there was no longer any question of exiling Rasputin."[8] Thus, while Kurlov defended the emperor's physical security, he opened the door to a process by which the monarchy was delegitimized, for few single factors occasioned greater damage in this regard than the proximity to the imperial court of the Siberian *muzhik* (male peasant). A few brave officials, including Stolypin, would later seek to dissociate Rasputin from the court, but the unofficial support for him that began during Kurlov's tenure became a permanent leitmotif until the monarchy's fall.

Even so, at the start of 1909 the Russian monarchy, in large part thanks to its security police, seemed unassailable. On 2 January a leading Socialist-Revolutionary, O. S. Minor, was arrested along with many other members of his party thanks to intelligence provided to the police by both E. F. Azef and T. M. Tsetlin. Eight days later the Moscow security bureau sent to St. Petersburg a list of thirty addresses of Social Democrats active in the region surrounding Moscow. In mid-February employees of the bureau arrested several of them.[9] These arrests were overshadowed, however, by the revelation that a leading Socialist-Revolutionary had been a police informant for over a decade.

UNMASKING AZEF

Vague suspicions had followed Evno Fishelevich Azef for years. As early as 1902, Krest'ianinov, a student and a member of the party, accused him of working for the police. A party commission investigated the matter, then dropped it. In 1904 the bibliographer N. A. Rubakin shared his suspicions about Azef with M. R. Gots, who apparently just passed the remarks on to Azef. Far graver, L. P. Men'shchikov, the renegade security police officer, anonymously denounced Azef to the Socialist-Revolutionary leadership in September 1905. The month before, E. P. Mednikov, the Police Department's director of plainclothes surveillance, who was then suffering from a progressive nervous disorder, apparently revealed some details about Azef's double role, without mentioning his name, to a surveillant in Saratov. This information wended its way to the Socialist-Revolutionary Party's central committee.[10]

Azef's closest party comrades knew he had some suspicious ways. A. A. Argunov later testified that Azef had ranged freely in St. Petersburg, apparently unconcerned with police surveillance. He also rarely drank, and he avoided sleeping in the same room with his comrades since he ground his teeth, groaned, and talked in his sleep.[11] It seemed, however, that no leaks, suspicions, or dubious behaviors could shake Azef's comrades' faith in him. Had he not masterminded major assassination plots against senior government officials and members of the imperial family? Only one radical activist, who tellingly was never a member of the Socialist-Revolutionary Party and therefore did not feel the profound loyalty that usually bound its members into a tight fellowship, suspected Azef and tenaciously sought to expose him and to destroy his career.

Vladimir L'vovich Burtsev was born in 1862, the son of a Cossack officer. He studied mathematics and law. He was exiled in 1886 to Irkutsk Province, then he fled abroad, where he spent most of the rest of his life. Burtsev claimed he had begun to suspect that Azef was a police informant in 1906 when he saw him riding in an open carriage down a busy street in St. Petersburg. If Burtsev had recognized him, he thought, so must have trained surveillants. After reflecting and doing some research, Burtsev began to make informal accusations against Azef in spring 1907. Burtsev moved to Paris in late 1907 and later claimed that he had done so "to wage a campaign against provocation and against the Police Department, because I consider provocation the greatest evil for Russia and the foundation of the Russian reaction." Spiridovich, jabbing at Burtsev, wrote that he "had his own *okhrana*, in every way like that of government."[12]

For ammunition in his fight, Burtsev had a list of fifty to seventy-five police informants that had been given to him by M. E. Bakai, a police official who had defected to the revolutionaries in 1906. In early 1908, Burtsev vainly tried to obtain further inside information on these police agents from the retired security officer S. V. Zubatov, who replied that such cooperation would require him "to delight in the destruction of what I hold most dear."[13] What were fallen angels to the revolutionaries were comrades-in-arms to Zubatov.

Burtsev began his crusade in March 1908 with M. A. Kensitskii, who was spying on the remnants of the Maximalists in Paris. Since Kensitskii had been an informant for the Warsaw security bureau in 1904 and 1905, it seems likely that Bakai betrayed him. A. M. Garting, the Paris security bureau chief, immediately warned his superiors that Burtsev's campaign could

Evno Fishelevich Azef, "star"
security police agent (1893–1909).

create a terrible scandal in the French press, could lead to the murder of informants, and in general threatened the Russian security police force's outpost in Paris. Therefore his bureau was transferred from the imperial embassy to a secret apartment. The French police, at Garting's behest, questioned Bakai, who admitted nothing, and threatened to expel him from the country—an idle threat, as the prefect admitted. Garting's force maintained tight surveillance over Bakai for several months, then gave it up as fruitless: Bakai lived in an idyllically quiet neighborhood (Parc Montsouris), and his socialist building superintendent would not help the Russian police.[14]

Probably emboldened by this first success, Burtsev formally accused Azef of spying in May 1908. The party leadership grew defensive. Did Burtsev have any idea of Azef's immense service to the party's program of terror? exclaimed O. S. Minor. Burtsev realized he needed a reliable witness from within the police apparatus. He approached several officials before turning to A. A. Lopukhin, an obvious target from Burtsev's point of view. Lopukhin had been removed from the directorship of the Police Department under a cloud of ignominy after the assassination of Grand Duke Sergei Aleksandrovich in 1905, and he was the only Police Department di-

Vladimir L'vovich Burtsev, the "revolutionary Sherlock Holmes";
he unmasked Azef.

rector in the history of the institution who had not been made a senator upon retirement. He had leaked information about the Kommisarov affair in 1906, had publicly criticized the police apparatus in 1907, and had persistently but vainly sought to join Kadet circles. Although he had once used the familiar form of address with Stolypin, whom he had known since childhood, he now appeared to be alienated from both the interior minister and the bureaucratic milieu. According to his cousin, career diplomat V. B. Lopukhin, the former Police Department director desired above all to take revenge on the government for the failure of his career in the civil service.[15]

Burtsev claimed that in early September 1908 he arranged to meet with A. A. Lopukhin, who was traveling home from a vacation in Germany. He wrote that an acquaintance had told him that Lopukhin would have to change trains in Cologne. Carefully concealing himself, Burtsev watched the former police official step off one train and onto another one bound for Berlin, which Burtsev discretely boarded. After the Berlin-bound train left the station, Burtsev sat down opposite Lopukhin and struck up a conversation with him. Although the former police official did not directly affirm that Azef was an informant, he decisively confirmed Burtsev's suspicions in that regard. Soon thereafter, Burtsev reported his findings to B. V. Savinkov and other Socialist-Revolutionary leaders. As late as 1916, Burtsev affirmed that Lopukhin was "entirely pure before the government."[16]

The trouble with this version of the story is that it is almost entirely false. It seems that Lopukhin was just as eager to talk to Burtsev as Burtsev was to speak to Lopukhin. Recently declassified party archives carefully researched by two Russian historians suggest that Lopukhin himself sought, through a variety of means, to expose Azef's police ties to his party comrades. Back in May 1908, N. A. Morozov, an old revolutionary who had spent twenty-four years in prison, had already traveled to Paris to denounce Azef to M. A. Natanson, but Natanson had rejected the allegation and warned Morozov not to repeat it. Morozov later revealed that he had learned Azef's secret from A. A. Orlov-Davydov, a Kadet and leading Freemason with close ties to S. D. Urusov, another leading Freemason and Lopukhin's brother-in-law. Probably Lopukhin had told Urusov, who had told Orlov-Davydov to pass the information on to Morozov, who supposedly was also a Freemason. In August 1908, A. I. Braudo, an employee of the St. Petersburg Public Library and a Freemason who had previously facilitated contacts between Burtsev and Lopukhin, visited Burtsev and told him when Lopukhin would change trains in Cologne—surely he was the acquaintance Burtsev had mentioned in his own account. In May 1910 Burtsev admitted to a party investigating commission that Lopukhin had told him "absolutely everything about Azef."[17]

Azef's party comrades reacted with disbelief and anger. "Azef and the party," Burtsev was told, "are one and the same." They tried Burtsev for libel in an intraparty arbitration court in Paris and persuaded him to name his source of information. Then A. A. Argunov, a staunch defender of Azef, was sent to Russia in early November to assess Lopukhin's credibility. While he consulted with some of Lopukhin's acquaintances in Moscow, Azef and Gerasimov met separately with the former police chief, urging him to protect Azef.[18]

Braudo and S. E. Kal'manovich, a Freemason and radical attorney, arranged for Argunov to meet with Lopukhin on the 18th of November. Meanwhile, Braudo had passed a letter to Lopukhin from Burtsev saying Burtsev might commit suicide if Lopukhin refused to back him up.

Aleksei Aleksandrovich Lopukhin,
director of the Police Department
(1902–1905) who denounced Azef to
Burtsev in 1909.

Argunov thought Lopukhin "did not look like a policeman. Rather it was a
noble landlord, in his manners, tone of voice, and gestures. . . . His eyes
were cold. . . . Yet these were not the eyes of a policeman. . . . They did not
roam about or squint but . . . withstood my unyielding, insistent stare."
Lopukhin told him that he was "not a revolutionary . . . but only a witness"
and that he had unintentionally divulged *(sluchaino progovorilsia)* information
about Azef, but that he would not take back what he had revealed. The next
day they met again, and Lopukhin was very forthcoming.[19] Soon after this
meeting and another on the following day, Lopukhin wrote letters denouncing Azef to Stolypin, Makarov, and Trusevich. He gave the letters to Argunov,
who asked Braudo to mail them. Braudo apparently sent a copy to the London
Times, causing a huge sensation.[20]

On 21 November Gerasimov apparently visited Lopukhin a second time.
Did Gerasimov threaten him? Lopukhin sent word to Argunov that he was
"more afraid of Gerasimov than of anyone else." He vowed to "travel anywhere you want in order to testify." Since Lopukhin was planning to travel
to London in early December, they agreed to meet there. On 10 December
Lopukhin met with members of the intraparty arbitration court in the
lobby of the Waldorf Hotel in Charing Cross and revealed to them facts
about Azef, the totality of which only a few party leaders knew. There
could be no doubt that Azef had betrayed them.[21]

In early December the intraparty court in Paris sentenced Azef to death. On 7 January he slipped out of Paris—Gerasimov had given him several passports and between two thousand and three thousand rubles. The next day the party leadership publicly denounced Azef as a police informant and published a list of the terrorist acts in which he had allegedly taken part. The party's central committee proclaimed in February that they were dissolving the combat organization, but it continued to function weakly under the direction of Savinkov. Azef settled in Berlin as A. Neimaier, merchant. Allegedly V. M. Chernov wished to kill his former comrade soon after his exposure, yet when a Russian official in Belgium allegedly offered to give Azef's address to a Socialist-Revolutionary terrorist, the party declined to receive it, presumably so as to let sleeping dogs lie. Azef lived comfortably until 1915, when he was imprisoned by the German police as an enemy agent; he died in a German prison in 1918.[22]

The tempestuous public reaction to the Azef affair merits discussion, but first it is well to take a stab at several vexing questions: Was Azef a double agent? Was he a provocateur? Why did so many revolutionaries refuse to believe the allegations that their milieu was pervaded by informants?

Nearly all contemporaries and commentators have rightly presumed that Azef served both the security police and the Socialist-Revolutionaries, sometimes leaning more toward the one, sometimes leaning more toward the other.[23] Indeed, it seems clear that during some periods of his career as a police informant Azef was unfaithful in his service to the police—for example, during the period from 1902 to 1905, when he answered to L. A. Rataev, he apparently masterminded the assassinations of Interior Minister V. K. Plehve and Grand Duke Sergei Aleksandrovich. R. A. Gorodnitskii has called the time from summer 1903 to March 1905 "an unconditionally revolutionary period" in Azef's life.[24]

The argument that Azef served the police entirely loyally during the years when Gerasimov directed his actions (1906–1908), moreover, is undermined by the fact that in 1907 Azef failed to report on several terrorist plots, most grievously the assassination attempts on the emperor's life in 1908 in Reval and Kronstadt. Gerasimov mentions neither plot in his memoirs. Gorodnitskii is right to argue that the "blindness of the police can only be compared to the blindness of leaders of the party and the combat organization." It is hard to say which side Azef betrayed more. Gorodnitskii has gone so far as to call Gerasimov "criminally negligent." It is hard to argue with that assessment: Gerasimov was essentially willing to place the security of the emperor and senior officials in the hands of a man with close ties to political terrorists who never revealed to him the full details of the terrorists' operations. "I had total confidence in Azef," he wrote, "and gave him freedom of action."[25]

So long as the plots failed, Gerasimov seems to have been justified in his approach. But how could he have been sure that Azef was truly loyal? For their part, his party comrades racked their brains trying to understand how he could have taken them in. Natanson believed Azef "calculated fifteen moves—and more—ahead." G. A. Lopatin called him a "professional in the best sense of the word."[26] But why did Azef place himself in such danger, especially if Anna Geifman is correct that he engaged in a "lifetime struggle with fear"? M. O. Levin, who knew Azef from their school days, was probably right to argue that what attracted him to his role as a double agent was not simply a desire for money—as an outstanding engineer he could have earned a good salary—but lust for power and adventure, the "idea that a humble person held the fate of so much in his hands."[27]

So he was a brilliant double agent, but was he a provocateur? Few Russian police informants were provocateurs in the strict sense—that is, few of them incited revolutionaries to commit crimes in order to betray them thereafter to the police. It is clear that Russia's revolutionaries continually broke the law—and were committed to breaking the law—without any help from informants. Yet Azef did engage in provocation. Leaving aside the terrorist acts he personally masterminded and the plots he inspired and organized before helping the police to undo them, Azef also continuously incited his comrades to violence.

I. Skalichev, a minor Socialist-Revolutionary activist, recalled how in 1902 Azef, upon seeing contraband pamphlets smuggled from Finland into Russia, gnashed his teeth and said: "because of these books in five years the very bones of Russia will crack." Skalichev soon found himself in a police cell and thereafter was exiled to Siberia, presumably because Azef had betrayed him. Although he publicly called for an end to his party's campaign of terror in October 1905, during a private conversation with V. M. Chernov, Azef apparently advocated blowing up the Moscow security bureau. In spring 1908 N. A. Lazarkevich rejected Azef's request that he set up a big dynamite workshop in St. Petersburg because Swedish manufacturers would ship as much as Lazarkevich wanted through Finland. Azef's typical stance with party comrades seems to be revealed in the words that, according to A. A. Argunov, he regularly uttered: "Terror is the main thing."[28]

Bakai lamented that for years most revolutionaries disbelieved the repeated warnings about the ubiquity of informants in their midst. "They seem," he wrote, "to flee from it completely, to ignore it, thereby causing themselves the most serious and irrevocable harm."[29] Why was this so? There seem to have been five reasons. First, any admission by party members that their ranks were penetrated by police spies was likely to diminish the prestige of the party and make it harder to recruit and retain new members. Second, revolutionary activists formed tight bonds of loyalty and trust with one another and therefore found it hard to believe there might be traitors in their midst. Third, it may have been quite reasonable to prefer blissful ignorance to the anxiety, even paranoia, that would inevitably follow the acknowledgment that traitors lurked among one's comrades.

Fourth, those revolutionary leaders who emphasized spreading propaganda rightly believed that even informants, who had to abet this work, served a useful purpose in the organizations they spied on. Finally, and most important, all the revolutionary leaders were fanatically committed to their cause, which they held sacred and pure. Any apostasy from that cause, from the revolutionary faith, by other righteous fighters, especially by a member of the inner circle, a "high priest," would traumatize the true believers and might shatter their worldview.

REACTIONS TO THE AFFAIR

The unmasking of Azef stunned and outraged the educated Russian public. The press feverishly discussed the nature of the Russian security police. On 20 January the Kadet daily, *Rech'*, alleged that the work of the security police had been given precedence "over all other higher tasks of state," a silly assertion considering the institution's exiguous budget compared to those of a dozen other government agencies, the disdain with which the imperial court and much of senior officialdom regarded security policing, and the greater importance Prime Minister Stolypin attributed to his reform program, now that the administration as a whole had crushed the popular rebellion. Commentators also implicated the Russian government in the orgy of political terror of the previous four years. Thus the Duma deputies who had refused to condemn revolutionary terror in 1907 had been justified, argued V. P. Obninskii, because they had seen "the links between terrorism and the policies of the government, which created the Police Department and became its slave and its victim." The name Azef became shorthand for police informant. In late 1911 the liberal *Birzhevye vedomosti* referred to an "Odesskii Azef" who had been unmasked in that city. The legal scholar N. S. Tagantsev later remarked that the name Azef had become a cultural icon, like the character from Russian folklore "Zmei-Gorynich" and the leader of Ivan the Terrible's reign of terror, Maliuta Skuratov-Bel'skii.[30]

The Duma saw intensive debates on the Azef affair. On 11 and 13 February Social Democratic and Kadet deputies lodged two interpellations asking the interior minister to clarify whether Azef had taken part in revolutionary activities. Kurlov and Trusevich, at Stolypin's behest, conferred at length with Zubatov, Rachkovskii, Rataev, N. N. Kuliabko, and other current and former security policemen. Kurlov then reported to the Duma that the interpellations contained no facts and therefore required no explanation. Social Democratic deputies took this occasion to bring to public attention numerous details about Azef and about the security system in general, for example that several erstwhile informants were at the time employed in the Police Department (M. I. Gurovich, N. V. Dobroskok, and

N. E. Pankrat'ev). There was also plenty of vitriol, as when I. P. Pokrovskii, a Social Democrat, declared that "the system of provocation, the system of political policing has at the current moment become a system for controlling the entire country. . . . An Asiatic despotism, a cannibalistic, bloodthirsty government needs provocation."[31]

When the Kadet deputy O. Ia. Pergament called Stolypin's honesty into question by pointing to his assurances to the First Duma that he would not tolerate provocation, Stolypin decided to present spontaneously his ministry's response to the interpellation. First, he challenged the use of the term *provocateur*. Providing information, he argued, is not provocation. He then claimed that Azef had become fully aware of the terrorist activities of the Socialist-Revolutionary Party only beginning in May 1906. It is unclear whether Stolypin knew that this statement was false: Azef had been a member of the inner circles of the party and the head of its combat organization since 1903. Stolypin then alleged that Azef had helped the government to avert terrorist plots beginning in 1906. In this sense, he argued, informants were extremely valuable for the government and dangerous for the revolutionaries. "It is a sad fact," he said, "that as long as there is political terrorism, there must be a political police." He reaffirmed his commitment to the rule of law and to the rooting out of administrative abuse. "We have prosecuted every case [of provocation] that has come to our attention," he added. Yet the government had to function in the face of grave danger. "When I was in Saratov," he noted, "both security bureau chiefs asked me, in the event of their death, to take care of their families. Both were killed while conscientiously serving the tsar and the motherland." Combating revolutionary terrorism is "not our goal," he explained; however, "it is the means to create the opportunity to legislate."[32]

Following two more opposition speeches, the Kadet leader V. A. Maklakov asked rhetorically, "Do you think that this okhrana, full of hidden Azefs, will tell the truth about an exposed Azef?" He then inquired how one could be a member of the central committee of a revolutionary party without taking a direct part in the work of the party. He concluded with a rhetorical attack on the government. "There is," he intoned, "no more state (which is a juridical entity), but only a gang *[shaika]* that has become the captive of these criminals. . . . Here we have a fateful influence of the okhrana on every aspect of our [national] life, a Babylonian captivity of our governmental authority." The Police Department, he asserted, "wishes to alienate the government from the population and is succeeding masterfully."[33] This was an astonishing tirade for a moderate Kadet.

Several rightists defended the government. G. G. Zamyslovskii likened provocation to bribe taking: "Just because some officials take bribes it makes no sense to abolish officialdom." He cited the planned attempt on the life of Shcheglovitov in early 1908. Thanks to Azef, the police had established surveillance over Anna Rasputina, who was to kill him. The surveillance permitted the police to gather incriminating information against her and to foil the plot. It was impossible for the police to arrest her without further incriminating evidence; if they had the Duma would have lodged an interpellation for abuse of power. Ultimately, the mission was aborted and Rasputina fled.[34]

N. D. Sazonov, an independent nationalist, argued that by joining revolutionary leaders for a meeting in Paris in September 1904 the Kadet leaders had encouraged them in their radicalism, which constituted a form of provocation. The Octobrist N. P. Shubinskoi stated that though he was "no partisan or admirer of the security bureaus," when violent political activity "threatens human life, it is necessary to put up a defense." He pointed out that the entire case against the government and Azef rested on two letters, one written by Azef after his exposure and the second produced by V. M. Chernov, a party leader. Neither source, he contended rightly, merited much credence. Shubinskoi concluded dramatically. Political terrorists, he said, were generally "youths, doubtless full of enthusiasm, sent off by revolutionary leaders . . . [who] are themselves inciters, provocateurs."[35]

The Duma ultimately rejected the proposed interpellations, and on 13 February it adopted a motion accepting the government's explanation of the Azef affair as adequate and expressing reliance on the government to combat terrorism using every legal means at its disposal—implicitly, according to Spiridovich, approving the use of secret informants.[36]

A former French police official allegedly said in 1870 that "In a group of ten secret society members there are always three *mouchards* [informants], six well-meaning imbeciles, and one dangerous man." There were never so many informants among Russian revolutionaries, except perhaps in their leadership circles, yet the Azef affair brought home to revolutionary activists just how beset they might be. Underground revolutionaries grew suspicious and fearful. Even Chernov was suspected of being an informant.[37]

Burtsev considered his revelations about Azef an invaluable service to the revolutionary movements, yet they devastated the Socialist-Revolutionary Party. He had, he later wrote, "exposed one of the most terrible aspects of my country," something that people would "still be talking about as of a nightmare" even in the distant future. V. N. Figner also thought Burtsev's "service" a nightmare. "You sow suspicion," she wrote, "you sow loathing and contempt for people, for mankind in general. . . . You are . . . darksouled." Chernov believed Burtsev's relentless unmasking of traitors caused a massive exodus from the party. The main party organ lamented that "the Azef affair tarnished with mud the most glorious pages of our recent history, shook among many their faith in the great moral values of the party . . . was shaking the very foundations of our party."[38]

Many must have feared that by discrediting the party, Azef might have driven a wedge between it and its mass constituency. One party member, S. Zorin, wrote that the unmasking of Azef, "as with a club to the head, struck the workers who at that time of dark reaction had been straining every nerve in their struggle with tsarism." When V. M. Zenzinov traveled around the country in February and March 1909 to contact local party organizations, he found "apathy, disaffection, detachment." He waxed apocalyptic. Azef, he wrote, "forced us to look at the world, people, and life with different eyes." The party's fortunes suffered further when later in the year B. V. Savinkov, under the pseudonym V. Ropshin, published *Kon' blednyi (Pale Horse)*, a novella depicting revolutionary terrorists as cynical, amoral, and purely criminal. Because Burtsev continued to unmask informants over the next three years, the party was obsessed with the question of provocation until the First World War. Although the party clung to an ideology of terror, and isolated terrorist acts continued to take place, the Azef affair marked the end of large-scale revolutionary terrorism in Russia.[39]

Social Democratic activists tended to imagine, complacently but not entirely falsely, that their organizations were less infiltrated by informants. After all, government officials were more afraid of acts of terror than they were of activists spreading propaganda among the population. Social Democratic leaders also argued that individual leadership played a far less vital role in their party than in a party emphasizing individual acts of terror. One could not gain the trust of the Social Democrats without spending countless hours spreading Marxist propaganda among laborers, and that activity, even coming from a police agent, could not but advance the Social Democratic cause. In this sense, Zubatov and G. A. Gapon increased the receptivity to radicalism of the industrial workers more than they diminished the influence of the Social Democrats among them. Yet the number of informants operating among the Social Democrats was considerable, and in absolute terms it surpassed the number within Socialist-Revolutionary ranks beginning, at the latest, in 1912, presumably because of the decline of political terror and the growth of the labor movement. Moreover, police repression gravely weakened Social Democratic operations during the years before the First World War, despite the Bolsheviks' February 1910 creation of a special investigative section headed by F. E. Dzerzhinskii "to expose and isolate provocateurs."[40]

Figuring out who was a police informant was a tricky business. For one thing, the revolutionaries knew, or at least suspected, that the security police occasionally sought to cast doubt upon the loyalty of individual members in order to sow discord within the party membership. Given the atmosphere of suspicion and uncertainty within the revolutionary underground, an unfavorable coincidence of circumstances could turn comrade against comrade unjustly. For example, I. V. Orlovskii, an activist in the Social Democratic organization in Moscow, fled abroad in early January 1909 on the eve of a series of major arrests in that organization. His party comrades thereupon accused him of spying for the police. He returned to Russia to try to clear his name and was arrested and exiled to Siberia. His former comrades remained falsely convinced of his guilt.[41]

The leaders of the major revolutionary parties were not the only ones profoundly shaken by the exposure of Azef. Kurlov railed against Lopukhin and Trusevich: if Azef had really taken part in terrorist acts, then he should have been arrested. He certainly should never have been betrayed to revolutionaries. Stolypin concurred and requested the emperor's permission to punish Lopukhin. Nicholas readily consented and, after Lopukhin's arrest, jotted: "I hope he'll get hard labor."[42]

It was unclear, however, with what crime Lopukhin should be charged. The government could hardly try him for revealing the identity of a government employee who had helped organize the assassination of government officials, as Maurice Laporte remarked. Kurlov later admitted that Lopukhin had violated no law. He had not violently attacked the emperor (Article 99 of the criminal code) or violently attempted to alter the duly constituted order of Russia (Article 100). Nevertheless, the ministers of interior and justice, N. A. Maklakov and I. G. Shcheglovitov, as well as the chief prosecutor of the St. Petersburg judicial tribunal, P. K. Kamyshanskii, resolved to prosecute him under Article 102 of the criminal code of 1903, that is, for participation in an association *(soobshchestvo)*, in this case the Socialist-Revolutionary Party, constituted for the purpose of committing crimes described in Article 100. Apparently many jurists, including Kurlov, thought the charge, and therefore the trial, illegitimate.[43]

Lopukhin's case was heard by a special commission of the Senate from 28 to 30 April 1909. The state argued that Lopukhin's revelation of the identity of the security police force's key informant within the Socialist-Revolutionary Party constituted a state crime, for it had provided "significant assistance to the criminal organization of Socialist-Revolutionaries," which was indeed true, despite the negative impact the exposure had on the party in the long run. It is curious therefore that so staunch a monarchist hard-liner as Kurlov would consider the trial legally baseless. In any event, Lopukhin argued that he could not help but believe Burtsev's assurance that Azef had taken part in numerous crimes. "Perhaps I believed him too carelessly *[legkomyslenno]*, but since I did believe him, I considered it impossible to keep silent."[44]

The prosecutor's heart was not fully in the case. He accused Lopukhin of bringing great harm to the Russian state but also called Azef a traitor. "If he were an agent of the government, a man of duty, a man who has sworn to serve loyally, one might have been surprised by his courage . . . [but] he was a revolutionary . . . betraying his own people to the enemy for money, and of course this activity is not worthy of anybody's sympathy."[45] It is astonishing that a government prosecutor would refer in a court of law to his own government as "the enemy," even by analogy. Perhaps his statement bespoke a secret admiration for the revolutionary opposition; perhaps it revealed an instinctive revulsion for any tattler and an antipathy toward the security police; certainly it stemmed in part from the immense value the Russian public ascribed to loyalty to one's comrades.

On 1 May Lopukhin was sentenced to five years of penal servitude. Nicholas wrote one vehement word on the report: "Splendid" *(Zdorovo)*. The Senate's cassation department commuted the sentence to the deprivation of all rights and exile, which he served in Minusinsk in Siberia. Lopukhin later benefited from an amnesty, announced on 21 February 1913, that fully restored his rights, so it was as though he had never been convicted. If the government had had no right to try him under Article 102 of the criminal code, it also had no right to amnesty him at this time, since the amnesty was not supposed to apply to criminals convicted under Article 102. Clearly Russian governmental arbitrariness could work both for and against a given individual. After his release, Lopukhin first worked as a lawyer, then became vice-director of the Siberian Commercial Bank in Moscow. In 1913 he was appointed assistant director of the Moscow branch of the St. Petersburg International Bank of Commerce. After October 1917 he remained in this position briefly, then emigrated to Paris and found work in another bank. He died in 1928.[46]

ASSAULT ON THE SECURITY POLICE

On the eve of Lopukhin's day in court, M. F. von Koten faced his own trial in Paris. He had traveled there to meet with Mikhail Ripps, a veteran Socialist-Revolutionary terrorist whom he hoped to recruit as a police informant, but who intended to lure *him* into a trap. In 1906 von Koten had arrested Ripps, who was then exiled to Turukhansk in Siberia, from whence he escaped at the end of 1908. Von Koten arrested him again in February 1909, and knowing Ripps had taken part in three bombings in 1905 and 1906, he supposedly gave him a choice: either infiltrate the terrorist milieu in Paris or return to Siberia. Ripps chose Paris but resolved to kill von Koten, or so Burtsev asserted. The latter urged him simply to write an exposé on the Russian security police and certainly not to commit murder in France, a refuge for Russian revolutionary émigrés. Ripps insisted on going through with the act, but he vowed, at Burtsev's entreaty, to stand trial for the offense and to profess that he had acted alone.[47]

Ripps persuaded von Koten to meet him in Paris. After his arrival on 18 April (all dates Old Style), von Koten introduced Ripps to Garting, who, impressed with Ripps's knowledge of the Socialist-Revolutionary milieu, agreed to pay him 500 francs (or 250 rubles) per month as an informant. On 25 April Garting drove von Koten most of the way to 4 rue Bolivar. They then proceeded on foot, and finally von Koten went alone upstairs to Ripps's apartment. Ripps inquired, "Where is your friend?" Upon hearing he was waiting below, Ripps said, "It is very dangerous to be seen with Garting." Von Koten suggested inviting him upstairs. Ripps replied that he needed to talk alone. "It's very dangerous in Paris," he said. "There are traitors. Garting himself must be a traitor." Von Koten then looked out the window. Suddenly he heard three shots and realized that he was wounded. Ripps shot a fourth time. Von Koten managed to push Ripps's arm away, but the report shattered his left eardrum. They struggled, and von Koten fled. He provided a detailed account of the incident to the police and a judicial investigator, who requested that he remain in Paris. Newspapers reported that one bullet had pierced a wall and just missed a woman sitting with her child and that von Koten had fled Paris, fearing reprisals.[48]

The Russian government pressed charges in France against Ripps. The trial, which did not take place until mid-July 1911, was a political sensation. Fernand Labori, the "greatest criminal lawyer of his day," who had defended Alfred Dreyfus, stood by von Koten. Ripps's defense called Jean Jaurès, the socialist leader, who presumably had nothing to say about the case, to the witness stand. Ripps told the court he had shot von Koten because the latter had tried to make him a provocateur. The French press raged against the Russian police, and the jury acquitted Ripps.[49]

Like a man possessed, Burtsev continued his hunt for informants. His next target was a woman. Back in December a prominent public figure, almost certainly S. D. Urusov, had revealed to revolutionaries in Paris that a long-serving woman informant was still active within the Socialist-Revolutionary Party. Urusov apparently had received the information from an incautious former director of the Police Department, S. G. Kovalenskii (though he might just as well have gotten it from his brother-in-law). Burtsev publicly made this known in September 1910.[50]

The informant in question was Z. F. Gerngross-Zhuchenko, but Burtsev's suspicions initially fell on T. M. Tsetlin (or Tseitlin), whose real name was M. Ia. Tsikhotskaia. An informant for Gerasimov since 1907, Tsikhotskaia had infiltrated the Socialist-Revolutionary combat organization and was involved in late 1908 in a plan for regicide, which was postponed by the arrest of O. S. Minor and the exposure of Azef. She then grew closer to Savinkov, who was plotting the assassination of Gerasimov, Kurlov, and other police officials.

In March, Tsikhotskaia summoned N. V. Dobroskok, a security police official, to Paris to divulge these plans to him, and revolutionary activists observed their encounter. That evening she received a cable from Savinkov, requesting that she visit him at rue Azelin in the Latin Quarter at the apartment of M. I. Deev (pseudonym: Sin'kovskii), whom they also suspected of informing. Ten revolutionaries, including Savinkov, met her there on 10 April. They pointed a gun at her, searched her, and divulged to her little-known information about the Russian security police, such as the location of a secret apartment in St. Petersburg. She assumed her fate was sealed.

The next morning, Burtsev arrived with five "judges," including Savinkov and V. M. Chernov. Burtsev took her to her apartment, where he found postcards from Dobroskok, whose handwriting he identified. Meanwhile the "judges" interrogated Deev. Later, Tsikhotskaia admitted to being a police agent, and the revolutionaries decided to execute both of them. Party activists kept them under armed guard for several days; then on 19 April their "sentences" were rescinded for want of evidence that "their hands are stained with blood," as Savinkov remarked. Instead they were merely expelled from the party and ordered to keep the party informed about their places of residence. In Tsikhotskaia's own account of these events, which coincides in nearly every particular with that left by her opponents, she added that the revolutionaries offered her a chance to rehabilitate herself by killing Dobroskok. She refused and left for Germany under the surveillance of three revolutionaries, then escaped their gaze and made her way to Russia, where she tried to bring charges against her tormentors but then dropped them. Ironically, in 1913 she was sent abroad again and would have been killed by revolutionaries had not Burtsev intervened; in thanks, she gave him information about police operations.[51]

The next exposure of a police spy ended tragically. During Tsikhotskaia's interrogation, Burtsev realized she was not the informant they were after. The party leadership had for some time suspected E. M. Lapina, a longtime Socialist-Revolutionary and a member of the combat organization since 1905. In spring 1909, Lapina sensed that the party leaders' attitude toward her had changed. They sent two representatives to St. Petersburg to verify their suspicions. On 3 May (New Style) she told party leaders that she intended to leave the party because the current "atmosphere is killing all faith in the sanctity of party work." A few days later an unidentified comrade, possibly a police agent, informed her that she was suspected of "provocation." On 12 May (New Style), in a letter to the Russian Police Department, she detailed her work as a revolutionary activist and asked to be arrested. She sent a copy of the letter to party leaders, who were then meeting at the fifth party council in Paris. In a separate message for them, she wrote that they had driven her to throw herself upon the mercy of the Russian government, which was "humiliating and unworthy of any revolutionary." She attached to this message her resignation from the party. Five days later she fatally shot herself. She was not a police agent.[52]

At the fifth party council, which was still in session, the party leadership elected a commission to investigate the Azef question. P. V. Karpovich, a close associate of Azef who soon quit the party, referred to the commission as "the gendarme station." The commission issued its conclusion in February 1911. It largely blamed the leadership of the combat organization and exculpated the central party leaders. The leadership also decided to spend more money on conspiratorial operations to thwart penetration by informants. Finally, after heated debate, they agreed to continue to support extensive terrorist operations and approved a plan to target Nicholas II and Stolypin. But the era of big terror was over.[53]

May was a busy month for Burtsev. L. P. Men'shchikov, in retirement from the security police since December 1906, traveled to Paris via Sweden and tentatively offered his services to Burtsev and to representatives of the Social Democratic Party. Now it was their turn. In all, he supplied lists of names and pseudonyms of some two hundred alleged informants, including ninety Social Democrats, twenty-five Socialist-Revolutionaries, and twenty Bundists. Since the "life-expectancy" of informants was on average three years, some (if not most) of those on his lists were presumably no longer active. Men'shchikov later claimed that he had "entered the camp of security officers in order to uncover their methods of operation and . . . to unmask spies." It is documented, however, that Men'shchikov had been an extremely loyal and effective police employee for over twenty years. It is also known that he had felt great resentment over receiving a meager pension in 1906, and he may have had trouble finding employment. It was apparently difficult for former security police employees to find jobs in any other official or private organization.[54] At age thirty-eight, Men'shchikov must have wanted to do something more with himself. Perhaps the revolution of 1905–1907 had shaken his faith in the Russian government. Maybe he had also felt remorse over the harm his work had brought to revolutionary activists. With sensitive police documents in his possession, the king of informants unmasked, and a disloyal former police chief harshly punished, Men'shchikov was moved to action.

Burtsev used Men'shchikov's expertise to score more coups against the Russian security police, beginning with the security chief in Paris, A. M. Garting. He was the Arkadii Mikhailovich "Landezen" who had allegedly organized a terrorist plot in Paris in 1890 in order to precipitate the arrest of several Russian revolutionaries. The revelation of Garting's true identity stupefied the French public. Jean Jaurès launched an interpellation in the parliament in June and claimed that he could have set off a revolution in France had the government dared to expel Burtsev. President of the Council of Ministers Georges Clemenceau vowed before the Chamber of Deputies to banish the Russian security police from France. In reality, however, Clemenceau immediately ordered the Prefecture of Paris and the Sûreté Générale to maintain their previous relations with the Russian police, as did the socialist Aristide Briand, who became president of the Council of Ministers in July. Garting returned to St. Petersburg in haste, where he became the subject of a Duma interpellation. Meanwhile, his assistant, V. I. Andreev, concerned about continued leaks to Burtsev, proposed to play possum: to fire all of the bureau's informants but secretly keep a few of the best ones.[55]

In November a gentleman who was a retired cavalry guard officer was sent to Paris in an ostensibly diplomatic capacity, but his job was to replace Garting. Aleksandr Aleksandrovich Krasil'nikov, according to Spiridovich, was a charming man who "knew Paris like the back of his hand." S. P.

Beletskii testified that he was a "perfect example of a spendthrift who lived lavishly and had huge debts. . . . He knew nothing about security policing, but what saved him was that he was educated, experienced, and mature, and he spoke many languages." Krasil'nikov's key asset, it seems, was that he had served in the same regiment as both Kurlov and V. B. Frederiks, the minister of the imperial household.[56]

Krasil'nikov's first deputy, A. V. Ergardt, carried out the day-to-day affairs of the bureau. It was he who set up a fictitious private detective agency to conduct surveillance over émigré Russian revolutionaries. The agency, located at 3 rue Chomel, was ostensibly owned by a French citizen, Marcel Bittard-Monin, who employed another Frenchman, Henri Bint, both of whom actually assisted four Russian police officials. In January 1911 Krasil'nikov reported that throughout 1910 his bureau had expanded its relations with foreign police forces. The French government's support in particular "could not be better." (In fall 1913 a new "private" detective agency, Bureau de Renseignements, Bint & Sambain, replaced that of Bittard-Monin.)[57]

Within a few days of Lapina's suicide, Burtsev, with the help of Men'shchikov, became convinced that Zinaida Fedorovna Gerngross-Zhuchenko was the informant he was seeking. According to A. V. Pribylev, she was "tall and thin with a pretty face, a high forehead, light-colored thin hair, and gold-rimmed glasses." Behind her glasses were "grey, slightly thoughtful eyes, always looking straight and self-confidently but giving nothing away of emotion or intention." She was "businesslike but also greatly modest, even self-deprecating," which helped her to gain her comrades' trust. In early August 1909, Burtsev wrote to her. He tried both blackmail and wooing. "I love Bakai," he wrote, "like my conquest or protégé," implying that she could follow in Bakai's footsteps.[58]

They met in Berlin on 11 August. She declared she had always been a convinced monarchist and called the Police Department a "sacred institution" employing the "best people in Russia." Burtsev was stunned. He never expected to find intelligent and attractive defenders of the Police Department, he later wrote. On 14 August she wrote to von Koten that she feared that the revolutionaries, out of vengeance, might throw acid at her face or kidnap her son. Zhuchenko's discussion with Burtsev permitted her to wreak her own revenge: she guessed by Burtsev's words that his source of information was Men'shchikov. She denounced Men'shchikov to the Police Department, which cancelled his pension. *Znamia truda* wrote that her unmasking had harmed the party even more Azef's had, because it had exposed a "broad contagion in the [party's] mass work."[59]

In recognition of Zhuchenko's immense contribution to the work of the Police Department, in October 1909 Stolypin secured for her a yearly pension of 3,600 rubles—nearly three times Men'shchikov's. A later government report noted that of the many informants unmasked by Burtsev only

Zhuchenko had openly told the world that she had served out of conviction. In response to a request by the Russian Police Department, the police president of Berlin authorized Zhuchenko to remain in Charlottenburg, and the German interior ministry ignored Karl Liebknecht's demand for her expulsion in February 1910. With the outbreak of war, however, Zhuchenko was interned. In 1918 she was released, and she moved to Belgium.[60]

In the first issue of a new journal, *Obshchee delo* (Common Cause), which appeared in mid-October 1909, Burtsev published a list of informants provided by Men'shchikov. One was Anna Egorovna Serebriakova, a longtime Social Democratic activist. Several other newspapers, including *Russkoe slovo* (Russian Word), immediately published the allegation about Serebriakova. V. M. Doroshevich, the editor of *Russkoe slovo*, complained to Burtsev that he was besieged by readers rejecting the allegation. "Why don't you just write imaginative literature. We'd love to publish you," he wrote. Burtsev wrote back that unmasking informants was his "grave duty," the "tragedy" of his life. In Paris a prominent Social Democrat bullied him: "I'd sooner believe my own mother was a provocateur," than Serebriakova. Ironically, the security police called her Mommy *(Mamochka)*. In a letter dated 8 November Serebriakova herself railed at Burtsev. Why had he not first made an informal accusation against her? Why had she not been convoked before a party court of arbitration? He replied that it was up to the established parties to order such a trial. As for himself, he never published information about police spies without first presenting it to the relevant party leaders.[61]

Thanks to Burtsev's revelation, Serebriakova's husband lost his job at the Moscow provincial zemstvo board. He sued *Russkoe slovo*, which agreed to pay him one thousand rubles in an out-of-court settlement. In 1911 the emperor, at Stolypin's behest, bestowed on Serebriakova, as a "committed enemy of sedition," a yearly pension of 1,200 rubles. A Soviet court found her deserving of the death penalty in 1926, but because it considered her no longer socially dangerous, it sentenced her instead to seven years' imprisonment.[62]

Other people on Burtsev's list were soon unmasked. The Bund leadership denounced I. M. Kaplinskii, a metalworker and party activist. Recruited by S. V. Zubatov back in 1899, he had served for years, reporting on the party's members and operations. He was apparently shot by the Cheka in 1922.[63]

The details about the unmasking of O. F. Putiata (Rusanovskaia) are far more dramatic. In May 1910 she appeared at Burtsev's editorial office demanding to know how he dared to accuse her of informing. "Am I in a revolutionary security bureau," she inquired, "and are you the same as von Koten?" He warned her that he had enough evidence against her to convince her comrades of her guilt. "If they agree with me," he said menacingly, "you know what will happen." It would be better, he urged, to confess. She consented, and they met several times. She claimed to have joined the Moscow security bureau in order to denounce a woman competing

with her for the affection of a man. At the bureau, L. P. Men'shchikov became a father figure to her. Gradually she developed into an important
agent. She was a "wonderfully bold woman, who works not out of fear but
by conscience," wrote one security policeman.[64]

Now, with Burtsev accusing her, she thought of committing suicide, but
she decided to confront him instead. On her way back to Russia she wrote
him, saying "I hate myself for all I did, how I lied, what I did to people; but
at the same time, I despise people." Putiata told Burtsev that although her
husband, a writer called S., was a "decadent" and had neither knowledge of
nor interest in her antirevolutionary activities, a reporter for *Russkie vedomosti* portrayed S. as her assistant. When a party court of arbitration
cleared him of that charge, he sued the newspaper and collected several
thousand rubles out of court, then disappeared from literary life.[65]

Burtsev decried police tactics in open letters to senior officials, members
of the Duma, public figures, and even Nicholas himself. In one letter, published in Paris, he denounced Azef for his involvement in a 1908 attempt
on the life of the emperor and demanded that he be brought to trial. Burtsev's unrelenting counterprovocation efforts rankled both revolutionaries
and police officials. P. A. Kropotkin argued in a 28 February 1911 letter to
Burtsev that it was absurd for a revolutionary to demand that Azef be tried
for his attempt on the life of the tsar. "Even if it is true that Azef was involved with terrorist acts," wrote Kropotkin, "to prove it would only make
the revolutionaries look bad. Even in France, everyone knows that all
agents serve both sides." The Russian security police, for their part, worried
about Burtsev's campaign and kept pressure on him. In early 1910 security
policemen received orders to watch their employees carefully and to prosecute any officials found leaking documents. Police officials launched their
own publicity campaign against Burtsev, spreading negative rumors about
him in émigré circles, then ordered his arrest. Meanwhile, Men'shchikov,
shunned by the revolutionaries, fled in 1911 to the United States.[66]

Other informants were unmasked without Burtsev's intervention. In fall
1909 suspicions fell on Iu. O. Serova, who reported on the Social Democratic
underground in St. Petersburg. She was unmasked sometime in 1910. In
late 1912, her husband, the former Duma deputy V. M. Serov, repudiated
her publicly. Meanwhile, Serova pleaded with von Koten for financial support, painting a grim picture of her three shoeless and coatless children
and threatening suicide. The government provided modest sums of money
and found her work in railroad administration.[67]

Three more cases ended tragically. L. A. Liberman, a member of
Savinkov's combat organization, was arrested in February 1910. Savinkov
and the other members managed to escape thanks only to a leak of information from a government official. Now Savinkov disbanded his organization and nervously searched for the traitor. In September he and his comrades exposed I. P. Kiriukhin, who then fled. Von Koten arranged for

Kiriukhin to live well on false documents in Pskov and Terioki for two years. Next the suspicions of Savinkov and his comrades fell on Ia. F. Berdo. Cornered in late 1910, Berdo shot himself. Finally, they turned against V. M. Kamorskii, and in 1911 he too shot himself. Historian K. N. Morozov concludes that, of the three, only Kiriukhin had served the police. When the war began, von Koten obtained a senior position in military counterintelligence and hired Kiriukhin as his subordinate. Arrested and imprisoned in 1917, Kiriukhin was probably shot to death by the Bolsheviks.[68]

The loss of so many valuable informants may not have undermined the effectiveness of the security police system as a whole, since the revolutionary movement in general and the revolutionary parties in particular reached their nadir in 1909–1911, but police officials did scramble to hire new informants and to tighten control over the existing ones. They also increased their reliance on perlustration.

Informant recruitment spiked in the years 1910–1911. The security bureau and the gendarme station in Moscow collectively recruited ninety-six informants in 1911. Similarly, all but sixteen of the ninety-four informants employed by the St. Petersburg security bureau in 1913 had been hired during the previous three years. Some existing informants recycled themselves. A. M. Romanova informed on the Socialist-Revolutionaries in Moscow in 1908 and 1909, then, after a period of incarceration, changed her hair color and informed on university student organizations in St. Petersburg in 1911. Police officials also sought to retain the services of existing informants. They urged reassuring them by emphasizing that the Police Department had protected Azef's identity for sixteen years.[69]

Recruitment in the provinces proved less successful. In summer 1909 Gerasimov inspected the security police in Perm, Samara, Kiev, Odessa, Riga, Saratov, Nizhnii Novgorod, Sevastopol, Kazan, and Taurida provinces. He found mediocre cadres of informants everywhere but in Saratov under A. P. Martynov. An important stumbling block was inadequate funding. Throughout the Moscow region in 1909 only the Moscow and Orel gendarme stations and the Iaroslavl and Nizhnii Novgorod security bureaus had annual budgets for informants of over 2,500 rubles. This was in itself a paltry sum in comparison with the 40,000 rubles von Koten had at his disposal for paying informants. None of the security police institutions Gerasimov inspected employed more than fourteen informants; the majority had fewer than eight. Since the actual amount spent each year on informants was to some extent left to the discretion of individual chiefs of security bureaus and gendarme stations, police authorities ordered them—ten times in 1909–1912—to devote more of their budgets to recruiting informants.[70]

To compensate for the loss of valuable central informants, police officials sought to improve the interception of mail. A survey of officials in most major cities without specially outfitted perlustration offices suggested that the postal authorities were more than willing to cooperate with the security police. (A secret rule of 1903 obligated postal officials to render such assistance, and a directive of 20 March 1909 recommended that the security police make circumspect use of their right to demand assistance from postal officials.) Funding for the system had increased from 92,000 rubles in 1882 to only 107,000 rubles in 1909. During this period, the annual number of letters opened hovered around 400,000, but the number of letters copied increased from 3,600 to some 10,000. This increase was quite small in view of the expansion of revolutionary organizations and the increase in the volume of mail delivered. In February 1910 N. P. Zuev proposed that the perlustration budget be raised from 107,000 to 135,000 rubles per year. An investigation showed that although it employed highly sophisticated equipment, the system did not always function effectively. The performance of the seven provincial offices proved uneven: that of the Warsaw office was excellent, that of the Moscow office, mediocre. Police officials recommended opening additional perlustration bureaus in Rostov-na-Donu, Saratov, and Ekaterinoslav.[71]

Government and police officials probably yearned to relax after a year fraught with scandals. Yet the fateful year of 1909 had one more debacle to visit upon the officials and institutions of the imperial Russian security police—the most dramatic one yet.

UNWARRANTED TRUST?

In October 1909 Sergei Georgievich Karpov became chief of the St. Petersburg security bureau, replacing Gerasimov, who took an extended leave of absence (Stolypin intimated that upon Gerasimov's return he would like to appoint him deputy interior minister for police affairs). A Cossack born in the Don region in 1864, Karpov had previously served in middle-level posts in several far-flung railroad gendarme stations. Spiridovich laconically called him "not up to the task," and Vissarionov admitted that Gerasimov's replacement "could not easily fill his shoes." Why was he chosen to head the largest and most important security bureau in the country? Some claimed Gerasimov had wanted a nonentity to succeed him so that his own prowess would be underscored. Martynov, who met some of Karpov's subordinates in 1909, recalled that they were "baffled at why they had got such a strange boss. They said he met subordinates totally naked."[72]

Karpov's nemesis was a Socialist-Revolutionary named A. A. Petrov. Repeatedly arrested and imprisoned, often living underground or in European exile, Petrov had robbed banks and thrown bombs. An accidental explosion had deprived him of a leg. Betrayed by M. Ia. Tsikhotskaia, he had been arrested along with O. S. Minor. Interrogated in Saratov by Martynov and V. K. Semiganovskii, the chief of the Saratov gendarme station, and in St. Petersburg by Gerasimov, Petrov had consented to inform.[73]

The police facilitated his escape from prison since their need to recruit informants carried no weight among public prosecutors or prison officials: Petrov feigned insanity so as to be transferred to a psychiatric hospital, from which sympathetic doctors permitted him to flee. He then traveled abroad, ostensibly to reestablish his position in the Socialist-Revolutionary Party. Instead, he confessed to his party comrades, and they demanded that he redeem himself by killing Gerasimov. In late November Petrov left for St. Petersburg with dynamite provided by Savinkov, in the company of two Socialist-Revolutionaries and under the watchful eye of Russian surveillants.[74]

Karpov trusted Petrov so blindly that he outfitted a secret apartment specially for him at 25 Astrakhanskaia Street in the Vyborg district and vainly urged senior police officials to visit them there. Meanwhile, Petrov installed a bomb under a table in the living room. Karpov's impulsive arrival on the evening of 17 December with hors d'oeuvres and wine prompted the nervous Petrov to detonate the bomb, thus causing Karpov's death. Petrov was immediately seized by police in the street.[75]

The story of Petrov's motivations and those of his police supervisors and their superiors in recruiting him is fantastically turbid. Petrov later claimed that he had agreed to inform only in order to inflict damage on the security police system. Gerasimov and Kurlov, for their part, were apparently desperate to find a replacement for Azef. Although Trusevich and Klimovich were skeptical, Petrov did provide the police with some damaging information about Socialist-Revolutionary inner circles, according to a party investigating commission.[76]

There is also some evidence of complicity by various police officials in Petrov's actions. K. N. Morozov presents three separate versions of such a scenario. First, Petrov testified that Gerasimov had incited him to murder Karpov, Kurlov, and Vissarionov in the hope of taking Kurlov's place. Second, N. V. Dobroskok said that Karpov had asked him to obtain a ticket to a performance at the Mariinskii Theater for Petrov. Dobroskok had refused to comply once he discovered that Stolypin was scheduled to attend the same performance. Kurlov supposedly hoped to use Petrov to remove Stolypin so as to supplant him. Why else, argues Morozov, would Kurlov have approved of substituting Karpov for the highly professional Gerasimov? Kurlov claimed in his memoirs that, having grown suspicious about Petrov in fall 1909, he had ordered his arrest. Yet Morozov never found such an order in the police archives. Third, Kurlov may have wanted simply to discredit Stolypin in the emperor's eyes by linking Petrov to Gerasimov, who was close to Stolypin. Some circumstantial evidence supports this interpretation. For example, a letter from Petrov to Gerasimov dated 5 December mysteriously turned up in Petrov's apartment after the assassination. Morozov admits that insufficient evidence is available to render any one of these theories convincing.[77]

St. Petersburg security chief S. G. Karpov's apartment after the explosion that killed him, detonated by his informant A. A. Petrov in December 1909.

In any case, Stolypin apparently had no inkling of Kurlov's alleged evil designs. In January 1910 Kurlov was promoted to the rank of lieutenant-general. Gerasimov was not so fortunate. He was sent to Irkutsk on business so he would be out of the way during the murder investigation. The final report recorded Gerasimov's alleged suggestion to Petrov that it would be better to kill Kurlov than "that idiot" Karpov. After Petrov was hanged in January 1910, Gerasimov returned from Irkutsk and was shunned by police officials, including Stolypin. He was attached to the interior ministry for special missions but was assigned none. Also, he began to notice police surveillants following him. "As though" he wrote, "the security police had nothing else to do."[78]

The assassination caused a minor scandal. The Duma considered, but decided against, interpellating Stolypin. The ruble fell. The Socialist-Revolutionary leadership, aware that its own rules disallowed any contact of party members with the security police, rushed to its own defense. "It seems," said the Socialist-Revolutionary newspaper *Znamia truda*, that Petrov "was a sincere revolutionary, under the influence of an illusion but who realized his mistake and redeemed his guilt before it led to real betrayals." Any act of terror, "must be crystalline pure, transparently clear, free from any personal motivations, personal passions, from any extraneous elements." The party had not authorized Petrov's contacts with the security police, continued *Znamia truda*, but had nevertheless helped him "as a private person in an undertaking the party sympathized with."[79]

On 22 December M. F. von Koten, whom senior officials, including Stolypin, still esteemed highly, was appointed head of the St. Petersburg security bureau. Von Koten's replacement in Moscow was Pavel Pavlovich Zavarzin, until then chief of the security bureau in Warsaw. Born and raised in Odessa in 1868, Zavarzin had joined the Gendarme Corps in 1898, then served at various gendarme stations in the western and southern borderlands before being appointed as director of the security bureau in Warsaw in September 1906. He had learned the ropes of security policing and had been a tough security chief in Warsaw, but he was considerably less talented than von Koten. Martynov, who replaced Zavarzin in Moscow in 1912, called him neither "refined nor developed" and attributed his successes largely to his clever wife and relatively talented subordinates, such as V. F. Modl'.[80]

Beginning on 18 December a flurry of directives poured out of the Police Department to strengthen the system's defenses. One directive emphasized that case officers should not trust informants too fully or grow close to them on a personal basis and that they should meet with them only in secure conspiratorial apartments or in public places, like restaurants and parks. Kurlov later admitted that case officers had to walk a fine line when guiding informants. "Humans," he wrote, "gradually adapt to all things, like medical students to dissection. Case officers get used to informants, even grow close to them, trust them. This is important, for without feeling trusted, informants will often not be reliable." Referring to Karpov, he added, however, that "some case officers were too credulous, and paid for this with their lives." Other directives urged limiting access of police employees to the Police Department director and to the Special Section, tightening control over informants in prisons, watching out for efforts by revolutionary activists to infiltrate security police institutions, and ferreting out the source of leaks of information and documents to Burtsev. Police officials also redoubled their efforts to expose unreliable informants. In March 1910 alone seven of them were dismissed.[81]

Sitting alone in prison awaiting his execution and writing a brief memoir, Petrov issued a word of warning to his colleagues. "Don't even think about trying to serve the party by contacting the security police," he implored. "It would be better if you killed yourself at the moment when this idea entered your head. Either give it up immediately or kill yourself at once." Burtsev published the memoir with this cautionary plea in Paris in 1910.[82]

Perhaps in the long run the public perception of the Russian government and political system suffered the most from the unmasking of Azef and other informants, the violent attacks against von Koten and Karpov, and the rumors and accusations of malfeasance in high places related to these incidents. When even the moderate Kadet V. A. Maklakov could refer to a "Babylonian captivity of our governmental authority" by the security police,[83] then one can assume that the latter were helping to delegitimize that authority.

CHAPTER FOUR

THE APOGEE OF

THE WATCHFUL

STATE

■ As social calm returned, government repression diminished. In June 1909 P. A. Stolypin downgraded Moscow's security level from extraordinary to reinforced, fired Moscow's hard-line governor-general, S. K. Gershel'man, and ordered governors to use military courts and administrative punishments sparingly. He also reduced the number of jurisdictions under the various states of emergency from 120, including 45 full provinces, on 1 January 1907, to 50, including 27 full provinces, by November 1909. The number of such jurisdictions decreased again by half in 1911; by September 1912 only Voronezh, Ekaterinoslav, Kursk, Moscow, St. Petersburg, Samara, Saratov, Khar'kov and Chernigov provinces, plus four provinces of Poland, remained under reinforced security. Neither extraordinary security nor martial law was retained in any locality. Finally, the number of state-crime cases fell from 7,593 in 1908 to 4,616 in 1909 and 2,231 in 1910.[1]

Even so, the security police kept up an intensive counterrevolutionary campaign. In Moscow city and province security chief P. P. Zavarzin repeatedly struck at the Socialist-Revolutionary and Social Democratic parties, leaving them "disorganized" and "devastated."[2] In the northern capital, according to Robert McKean, "The underground still remained at the end of 1911 but in an atomized, cellular form. The price of its survival was its impotence." The same could largely be said of the revolutionary underground all across the Russian Empire. By the end of 1910 all regional and most provincial committees of the Socialist-Revolutionary Party had collapsed, while the amount of money in its central coffers slumped from 168,000 rubles in 1908 to 36,000 in 1910. According to A. I. Spiridovich, throughout 1910 there was "virtually no Social Democratic Party center in Russia." The police seized seven of the party's illegal presses that year, and its smuggling operation suffered a blow when its main organizer was arrested and replaced by M. I. Briandinskii, a police informant. The Bolshevik activist N. I. Podvoiskii admitted that "the party apparatus, because of provocation, could not recover from one series of arrests before being disorganized by a new one. . . . So they had almost no connections with the masses and the new worker movement. In their turn, the masses, for fear of provocation, avoided ties with party organizations. . . . The Azef syndrome put the working masses on their guard in relation to underground organizations."[3] The revolutionary parties were left with no choice but to channel more and more of their energy into legal activities.

STRENGTHENING THE SECURITY NETWORK

In the breathing space afforded by a weakened revolutionary opposition, police officials undertook both to make the security system more responsive to the Special Section and to raise the overall level of competency of the mass of gendarme and security officers. Aleksandr Mikhailovich Eremin, who replaced E. K. Klimovich as head of the Special Section in January 1910, was the driving force behind these efforts. S. P. Beletskii, a vicedirector of the Police Department, called Eremin "a rank-and-file Cossack, very straightforward, very honest, old-school, hardworking, constantly fighting provocation." Born in 1872 in the Don region, he had served in a Ural Cossack unit until his induction into the Gendarme Corps in 1903. From 1905 on he headed the security bureau in Kiev, worked at the Special Section, and directed the regional security bureau in Tiflis. He was only the second gendarme officer, after Klimovich, to head up security policing in Russia, though, as usual, his three assistants, N. A. Peshkov, M. E. Broetskii, and N. D. Zaitsev, were all jurists with years of experience as prosecutors. Working closely with a vice-director of the Police Department, S. E. Vissarionov, Eremin further systematized the security system. The chief means he employed were the painstaking analysis of domestic intelligence, myriad official directives, inspection tours, and standardized training courses.[4]

The Special Section was a small but highly efficient operation. In addition to his three assistants, Eremin supervised eight heads of divisions, seven junior clerks, one translator, seventeen temporary employees, and twenty-two copy clerks (eleven of them without rank), who had at their disposal seven typewriters, one with Latin characters. The senior staff were well-trained, intelligent, and knowledgeable. By analyzing and cross-checking intercepted letters, illegal and legal publications, and reports from gendarme and security officers in the field, they often managed to identify individuals on the basis of their initials, to catch discrepancies in information reported from the provinces, or to tease out of cryptic or even encoded messages incriminating data about the revolutionary underground. Of course, they had at their disposal both a massive card catalog, which by 1917 contained some half-million cards, and tens of thousands of files, all carefully cross-referenced. In one case, an agent in Constantinople referred to a "well-known Savitskii." An official of the Special Section soon responded that "we know twelve Savitskiis; three are revolutionaries. None can be called 'well-known.'"[5]

Between 1910 and 1912, the Special Section distributed roughly 100 operational and 250 informational circular directives yearly, in addition to hundreds of instructions to specific security and gendarme chiefs—855 of them in 1910 alone: 176 on working with informants, 114 on external surveillance, 210 concerning financial reporting and record keeping, 229 about reporting procedures, and 126 explaining how best to carry out security policing operations.[6]

Many directives emphasized preserving secrecy and camouflaging sources in official reports, forbade supplying official government documents to third parties, and provided detailed instructions on safeguarding secret documentation. Others regulated the cooperation between security and regular officials: security officials were to use tact when warning government officials of impending terrorist acts, since such news had once caused an official to die of a heart attack; to report to governors all they needed to know about security operations but nothing related to the acquisition of secret information; and, whenever relevant, to request information from the criminal detective police. Still other directives spelled out and reiterated the rules circumscribing security police operations. Suspects in political cases should be searched or administratively exiled only on the basis of "detailed and thoroughly verified information." Intelligence furnished by informants should be used very carefully as evidence against suspects. If a suspect denies he wrote an incriminating document, then an expert must be called in to determine its authorship. The interrogation of political-crime suspects had to occur within the first twenty-four hours of their arrest, and requests to prolong the detention of such suspects beyond the one-week period stipulated by the security law of 1881 had to reach the Police Department before the end of the week. Finally, numerous directives were aimed at ensuring that regional bureau chiefs kept on top of political investigatory work in their jurisdictions. "Security policing," noted one, "is a vital not a formal endeavor" and therefore demanded frequent personal interaction of local officials.[7]

Orchestrating security police work across the Russian Empire by means of written directives naturally had its limitations, since one could never know whether local officials would carry them out properly or even understand them. For example, when the Special Section requested copies of revolutionary publications for the collections of the Alexander III Historical Museum in Moscow, one gendarme chief shipped in 5,430 copies of a single confiscated publication.[8] One can imagine the derisive smirks at this blunder in the offices of the Special Section. What if such incompetence permeated the whole security system? The only way to know the answer was to send expert security policemen out into the provinces to find out for themselves.

Continuing M. I. Trusevich's program of regularly inspecting the empire's security system, in 1910 alone Vissarionov and other officials inspected security bureaus and gendarme stations in Siberia, Poland, Saratov,

Samara, Penza, Perm, Khar'kov, Kursk, Finland, Moscow, the Don region, and Turkestan. The inspections had a threefold purpose: checking up on specific provincial officials, providing in-depth data for police analysis, and encouraging gendarme and security chiefs not yet subject to inspections to do their best.[9]

Vissarionov found "serious improprieties" at the Moscow security bureau. An inspection in Warsaw found security chief K. I. Globachev "weak" and revealed that the assistant governor-general for police affairs, L. K. Utgof, had countermanded Police Department directives. Although it was not indicated in the inspection report, P. G. Kurlov later wrote that the inspectors had found "excessive activism"—a euphemism for provocation—on the part of the Warsaw security bureau's informants. The gendarme station in Finland, where there was no security bureau, was a case entirely sui generis. Inspectors said it was "organized very poorly for security policing." Most important, it employed only eighteen full-time informants, as compared with roughly fifty at the Moscow security bureau, despite Finland's larger population. The gendarme station chief, K.-R. K. Utgof, tried to justify his station's failing. "Those who don't work here," he wrote, "don't realize how hard it is." There were many private oppositional associations to which "everyone belongs, even civil servants." The police were not obligated to lend assistance to the security police, he argued, and anyway, "most are unreliable." It was hard to recruit informants, since "people avoid the gendarmes." Perlustration, moreover, was utterly impossible, since postal officials feared criminal charges. "But *our* mail," he wrote, "is opened."[10]

Overall the inspections produced sobering results. In November 1911 Vissarionov reported that 50 percent of the gendarme officers engaged in security policing were "unfit for their work." As a result of inspectors' reports in 1911 and 1912, thirteen gendarme station chiefs were dismissed, and thirteen more were placed on probation. Of course, the delinquents were mostly out in the provinces where serious revolutionary threats were infrequent and the gendarmes' main task was to watch out for suspicious activity in general and to report on broad trends in social and political life. The inspection tours grew more standardized in 1912 when officials drafted detailed lists of matters to investigate, including the monitoring of public associations and political and revolutionary organizations, the general political situation among all classes, and the public attitude toward the police. Beginning in late 1912 inspections were conducted by teams of officials consisting of permanent inspectors, experts in general bureaucratic affairs, and specialists in security policing.[11]

Also important were efforts to train gendarme officers better. Beginning in April 1910 some officers were stationed periodically at the regional bureaus to learn from experienced security officers. The busy regional chiefs found little time for training them, however, and used them instead for menial tasks. Next, the gendarme officer training course was improved. The new four-month course began in November 1910 at Tsarskoe Selo. It included lectures on gendarme investigations, anthropometry, law and government, and codes, plus instruction in telegraphy in case telegraph workers should go on strike.[12]

The only subjects related exclusively to security policing were presented by A. I. Spiridovich, starting with a cycle of twenty-seven lectures on the history of socialist political movements in the West and in Russia. Spiridovich found the sixty officers in his course enthusiastic and highly curious. He handed out programs, leaflets, and other brief imprints from the main revolutionary parties, but ironically he could find no other text to assign his students than Alphons Thun's history of the Russian revolutionary movement, which had been translated by the former terrorist V. N. Zasulich, among others, and published with a preface by G. V. Plekhanov, the "Father of Russian Marxism." Spiridovich also lectured on security police operations. His approach was mostly theoretical, though he did provide practical training in external surveillance, which he set up as "police games" with his trainees trying to shadow Spiridovich's agents, who pretended to be revolutionaries. This playacting raised some eyebrows among his superiors but won converts to security policing among the officers in his charge.[13]

Security police officers devised a variety of pedagogical aides to assist with the training of gendarme officers. Klimovich, Eremin, and Broetskii composed brief treatises on the revolutionary and oppositional parties. F. S. Rozhanov and Spiridovich wrote lengthy textbooks on the revolutionary parties and movements. Special Section clerks drew up at least twenty-one poster-sized, multi-colored organizational diagrams of the major revolutionary parties. Rozhanov also prepared a complicated chart detailing the historical development of the Socialist-Revolutionary and Social Democratic parties, tracing their origins in terms of ideas, events, and institutions back to the Enlightenment. The chart is very detailed, with several parallel columns that indicate contemporaneous historical developments in Russia and Europe and a welter of offshoots from the two main branches; the whole entity confers the impression of a luxuriant vine.[14] In general, the chart was quite comprehensive and accurate and probably would have been no different had Thun himself produced it.

There remained two impediments to raising the professional level of gendarme officers. The first was the Gendarme Corps itself. In November 1911 Vissarionov complained that the Corps objected to the rapid promotion of security officers, appointed weak officers to railroad gendarme stations, and simply transferred to other posts gendarme officers dismissed by the Police Department for inefficiency or insubordination. The Police Department, not the Corps, he argued, should have the decisive voice in the selection, discipline, and promotion of gendarme officers engaged in security policing. True, the Police Department controlled a variety of enticing means to spur security policemen to greater productivity, including comparatively higher pay and faster promotions. Even so, the Police Department did not establish criteria for the selection of gendarme officers until December 1913, and even then it is not clear that the criteria then established were well enforced.[15]

The second impediment was the deeply rooted customs of patronage and nepotism. When transferred to new posts, security officers often sought to bring with them trusted subordinate officers. Senior officials occasionally thwarted such efforts, for example prohibiting Zavarzin from bringing a protégé named A. M. Shostakovskii to Moscow. Far worse, N. N. Kuliabko, appointed security chief in Kiev in 1907, apparently owed his rise from the position of a simple district police captain in Moscow to the fact that he had studied with Spiridovich and had married his sister.[16] Yet in a relatively small-sized bureaucratic world of often stifling formalism, intense institutional rivalries, and scarce resources, officials naturally gravitated to people they knew.

EYES AND EARS OF THE TSAR

As revolutionary activism dwindled in 1910 and 1911, the security police force concentrated more of its time and energy on broad surveillance. The expansion of civil society and the means it provided for expressing political opposition meant that the security police force could draw into its field of vision a much smaller proportion of the full range of social phenomena than was previously possible. In Moscow Zavarzin, with nine officers, ten clerks, seventy-two surveillants, and fifty-five informants, could maintain loose surveillance over only some three thousand people in 1912.[17] The total number of people under surveillance by the entire security police system—a larger number and far broader range of people were subject to perlustration—may have reached twenty to thirty thousand (not counting, of course, the entire memberships of organizations under surveillance, such as trade unions), if one supposes that the security bureau in St. Petersburg watched approximately five thousand people; the Warsaw bureau, two thousand; the fifteen provincial bureaus, five hundred each; and the eighty gendarme stations, one to three hundred each.

In their effort to widen their scope of observation, the security police relied upon the regular police for assistance. In some cases, requests for intelligence were quite specific, such as: "Send information on all boot makers who recently arrived from Warsaw." Usually within a few days, the regular police would submit a report listing each person's name, age, occupation or social status, religion, profession, type of passport, and location where the passport was issued. The regular policemen in urban areas were supposed to display a continuous watchfulness, but as a directive from December 1910 insisted, they should avoid "mere formal observation," since "the smallest details can sometimes provide leads toward uncovering criminal plots."

The police should watch for "any questionable activity, anything suspicious about the lifestyle, behavior, or relations of people in their districts." They in turn should call upon building superintendents *(dvorniki)* and household servants for information on "those who, by their person and conduct, raise suspicions." In the countryside, regular policemen were supposed to detail, first, the "mood of the peasants," peasant unrest, and troubling rumors circulating in the countryside; second, the mood and general situation among students, professionals, and members of the intelligentsia and political parties; and third, the incidence of regular crime. More concretely, they should keep tearooms and tearoom newspapers *(chainye gazety)* under close supervision and watch for agitators seeking to exploit popular rumors—such as one about an allegedly imminent land repartition that would supposedly be part of the commemoration of the 1812 defeat of Napoleon.[18]

That the security police still devoted the lion's share of their attention to revolutionary activists is clear from the identity of the people police informants watched. Zavarzin employed fifty-five informants in 1912, of whom seventeen worked among Socialist-Revolutionaries and twenty among Social Democrats; these groups were thus the subject of the work of 31 and 36 percent of all informants, respectively. As a group, the informants among the Social Democrats received an even larger proportion of the total pay, or 38 percent versus 26 percent for informants among the Socialist-Revolutionaries, and a higher average pay, namely, forty-two rubles per month, versus thirty-four for the counterparts among the other party. Thus Nurit Schleifman's undocumented assertion that informants among the Socialist-Revolutionaries "continued to make up the majority of the highest paid secret agents" was not true of Moscow. (Informant lists for St. Petersburg have not been preserved.)[19]

In 1913 the number of informants working among the Socialist-Revolutionaries for the Moscow security bureau fell to eleven, and of those working among the Social Democrats fell to eighteen; their pay then represented 14 and 20 percent, respectively, of the total salary pool. The numbers for most of the other main categories of informants also fluctuated, with ten in the university student movement in 1912 and thirteen in 1913; three among the anarchists in 1912 but only one in 1913; and four in public organizations in each year.[20]

A major difference in 1913 was the dramatic increase in the number of so-called auxiliary informants *(vspomogatel'nye agenty)*, to forty-one from only about six in 1912. Payments to these informants accounted for nearly 40 percent of the total monthly informant budget of three thousand rubles in 1913, which was up by nearly eight hundred rubles from the previous year. An instruction on working with informants stated that auxiliary informants could be either temporary or permanent, though it is hard to tell whom exactly these informants reported on. The six in 1912 infiltrated several milieux, including the Moscow press, the Octobrists, the Armenian movement, rightist organizations, and the Jesuits, though in some other contexts and periods informants reporting on military units were designated as auxiliary. Yet the report for 1913 gives no breakdown at all. The record does show that a few of the informants who were assigned to watch Socialist-Revolutionaries and others in 1912 bore the designation of auxiliary informants in 1913. Maybe these informants were reporting on broader social trends, though one official later wrote that auxiliary informants were those who were "not currently active or useful in those relatively quiet times, but who, because of their revolutionary connections or their cunning [*pronyrlivost'*], at the right moment could become useful."[21] Perhaps most of those in the report for 1913 fit that description.

Subversion in the military worried security police officials, especially after the Socialist-Revolutionaries organized a conference in Zurich in October 1910 to unify the efforts of all revolutionary parties to penetrate military units. Later that month N. P. Zuev launched a campaign to "vigorously but cautiously" recruit informants from among those serving in military units. Countermanding an earlier directive, he advised that they report on their findings directly to the Police Department, bypassing the local military leadership. In June 1911 Zuev urged that the recruitment of low-paid auxiliary informants be conducted in the small shops and tearooms off base where soldiers tended to congregate. By early 1912 Zavarzin had eighteen minor agents operating in military units stationed in Moscow. To direct their work, he composed a detailed inventory of the information that such auxiliary informants should provide. He was most interested in the mood of the soldiers, where they gathered, what they read, and whether there were signs of insubordination or of collusion between officers and enlisted men. Meanwhile, in 1910 a bureau was created in Kronstadt to coordinate surveillance in the Baltic fleet. Three gendarme officers who reported to M. F. von Koten were supposed to deploy thirty surveillants and dozens of auxiliary agents, six on each large ship, two on each medium-sized one, and one for each squadron of smaller boats.[22] Given the important role the military played in preserving the Russian state in 1905, this was a smart policy.

The revolutionary leaders were hard-pressed to cope with their "informant problem." The Bolshevik central committee discussed the matter three times from 1912 to 1914. The year 1911 marked the pinnacle of "spymania," Lenin later said. Many Social Democratic leaders were torn between acting decisively on their suspicions and remaining loyal to their party comrades or even trying to believe that informants could serve the party well. Ia. A. Zhitomirskii, for example, caused immense and repeated harm to the Social Democratic Party from 1907 to 1911. Notably, he helped prevent its leaders from recovering the money stolen in the Tiflis Bank robbery of June 1907. Although V. L. Burtsev managed to cast so much doubt on his loyalty that in 1911 the Bolsheviks removed him from his leadership role, even later Lenin allegedly remarked of his contribution to the party that "in any big operation all sorts of rubbish can prove useful."[23]

Besides Zhitomirskii such important party activists as M. E. Chernoma-zov, A. S. Romanov, and M. I. Briandinskii were informants. The most highly placed informant in any Russian political party during this period was Roman Vatslavovich Malinovskii, a Polish nobleman who had repeatedly been tried and found guilty of burglary. Recruited in July 1910, he initially earned one hundred, then eventually five hundred rubles a month and caused major damage to the Social Democratic organization. To keep his double role secret, the police arrested him briefly three times before 1912.[24]

Historians have drawn upon the massive documentation derived from informants' reports to write hundreds of studies on the Socialist-Revolutionaries, the anarchists, and especially the Social Democrats. There is a general consensus both about the accuracy of the documentation and about the necessity of using it to write a full account of any radical Russian political organization in the final two decades of imperial Russia.

The Russian security police were not omniscient, though the mistakes in their assessments were often minor. A systematic compilation of police reports, mostly reports from the Moscow security bureau on the Social Democratic Party published in 1918 and reissued in 1990, points out, for example, misinterpreted party nicknames, misreported information about party membership and relationships among party leaders, and misdating of important meetings. Thus, the list of central committee members elected at the fifth congress in London in May 1907 was only about three-quarters accurate. The security police believed that Plekhanov had actually joined Lenin in 1910, whereas in reality he had only formed an alliance with him, and the Zimmerwald conference was reported as having taken place on 9–12 September, instead of 5–8 September 1915. For the most part, however, the reports are taken to be quite reliable and accurate. There exists no analytical compendium of police reports on the Socialist-Revolutionary Party, but the authors of recent monographs on the Socialist-Revolutionaries rely heavily on the police archives, and one noted that security police reports are, for his purpose, "extraordinarily informative."[25]

The security police used their informants subtly within the labor movement. Informants tried to establish the reasons for worker dissatisfaction with their employers and, at the same time, allowed the police to discriminate between revolutionary activists among industrial workers, whom they repeatedly arrested, and union members, who largely escaped arrest. Surveillance over ordinary workers usually fell to regular policemen.[26]

A few talented informants infiltrated the Kadet Party and other opposition forces. One was Ivan Iakovlevich Drillikh, an Austrian subject. He was arrested in Kiev in mid-1910 for penning a "subversive" newspaper article and was exiled to Tomsk, but he escaped. He settled in Moscow under a false identity and foolishly trusted the postal service. His letter was intercepted, and within four days Zavarzin had him in custody. Zavarzin then presented him with a dilemma: he could either serve his term of exile or "remain in Moscow and serve us." Drillikh chose the comforts of the ancient capital. Under the pseudonym Blondinka ("Blondie") this physically strong, dark-haired journalist worked for the Moscow-based mass-circulation newspaper *Russkoe slovo* and informed for nearly seven years on liberal activists.[27]

According to the Soviet historian A. Ia. Avrekh, Blondinka furnished most of the security police force's information about the Kadets and other liberals, even those in St. Petersburg. Yet Avrekh charged that the informants reporting on Kadet circles were generally ill informed and that Blondinka "lied all the time . . . . got things confused, made things up." Although Avrekh was undoubtedly exaggerating, Blondinka did puff up his ability to acquire first-rate information about the liberal opposition. In September 1914, for example, he reported that leading Kadets in St. Petersburg had met several times in private apartments, at the editorial offices of *Russkie vedomosti* (Russian News), and in the restaurant Ermitazh, yet he provided concrete details only about the collective repast, where presumably little of political substance was discussed. Moreover, he listed as a leading Kadet G. A. Fal'bork, who in actuality belonged to no political party, though he had ties to numerous Kadets.[28]

In one clear-cut, important case, though, Avrekh himself was wrong. He called spurious Blondinka's late September 1915 report that the Kadet leadership had agreed earlier in the month to stand behind Prince G. E. L'vov as the best candidate for the premiership. Avrekh countered that L'vov was not even a Kadet at the time and that the Kadet leadership definitely did not have him in mind as a future prime minister. Avrekh also called into question the work of an early Soviet historian, B. B. Grave, who published in 1927 a compilation of security police reports on the liberal opposition and had found them very valuable. Grave, according to Avrekh, had never seen the minutes of the Kadet central committee, which Avrekh used to verify the accuracy of security police reports. Precisely in these minutes, however, one finds a clear confirmation that the central committee of the Kadet Party voted on 16 September 1915 to support L'vov for the premiership; indeed, at several meetings of the central committee from June through September most of the leadership consistently supported him.[29]

The political activists who, though they were intriguing, proved the most resistant to security police surveillance were Russia's Freemasons. After their almost complete suppression in Russia in the 1820s (many Decembrists were Masons), the movement gained a second life during the revolution of 1905. By 1908 there were perhaps one hundred Masons in Russia, most of them Kadets. Their main purpose was political: to unite secretly as much of the opposition to the government as possible.[30]

The security police had been vaguely aware of the reemergence of Freemasonry in Russia and had produced inconclusive reports on its activities. Then in November 1908 an article by the Kadet Duma member E. I. Kedrin in *Russkoe slovo* made the security police take notice of Freemasonry as a movement. Kedrin, avowing himself a Mason, argued that Masons had not caused the Revolution of 1905, doubtless prompting some officials to wonder if he was protesting too much. In December S. E. Vissarionov suggested to Trusevich that Masons were dangerous political activists. Interior ministry official G. G. Mets concluded that disorder would soon strike again and that the blow would probably come from "people who do not yet enjoy civil rights in Russia," by which he undoubtedly meant the Jews. Police officials often linked Freemasonry, either explicitly or implicitly, to the Jews, as the lists of publications on the Freemasons collected by police officials makes clear. In reality, nearly all Russian Masons were Russian Orthodox.[31]

In 1910–1912, B. K. Alekseev, a police official, and L. A. Rataev submitted reports to Kurlov and Stolypin on the activities of Freemasons. Avrekh rejected these reports as trivial, fraudulent, even irrational. Mets was arguing, as Avrekh saw it, that Masons had not been discovered in Russia; therefore, they were omnipresent. Avrekh's own argument is similarly irrational, though it is constructed contrariwise: the Russian security police found little evidence of Freemasonic activity in Russia; therefore, almost none existed.[32]

Yet recent research in long-closed Russian archives shows that Freemasons were far more active in Russia than Avrekh allowed. The entire leadership of the Kadet Duma fraction save P. N. Miliukov and F. I. Rodichev were Masons; so were a few of the key Social Democrats and Socialist-Revolutionaries, such as N. S. Chkheidze and A. F. Kerenskii. Around the time of the Azef affair, they began to cooperate intensely and to employ rigorous strategies for maintaining secrecy in order to avoid police detection. In 1910 and 1911 a few leading Masons, most importantly the left-leaning Kadet N. V. Nekrasov, closed down several existing lodges and created a supreme Masonic council that focused on secrecy and political coordination.[33]

In the absence of completely free forums for public expression and political organization, it is understandable that political activists would seek within the cover of such a secretive association a means to break out of their rigid political parties and to develop ties among diverse members of the opposition. Although individual Masons held to and defended their own political interests, they pledged to support each other in public, for example by signing onto each others' Duma interpellations. They also vowed never to divulge anything about the Masons, even in court. B. I. Nikolaevskii, who interviewed several Freemasons after 1917, claimed they had pledged to sacrifice the interests of family and friends on behalf of their fellow Masons. It was easy to keep silent under the imperial Russian regime, and no Mason broke the pledge before 1917. Thus, the security police were unable to shed light on their organization or activities. It was more dangerous to remain silent under Stalin. In 1939 the NKVD apparently interrogated Nekrasov, who told everything he knew. That report supposedly reposes in the KGB archives in Russia.[34]

If the prerevolutionary security police were almost completely in the dark about the Masons, they were also unable to protect the government against one powerful figure whose every move they scrutinized—G. E. Rasputin. A. V. Gerasimov's surveillants started watching him in late 1908, using the moniker Temnyi ("Shady") for him. In early 1909 Stolypin authorized Gerasimov to exile Rasputin to Siberia as an immoral person, but he presumably got wind of the plan and returned to Siberia of his own volition. Restricting press reporting on Rasputin was also difficult. By law, articles concerning the imperial family were subject to preliminary censorship by the court ministry, but in practice only articles in which the name Rasputin appeared juxtaposed with names of members of the imperial family could be banned. True, in January 1912 two publications of the religious philosopher M. A. Novoselov denouncing Rasputin as a member of the Khlyst sect were confiscated because they violated a law banning pornography. Yet the measure backfired when the public joked that Rasputin's "very name is pornographic." Neither Nicholas nor Alexandra nor senior court officials could understand the court ministry's powerlessness in this matter.[35]

The purpose of censoring public mention of Rasputin, as well as watching him and attempting to exile him to Siberia, was to protect Nicholas's image and prestige within society. The security police also devoted much effort to protecting the persons of the emperor, members of his family, and senior officials. Various guard detachments, including that of A. I. Spiridovich, ensured Nicholas's security at his residences in and around St. Petersburg—at a cost of some three hundred thousand rubles in 1909–1911 and six hundred thousand in 1912. When Nicholas traveled, P. G. Kurlov coordinated all local security measures. In December 1910 he approved the reorganization of the mobile surveillance brigade into a security service for the emperor during his travels in the empire. In June 1911 the Special Section explained in detail how to protect the imperial family and senior officials. The security police were to verify with the regular police the identity of all the people living in the vicinity where the important person was supposed to appear and order surveillants to watch all suspicious people, paper sellers, cabbies, and vendors in the district.[36]

Ensuring the security of members of the imperial family was mostly routine but occasionally operatic. In early 1912 Gerasimov was instructed to prevent the marriage of Grand Duke Mikhail Aleksandrovich to a twice-divorced woman. The Paris security bureau assisted Gerasimov, as did the French police; they watched the grand duke like hawks. Yet he gave signs he would depart for Nice, and Gerasimov and his agents sped thither. Meanwhile the imperial elopers were married in a Serbian church in Vienna. Gerasimov traveled there and procured a copy of the marriage document, which he presented to his superiors in St. Petersburg.[37]

The security police frittered away more of their meager resources on counterespionage. For decades, gendarme chiefs were supposed to report to the Police Department any evidence of spying by foreign powers, yet even during the war with Japan no office or institution in Russia bore sole responsibility for counterintelligence operations. In early 1909 a commission of police, military, and administrative officials headed by M. I. Trusevich, recommended the creation of semiautonomous counterespionage bureaus *(Kontrrazvedyvatel'nye otdeleniia)* that would serve under the direction of gendarme officers and be organized along the lines of the security bureaus. Eleven bureaus were created in mid-1911 in Warsaw, Kiev, Vilna, Odessa, Moscow, Tiflis, Tashkent, Irkutsk, Khabarovsk, and St. Petersburg (one for the metropolitan area and a second for the military district). Their combined budget of 251,520 rubles per year was smaller than that of von Koten's bureau alone. Headed by gendarme officers but staffed by military personnel, the counterespionage bureaus were formally subordinated to local and central military authorities. Had the bureaus answered to the Police Department, as the Trusevich Commission had advocated, security policemen would have played a major role in counterespionage. Instead, a series of directives instructed them to participate actively in that work only on exceptional occasions. The security police preferred this outcome, though in consequence Russia's military counterespionage capabilities were comparatively weak on the eve of the First World War.[38]

"A CONSPIRACY OF MEDIOCRITY"

Although historians agree that Stolypin was Russia's last great statesman, by the end of his term of office he had lost the confidence of most of his contemporaries. Indeed, a large number of the generally polarized elites despised him. As Stolypin's power and authority waned, he failed to realize most of his reform goals, and even rightists came to oppose him and his government. On 3 March 1911, for example, the son of the conservative editor and publisher M. N. Katkov sent a long, impassioned letter to Stolypin expressing outrage. "My letters are being opened," he asserted, "because a newspaper critical of the government is being published in my building." He concluded with rhetorical questions, "Can't you tell right from left? Do you support all local officials without question?" Later in the month the Police Department reported that they had given no such orders and had no information about Katkov at all.[39] The editor's fears may have arisen from an unusually feverish mind, but more likely they resulted from a broadly based dislike of, or irritation with, the government.

Illustrative of Stolypin's growing weakness was his manner of dealing with Iliodor, a notorious right-wing monk and one of the founders of the Union of Russian People. Because of his antigovernment rhetoric, Iliodor had been exiled to a monastery in Vladimir Province, but in March 1911 he fled exile and returned to his former monastic redoubt in Tsaritsyn. Thence he launched a verbal campaign against the government, threatening to whip all the ministers, whom he called Yid-Masons *(zhidomasony)*. The Police Department immediately authorized his arrest. Yet the monk was adulated by right-wing activists and members of grassroots Russian Orthodox organizations who likened him to the revered St. John Chrysostom. Archpriest I. I. Vostorgov, president of the Moscow branch of the Union of Russian People, spoke vehemently in early March against the "all-powerful autocratic bureaucracy, which is destroying the foundations of the church and people" by persecuting Iliodor. Even within officialdom Iliodor enjoyed strong support. Martynov recalled that his own failure to succor the monk strained his relations with the Saratov gendarme chief V. K. Semiganovskii (Tsaritsyn fell within the diocese of Saratov). Finally, Iliodor had friends at court. In the end, Stolypin forbade his arrest.[40]

Liberal and moderate political activists staunchly opposed Stolypin on many grounds. Foremost among these was continued administrative arbitrariness. Tensions ran high during the Duma's discussion of the interior ministry's budget in January 1910. V. A. Maklakov declared that the ministry dominated the government as a whole and that its policies "Are now the primary content and chief evil of our time." Later in the debates the Octobrist prince A. D. Golitsyn claimed that the activities of the security bureaus "extend to all areas of the administration." Again, in February 1911 during the Duma's debate over the interior ministry's budget, the Octobrist S. I. Shidlovskii claimed that the ministry had become a huge police agency. Stolypin's newspaper, *Rossiia,* retorted that it was "necessary to accord to police activity more attention than the government would like to give it." Even so, public opinion forced the government to hew more closely to the rule of law: Duma deputies' complaints of improper treatment of themselves by police and local administrators in 1911 provoked the interior ministry to order its officials to put an end to such practices.[41]

During the controversy over Iliodor, the political right in the State Council dealt Stolypin the most damaging blow of his political career by rejecting his bill on the western zemstvos. His subsequent flouting of parliamentary procedure to get the bill passed turned the premier's remaining liberal and moderate supporters against him. The security police intercepted a revealing letter of 8 June 1911 addressed to A. M. Koliubakin, a Kadet Duma deputy, that claimed that Russian society was more wholeheartedly opposed to the imperial government than at any time since late 1905 and that all the opposition leaders believed the Fourth Duma would veer left. On the basis of this and other sources, in July Zuev warned that Progressists were allying themselves with left-Kadets and in some cases even with the revolutionary parties, while the Kadets were seeking to cooperate with Socialist-Revolutionaries and Social Democrats.[42]

At the end of August 1911 Stolypin traveled in the emperor's entourage to Kiev to celebrate the unveiling of a monument to Alexander II. As during previous state visits, Kurlov bore responsibility for ensuring the emperor's security, but since Kiev had a governor-general, who could not be legally subordinated to Kurlov, the actual security arrangements were divided among several officials. For example, Spiridovich ensured the emperor's physical security, and N. N. Kuliabko, the local security chief, handled general security policing and Stolypin's physical security. The situation was complicated by police intelligence warning of an impending attack against the emperor, allegedly to be organized by B. V. Savinkov. To make matters worse, the Kiev security bureau did not have any high-level informants.[43]

Kurlov arrived in Kiev on 14 August to await Nicholas's arrival. The next day he suffered a minor stroke that kept him in bed for ten days. Toward the end of the month Kuliabko reported that a reliable erstwhile informant, D. G. Bogrov, whom he had arrested as an anarchist-Communist in 1907, had returned with allegations about imminent terrorist plans. Kurlov urged Kuliabko to learn everything he could from Bogrov, who claimed that terrorists were scheduled to arrive in Kiev and that he would enable Kuliabko to foil their plot.[44]

Stolypin brushed aside concerns about security in Kiev and refused to permit increased protection for himself. A senior medical official of the interior ministry, G. E. Rein, had warned Stolypin earlier in the summer that Kiev was a dangerous city and had urged him to wear a bulletproof vest. Stolypin quipped in response that a vest would not protect him from a bomb. Minor conflicts ensued between Spiridovich's forces and those sent by von Koten: the emperor's mobile security service, which operated out of von Koten's security bureau. Then on Friday, 1 September, Kuliabko awoke Spiridovich at 6 o'clock in the morning and informed him of Bogrov's recent appearance and his allegations. Spiridovich was stupefied. That evening, Nicholas and his entourage were to attend the opera. Surely no terrorist could reach him there. Ninety-two of Spiridovich's agents permeated the Municipal Theater, plus he had seated handpicked officers in the first four rows on the main floor. Representatives of all the services, professions, and civic corporations in Kiev helped verify the identity of those seeking to enter the theater, and anyway only people with official connections had received tickets.[45]

Nevertheless, supposedly unbeknownst to Kurlov and Spiridovich, Bogrov entered the theater during the performance. During the first intermission, he met with Kuliabko to report about the alleged terrorists. Then he left. Bogrov later testified that he was still unsure whom to kill. He apparently returned during the second intermission, and Kuliabko told him to leave right away. Instead he entered the main hall and, seeing Stolypin up by the orchestra, approached him and shot him in the chest. Stolypin apparently exclaimed, "I am happy to die for the tsar." Members of the public threw themselves on Bogrov, and only police intervention saved his life. In five days Stolypin died. In five more Bogrov was hanged.[46]

The most incredible fact in the entire story is that Kuliabko had furnished Bogrov with a ticket to the performance—but it was perhaps not entirely surprising. P. T. Samokhvalov, Kuliabko's assistant since 1909, testified that his boss had little understanding of security policing, paid almost no attention to his informants, let important documents from the Police Department pile up, and "always said, 'don't worry. Spiridovich has already taken care of it.'" (Spiridovich was his brother-in-law.) Bogrov, the son of a wealthy assimilated Jewish lawyer and himself a convert to Russian Orthodoxy, claimed to have joined the police because he had found the anarchists to be "bandits." He informed on the anarchists as well as Socialist-Revolutionaries.[47]

It seems that some of Bogrov's comrades—anarchists, apparently—had discovered his police connection and had threatened to kill him unless he assassinated a government official. He had found it psychologically impossible to kill his first target, Kuliabko, who, when Bogrov returned to Kiev, greeted him in his underwear and with a blanket draped around him, saying "Hello, dear friend." Bogrov then resolved to kill either a senior official or even the emperor himself and therefore invented the story about an imminent terrorist attack. In order to thwart the plot, he explained, he would need to enter the theater on the night of the performance. Bogrov admitted during the criminal investigation that his story had not been entirely credible. Suspicion naturally fell on Kuliabko, Kurlov, and Spiridovich. So insistent were the suspicions that rightist activists demanded to be present at Bogrov's execution to make sure it was indeed Bogrov who was being executed. Within a month Nicholas accepted Kurlov's resignation.[48]

Nicholas appointed Finance Minister V. N. Kokovtsov to replace Stolypin as prime minister (A. A. Makarov became the new interior minister). The new premier received reports from Kiev of massive anti-Jewish ferment and of insufficient police and military forces in the area. Kokovtsov ordered three Cossack regiments back from maneuvers. They occupied whole Jewish areas, and the agitation quickly subsided. Kokovtsov also ordered the empire's governors to use all the means authorized by law, including the force of arms, to prevent pogroms. Nicholas later thanked Kokovtsov warmly for having done so.[49]

On the advice of Justice Minister I. G. Shcheglovitov, Nicholas appointed Senator M. I. Trusevich, a bitter enemy of Kurlov, to investigate Stolypin's murder.[50] Trusevich and Senator N. Z. Shul'gin, who completed the investigation, interviewed the principal defendants and dozens of witnesses, including numerous security police officials. Some of Kuliabko's testimony was contradictory, confused, and almost irrational. He admitted that Bogrov had lied to him about the supposed plot, but that he had trusted him and had believed the plot was real. He claimed he could not understand why Bogrov would have lied to him, since he would have given him a ticket to enter the theater no matter what. He knew about the Police Department directives warning against placing great trust in informants, and he knew that S. G. Karpov had been killed in 1909 because he had trusted his informant too fully, yet he asserted, "I believe you cannot work with informants without strong trust. Plus, I did not really think about these directives at the time." After all, senior police officials were on the scene, and they "gave me no precise orders on this matter," he said.[51]

Asked why he had not searched or established surveillance over the apartment in which the alleged terrorists were supposedly living, Kuliabko replied, "We had never done anything like this before." He also claimed that both Spiridovich and M. N. Verigin, a vice-director of the Police Department, had agreed to Bogrov's entry into the theater. Yet Spiridovich himself testified, quite plausibly, that they had not discussed Bogrov or the arrival of terrorists, "since this was a security policing matter, which Kuliabko was in charge of." In later testimony Spiridovich suggested that Kuliabko probably would not have allowed Bogrov to enter the theater without authorization, implying that Verigin must have been in on the plan.[52]

Kurlov admitted to having received negative reports about Kuliabko's performance, including evidence of financial irregularities and other manifestations of administrative mismanagement. Kuliabko had been slow in replying to requests for information from the Police Department, had failed to maintain an adequate informant network, and had displayed a rude attitude toward officials of the Police Department. Kurlov also let slip a remark about Spiridovich that suggested the latter's ministrations had helped to squelch any misgivings about Kuliabko, who was his brother-in-law.[53]

In the end, the investigation turned up only two important facts. First, periodic inspections of Kuliabko and his security bureau had deemed both unsatisfactory, yet Spiridovich and Kurlov, his patrons, had made it impossible to censure him. Second, a rivalry between M. F. von Koten, who had once supervised Bogrov, and Spiridovich and Verigin prevented von Koten from informing them of his certainty that Bogrov was not to be trusted. Trusevich concluded that if these officials had shared the information at their disposal, the murder might have been avoided.[54]

Kuliabko was dismissed from service and imprisoned for the loss of 8,147 rubles in state funds, though embezzlement could not be proved. Kurlov, who received a small pension, returned to service only when war was declared; Verigin never returned to service; and Spiridovich, at the insistence of the emperor, remained at his post even during the investigation. Nicholas liked and trusted the man who acted as an unofficial photographer in the emperor's entourage. In January 1913, while the State Council was considering whether to send the case up to the Senate for a trial, Nicholas confided to Kokovtsov that he had granted clemency to all the defendants. "I would like to mark the healing of my son with a good act," said Nicholas. "Especially Spiridovich. . . . He is guilty only of failing to take all precautions."[55]

Contemporaries and historians have assessed blame variously. V. F. Dzhunkovskii faulted Stolypin himself for concentrating so much supervisory authority in Kurlov's hands. Gerasimov considered it "gross stupidity to trust Bogrov, to let him enter the theater without strict surveillance." He surmised that Kurlov and Kuliabko had run the risk "in order to be able to foil a plot against the tsar" and therefore to win accolades and monetary rewards. A. Ia. Avrekh asserted forcefully in 1968, but less so in 1989, that Kurlov, in league with Spiridovich and Kuliabko, had masterminded Stolypin's murder. His case against them rests on two pieces of circumstantial evidence. First, they failed to pursue aggressively the lead Bogrov had furnished them. Second, they allowed Bogrov to enter the theater.[56]

S. A. Stepanov recently subjected these and other speculations and allegations to careful scrutiny. He begins by arguing that Kurlov would hardly arrange to kill one of the people whom it was his official duty to protect, unless he simply hated him blindly, which did not seem to be the case, and did not care about the likelihood of damaging his own career should he fail miserably in carrying out his duties. (One could add that everyone believed that Stolypin's days in office were numbered.) Stepanov then draws a parallel with A. A. Petrov, who killed S. G. Karpov out of anger at having been used by the police and having come under pressure from his erstwhile comrades who had found him out. It seems likely that Bogrov underwent similar psychological pressure and would find some way to kill an official or other important person. Finally, as Stepanov argues, for years publicists and rumormongers had lodged wild accusations against Russia's security policemen. Fantastic stories had long circulated that G. P. Sudeikin had wanted to become a dictator and that Gerasimov had sent terrorists to kill Kurlov. Moreover, V. D. Novitskii, a retired gendarme officer, believed that Zubatov had organized assassinations, and D. F. Trepov had called A. A. Lopukhin a murderer after Grand Duke Sergei Aleksandrovich was killed. Stepanov concluded that "There was no carefully planned conspiracy against Stolypin. He fell prey to a different, a more terrible kind of conspiracy that rendered the monarchy powerless and in a few years led to its collapse. It was a conspiracy of mediocrity and incompetence."[57]

In the wake of Stolypin's assassination, public figures, journalists, and Duma deputies called into question both the emperor's security service and the entire imperial security police system. Criticism came from nearly every political quarter. The Duma devoted to Stolypin's murder an entire session, during which A. I. Guchkov attacked the defendants in the case. Both Spiridovich and Kuliabko were so outraged, they wanted to challenge him to a duel, but senior officials dissuaded them from doing so. When the Kiev newspaper *Kievskaia mysl'* (Kiev Thought) printed damning allegations against Kuliabko, he persuaded his successor at the security bureau, I. A. Leont'ev, to pressure the editor to reveal his source of information. The effort backfired, however, when a senior police official chided Leont'ev for summoning the editor to his bureau and threatening him with mistreatment. Prince V. P. Meshcherskii, the editor of the right-wing *Grazhdanin* (Citizen), called for the abolition of the security service, which "toyed with the life of the emperor . . . in some kind of mad interlacing of infernal terrorist plots and the police organization. . . . How can one trust and make deals with a terrorist? . . . The people's love for the tsar is a far better source of security."[58]

Toward the opposite end of the political spectrum, N. A. Gredeskul, a well-known Kadet jurist, wrote in 1912 that to combat terror with only honest and open means was to condemn oneself to failure, but to fight it with secret and underhanded methods could only lead to the calamities of Azef and Bogrov *(azefovshchina-bogrovshchina)*. He likened security policemen to the terrorists they combated. Both lacked a sense of limits and drew into their ranks unreliable and dangerous people, like Petrov, Mikhail Ripps, and Bogrov. In Russian life, he contended, there had arisen two large organizations, the revolutionary movement and the security police, "each one of which, in the name of its supreme goal, considers itself permitted to do virtually anything considered morally and socially reprehensible. And these two organizations . . . became intertwined in an unimaginable mutual betrayal." Yet Gredeskul remained optimistic. The social and political maturation of the Russian population had "morally and politically" dissipated the impulse to political terror. Therefore, the time was ripe to reform the security police force—that is, to dismantle it as then constituted.[59]

Major security police reform seemed unlikely, however, for want of dynamic, visionary leadership and because of structural problems and bureaucratic inertia. Henceforth no statesman would appear who even vaguely approached Stolypin in character and ability. The new interior minister, A. A. Makarov, had been Stolypin's deputy for police affairs and then the administrative secretary for the State Council for nearly three years. K. D. Kafafov called Makarov, who unlike Stolypin was a lawyer, "excellent, honest, noble, with a deep Christian faith." Spirodovich agreed that "he was fully honest," but objected that he "rather resembled a decent and calm provincial notary" who "was not made for the capital . . . and understood nothing of security policing."[60]

Makarov selected I. M. Zolotarev, the prosecutor of the Novocherkassk judicial tribunal since 1907, to be his deputy for police affairs. Dzhunkovskii described Zolotarev as a "well-educated, well-read jurist; as a man . . . most noble, honest, deserving of respect. Yet he was very lazy by nature and hated work and preferred a comfortable, peaceful life." Spiridovich concurred, "He was charming, honest, in every way irreproachable, a grand lord, but because of these very qualities unprepared for his task."

Aleksandr Pavlovich Martynov, chief of the Saratov security bureau (1906–1912) and chief of the Moscow security bureau (1912–1917), sits in a garden with his wife.

Thus, Zolotarev shifted nearly all the responsibility for police affairs to the new Police Department director, S. P. Beletskii, whom he charged with renovating the institution.[61]

Beletskii's first important task was to tighten the emperor's security during his travels. In January 1912, while still vice-director for legislative affairs, Beletskii had joined senior police officials from St. Petersburg and Moscow to plan the security measures for Nicholas's impending trip to Moscow. They agreed that city or provincial governors would bear the chief responsibility for ensuring Nicholas's security, while the security police would report to the governors. Officials from St. Petersburg would oversee the operations but would not intervene in them. Then in April Vissarionov convened a meeting of all the security and gendarme chiefs in the Moscow region to discuss the necessary concrete measures.[62]

At the same time, Vissarionov inspected the security arrangements in Moscow. He lodged numerous criticisms against Zavarzin, claiming that he lacked adequate informants among the anarchists and Socialist-Revolutionary terrorists, that he had failed to detain people who might endanger the emperor's security, and that he pressured his staff too much and was in a perpetual state of nervous tension. Zavarzin might have kept his job if Makarov had not seen him at a reception for the emperor when he was supposed to be at the security bureau. Makarov transferred him to the Odessa gendarme station and summoned Aleksandr Pavlovich Martynov from Saratov to take his place. M. S. Kommisarov, whose rehabilitation Beletskii had facilitated, was sent to Saratov to replace Martynov.[63]

Martynov, who directed security policing in Moscow from July 1912 to February 1917, later claimed that he worked extremely long hours, seven days a week, and took no time off while he was director, except one month in May 1914. He was eager to work hard, since a security officer could scarcely rise higher in terms of power, prestige, and earnings. He earned a "governorly income"—"1,000 rubles per month, if one counted the eight-room apartment with heat and light, a carriage, a clothing allowance, 300 rubles as a lieutenant-colonel, 150 rubles as the director of the regional bureau, free train tickets, a travel allowance of 150 rubles, plus bonuses equaling an average of 400 rubles." Martynov might also have mentioned that he controlled a yearly budget of 189,000 rubles (compared to 282,000 for the St. Petersburg bureau) and employed well over one hundred people.[64]

THE LENA GOLDFIELDS MASSACRE AND AFTERWARD

Even as the security police laid their plans for the emperor's trip to Moscow, which was intended to bring him closer to the Russian people, a tragedy occurred far away in the largely British-owned Lena goldfields on the Vitim River some two hundred miles northeast of Lake Baikal. On 4 April 1912 troops opened fire on a crowd of miners peacefully bearing hundreds of individually written complaints. Some 170 workers were killed on the spot; sixty more succumbed later from their wounds. A government investigation, carried out by Senator S. S. Manukhin, laid all the blame for the tragedy on the mining company and the government. It recommended criminal prosecution for N. V. Treshchenkov, a gendarme captain with expertise in security policing, whose heavy-handed arrest of members of the workers' strike committee against the wishes of the Irkutsk governor, A. F. Bantysh, precipitated the shootings.[65]

From the revolutionary left to readers of Meshcherskii's right-wing *Grazhdanin*, the public was shocked and indignant. All of the newspapers except the official *Rossiia* criticized the government for its handling of the tragedy, though the sensationalist *Kopeika* (Kopeck) printed nearly as many stories about the *Titanic*, which had sunk two days before the massacre (15 April, New Style). On 11 April Makarov was called before the Duma to defend his ministry's actions. Arguing inaccurately that the miners had attacked the troops who had been called in to maintain order, Makarov contended that in all such cases the troops have "no choice but to fire. That is how it has always been and will be in the future." Although the rightist deputies applauded the speech, deputies from the left of the chamber called Makarov a "bloodsucker."[66]

Like many senior officials, Makarov had no idea of the necessity of culti-vating public opinion under the conditions of participatory politics. Even so, at the very least Makarov had the responsibility to try to answer some fundamental questions about his ministry's action, such as one posed by Prince Meshcherskii, who sensibly wondered why the main local govern-ment protagonist in such a delicate affair had been a gendarme captain. In-deed, not only was Treshchenkov of low rank, but he was primarily a secu-rity policeman.[67] Meshcherskii probably had no idea that it was exceedingly rare for gendarme officers to involve themselves in major re-pressive actions and unheard of for them to command troops, defy gover-nors, or act with as much authority as Treshchenkov did.

The shootings provoked a groundswell of popular dissatisfaction that re-sulted in worker protests, collections of funds to assist the families of vic-tims of the massacre, and a huge wave of strikes between 14 and 22 April. Although 1911 had witnessed an increase in labor agitation, Lena marked a watershed: over the next two years the government would have to face a qualitatively and quantitatively new workers' movement.

The government responded to the strikes and demonstrations with mi-nor concessions and with repressive measures. The concessions were two social insurance laws, on worker disability benefits and on sickness funds, adopted on 23 June. Though limited in scope, these legislative acts were a comparatively enlightened response. By 1914 some two million members belonged to 2,800 sickness funds, which often resembled trade unions and which the Bolsheviks sought assiduously to penetrate and control. Robert McKean has concluded that police officials felt a "far from groundless ap-prehension that the sickness insurance funds would afford a legal covering for socialist activists."[68]

As for repression, on 19 May the Police Department directed security po-licemen to acquire informants within factories to prevent political strikes and to keep out revolutionary propaganda. Over the next several months senior police officials entreated regular and security police officials to coor-dinate their efforts to contain strikes, to arrest and exile strike instigators, to prevent worker demonstrations, to plan to suppress worker disorders, and to use force—and even to summon military detachments—if needed. Be-ginning in the fall the Police Department sought to increase its surveillance of and control over trade unions and other legal workers' organizations. Yet the task appeared daunting to senior Police Department officials and gen-darme and security chiefs meeting in September and November 1912. Even keeping watch over those organizations dominated by revolutionaries ex-ceeded the capacities of government institutions, the officials agreed.[69]

During the summer of 1912 revolutionary agitation increased dramati-cally in the Baltic fleet, where, despite years of repression, revolutionary ag-itators had "multiplied like mushrooms after a rainfall." P. E. Dybenko, who was later the commander of the entire fleet and who married A. M.

Kollontai, a senior Bolshevik official after the October Revolution, helped organize the mutiny that broke out on the *Emperor Paul I* on 22 July and spread to other ships in the Baltic and Black Sea fleets. The unrest prompted Police Department officials to advise the setting up of more barriers to revolutionary agitation within naval units. Their report of 2 August urged that ships cease wintering in Finland, where the local authorities "constantly resist imperial orders"; that the "political reliability" of port workers be scrupulously verified; that civilians wishing to visit ships be carefully screened; and that Russian ships be stationed as seldom as possible in European ports, where Russian revolutionaries could not be prevented from boarding them.[70]

The report's authors admitted that sailors' discontent often stemmed from harsh treatment by noncommissioned officers, from bad rations, and from the distance between sailors and officers, who usually did not know the sailors' last names and often confused breaches of discipline with revolutionary ferment. The relationship between officers and sailors was an echo of tensions between elite society and the masses. Makarov approved most of the recommendations in the report to the naval ministry, including measures to improve the living conditions of sailors. To improve surveillance over Baltic sailors, a regional security bureau comprising the gendarme stations in Finland, Estland, Kurland, and Lifland was set up.[71]

This effort may have been for naught: police officials continued to deem sailors, unlike army personnel, too unreliable for recruitment as regular policemen. Indeed, an object of fear throughout the government and among conservative political commentators was the potential for a military coup along the lines of the takeovers by radical officers in Portugal, Turkey, Persia, and China during the previous three years. The fear of disorder in the military was so great that in November Beletskii ordered security policemen to avoid arresting soldiers since "they sit in jail with political prisoners and end up more propagandized."[72]

The Lena tragedy caught the major revolutionary organizations off guard. The Social Democrats were seriously divided among themselves; they traded accusations of provocation at their party conference in January 1912. Moreover, the arrest of leaders of the major revolutionary organizations had continued apace across the empire, both in the months before and immediately after the Lena events. In August Lenin complained to Gorky, "Things are brewing in the Baltic Fleet . . . [but] there is no organization—I could simply weep." A Bolshevik committee reconstituted itself in Moscow in August, but soon most of its members fell into the security police force's nets. I. F. Armand organized a Bolshevik committee in St. Petersburg only in December. The Mensheviks, who had maintained a committee in the capital all year, had carried on little underground work. The Socialist-Revolutionary underground had "scarcely survived as an organizational entity."[73]

Revolutionary activists turned to legal publishing ventures, for which the Lena shootings caused donations to flow into party coffers. The three major revolutionary parties launched daily newspapers: the Bolshevik *Pravda* (Truth), the Menshevik *Luch* (Ray), and the Socialist-Revolutionary *Trudovoi golos* (Voice of Labor). They persisted for two years but suffered considerable repression in the interim. During the twenty-seven months of *Pravda*'s existence, for example, a variety of repressive measures, mostly administrative, were imposed on 194 issues out of 645. Several of its editors spent a combined total of forty-seven months in jail and paid 16,650 rubles in fines. Judicial punishments, which were generally harsher, occurred more rarely. All told, thirty-six judicial cases were brought against *Pravda* during its existence.[74]

The revolutionary publicists played a clever game of cat and mouse with the censors. For example, the editors of *Pravda* always sent some copies of each issue right out to factories and railroad stations in St. Petersburg before the print run's formal distribution. One worker recalled regularly carrying one thousand issues of *Pravda* to the Putilov factory. Catching onto this trick, the authorities stationed policemen in the neighborhoods around the relevant printers' shops each night. In violation of the press law, they also sometimes seized issues before word came from the censors. Then the printers tried to hide as many copies as possible all over their shops, including inside the covers of the right-wing *Zemshchina*, which they also printed.[75]

A member of the editorial board, A. E. Badaev could take part in these efforts with impunity because of his parliamentary immunity. Moreover, Matvei, a seventy-year-old watchman, always made the trip to the censor. He walked the half-kilometer as slowly as possible, often taking up to two hours. Once he had handed the issue to the censor, he carefully watched him reading it. If the censor read it then moved on to another paper, Matvei left calmly. If he knit his brows and telephoned the police station, Matvei slipped out, jumped in a cab and dashed off to press. There a sentinel was watching for him, ready to sound the alarm. Several printers were usually ready to carry off as many issues as possible to the workers' neighborhoods.[76] Though these ruses perhaps infringed on the spirit of the law, they were perfectly consistent with its letter.

Occasionally the security police knew exactly what the revolutionary activists were up to. For example, already on 13 April 1912, that is, ten days before the first issue of *Pravda* appeared, the Police Department received detailed information about the activists involved and their strategy and organization. Yet although the security police were often quite aware of revolutionary activists' journalistic work, they could not easily stop it, as Beletskii conceded in October 1912. At times, he later testified, the police were reduced to buying up issues of *Pravda*. He undoubtedly knew, as Badaev admitted, that *Pravda*'s editorial offices were "in fact the legal headquarters of illegal Bolshevik work," where Bolshevik activists met with worker representatives, discussed illegal meetings, planned rallies, raised funds for revolutionary purposes, and organized strikes.[77]

It seems, therefore, that it was almost out of desperation, in order to penetrate to the heart of the Bolshevik leadership, that senior officials abetted the election of R. V. Malinovskii—by far the most talented of the six Bolshevik deputies in the Fourth Duma. The authorities in Moscow, with Makarov's and Beletskii's approbation, neglected to provide any information about Malinovskii's regular criminal past to the election authorities and actively removed obstacles from his path to the Taurida Palace. Once elected to the Duma, Malinovskii received a monthly salary of five hundred rubles and a transfer from Martynov to Beletskii's supervision.[78]

It is legitimate to ask who gained the most from this gambit. A fiery orator and a gifted revolutionary activist, Malinovskii enjoyed great popularity among Moscow's workers. Lenin, who apparently trusted him completely, exulted at the news of his election. Malinovskii's reports to the police had wreaked havoc on the Social Democratic underground in Moscow, yet his fervent speeches, which Beletskii edited, ridiculed and excoriated the government. Beletskii put up with his inflammatory rhetoric—though he sometimes softened it—because he hoped it would tend to discredit the Bolsheviks and drive a wedge between them and the Mensheviks, "to divide and conquer them," as Beletskii himself remarked.[79] It may have divided the Social Democrats, but it also helped make the Bolsheviks the dominant force within the Social Democratic coalition.

Aside from meddling with internal Social Democratic politics, Beletskii responded to the increase in antigovernment activism with a string of directives and conferences. In October 1912, for example, he underlined the crucial importance of recruiting and directing secret informants. "Materially speaking," he wrote, "security policemen enjoy better pay and faster promotions than in any other branch of state service." They would have to work hard to continue to receive them. Later in October Vissarionov presided over a conference of security police officials convened to recommend improvements in the recruitment and training of gendarme officers. Finally, in late November and early December Beletskii convoked a dozen specialists in security policing, including Gerasimov, Martynov, von Koten, Vissarionov, and Eremin, all gathered under the chairmanship of I. M. Zolotarev, to discuss how best to combat revolutionary activism.[80]

The lengthy final report summarizing the conference participants' conclusions suggested that the recent security police reforms—especially the improved training of officers and the creation of regional security bureaus—had contributed to the weakening of revolutionary organizations throughout the Russian Empire. Yet because agitators were exploiting the relatively liberal laws on voluntary associations and the press, because large numbers of revolutionary activists were scheduled to return soon from exile, and because revolutionaries were engaging in renewed efforts to spread propaganda in the military and to reestablish postal-telegraph and railroad unions, which had played such an important role in the revolution of 1905, it was necessary, according to the conferees, to take some strong actions. They would have to reorganize the security bureau in Paris along the lines of the bureaus within the Russian Empire, improve the training of lower-ranked gendarme officers, recruit more auxiliary informants in military units and other sectors of society, recruit more full-time informants within the legal opposition, maintain careful registers of professional and cooperative organizations, hire a few more well-educated surveillants to watch intellectual revolutionaries, and employ informants within all institutions of higher learning and in the upper grades of high schools, especially in such borderland areas as Poland and the Caucasus.[81]

Concretely, scarcely a whit of this agenda came to fruition. Beletskii's ominous warning to Makarov that "The tragic events of 1905 . . . have underscored the common goals of both the public opposition and the revolutionaries and the need to suppress both,"[82] was perhaps expressing a heartfelt goal of many administrative officials at a time when the suppression of either was beyond the moral and material capacities of the imperial Russian government. Furthermore, within days of receiving this report Makarov was dismissed from office, and his successor, V. F. Dzhunkovskii, began a series of reforms that both weakened the security police and was aimed at decreasing popular animosity against them.

CHAPTER FIVE

A MORALIST

RUNNING THE

POLICE APPARATUS

■ Maurice Laporte, the only foreigner to gain access to the imperial Russian police archives before 1989, ended his history of the Russian security police with the death of Stolypin. From then until 1917, he argued, foreign policy overshadowed domestic politics. Moreover, the power of the security police was at its apogee, with the revolutionary organizations in disarray and with terror for the most part abandoned. Most of the leaders of revolutionary organizations were in exile, and the Paris security bureau watched them by habit, but not because they seemed particularly dangerous at the time.[1]

Yet, in truth, the story of the Russian security police contained many twists and turns in the final years of the old regime. None was more important than the reform program V. F. Dzhunkovskii launched in 1913. A man with a profound sense of honor, or at the very least obsessed with giving that impression, Dzhunkovskii devoted much of his energy and attention to cleaning up the police institutions. He wanted to defend and uphold the state order but abhorred the methods traditionally used to that end. It was perhaps a testimony to the elite's public disgust with the security police, especially in the wake of the *azefovshchina-bogrovshchina,* that Dzhunkovskii's efforts to rein in the police met with little resistance within officialdom, the court, or rightist circles. The police apparatus had won the war against revolutionaries and terrorists, yet it had lost the battle of public relations. Perhaps the decent Dzhunkovskii could win the trust of society.

A FRIEND OF A FRIEND

On 26 December 1912, the emperor appointed Nikolai Alekseevich Maklakov as interior minister. Born in 1871, a year after his brother Vasilii, the celebrated Kadet jurist, Maklakov graduated in history and literature from Moscow University and had previously worked in various provincial offices of the finance ministry. V. I Gurko described him as "a fat, rubicund, cheerful man, a typical provincial dandy, a ladies' man, a highly diverting raconteur and reputed to be an inimitable anecdotist." A hard-line administrator, "decent but irascible," in the words of K. D. Kafafov, Maklakov owed his appointment as interior minister to the high opinion Nicholas had formed of him during the emperor's official visits to Poltava in 1909 and Chernigov in 1911, where, in both cases, Maklakov was governor at the time.[2]

The emperor undoubtedly prized Maklakov's explicit rightist convictions and adamant defense of the prerogatives of the supreme authority. A. V. Krivoshein wrote that he had a "psychopathic adoration" for Nicholas, who counted him among his three closest friends. Yet Maklakov lacked allies in the upper echelons of officialdom, which left him vulnerable to bureaucratic intrigues. His avowed program was modest and conservative: he proposed to strengthen the power of provincial governors, increase funding for the police, tighten the passport system, and enhance government control over the press.[3] He managed to accomplish none of these goals.

Maklakov selected Vladimir Fedorovich Dzhunkovskii, a personal friend, to replace I. M. Zolotarev as his deputy for police affairs. Nicholas approved the choice. The well-connected Dzhunkovskii, a former Preobrazhenskii Guards officer, had made a good impression on the emperor and his entourage during their celebration of the centennial of the war of 1812 that was held in Moscow, where he was governor. Dzhunkovskii later admitted that he was "not enthusiastic about being in charge of the police," for he "was aware of the negative aspects of security policing." He accepted the position out of duty and "to help maintain order."[4]

Although numerous rightists disliked Dzhunkovskii, he enjoyed the respect of much of the moderate and liberal public in Moscow Province. P. P. Riabushinskii, the Progressist leader, wrote in the Moscow Progressist daily, *Utro Rossii* (Russia's Morning):

> Something very strange is going on in Moscow; for the past two weeks they have been saying goodbye to Dzhunkovskii, and saying goodbye brings together all of Moscow city and province, all public activists and officials, as well as representatives of the clergy, the army, the nobility, the petty urban dwellers, and the peasants. Even his worst enemy would not call him a liberal or a political gradualist; he's just like any other convinced orthodox conservative, like his unpopular predecessor. The secret is that, being a truly decent man in his private life, Dzhunkovskii carried this decency over to his official life. How little is necessary from a representative of authority to ensure a certain share of public sympathy: personal honesty, a lack of impulsiveness, and a respect for the law.[5]

After he had taken up his post on 25 January 1913, however, Dzhunkovskii caused some consternation with an order of 6 February to the personnel of the Gendarme Corps, presumably because of its apparent anachronism. Recalling Nicholas I's alleged bestowal of a handkerchief on

Vladimir Fedorovich Dzhunkovskii, deputy interior minister (1913–1915).

the first gendarme chief ("to dry the tears of the sorrowful"), Dzhunkovskii proclaimed that "the holy testament of mercy, which called for drying the tears of the sorrowful, will remain the unalterable motto of each one of us." He also expected all gendarme officers to cherish those qualities of which the Russian military was justly proud: "corps d'esprit, mutual trust, noble straightforwardness *(priamodushie)*." I. Lopatin mused in *Utro Rossii* in regard to this order that "we inhabitants are trying to guess who will reshape whom sooner: the superior the gendarmes or the gendarmes their superior."[6] Several vigorous actions early in Dzhunkovskii's tenure suggested he meant to prevail.

He started with a campaign to oblige gendarme officers, even those performing only administrative duties for the Corps, to wear their full gendarme uniforms. He insisted on wearing his own wherever he went, although he later noted that it had been "unpleasant to put on the uniform, since it was discredited, disapproved of by society." He recalled that when he first went to a party wearing the uniform, "people all looked at him with condolence." He nevertheless felt it his duty to wear it, even though he had the right to wear the uniform of the imperial retinue, and he was determined to make his subordinates do likewise.[7]

It seemed to him that this decision won him popular sympathy. When he first appeared before the Duma on 15 February, apparently the first official to do so in the distinctive midnight-blue garb, all eyes fixed on him in astonishment; yet, he wrote, "most of the deputies, even the extremists, respected my courage." This act must have taken great courage indeed, since Dzhunkovskii had confided to Maklakov that he would have preferred not to speak at the general assembly of the Duma at all. Throughout his tenure, however, he enjoyed regular meetings with Duma deputies in the commission on police reform, where he found the atmosphere "amiable," and he wrote that he never met with any problems or misunderstandings when attending meetings of the budget commission.[8]

At the start of Dzhunkovskii's administration Nicholas declared an amnesty in honor of the tercentenary of the Romanov dynasty. Thousands of political prisoners serving sentences under various articles of the criminal code and the statute on criminal procedure were released—1,252 out of 3,074 inmates in five prisons in St. Petersburg alone. Meanwhile 6,185 administrative exiles received their freedom, and by September there were only 1,217 left (2,295 had fled their places of exile). Even many who had escaped from exile benefited from the amnesty. Dzhunkovskii later wrote that he had considered administrative political exile a form of "self-deception" in which antigovernment activists in one place were simply transferred to another place, all while the arbitrary nature of the practice increased discontent among the exiles and their friends and families. He sought, therefore, to diminish the use of exile, and later he implied that he had hoped to abolish it outright, but that the war had intervened.[9]

The government sought to use the tercentenary festivities to project the image of a confident monarchy. Yet because of alleged bomb threats and leaflets calling for mass protests, St. Petersburg was so filled with police and troops that, according to Dzhunkovskii, it took on the appearance of a "military camp," which must have made an unfavorable impression on the public and on the soldiers themselves.[10]

SHAKING UP THE SECURITY POLICE

Dzhunkovskii almost immediately set about reforming the security police system. Although he later admitted that he had been quite unfamiliar with police methods and institutions, he enjoyed something like carte blanche in running the police apparatus, since Maklakov apparently felt toward Dzhunkovskii "unlimited trust and he accorded me complete freedom of action." Among his first acts was to curtail the security police force's meddling in the military. As a staunch defender of military honor,

Dzhunkovskii considered it imperative to keep soldiers separate from the police apparatus in all its forms. Moreover, he frowned on the whole idea of police informants. Zavarzin found it preferable, when briefing Dzhunkovskii, to refer to them as plainclothes officers. Thus, although an investigation of the summer 1912 unrest in the navy had indicated that informants had prevented mutinies on some ships and although the security policing conferees in late fall 1912 had stressed the importance of maintaining informants in military and naval units, on 13 March 1913 Dzhunkovskii banned the deployment of informants within the military. He apparently took this step not to increase the effectiveness of the security police but primarily as a matter of principle, of honor. Although the emperor had been uncomfortable with the use of informants in the military, neither he nor the navy or war ministry had demanded its abolition; that was apparently entirely Dzhunkovskii's initiative.[11]

Reacting to public outrage at the March 1913 arrest of two high school students from the Vitmer Gimnaziia in St. Petersburg, Dzhunkovskii investigated the case and found, to his horror, that security policemen deployed informants among high school students. He considered this practice an "egregious corruption" of schoolchildren. In a directive of 1 May 1913, therefore, he forbade it. Dzhunkovskii argued that previous directives were correct to advocate recruiting informants among university students, some of whom, he admitted, were very active in the revolutionary movements. The policy should not, however, be applied to students in secondary schools, for they were only the target of revolutionary propaganda and never participants in revolutionary activity—a dubious assertion. When he ordered the dismissal of all informants in secondary schools, he did allow, however, that informants might be recruited among outsiders seeking to influence schoolchildren.[12] While it is true that a directive of 25 January 1908 advocated recruiting such informants,[13] it seems unlikely that the security police had until then recruited many informants in secondary schools. Lists of informants never refer to high school students *(ucheniki)* but only to university students *(studenty)*. Given officials' fear of seditious activity in universities, it seems unlikely that many security policemen had diverted scarce resources toward secondary schools. The banning of informants in high schools was therefore an action on principle with few practical consequences.

Far more important, Dzhunkovskii dismantled the networks of provincial and regional security bureaus. He objected vehemently to the existence of these institutions because they had been created by administrative fiat, drew upon secret funds, and raised junior gendarme officers above their seniors. He thought that the network of regional bureaus had been established in part because some gendarme officers "wanted to occupy a completely isolated position, far from any supervision." He abolished the networks in two stages, beginning with most of the provincial security bureaus. Regarded since their creation in 1902 and 1903 as the backbone of the security police system, by 1912 the provincial bureaus had numbered fifteen. As late as 9 January 1913 senior police officials were seriously considering creating six more bureaus in border provinces. The latest draft of the Makarov Commission's proposals for reforming the police system, discussed in early February, had proposed no changes in the security police system.[14] It seems that the initiative for abolishing the security bureaus was again entirely Dzhunkovskii's.

In a directive of 15 May 1913, Dzhunkovskii justified the move by underlining the importance of "unifying the security system." The same day, S. P. Beletskii, the director of the Police Department, announced the abolition of ten security bureaus (in Baku, Ekaterinoslav, Kiev, Nizhnii Novgorod, Lodz, Sevastopol, Tiflis, the Don military district, Nikolaevsk, and Iaroslavl). No legislative act was needed: only the bureaus in Warsaw and the imperial capitals existed formally, and only the one in St. Petersburg on a legal basis. The former security bureau chiefs were thenceforth subordinated to the appropriate gendarme station chiefs, who became the sole directors of security policing in their provinces and were instructed to dismiss, insofar as possible, employees of the former security bureaus. This policy was expected to result in a major financial savings. Although Dzhunkovskii's directive asserted that "uniting this work in one office will simplify and accelerate it,"[15] the reform probably also undermined the effectiveness of the security system, since in most cases the displaced bureau chiefs were better security policemen than their new superiors.

The abolition of the network of regional security bureaus, which Dzhunkovskii later called a "state within a state," may have made more practical sense. A conference of police officials held on 11 July 1911 had concluded that the regional bureaus engaged in excessive paper-shuffling and were ineffective overall and had proposed abolishing them everywhere except in Siberia and a few other areas. Even so, police officials incessantly criticized provincial gendarme officers while often praising the security bureau chiefs who headed the regional bureaus. Most important, a high-level Police Department report of December 1912 referred to the "excellent idea" of the regional bureaus, which had permitted "the annihilation of the revolutionary movements" and had increased interest in security policing among local police officials, especially provincial gendarmes. True, a Police Department report of November 1913 requested by Maklakov concluded that the regional chiefs' authority to check up on the local bureaus' informants was really only a "license to meddle, to play inspector." The report advocated dismantling all the regional bureaus, save those in border areas. Yet it was likely that the official who drafted this report, S. P. Beletskii, knew what Dzhunkovskii wanted to hear. In any event, a directive of 22 February 1914 implemented the recommendation, preserving the regional bureaus only in Siberia, the Caucasus, Turkestan, and Poland.[16]

Dzhunkovskii's ability to effect change did not always match his zeal. He felt uncomfortable about perlustration, the interception of private correspondence, but he failed to change the system, much less to abolish it. Indeed, many intercepted letters passed over his desk. He sought to justify his involvement by claiming that reading the letters permitted him to curb the number he passed on to the Police Department director. Predictably, he did not trust the director of the "black offices" where the letters were opened, M. G. Mardar'ev.[17]

Much of the public knew about the practice of perlustration. In 1911 and 1912 several correspondents, including some notable individuals, had alleged mail tampering in complaints to the Police Department. A secret investigation concluded in May 1912 blamed provincial gendarme officers for sloppy letter opening and urged that they employ more sophisticated methods. In late February 1913 a commission that Dzhunkovskii had set up agreed that perlustrators should receive better training, that mail should be intercepted and opened only in the black offices, and that the utmost caution should be exercised when admitting security policemen to view intercepted letters. The commission also decided that more black offices should be created, in Vilna, Riga, Belostok, Saratov, Nizhnii Novgorod, Rostov-na-Donu, Minsk, and Irkutsk, and at three border points. The plan was not implemented, probably for want of funding, but it is reasonable to presume also that Dzhunkovskii did not support it.[18]

Public concerns about perlustration remained. On 4 July 1913 *Utro Rossii* published an anonymous, well-informed, detailed exposé on the letter-interception system, apparently by a disgruntled former perlustrator, V. I. Krivosh. The article provoked a minor scandal in the press. Six months later, V. V. Musin-Pushkin sent a letter to his father-in-law, I. I. Vorontsov-Dashkov, the viceroy of the Caucasus, in a package containing sausage. "My wife will have informed you by cable about how this letter will reach you," he wrote, "but I still worry that Maklakov's minions may catch it, and so please cable me to say you have received the letter."[19] The censors did not intercept it.

Dzhunkovskii considered it essential to trim police expenditures. He reported to the emperor in July 1913 that he hoped the abolition of the provincial and regional security bureaus would save the treasury half a million rubles. He testified in 1917 that he had cut the budget of the St. Petersburg security bureau four times. Also in July 1913 the Police Department, citing high cost and undoubtedly with Dzhunkovskii's blessing, urged a reduction in the foreign travel of surveillants. Around the same time, Dzhunkovskii slashed the Police Department's budget for ensuring the safety of government officials and members of the imperial family. He also ordered police officials to write fewer and shorter telegrams. By August 1915, all these budgetary reductions had permitted Dzhunkovskii to amass a surplus of over 1.5 million rubles in secret funds. This was a significant proportion of all such funds disbursed in a given year—for example, 5.3 million rubles were disbursed in 1913.[20] It is unknown to what purpose he devoted the savings.

Dzhunkovskii later testified that his first priority upon entering his position had been to get rid of S. E. Vissarionov and Beletskii. The first to go was Vissarionov, though Dzhunkovskii "felt unable to dismiss him right away before having familiarized myself with the workings of the Police Department." In the fall he transferred Vissarionov to the censorship department and appointed as first vice-director of the Police Department M. K. Lerkhe, of whom he wrote: "irreproachably honest, a legal expert; by his nobility and decency he set himself apart from all other police officials."[21]

Dzhunkovskii also selected A. T. Vasil'ev as the vice-director in charge of security policing. Ironically, Vasil'ev had assisted M. I. Trusevich in the creation of the network of regional security bureaus over whose abolition he now presided. Dzhunkovskii apparently thought that Vasil'ev had left the Police Department in 1909 because he did not like its methods of operation, but it seems more likely that Trusevich had purposely replaced him with the more energetic A. M. Eremin. In any case, Dzhunkovskii admitted that Vasil'ev "turned out lazy, not very capable, not immune from using negative approaches in security policing, though quite a decent man."[22] The record is unclear on why Dzhunkovskii retained Vasil'ev in such a sensitive position, though it is safe to say that he always preferred a lazy and incompetent but "decent" official to a clever, hard-working, and proficient one whose uprightness was uncertain.

Removing Beletskii, who had good connections, required tact. The exact grounds and circumstances of his dismissal are uncertain. One version alleges that Belteskii had placed A. F. Koshko, the director of regular criminal investigation in Moscow, under close police surveillance for an unknown, presumably spurious reason. Another version suggests that an audit of the Police Department had uncovered an improper use of funds by Beletskii. Dzhunkovskii claimed that he had distrusted Beletskii from the first but also that he had disliked his approach to work: he had "a phenomenal capacity for work. He could work twenty-four hours a day, grasped very quickly the essence of any matter, could orient himself and adapt himself to any circumstances, but what he really did superbly . . . was pull the wool over people's eyes. . . . Twice weekly he reported to me for four hours at a time. Afterwards I felt completely exhausted. . . . He wore me down with all kinds of insignificant details, . . . trying to divert my attention from the most important matters."[23]

As important as Beletskii's annoying industriousness was their conflict over security policing. Dzhunkovskii recalled that Beletskii had been fired for his strong opposition to removing informants from the military. Beletskii himself testified that, beset by bureaucratic intriguers, he had complained to Maklakov and, finding him unsupportive, had voluntarily retired. When Maklakov offered him a governorship in either Olonetsk or Vologda province, both in the far north, Beletskii indignantly refused. On 30 January 1914, as a compromise, he was made a senator, the usual portion of retiring Police Department directors.[24]

Beletskii's replacement was Valentin Anatol'evich Brune de St.-Hyppolite, a Russian of French origin who had recently served as prosecutor for the Omsk judicial tribunal. Martynov described him as "tall, handsome, with auburn hair, very imposing and 'proper,' 'proper' to the extreme. So to speak the ideal type of prosecutor, but cold in his relations with others . . . a formalist to the marrow. . . . [His] face bore a perpetual air of, as it were, squeamishness about dealing with cases handled by gendarmes." Dzhunkovskii had known Brune de St.-Hyppolite previously as an assistant prosecutor for the Moscow district court and considered him a man of "crystalline purity, intelligent, businesslike, very well acquainted with security police affairs." Dzhunkovskii was pleased with his choice. "The regular reports of the Police Department director," he wrote, "were no longer a nightmare for me; they lasted not four hours but two, because Brune did not burden me with trivia and nonsense but reported only on essential matters. And in the Police Department one began to feel a new atmosphere, a sense of nobility." By February Dzhunkovskii "was able to breathe freely." The only problem was, according to three police officials, Brune did not much like police work in general and security policing in particular.[25]

Dzhunkovskii did not mind Brune's distaste for police work because he himself disliked security officers and nearly anyone involved directly with security policing. He did like A. A. Krasil'nikov, the director of the Paris security bureau, and tried unsuccessfully to increase his status in the service because of his "decency and honesty," but apparently no police officials considered him knowledgeable or energetic.[26]

Dzhunkovskii appreciated no other officials who were directly in charge of security policing, and he gave the ax to several. For example, during an inspection tour of three cities east of Moscow in March 1913, he concluded that the security chief of Nizhnii Novgorod, V. A. Strekalovskii, was a "typical *okhrannik*, . . . deft, cunning, inclined to provocation, smart, played close to the chest." Dzhunkovskii made sure to get rid of him as soon as possible. About the best he could say of a security officer was, in the case of Petr Pavlovich Martynov, the brother of Aleksandr Pavlovich Martynov, that he was "more decent" than the latter but "also sly, which was for the most part a characteristic of all security officers." As for Aleksandr, Dzhunkovskii "did not trust him much." He was "clever, but not sincere, cunning, intelligent, and egotistical. I knew he was ambitious, so I expected him to follow trends I was establishing." Although an inspection in May 1913 of Aleksandr's security bureau in Moscow found things in excellent order, in August 1913 Dzhunkovskii personally rebuked him for permitting a loud altercation to take place in one of his conspiratorial apartments.[27] Dzhunkovskii may have been looking for an excuse to remove him.

The next head to roll was M. F. von Koten's. In May 1913 it had come to light that he had waited over a month to notify A. P. Martynov that one of his informants had been residing in Moscow. Dzhunkovskii called this inaction "totally inadmissible" and demanded a detailed written justification. Von Koten explained cogently that he had considered it unnecessary to report on the matter so long as his informant had not entered into contact with revolutionary activists in Moscow, which might have led to the informant's arrest by the security police.[28]

The issue was apparently dropped, but Dzhunkovskii ordered the inspection of von Koten's security bureau in St. Petersburg in November 1913. This fishing expedition yielded enough ammunition to effect an ouster. The report detailed evidence of "far too many fruitless arrests" and "insufficient cross-verification" of informant reports, sins probably being committed at all the security bureaus, to say nothing of the gendarme stations. Thus, although the city governor, D. V. Drachevskii, warned that he could not guarantee the maintenance of security in the capital without von Koten, the security chief was offered a "promotion" to the headship of a provincial gendarme station, which he politely declined. He then retired voluntarily from the Gendarme Corps in January 1914 in order to develop Russia's counterintelligence capabilities for the imperial general staff. Von Koten's successor was P. K. Popov, until then the gendarme station chief in Sevastopol. Unskilled as a security policeman, Popov had begged Dzhunkovskii to pass him over, then had agreed to take the job, but only for three months. He remained in the new position for a year.[29]

In late January or early February 1914, Dzhunkovskii also dismissed A. V. Gerasimov, who was still a special agent of the interior ministry. Although Dzhunkovskii knew that Gerasimov had for some time received no assignments at all, he disliked his preference to dress in civilian clothes and thought it discredited the interior ministry to have a "provocateur so close by."[30]

Dzhunkovskii next looked to revamp the lines of authority of the police apparatus. He abhorred the way security policemen sometimes acted on their own initiative—for instance when Zavarzin took it upon himself to send a copy of a report requested by Dzhunkovskii to the Police Department. Dzhunkovskii also believed that the security police should be closely supervised by local administrative officials and not the other way around. Thus, he rescinded a directive ordering gendarmes to report on the workings of the provincial administration to the Police Department, a practice reminiscent of Nicholas I's use of the gendarmes as an elite superbureaucracy. One can imagine Dzhunkovskii's distaste for an office as powerful and seemingly unregulated as the Special Section. He probably would have removed its talented and highly competent director A. M. Eremin had not Beletskii already transferred him to the Finnish gendarme station in June 1913. Eremin's replacement, M. E. Broetskii, a former jurist with several years' experience as a prosecutor, had lately served as Eremin's assistant. Broetskii himself had warned Beletskii that an experienced gendarme officer would have made a better choice.[31]

Dzhunkovskii renamed the Special Section the ninth division, apparently in order to unify its structure and to eliminate its privileged position within the Police Department. In January 1914, the duties and responsibilities of all of the Police Department's nine divisions were spelled out. With nine offices (*otdeleniia*) and its mission delineated in an eleven-point roster, the ninth division remained by far the largest and most important unit in the Police Department. Its tasks included supervising all aspects of security policing in Russia and abroad, safeguarding all top secret Police Department documents, combating propaganda in the military, involvement with military espionage and counterespionage, managing communications with the foreign ministry, and ensuring the security of important persons and of large shipments of state funds. Of course, naming things is not the same as controlling them, and it is not surprising that the ninth division retained all of the importance and even quasi-autonomy of the Special Section. On 1 April 1915 Dzhunkovskii merged it into the sixth division. It thus grew even more powerful by gaining the sixth division's huge alphabetic registers and reference staff. In fall 1916 "Special Section" became the name of this combined entity.[32]

Sometime in early 1914, Dzhunkovskii authorized a revision of the instructions, directives, and regulations guiding security police work. This project was important, given the major changes in operations and organization he had wrought. Provincial gendarme officer V. E. Engbrekht worked on the task till November. The voluminous materials he compiled, essentially the reworking of existing instructions and the drafting of new ones, were sent for consideration to P. K. Popov. The manual on working with informants reiterated the ban on recruiting them in secondary schools and the military, but it also declared unequivocally that "the only totally reliable means for securing information about revolutionary activities is *vnutrenniaia agentura*," or the use of secret informants, and that security policemen "should never let pass a single chance that may offer even a remote hope of acquiring an informant or auxiliary agent." This manual was not distributed to security policemen, perhaps because it so vehemently underscored the centrality of informants to security policing.[33]

It seems that Popov then developed the materials further. He ultimately, in 1916, submitted to the interior minister two versions of an extensive handbook on security policing. It spelled out in minute detail nearly every aspect of the business, from where to recruit informants, including in prisons and secondary schools; to special strategies for plainclothes surveillance, such as the use of disguises, photographic albums, bicycles, and horses, as well as the impersonation of suspects. Despite all the work of Engbrekht and Popov, none of these efforts seems to have had any concrete impact.[34]

The only revised regulations actually adopted on Dzhunkovskii's watch were rules governing the induction of officers into the Gendarme Corps and tightening controls over the employment of surveillants and informants. The rules on hiring gendarme officers, affirmed on 24 December 1913, spelled out the subjects in which candidates required training, such as law, history, political economy, and geography. No mention was made of any aspects of security policing. But then, as Dzhunkovskii claimed, defending himself before an investigating commission in 1917, his "first idea was to cleanse the Gendarme Corps. I wanted to remove . . . all political tasks and create a special political section staffed by lawyers, prosecutors, and just decent people." Regulations laying out how to work with secret informants had no place in his mission, though in May 1914 the Police Department did establish rules requiring local security police officials to maintain, and periodically to furnish, careful records of when they hired informants and surveillants, how much they paid them, whom they watched over, and the like.[35] The point of these rules apparently was to tighten central control over the work with informants, not to improve its effectiveness.

SECURITY POLICE IN ACTION

Many security policemen loathed Dzhunkovskii. A. P. Martynov believed that Dzhunkovskii "hated security policing." A. I. Spiridovich called Dzhunkovskii "unprofessional." E. P. Florinskii, then gendarme chief in Perm since mid-1912, upon reading the decree abolishing regional bureaus, wrote, "they have given us a traitor for a chief; we are now blind and cannot work. We must now await a revolution." There is no denying that Dzhunkovskii's reforms, which one historian has recently called counterreforms, dismantled part of the security policing edifice built by S. V. Zubatov and M. I. Trusevich.[36]

Yet for all their apparent trepidation, security policemen maintained supremacy in the fight against revolutionary activism for two reasons. First, the main elements of security policing remained in place: the informant network, the squads of surveillants, the interception of mail, and the system's nerve center, at this time called the ninth division. Second, the revolutionary underground remained disorganized and demoralized. Not only were there fewer and fewer people involved in political activism: the number of administrative political exiles continued to diminish, to just over one thousand by late 1913, as did that of political *katorzhniki*, or hard-labor convicts, to just over two thousand by early January 1914.[37] And it was not because the security police were letting their guard down: security officers kept up their pressure on the remaining activists by arresting them in 1913 and 1914, mostly in Moscow and St. Petersburg.[38]

By May 1913 Socialist-Revolutionary activists were "fleeing from Moscow, fearing arrest," and the Social Democrats were "totally quiet." There was "no underground organization, just a few unconnected people."

By December only those Social Democrats eschewing illegal activities remained active in Moscow. Major arrests undermined the Social Democratic underground in such provincial towns as Kostroma and Ivanovo-Voznesensk, and even St. Petersburg was largely calm. The Bolshevik fraction's structure, while somewhat closer to the workers than that of the Mensheviks and possessing small-scale organizations in some of the industrialized parts of Ukraine, Poland, the Baltic region, and the Caucasus, weakened under the impact of continuous arrests. In a letter intercepted by police in April 1913, an unnamed Social Democratic activist admitted that within the Russian Empire it was "incredibly hard to build up the party."[39]

Hard-core revolutionary activists strained to preserve their significance. In December 1913, diverse Social Democrats created the St. Petersburg Interdistrict Committee of the Social Democratic Party, or Mezhraionka, to heal the rifts between Bolsheviks and Mensheviks while they remained committed to illegal, underground activity. By late 1914 it had some three hundred members. As police systematically closed the revolutionary underground's presses (the Social Democrats had only six such presses by 1913), they relied more heavily on hectographs, primitive copying machines of which the Social Democrats deployed twenty-six in 1912 and forty-six in 1913. In the face of harsh repression of legal revolutionary newspapers, including tens of thousands of rubles in fines, the editors undertook a massive fund-raising campaign. Six thousand collection drives yielded 44,000 rubles for *Pravda* alone. When these newspapers were shut down by court order for "systematic infraction of the press rules" and other crimes of "obvious party character" and "obviously harmful effects on the masses," the editors remained in business by changing the names of their publications—*Pravda* appeared under nine different titles. Meanwhile censorship officials and government prosecutors dutifully compiled detailed information proving that each successive publication was the same paper, with the same stationery, bank account, filing system, and branch in Moscow; the same price, layout, and list of subscribers; and even the same handwriting on each successive registration application.[40]

These shenanigans must have driven the straightforward Dzhunkovskii crazy. They certainly outraged N. A. Maklakov, who told the French newspaper *Le Temps* that "the police are like Offenbach's musketeers," sweeping comically into premises from which most copies of a censored issue had already vanished. He recommended that newspapers be sent to the censors three hours before they were to reach the post office for distribution; that if the issue was impounded and the newspaper fined by the court, then it would pay a fine, as well as two to three thousand rubles as a caution to cover future fines; that responsible editors be required to have a secondary education so the indigent or ignorant could not fulfill that important role; and that organizing collection drives for newspapers be prohibited. These proposed changes were rejected even by Maklakov's like-minded colleagues in the Council of Ministers as too radical. The final, more modest bill was leaked to the press and printed in *Novoe vremia* (New Times) in May 1913, then rejected by the Duma in the fall.[41]

In midsummer 1913 oil workers went on strike in Baku. Apparently fearing the growth of broad-based popular discontent, in late July Maklakov ordered security policemen to arrest political activists as soon as suspicion fell upon them, instead of waiting for their activity to develop more fully, as Zubatov had taught. From early August to as late as 3 October, reports from St. Petersburg warned that an empire-wide strike could break out at any time, since "among workers there is an opinion that all massive, large-scale strikes usually begin in Baku." On 14 October Maklakov recommended creating arbitration chambers in Moscow to mediate economic strikes. Toward the end of the month, however, the Council of Ministers worried that "the strike movement is assuming more and more a political coloring." Little wonder, then, that in late 1913 police officials created a special file on measures "to prevent a repetition of the revolution of 1905."[42]

In late July 1913, senior officials sought to defuse a brewing scandal. E. N. Shornikova-Iudkevich, the informant who had helped incriminate Social Democratic deputies in 1907, had at that time faced charges for her role in their alleged antigovernment plot but had avoided arrest thanks in part to police protection. In 1911, B. B. Brodskii asserted in an open letter to V. L. Burtsev's paper *Budushchee* (The Future) that he had been the key police informant in the affair; he was essentially claiming Shornikova-Iudkevich's role. His letter precipitated a 15 November 1911 Duma interpellation about these informants' roles in the 1907 case against Social Democratic Duma deputies. Then in summer 1913 Shornikova-Iudkevich, repeatedly snubbed by police officials, admitted her own role in an open letter.[43]

The revelation provoked an interministerial crisis. Sitting on the veranda facing the garden at V. N. Kokovtsov's official summer residence on a sultry August day, the Council of Ministers discussed her case. It would have been easy to give Shornikova-Iudkevich a false passport and money enough to emigrate to the United States, as Beletskii proposed. Yet Kokovtsov hesitated, worrying that he would be obliged to justify any scandalous government policy before the Duma. I. G. Shcheglovitov warned that if Maklakov refused to cover up the affair, the justice ministry would be forced to bring her to trial. Dzhunkovskii feared that "in America she would be unmasked by Burtsev, leading to more scandals." Krivoshein and others considered it "unseemly for the government to buy off agents of the Police Department." With the emperor's approval, a closed session of the Senate tried Shornikova-Iudkevich and exonerated her because she had acted under orders from the police. The Police Department gave her 1,800 rubles, and she vanished. A majority in the Duma, defending the police's right to employ informants, blocked a Social Democratic interpellation.[44] The government had averted a major scandal.

Antigovernment rhetoric in Duma speeches reached its zenith in early 1913. In December 1912 thirty-two members of the Duma had submitted to Kokovtsov a draft bill on the inviolability of the person, which Justice Minister Shcheglovitov rightly considered a violation of Russia's rules of parliamentary procedure, since the government had already submitted a bill on the same subject. He also considered unacceptable several provisions of the Duma's bill, including the abolition of administrative punishments, of temporary detention without a court order, and of the Pale of Settlement. The Council of Ministers concurred. The failure to reach an agreement on the matter prompted the Duma to declare in February 1913, during the debate on the interior ministry's budget, that the "continuing use of exceptional measures" was stirring within the population "a legitimate feeling of revolt" and that the interior ministry "prevents the establishment of legal order in Russia and destroys in the population respect for law and authority, and thus strengthens the feeling of opposition."[45]

The Police Department knew that revolutionaries in the Duma used the body as a staging ground for antigovernment activity. In February 1913, for example, G. I. Petrovskii, a Bolshevik Duma deputy, harbored the Bolshevik leader Ia. M. Sverdlov in his apartment, where he was arrested. Electors of the workers' curia helped coordinate the interaction of factory workers and Duma deputies of the Social Democratic Party, and the Bolshevik Duma fraction actively coordinated illegal Bolshevik activities inside the Russian Empire.[46]

In October 1913, reacting to antigovernment rhetoric in the Duma, Interior Minister Maklakov asked the emperor to authorize the government to warn the Duma that it was treading "an errant path; its job is to work with the emperor, not to promote revolution." Maklakov admitted that such a measure could "cause an explosion" necessitating the dissolution of the Duma and requiring that St. Petersburg and Moscow be placed in a state of extraordinary security. Nicholas not only approved the measure, he proposed reducing the Duma to a consultative assembly. Alas for Nicholas, as Maklakov confessed in a letter of 22 October, although the ministers approved making preparations to thwart unrest should it arise, the "overwhelming" majority so opposed issuing a warning to the Duma that Maklakov realized he dared not bring up the question of altering the Duma's constitution.[47]

Nicholas and Maklakov apparently contemplated what effectively would have amounted to a revolutionary act, but they found no support among the other ministers. Indeed, Maklakov was largely isolated in the Council of Ministers. He often refused to compromise, grew nervous and flustered, then fell prey to clever torment by spiteful colleagues. Even Shcheglovitov, who generally shared Maklakov's conservative views, would then look upon the agitated minister with disapproval.[48] Clearly many of Russia's most powerful officials remained committed to constitutionalism, the rule of law, the separation of powers, and a limited monarchy.

Dzhunkovskii's final major act in regard to the security police concerned the Duma. He later claimed he had learned that R. V. Malinovskii was playing a double role from Brune de St.-Hyppolite, "a disinterested person of crystalline purity." Stunned by the bombshell, Dzhunkovskii "without hesitating" ordered P. K. Popov to persuade Malinovskii to resign from the Duma, a task Popov quickly accomplished "with the tact characteristic of him." Martynov and Beletskii, by contrast, asserted that Dzhunkovskii had abetted Malinovskii's election to the Duma. As Martynov recalled, Dzhunkovskii had told him (Martynov) that "everything possible will be done." Martynov also claimed that Dzhunkovskii demanded that Martynov take personal responsibility in spring 1914 for removing Malinovskii from the Duma. Martynov argued that solving the problem depended entirely on how much money Dzhunkovskii was willing to offer Malinovskii. Martynov suggested ten thousand rubles; Dzhunkovskii proposed five thousand. Martynov met with Malinovskii at the last tram station near Khodynka Field, in Moscow's northwestern suburbs. They walked near each other for half a *versta,* or quarter of a mile, then sat together in the grass and hatched a plan: Malinovskii would propose an extremist resolution that most members of the Social Democratic fraction would reject, giving him an excuse to quit the Duma in consternation.[49]

The version of events supplied by Martynov and Beletskii seems credible for two reasons. First, it is highly unlikely that Beletskii would have been willing to run the risk of senior administrative officials in Moscow discovering and revealing to the public or to the prosecutor's office information about Malinovskii's criminal past, the more so because Dzhunkovskii was a direct subordinate of the interior ministry and had to obey its dictates. Second, as much as Dzhunkovskii preferred Popov to Martynov, he could have had no doubt about which was the more competent and experienced security officer and which knew Malinovskii more intimately.

Why, then, did Dzhunkovskii wait so long to remove the informant from the Duma? Perhaps Beletskii had managed to convince him that Malinovskii's presence in the Duma was invaluable. It is also possible that Dzhunkovskii did not consider himself sufficiently powerful or competent to take on the task so long as Beletskii remained at his post. In any event, it was a long time even from Brune's appointment in early February 1914 to Malinovskii's fiery speech on 22 April, which entailed his suspension, along with that of twenty other deputies, from fifteen meetings of the general assembly of the Duma. On 8 May Malinovskii resigned as deputy and left the country.[50]

How did Malinovskii's departure influence the security police and the Bolshevik organization? Beletskii later claimed that he had been an extremely valuable informant because he had shed more light on the revolutionary underground than any other police agent. A postrevolutionary investigation of his activities indeed revealed that from 5 July 1910 to 19

September 1913 he submitted eighty-eight reports on his Social Democratic comrades, causing serious harm to the Russian bureau of the party's central committee and to its Moscow organization. His work had led to the arrest of several members of the central committee, including G. K. Ordzhonikidze, I. V. Stalin, Ia. M. Sverdlov, and F. I. Goloshchekin. According to Spiridovich, without Malinovskii the security police were unable to fathom the activities of the Bolsheviks at the center of their organization.[51]

Senior Bolsheviks had recognized that an informant had been operating at the highest party level, and Malinovskii's loyalty had occasionally fallen under suspicion. His call for a popular uprising in April 1914 and especially his inexplicable desertion of the Duma precipitated a flood of accusations in the non-Bolshevik press and threatened to undermine the party's prestige in the way that Azef's exposure had five years earlier undermined the Socialist-Revolutionary Party. Indeed, Ralph Carter Elwood has argued in a clever and careful analysis of the evidence that Dzhunkovskii himself threw suspicion on Malinovskii for this very purpose. Dzhunkovskii may have been more beguiling than his overt persona would suggest,[52] though a machination of this caliber seems rather beyond his capacities or inclinations.

Malinovskii's first stop after he quit St. Petersburg and visited relatives in Warsaw was Lenin's residence in Poronino, Galicia. After they engaged in long discussions, apparently on 15 May, Lenin spent a sleepless night pacing back and forth. On 25 May, *Pravda* printed a statement from Malinovskii asserting he had left the Duma for personal reasons but remained a Bolshevik. That summer, Lenin undertook an "investigation," in collaboration with J. S. Haniecki and G. E. Zinov'ev, that confirmed "Malinovskii's political honesty." According to one scholar, Lenin was so preoccupied with the scandal that the strikes of July 1914 caught him entirely off guard. Upon returning to Russia in 1917, Lenin learned the truth about Malinovskii's treason to the party. "What a swine," he said to Zinov'ev. "He really put one over on us. The traitor! Shooting is too good for him." Still, in May 1918, Lenin continued to insist that "with one hand" Malinovskii "had sent to *katorga* and death dozens and dozens of the best activists of Bolshevism," yet he insisted that "with the other hand he had been obliged to prepare tens of thousands of new Bolsheviks by means of the legal press." The number of Bolsheviks on the eve of the war was probably around ten thousand, though it may have been as many as thirty thousand. The Menshevik fraction was even weaker, and its leaders' harsh invective against Malinosvkii and the Bolsheviks apparently only further undermined their support among industrial workers.[53] The war ravaged both fractions of the Social Democratic Party.

In late June 1914 a major strike broke out, again in Baku. On 3 July a scuffle between police and workers at the Putilov steel factory left fifty people wounded (the labor press claimed that two workers had been killed; Dzhunkovskii apparently denied it). The event touched off major labor unrest. Within a week 150,000 workers were on strike each day in St. Petersburg. Barricades went up. The security police accurately reported that the revolutionary newspapers were serving as centers of the unrest, so within days the major revolutionary newspapers were temporarily suspended by court order. On the 10th, Dzhunkovskii and Brune arrived in Baku to break the strike. They confiscated a strike fund of three hundred thousand rubles and oversaw an extensive mobilization of troops and police in the city. The strike soon collapsed.[54]

Overall, nearly two million workers struck in the Russian Empire in the first seven months of 1914, exceeding by 60 percent the number in 1913. Moreover, the proportion of strikes that were political allegedly increased from 63.3 percent in 1913 to 79.9 percent in 1914. Although the concept of a political strike was imprecise, the workers' movement did become considerably more politicized in the aftermath of Lena. Even so, it cannot be persuasively argued that these strikes were a sign of critical instability or weakness specific to imperial Russia. Labor unrest was endemic to nearly all of Europe during the years before the First World War. In Russia, moreover, the countryside was relatively quiet after the good harvest of 1913, the armed forces remained loyal, and the revolutionary parties had been all but incapacitated. On nearly every day from 14 to 25 July, P. K. Popov could report to Dzhunkovskii, still in Baku, that St. Petersburg was "completely calm" except for a few an anti-German and anti-Austrian demonstrations and disorders. Elsewhere in the empire, mostly in border towns, security policemen reported similar actions.[55] Officialdom fretted lest these patriotic manifestations get out of hand.

POLICE AND PUBLIC BEFORE THE FIRST WORLD WAR

Tensions between the educated public and the government increased in 1913 and 1914. Among important issues were the treatment of political moderates, the Beilis trial, and the banning of demonstrations commemorating the centennial of Ukrainian poet T. G. Shevchenko's birth.

Many moderate political and social activists felt alienated from the government. The lack of public involvement in the tercentenary celebrations in February 1913 was a manifestation of this alienation. Although the Octobrists faced no police repression—they gathered regularly at Fontanka 32, a few doors down from the Police Department—a fear that the government was leading Russia to social upheaval and that the educated public would abandon the Octobrists for the Progressists and Kadets drove A. I. Guchkov firmly into the opposition, thus dividing and weakening the party.[56]

The Kadets, already a bulwark of the opposition, faced police harassment nearly every time they sought to convoke a general meeting. Just as with the Social Democrats, only their Duma deputies could gather with impunity. Thus, in late May 1913 von Koten ordered the expulsion from informal Kadet gatherings in St. Petersburg of anyone who was not a member of the Duma. In early October Kadets had to meet in several different apartments successively in order to avoid police incursions, and in each apartment members of the jubilee committee of the newspaper *Russkie vedomosti* were present to provide cover.[57]

By spring 1914, even most of the contributors to the moderately conservative daily *Novoe vremia* had given up hope in the government. Both the Kadets and the Octobrists noted in their private meetings a leftward shift in public opinion and growing dissatisfaction with the government. In this context leaders of the two parties tentatively considered joining forces, in part because both were being outflanked by the new Progressist Party, whose leaders eagerly sought to develop ties to the revolutionary parties.[58]

Police and other administrative officials at times seemed overwhelmed by the extent of civic activism. In addition to contending with challenges from the press, the Duma, the labor movement, and political parties, the government faced massive growth in voluntary associations. The number of public policy and professional congresses held in Russia peaked in summer 1913, with twelve occurring in Kiev alone. The participants in these congresses, which were gradually extending their purview to include a wide variety of social and political issues (often only tenuously linked to the actual programs at hand) managed by the eve of the First World War to create a sort of "parliament of public opinion," in the words of Joseph Bradley, that was destined to rival the "ineffectual Duma" as a forum for expressing the public will and resolving public issues. The extent of their expansion makes one wonder whether the government could have hoped to continue to circumscribe their activities without adopting harsh new repressive measures.[59]

Police officials grew more concerned with voluntary associations as intelligence reports filed by Beletskii in March and December 1913 warned that Masons were using the associations as front organizations. Two further reports, prepared by P. K. Popov in March 1914 and by L. A. Rataev a month later, sketched a menacing picture of interlocking nongovernmental organizations with Masonic ties across three continents, prompting Brune de St.-Hyppolite, on 24 May, to issue to security policemen a directive that deserves to be quoted extensively:

> Our information indicates that efforts are underway to organize a secret Masonic order, which has developed significantly in Europe and America over the last decade. Its immediate goal is a struggle against "superstition" and "arbitrariness," by which is meant struggle against the officially reigning church and against the monarchical authority. The long-term goal is the establishment of a "Holy Empire," or the Kingdom of Reason, Truth and Righteousness. Freemasonry seeks to overthrow the existing social and political orders

in European states, to stamp out nationalism and Christianity, and to destroy national armies. . . . It has been persistently and steadfastly developing in the [Russian] Empire under the banner of all kinds of scientifico-philosophical, occult, and other analogous voluntary associations. . . . Their leaders act insidiously, pretending to support the government, while inconspicuously developing in their members a spirit of opposition and gradually inculcating in them Masonic ideas. . . . Please investigate such voluntary associations with this in mind and report to the Police Department.

The directive, which incorporated a detailed list of suspect associations, was sent to ninety-eight recipients, including all the gendarme stations and security bureaus. Over the course of more than a year, eighty-five of the recipients responded, though none of them had anything significant to report.[60]

Were Russia's voluntary associations riddled with Masonic activists? It is unclear, though it does seem that the security police were unaware of an important aspect of the Masons' endeavors. Recent scholarship indicates that in Moscow at the end of February 1914 a Masonic informational committee sprang up to coordinate the activities of opposition parties from the Octobrists to the Social Democrats. In March I. I. Skvortsov-Stepanov, a leading Bolshevik who was also a Mason, contacted Lenin on behalf of A. I. Konovalov, the committee's "supreme coordinator." Lenin was apparently interested, but only because he hoped to extract money from the committee. The Mensheviks found it easier to work with the committee's organizers, although N. S. Chkheidze, a Mason, admitted that "we had trouble agreeing" with the committee's organizers since "the Masons advocated a broad-based organization and frowned on violent action."[61]

One of Martynov's informants reported in September 1914 that various leftist groups were trying to coalesce into something called the *konvent* (from the French *Convention* of 1792–1795); the informant, named Mukhin, had no idea that this was an ultrasecretive organization formed in summer 1912 by N. V. Nekrasov and other leading Masons.[62] The obvious conclusion is that the efficiency of the Russian security police drove opposition activists to adopt forms of conspiratorial action that the established parties could only dream about and that made this new element of the opposition almost completely impervious to police incursion.

The biggest cause of public recrimination against the government in this period was the Beilis affair. It all began in Kiev in August 1911, when the police, mystified as to who had killed a schoolboy, Andrei Iushchinskii, three months before, arrested a Jew, M. M. Beilis, with a most tenuous connection to the crime in order to appear to wrap up the case before the emperor's impending visit. The murder of Stolypin by a Jew a few days later gave rise to powerful anti-Semitic rumors. Some people made the bizarre claim that the murder stemmed from a supposedly Jewish need for the blood of a Christian for ritualistic purposes. Rightist activists, who were especially prominent in Kiev, demanded a Jewish sacrifice. True, Kurlov ordered Kiev governor A. F. Girs to take the most decisive measures to prevent anti-Jewish violence, but all in all what ensued was a most sordid affair.[63]

Police officials intrigued against A. D. Margolin, a defense attorney. Margolin had allegedly bribed witnesses, news of which the police leaked. To cover up an amorous tryst, Margolin was forced to admit having been alone with Vera Cherberiak, a prosecution witness and the mother of a boy who had played with Iushchinskii. Other radical defense attorneys, including A. F. Kerenskii, were sentenced to several months in prison for publicly accusing the regime of staging the trial for political purposes. Meanwhile, rumor had it that the Police Department had paid four thousand rubles to one expert witness.[64]

The trial began on 25 September 1913. Two days later, and several more times over the next two weeks, N. A. Maklakov cabled the governors in Kiev and adjacent provinces, ordering them "to take all measures" to prevent demonstrations, agitation, disorders, and anti-Jewish violence. "Even the smallest outburst of intense violence, even if it is quickly suppressed," he warned, "will be held by me personally against the local police authorities." Maklakov later admitted that he had ordered the bringing in of surveillants from around the empire to keep strict watch over the jurors, perhaps also to maintain public tranquility. Beletskii corroborated this admission and further testified that interior ministry officials had urged prosecutors to cooperate fully with the police and gendarmes.[65]

The press roundly criticized the government and suffered for its coverage of the trial. Six editors were arrested and eight were brought to trial; thirty-six newspapers were confiscated and three were shut down; and forty-three periodicals had to pay fines worth 10,050 rubles. Among those faced with a lawsuit for "intentionally spreading false rumors encouraging hostile attitudes toward the government" was V. A. Maklakov, the interior minister's brother. Popular unrest spread across the empire. Strikes rocked the institutions of higher learning in St. Petersburg in the first days of October. Senior officials were worried. Beletskii, citing statistics on the use of troops to quell civil disorders, reported on 15 October that such recourse would remain necessary. On 30 October a jury found Beilis not guilty of murder, yet it concluded that the murder had been ritualistic in nature.[66]

It did not help the government's public image when Nicholas dismissed Prime Minister Kokovtsov on 30 January 1914 and replaced him with the aged I. L. Goremykin, who was then seventy-five years old. According to A. Ia. Avrekh, Nicholas disliked Kokovtsov's commitment to the rule of law "while the tsar was moving more and more toward the idea of patrimonial government." Kokovtsov was also up against a powerful coalition of courtiers and state counselors, including Maklakov, Prince V. P. Meshcherskii, Grigorii Rasputin, E. V. Bogdanovich, and S. Iu. Witte. Also important, the powerful agriculture minister, A. V. Krivoshein, pressed for the appointment of Goremykin, whom he believed he could manipulate. He hoped to be the real force behind the chair, but without any legal responsibility. Krivoshein apparently hoped for a resolution of tensions between society and the government. In a famous speech in July 1913 in Kiev, the capital of Ukraine, he had lamented the "deplorable division between the government and the public." Eventually, he said hopefully, "it should not be 'us and them' but only 'us.'"[67]

It was, however, precisely in regard to Ukraine that the government adopted its most unpopular policy of the first half of 1914: the ban on mass celebrations on the 25 February 1914 centennial of T. G. Shevchenko's birth. The radical defense attorney O. O. Gruzenberg called the policy "outrageous." Lenin exulted at "such a splendid, excellent, felicitous to a rare degree, and successful measure from the point of view of agitation against the government. One cannot imagine better agitation."[68]

The Duma interpellated both Goremykin and Maklakov over the ban. Dzhunkovskii, who had borne full responsibility for the policy, defended it before the legislators. His version of the events, which is corroborated by official correspondence and press reports, satisfied the Duma's majority, which withdrew the interpellation. On 20 February Dzhunkovskii explicitly authorized private indoor commemorations of Shevchenko but, citing the rules of 4 March 1906, prohibited public ones.[69]

Ironically, several towns did receive permission to rename streets, collect funds, erect monuments and commemorative plaques, and put on festivities in honor of Shevchenko. The key resistance to such actions came from Russian nationalists in Ukraine itself. Administrative officials there warned that Ukrainian nationalists were preparing mass demonstrations with a large quantity of yellow and light blue banners, the emblem of the future independent Ukraine, to promote territorial separatism. Numerous Russian nationalist organizations, meanwhile, appealed to the interior minister to ban *all* commemorations, and they planned to stage counterdemonstrations. For Dzhunkovskii, the danger of violent clashes provided the most valid justification of his ministry's policy. Yet notwithstanding the broader concerns for state and public security, the administrative detention of eighty-nine Ukrainian nationalists in Kiev alone, for periods ranging from three days to three months, merely because they had sung the Orthodox hymn *Vechnaia pamiat'* (Eternal Memory), only further worsened public sentiment toward the government.[70]

■ ■ ■

Dzhunkovskii was undoubtedly a well-meaning official. He hoped to clean up the Police Department and to rein in the security police in particular. The overall police budget grew smaller, Zubatov's network of semiautonomous security bureaus disappeared, Trusevich's regional bureaus were mostly dismantled, uniformed provincial gendarme officers bore a heavier burden of security policing, secret police informants no longer penetrated high schools and military units, and key security policemen whom Dzhunkovskii found untrustworthy or "too independent" retired from the service. Yet Dzhunkovskii seems to have had failed to inculcate much respect for the gendarme uniform, win public trust for his ministry, improve relations between the security police and the regular civilian administration, and root out unsavory methods in the secretive recesses of the Police Department, even though those recesses now bore the name "ninth division" instead of "Special Section." Most vital for this study, however, is the question of whether Dzhunkovskii's reforms undermined the government's ability to defend itself against revolutionary activism during the First World War.

■ The first months of 1914 had witnessed an intensification of political discord. Then suddenly war intervened, drawing the elites together in a short-lived paroxysm of patriotic fervor. A. S. Lukomskii, a senior military official, believed "the whole population was becoming as one and in a general excess of emotion wanted to throw itself upon the enemy." The optimism of senior officials is not hard to understand. The Duma, which met on 8 August, cheerfully voted to meet that day only. "We are all one," P. N. Miliukov exulted from the rostrum. Nearly the whole of civil society, including much of the left and a pleiad of major writers, echoed the Kadet leader. Immediately following the declaration of war, moreover, Petrograd witnessed scarcely any antiwar agitation or unrest. As was often the case, however, the pessimistic policeman, in this case Interior Minister N. A. Maklakov, had a clearer long-term perspective. He warned: "War cannot be popular among the broad masses of the people who are more receptive to ideas of revolution than of victory over Germany."[1]

TIGHTENED SECURITY IN WARTIME RUSSIA

Russia's troops began to mobilize on 16 July. The First World War began three days later. Over the previous several days the government had begun instituting myriad restrictions on public life. The police apparatus, its powers gradually augmented and its resources soon stretched to the limit, bore the primary responsibility for imposing this bureaucratic straitjacket.

On 12 July the government had banned the publishing of information on eighteen topics relating to military issues, including foreign espionage and the capture, trial, and sentencing of foreign spies. On 20 July most of the empire's eastern and southern provinces, twenty-six in all, including Petrograd province, fell once again under martial law, and military commanders were empowered, "in case of necessity for military success . . . to forbid . . . any assemblies whatever and temporarily to stop periodical publications."

That same day, by means of Article 87, the government issued temporary regulations on military censorship, dramatically expanding administrative control over speech, the press, and private correspondence.[2]

In the theaters of war this control was nearly absolute. Elsewhere the principal change consisted of the promulgation of extensive lists of topics not to be discussed in either the press or public speeches. The forbidden topics included Russia's external security, transportation and communication lines, armaments, and the location and movement of troops. Military censors, who were agents of the interior ministry, subsequently added many more prohibitions. It became unlawful to mention the emperor or the Council of Ministers when they were discussing military matters, to speculate publicly about future battle plans, and even to cite meteorological data.[3]

The temporary regulations, though never formally ratified by the Duma, remained in force until 1917. On 21 July 1914, Maklakov ordered all governors to nurture the patriotic sentiments of the population but "to crush and annihilate" any seditious activity. Finally, a state of extraordinary security was established on 24 July in all provinces not under martial law or a state of siege *(osadnoe polozhenie)*.[4]

Administrative officialdom's power thus expanded enormously in scope, yet its responsibilities increased even more. The new demands ranged from the trivial (that Russian words should be used whenever possible in official documents—an incident was to be called not an *intsident,* but a *sobytie)* to the greatly burdensome. The Police Department reported in December 1914 on its contributions to the war effort. The department was setting up draft stations; tightening control over internal and external passports; enhancing the protection of civilian government institutions; supervising the repair of roads and bridges and the transfer of private aircraft to military jurisdiction; combating espionage; and enforcing the ban on alcohol and the prohibition on importing arms, explosives, and homing pigeons. In most of these cases the police had to report to local military authorities. Subsequent events and orders required the police to oversee, inter alia, the granting of free railroad passes to relatives of combatants and the evacuation of government institutions from territory surrendered to the enemy. Some of the war-related activities of the security police plumbed the depths of triviality, as when Martynov ordered regular policemen to seize from Caucasian fruitmongers orange crates sporting a picture of a Turkish general.[5]

Despite this extra burden, the size of the Police Department's staff decreased in real terms: the draft of 112 men by the military offset the increase in the number of employees from 387 at the start of the war to 406 a year later. Police officials at every level were subject to conscription. By May 1916 two-thirds of interior ministry employees had been drafted. Land captains often had to bear responsibility for three wards *(uchastki)* instead of the usual single ward. Security policing suffered too. When the war began, many gendarme officers asked for a transfer to the regular army. According to one, "it became an epidemic." As early as 31 July 1914 the commander of the Gendarme Corps had recommended rehiring retired gendarme officers, and in December senior police officials proposed training newly hired gendarme officers for security policing duties. Despite the promise of an extra one hundred rubles per month, the appeal met with little success.[6]

In what was probably an isolated incident, on 21 July at the railroad station in Kovno gendarme officer A. D. Vedeniapin, apparently suffering from stress and fatigue, fatally shot himself. He had been chief of the railroad gendarme station in Verzhbolov (Virbalis), Lithuania, since 1907. By mid-1916 some one hundred gendarme officers had joined military counterespionage units, and many others had apparently abandoned domestic intelligence gathering in favor of higher-paid administrative jobs. By December 1916 it had become difficult to find enough officers specializing in surveillance, even though the total number of gendarmes grew from 14,306 in mid-1914 to 15,718 in fall 1916, an increase of nearly 10 percent (compared to 16 percent growth from 1907 to 1914). Among security policemen, only members of the emperor's personal security service were spared conscription.[7]

Police informants were also subject to the draft. Martynov alone lost twelve of them by December 1915. After putting up some resistance, the war ministry agreed to grant exemptions for individual informants. The archives contain a few lists of petitions to recall "the most essential" informants from military service, yet it seems few exemptions were granted.[8]

The Police Department's budget increased from 4.5 million rubles in 1914 to only 4.9 million in 1916, at a rate far less than that of inflation, and the money allotted to the security police was a fraction of the 58 million rubles projected to be spent on the regular police across the Russian Empire in 1917. The expenditures for security policing accounted for just over 70 percent of the total Police Department budget in these years, or 3.3 million rubles in 1914, nearly 10 percent of which went to the Petrograd security bureau. Of the 3.3 million, according to P. E. Shchegolev's calculations, informants and conspiratorial apartments consumed approximately 600,000, or 18 percent. The security police institutions in the two imperial capitals took about 20 percent of that 600,000, or 130,000 rubles. The smaller institutions spent far less money for informants; eighteen received less than 3,000 rubles; thirty-three between 3,000 and 8,000; and only ten more than 8,000. Also included in the 3.3 million were 323,549 rubles disbursed to the security brigade and the central surveillance brigade, both stationed in Petrograd and used for protecting important people.[9]

In order to coordinate and digest the huge flow of domestic intelligence, on 31 December 1914 V. N. Voeikov, the court commandant, created a central surveillance clearinghouse *(Osobyi otdel)* that might be called the emperor's information bureau. Located at 18 Moika Embankment and headed by V. V. Ratko, an old Zubatovite, it received detailed intelligence reports from all major security institutions, then systematized the material and prepared, every few days, special reports for the emperor.[10]

Cooperation with the military intelligence and counterintelligence services probably constituted the security police force's most important intermural contribution to the war effort. The security bureau in Paris played an active role. Henri Bint and Albert Sambain, the front men for its European operations, along with A. V. Ergardt and other employees, conducted espionage in the Germanic countries, to a large extent by means of Swiss-German operatives. Cryptographers in the Special Section placed their expertise at the service of military intelligence, lists of foreign subjects suspected of espionage were compiled, and a huge number of allegations of espionage were investigated. A decree on civilian preparations for war that came into force on 14 July 1914 required gendarme and regular police officers to arrest suspected spies and to recommend their administrative exile, a function the counterespionage bureaus exercised in the frontal areas. Three orders of mid- to late 1915 and early 1916 spelled out how the security police and the counterespionage bureaus should more effectively cooperate. Despite all these efforts, A. G. Shliapnikov recalled, among industrial workers there were widespread rumors of security police connivance with German military intelligence.[11]

Meanwhile, the military counterintelligence services expanded, opening offices at General Headquarters, at the fronts, in all the military districts and armies, and (in September 1915) in the navy. Yet they apparently harassed many innocent people and overstepped the bounds of their main tasks by combating speculation, inflation, and political propaganda. N. S. Batiushin, who headed counterintelligence for the northern front, gradually devoted all his energies to these tasks and neglected counterintelligence altogether. "As a rule," wrote A. T. Vasil'ev, "the military authorities showed a certain jealousy of the police," which was probably reinforced by their fear of a plot, allegedly emanating from the interior ministry, that aimed at wresting control of counterespionage from the military. L. S. Iakovlev has concluded that the counterespionage bureaus were quite effective overall; N. V. Grekov has reached the opposite conclusion.[12]

The military authorities gradually intervened in more and more aspects of Russia's administrative and even economic life, ordering the exile of huge masses of people; the evacuation and confiscation of industrial enterprises; and the regulation and restriction of economic, publicistic, and cultural activity. The supreme commander enjoyed nearly absolute authority in the entire military theater. By summer 1915 the cabinet ministers felt helpless. In July the interior minister, noting that governors were flooding his office with complaints, quipped, "Everyone is giving orders, beginning with any enterprising ensign." At the same time, he lamented, "the Interior

Ministry is responsible for maintaining order" and was inevitably blamed for all administrative problems. Kurlov rightly argued that the military's meddling in civilian affairs "had a large role to play in the general breakdown of the state."[13]

COUNTERREVOLUTIONARY OPERATIONS

The security police still concentrated most of their energy on repressing revolutionary activists. Time and again they routed the hard-core revolutionaries. During the war, according to one reckoning, they beset the Social Democratic (mostly Bolshevik) organizations in Moscow twenty-six times and those in Petrograd thirty-three times. In Petrograd they arrested some 600 party leaders and veteran activists, miscellaneous party workers, thousands of petty agitators, and two-thirds of the 101 members of the ten successive slates of the city party committee.[14]

The party organization in Petrograd, whose membership plummeted from six thousand in early 1914 to perhaps just over one hundred by November, collapsed. Efforts to reinstate party operations in Moscow failed. Party activists continually rebuilt their organizations, but in the face of methodical police repression, they failed to provoke any mass actions in the imperial capitals before early 1917. The security police repeatedly launched arrests against Social Democrats in other parts of the empire too, including Kiev, Ekaterinoslav, Khar'kov, and Irkutsk, and also sought to accentuate the divisions between the Bolsheviks and the Mensheviks. On 16 September 1914 Brune advised instructing police informants "steadfastly and persistently" to oppose "any organizational merger whatsoever" of the various Social Democratic currents and "especially . . . the unification of Bolsheviks and Mensheviks." Spiridovich argued that all such efforts of the police, both repressive and broadly tactical, put an end to any systematic activity in Russia by the Bolsheviks during the monarchical period. Security police reports on the Socialist-Revolutionaries were no less sanguine. Fallout from the Azef affair, along with tensions over how to react to the war, had split party activists, while the numerous arrests had undermined all their efforts to build up their organization. By late 1916 a Police Department report claimed proudly that "in Russia such [a party] does not exist."[15]

During the war the security police combated the Social Democrats more energetically than they did the Socialist-Revolutionaries. Available statistical data indicates, for example, that in 1915 Martynov ordered the arrest of 441 people, including 210 Social Democrats and only 29 Socialist-Revolutionaries, and that in early 1916 the Petrograd security bureau fielded 14 informants among the Socialist-Revolutionaries and 27 among the Social Democrats. The police had grown less anxious about the Socialist-Revolutionary Party not only because it had declined in strength but, more important, because it apparently had abandoned its program of terror. Among similar reports, one may read A. A. Krasil'nikov's December 1915 assurance that "for now terrorist acts are unlikely," since the party leadership advocated combating the "foreign enemy first, then the internal enemy."[16]

The most sensational antirevolutionary operation of the war involved the arrest of the five Bolshevik Duma deputies in early November 1914. Police intelligence, corroborated later by A. E. Badaev, indicated that they planned to meet with other party activists to prepare to launch an underground periodical and to seek ways to stir up worker protests. A. P. Martynov's agent A. S. Romanov ("Pelageia") and P. K. Popov's agent V. E. Shurkanov ("Limonin") revealed details about the planned meeting, including its location, the home of Iu. G. Gavrilova in Ozerki, Finland, a suburb of Petrograd. Senior officials in the government and at headquarters followed the developments closely. A. V. Krivoshein called the matter "of great importance" but "very delicate."[17]

On 4 November police and gendarmes burst in on the secret meeting of the Bolshevik Duma deputies and six other party activists. The police got a break of sorts when Gavrilova's husband repudiated their claim that they had gathered to celebrate the couple's eighth wedding anniversary. While the other party members meeting with them were detained, the deputies were released and proceeded to destroy incriminating materials. Several days later, however, the deputies also landed in jail. Shcheglovitov had interpreted the statutes of the Duma to allow for the arrest of its deputies without its permission when the body was not in session. Popov reported on 12 November that apart from a relatively small number of industrial workers and students, few people reacted strongly to the raid or the arrests.[18]

Senior officials debated strenuously whether to try these revolutionaries in a regular or a military court. Popov urged the former, citing fears of provoking unrest and the greater importance of curtailing revolutionary activism than punishing revolutionaries. "Since internal calm is the most important goal," he wrote, "it would be most consistent with the government's policy to use repression only when absolutely necessary." In contrast, Justice Minister I. G. Shcheglovitov, fearing bad publicity for his ministry, argued that since Ozerki was under martial law, the prisoners had to be tried in a military court. But the military court probably would have sentenced the activists to death, and the senior military authorities, Dzhunkovskii, various courtiers, and Nicholas himself, who closely monitored the case's progress, loathed the prospect of making martyrs of them. The defendants therefore appeared before a civilian court, which exiled them to the Turukhansk region in eastern Siberia. Deprived of their daily newspaper and their Duma fraction, the Bolsheviks lost their ability to organize underground revolutionary activity inside the Russian Empire.[19]

The experiences of individual revolutionaries varied. According to the worker-Bolshevik A. G. Shliapnikov, most activists in Petrograd managed to evade police detection for only about three months; he and others who were extremely careful held out longer. Shliapnikov claimed that during his wartime stays in Russia, from November 1915 to early 1916 and after November 1916, he never slept in the same place two nights in a row, he hid the location of his eight conspiratorial apartments even from party comrades, he changed hats and coats frequently, and he regularly walked through the forest to lose surveillants.[20]

It apparently helped Shliapnikov that he possessed a French passport, which he, muttering in French, sometimes proffered to credulous policemen. Luckily, too, the surveillants posted in railway stations did not know him by sight. Despite her revolutionary activism, the Bolshevik Ts. S. Zelikson-Bobrovskaia also avoided arrest, even though she remained in Russia throughout the war. After being continually harassed while living in Moscow in the second half of 1914, she had complained to a senior gendarme officer, threatening to move to another apartment, even to a hotel. The officer declared that they would find her wherever she went. Zelikson-Bobrovskaia then "swore at him for all I was worth." Two days later, they stopped bothering her.[21]

Many revolutionary and opposition activists returned to Russia in the first months of the war, some out of patriotism. In September Krasil'nikov warned that thousands of Russians, many with false documents, were leaving Genoa bound for Arkhangel'sk and Odessa. In late August 1914 Maklakov ruled that fugitive émigrés would have to face criminal proceedings upon returning. V. L. Burtsev was among those who decided to take their chances. "Now is not the time to fight the government," he said, and he left for Russia. He was arrested on the border in August, sentenced to Siberian exile in January 1915, then amnestied at the end of the year thanks to intercessions by the Allied governments. Once he was back in Petrograd, the police watched him closely, "like a shadow or a faithful wife." Irritated, he approached each surveillant and barked: "Why are you following me? You are either a spy or a thief!" Sometimes he demanded that a nearby policeman arrest the surveillant. Once while Burtsev was attempting a citizen's arrest, the surveillant hopped on a streetcar, and Burtsev shouted, "Grab him!" People on the street echoed the plea, and the conductor stopped the streetcar. A crowd seized the surveillant, sure he was a thief. K. I. Globachev, who had ordered the surveillance, corroborated Burtsev's account, adding that Burtsev "jumped at absolutely innocent people . . . and in general gave the impression of being an abnormal man."[22]

Life for revolutionary activists in Siberian exile during the war was about as good as it got. E. M. Iaroslavskii recalled a life of "relative freedom" with no gendarme supervision in Iakutsk and "relatively loose police supervision in other areas." Some political exiles, he wrote, "even engaged in commerce, settled down firmly, built themselves houses, and were not preparing to return to political activity." When Iaroslavskii tried to revolutionize the Iakuts, others denounced him, saying, "you will wreck everything for us." The police chief, I. Rubtsov, searched Iaroslavskii's office at the ethnographic museum, but, as the revolutionary observed, Rubtsov "preferred not to find anything," so as to avoid charges of negligence.[23]

Ia. Papernikov found similar conditions in Irkutsk, where he worked with twelve other political exiles in a leatherworking factory, even though political exiles were not allowed to work in factories, where they might spread revolutionary ideas to vulnerable segments of the population. The police chief, he wrote, turned a blind eye to this activity. Under forged documents, political exiles also worked in the chancellery of the governor-general. Perhaps less surprising was their influence on public organizations. L. P. Sosnovskaia, a Soviet historian, bolsters this assertion, noting that numerous Socialist-Revolutionaries and Social Democrats contributed to a host of Siberian newspapers and journals and actually "dominated public opinion" in Siberia.[24]

Exiled revolutionaries also benefited from help afforded by the "revolutionary red cross,"—that is, efforts by revolutionary activists to help their comrades who were in prison or exile—and from a careful reading of law codes, as when the Bolshevik E. D. Stasova "dug out an article in the law, according to which court-sentenced exiles, having completed a part of their time in Siberia, had the right to visit their elderly parents in European Russia." From September 1916 Stasova spent four months in Petrograd. Her comrades at first "laughed at my juridical knowledge," but later followed her example.[25]

While continuing to draft surveys on the main revolutionary organizations—several were drafted in December 1914, for example—Special Section analysts for the first time began spilling ink in regard to the nonrevolutionary opposition. One survey bearing Brune's signature and sent to all security policemen in the field on 2 September 1914 traced the development of the major revolutionary and opposition groupings and parties since before the 1905 revolution. It argued that radical political organizations typically pass through twelve stages, from spreading socialist ideas to engaging in general armed uprisings. Whereas the revolution of 1905 had reached the eleventh stage (partial armed uprisings), according to the survey, the revolutionary movement in mid-1914 had attained only the sixth stage (armed demonstrations). The survey recommended taking "decisive and . . . efficacious measures" to neutralize revolutionary leaders without harassing the masses, most of whom were "victims of propaganda and agitation." Marking an important shift in strategy, it also recommended establishing which representatives of the Kadet Party "are secret leaders of revolutionary organizations," because the liberals "have provoked and supported opposition sentiment in all layers of society, creating favorable soil for the propagation and agitation of clearly revolutionary ideas."[26]

Given the major role liberal activists would play in undermining the government's legitimacy over the next two and a half years, perhaps this proposal made sense. By December 1915, A. P. Martynov deployed six full-time informants within unaffiliated public organizations, including the war industries committees, cooperatives, and the press. They earned among the highest monthly salaries paid by the bureau—ranging from 75 to 125 rubles; in comparison, only five of the twenty informants among the Social Democrats earned over 75. As late as 1916 the security bureau in Petrograd, however, employed twenty-seven informants among the Social Democrats and only four within Kadet circles and amid the broader public movement.[27]

Konstantin Ivanovich Globachev replaced P. K. Popov in February 1915. Born two days before V. I. Lenin in 1870, Globachev graduated from both the Polotskii Cadet Corps and the Nikolaevskaia Military Academy of the General Staff in 1890, one year before M. F. von Koten. Thus, he was among Russia's more highly trained gendarme officers. Globachev began directing the Warsaw security bureau in 1909. S. E. Vissarionov twice inspected the bureau when it was under his charge and deplored Globachev's "weakness, slackness [vialost'], lack of energy, . . . and poor leadership." Consequently, he was demoted to gendarme station chief in Nizhnii Novgorod in November 1912. Dzhunkovskii met him there in 1913 and later wrote that "he proved to be an excellent officer in every way, who understood security policing extremely well; calm, of a gentle disposition, honest, he comported himself with modesty and did not try to stand out."[28]

Globachev's own reports give the impression that he was a less talented security officer than Martynov. Globachev used subjective expressions like "the inveterate opportunist Miliukov," whereas Martynov always wrote with scholarly detachment and objectivity. Spiridovich, who frequently met with Globachev in his oak-paneled office in the vast mansion of Prince Ol'denburgskii, found him "clever, industrious, efficient, dependable, and profoundly decent. He was a typically good gendarme officer, with a profound sense of duty and love for the tsar and the motherland. But he was soft. . . . He was good for peacetime, but soft for the coming time of troubles."[29]

GOVERNMENT AND SOCIETY IN SUMMER 1915

Despite earlier defeats resulting in enormous losses of men, the Russian public remained essentially supportive of the government's war effort until spring 1915. Then a concerted German and Austrian attack in Galicia forced the Russian army to retreat, which altered the domestic situation considerably. Although the revolutionaries had been unable to organize more than a few large-scale May Day demonstrations because of systematic police repression (only one thousand strikers came out in Petrograd, though nineteen thousand did in Moscow), popular anger expressed itself in various forms of urban unrest, including a massive anti-German pogrom in Moscow in May.[30]

In an age of nationalism and in the midst of a total war, Russia's huge enemy-alien population posed an enormous problem. Some six hundred thousand subjects of enemy states lived permanently in Russia at the outbreak of war. Roughly two million people had immigrated to Russia and had become Russian subjects over the previous half-century from those countries. In 1912 alone two and a half million Germans had visited Russia for brief periods. It is not surprising, therefore, that the spy fever that was prevalent in all the belligerent countries gripped both officialdom and the population in Russia. "The mobilization against enemy aliens," according to Eric Lohr, "brought revolutionary methods into domestic politics on a large scale, in a sense, bringing the external war to the home front."[31]

Since aliens constituted a large portion of elites, the antialien movement had an antielite undertone. Two days after Germany declared war on Russia, the interior ministry directed governors to tolerate no violence against peaceful foreigners. Yet much of the popular press repeatedly demanded the dismissal of officials of German heritage and the expropriation of their land. Voluntary associations sprang up with the express aim of "combating Germans inside Russia." The military leadership, much of which considered all Russian Jews and Germans, as well as foreigners, traitors, pushed more than one million such people into the interior provinces, despite resistance by civilian officials.[32] The interior ministry and its Police Department were immediately drawn into this work.

On 12 August 1914 Maklakov, in accordance with a military directive, ordered the immediate arrest and exile of all German and Austrian men of eighteen to forty-five years of age. In exile they were placed under police supervision, one policeman per one hundred prisoners, though some faced greater limitations on their movements than others. The military authorities monitored this supervision by watching press reports and occasionally initiating inspections. By January 1915 there were nearly 66,000 enemy-alien exiles, including Hungarians and Turks, in twenty provinces.[33] In principle, therefore, some 660 policemen devoted much of their time to keeping track of these exiles.

The police also watched a wide variety of other population groups, from religious sectarians and Jews, to Ukrainians and Chinese, to military personnel and employees of charitable organizations and rural administrative institutions. As early as 28 July 1914 Dzhunkovskii warned governors and security policemen to maintain close surveillance over Chinese visitors, whom the Japanese were allegedly using as spies. In September all Chinese traders were banished from Petrograd city and province, and those in Moscow faced continuous police harassment. Police directives in early 1915 alerted regular and security policemen to the dangers of sectarians spreading antigovernment and antiwar propaganda among military personnel. The Baptists, according to one directive, were a "seedbed of Germanism." Beginning in fall 1914 the military authorities—and some civilian authorities—seized or placed under house arrest people from Jewish communities within the military theaters in order to use them as hostages: they threatened to kill them should spies or traitors be found within their communities; in most cases it seems the police had to maintain surveillance over the hostages. In June 1915 the regular police who were not in the frontal areas received orders to watch for Jews who had been released from German prisoner-of-war camps.[34]

Ukrainians endured no systematic restrictions on their activities, though police sometimes maintained close surveillance over Ukrainian nationalist activists. Take the case of M. S. Grushevskii (Hrushevskyi). A historian who argued that Kievan Rus' was Ukrainian, not Russian, he traveled at the war's outset from Austria to Kiev, where the police, apparently on orders from the military, arrested him and exiled him to Simbirsk purely on the basis of his beliefs. Without Dzhunkovskii's intervention, he would have ended up in Tomsk. Intercessions by S. F. Platonov, a major historian, and Grand Duke Konstantin Konstantinovich won his release to Moscow.[35]

In March 1915 Brune ordered the security police to check very carefully the "political reliability" of both military recruits and employees of charitable organizations, hospitals, and other institutions serving sick and wounded soldiers. In both cases his concern was that revolutionary activists would attempt to gain access to military personnel with the intention of spreading antigovernment and antiwar propaganda among them. Finally, in May 1915 Brune, fearing political agitation in the countryside, directed the security police to verify the moral character and "political reliability" of employees in peasant administrative institutions.[36] A major portion of these activities represented an increased burden imposed on the security police force by the war effort.

In all of these cases, beyond serving the demands of the military, with its sometimes irrational concerns about espionage, the Police Department's primary interest lay in maintaining order and averting unrest. For half a year Russia had witnessed large-scale manifestations of public joy at its military victories and anger at its reversals. Employers often did not dock their workers for time spent in these displays, which occasionally involved violence against German-owned shops. Senior officials worried about such events.

After a crowd looted the German embassy on 4 August 1914, killing an employee, Foreign Minister S. D. Sazonov cautioned Nicholas that news of this "shameful event" would "travel all over the world," negatively influencing international public opinion. And in late October, following vandalism against German-owned stores, Maklakov warned the Moscow city governor A. A. Adrianov to place a higher value on the preservation of order than on public expressions of patriotism. Among more general appeals to police and administrative officials to strive to prevent popular unrest and disorder was a directive issued by K. D. Kafafov on 21 May 1915 warning of a "strong anger against Jews." Pointing to the Jews' alleged "efforts to increase prices on items of primary necessity," as well as "official news confirming Jewish participation in espionage in the current war," the directive warned governors and security policemen of widespread propaganda inciting the population to anti-Jewish violence. It enjoined the governors "to take the most decisive measures" to nip anti-Jewish agitation in the bud.[37] Mass violence would soon ensue, but it would be directed against Germans, not Jews.

The anti-German pogrom that rocked Moscow from 26 to 29 May destroyed close to eight hundred businesses and residences, some of them owned by ethnic Russians, inflicting a total of some seventy million rubles in property damage. It was as if the German army had bombarded the city, according to a witness. Just after the pogrom began, Adrianov ordered all factory owners to fire their German employees immediately and refused to authorize the use of violence against patriotic crowds. Troops were not deployed until the morning of the 29th. They restored complete order in the city only by evening, and peasants continued to attack landed estates for another week.[38]

Eric Lohr found that the pogrom was entirely spontaneous; that most of the participants were factory workers, women, and adolescents; and that antialien hatred was what drove them. A German shopkeeper could save himself from a beating and his store from destruction if he were willing, upon command, to spit on a portrait of the kaiser or to sing "God Save the Tsar." Overall, only ninety out of 735 people who filed damage claims had Russian names.[39]

The pogrom frightened both officialdom and public. The specter of the Pugachev Rebellion and of the December 1905 armed uprising haunted many contemporaries.[40] A high-level investigation led by Senator N. S. Krasheninnikov concluded that Moscow officials had been adhering to an interior ministry policy of nonviolent crowd control established in April 1915 following a bout of popular unrest allegedly caused by armed police intervention. Adrianov had apparently hoped to convince the crowds that the government could be trusted to handle the problem of German influence, and he had opposed shooting at crowds containing many women and children. Intercepted letters, moreover, revealed extensive discontent among soldiers of the garrison.[41]

Only a very narrow circle of officials—not even all the ministers—were allowed to read the final report of the investigation, of which only four copies were made. According to Lohr, "It revealed not a strong state orchestrating a pogrom, but a weak state unable to control the streets, gripped with fear that the situation would spin out of control into general chaos or revolution." It seems that senior officials feared, as Orlando Figes has argued, that the Moscow pogrom was "the first sign of an upswing in the popular revolutionary mood."[42]

Tensions in the country remained high following the pogrom. Maklakov ordered governors to nip all disorders in the bud and to disallow all rallies, even patriotic ones. The interior ministry also abandoned its no-shooting policy, and on 3 June twelve demonstrating workers were shot dead and forty-five injured in Kostroma. On 4 and 5 June A. P. Martynov pointed to widespread rumors in Moscow of treasonous Germans in the Russian officer corps, and he warned that the pogrom might portend the coming of a "truly serious explosion." "Military reversals," he predicted, "will accelerate the course of events and will give birth to such forces as are now difficult to imagine."[43] This was a most prescient assessment.

Workers demanding the removal of Germans from their factories went on strike across the empire for weeks after the pogrom, and many soldiers distrusted their officers with German surnames and sometimes mistreated them. It was rumored that German saboteurs were active within Russia, that workers were being poisoned in German-owned factories, that officers of German origin were surrendering without a fight, that Germans had caused a recent outbreak of cholera, that the "insolent behavior of Rasputin" demonstrated the influence of the "pro-German party" in Petrograd, and that the pogrom had been organized by policemen in order to divert popular discontent away from the government. The respected Kadet V. D. Kuz'min-Karavaev had "no doubt that it was organized" in the way rumor alleged.[44]

Back in fall 1914 moderate cabinet ministers, in cahoots with Grand Duke Nikolai Nikolaevich and the courtier V. N. Orlov, had been plotting against Maklakov. The emperor's staunch support for him began to erode by May 1915 in the face of military failures and public pressure. An assistant to A. V. Krivoshein, who was the plot's mastermind, compiled three hypothetical cabinet configurations, in two of which Dzhunkovskii figured as interior minister. The intriguers aimed at bringing down other conservative ministers as well, including I. V. Shcheglovitov and War Minister V. A. Sukhomlinov. Prime Minister I. L. Goremykin's participation in the plan was crucial, for Nicholas apparently hated the prospect of dismissing Maklakov, probably because of Maklakov's almost fanatical devotion to him. Maklakov was dismissed on 5 June 1915. After that he remained a state counselor, yet he felt deep bitterness toward his former colleagues.[45]

The new interior minister, N. B. Shcherbatov, Krivoshein's protégé, was by most accounts not well selected. For several years the gentry marshal of Poltava Province, he had served as director of the imperial horse stables since 1913. Apparently hoping to win over public opinion, he soon received members of press. He told them he was a "zemstvo-style public activist" without an official political party and therefore was "free from political influences."[46]

Dzhunkovskii, who regretted Maklakov's departure, called Shcherbatov "insincere and sneaky" and said that he was "little interested" in the work of his ministry. Maybe Dzhunkovskii regretted having been passed over by the emperor. Shcherbatov considered Dzhunkovskii "very honest, thrifty," but "not fully in charge." He considered replacing him with R. G. Mollov, a longtime prosecutor whom he knew from their service in Poltava in 1907–1909, but settled instead on substituting Mollov for Brune, whom he called "very honorable, but not aggressive enough."[47]

Born in 1867 to Bulgarian parents, Mollov had taken Russian citizenship, studied law at the prestigious Imperial School of Jurisprudence, married an heiress to large landed estates in Poltava, and served in the justice ministry beginning in 1889. Globachev called Mollov "incompetent" and wrote that Shcherbatov himself "did not understand political questions." According to A. N. Iakhontov, Shcherbatov "felt open disgust" toward the police and, distrusting his assistants, left the various department heads to their own devices. N. P. Muratov, a senior official, wrote that under Makarov the minister's office had lost its awesomeness; under Maklakov it had lost its seriousness; and under Shcherbatov it had become a ludicrous place where one only brought papers to have them signed.[48]

From 10 to 14 June, the emperor agreed to further ministerial changes. A. A. Polivanov, a darling of the moderate public, was to replace Sukhomlinov, who retired amid allegations of treason. Nicholas selected as justice minister Senator A. A. Khvostov, whom many officials considered "smart, businesslike, and completely honest." Khvostov later testified that he had advocated abolishing perlustration, which he considered pointless. Liberals greeted these changes with some optimism but also urged caution.[49]

Industrial workers, who had been largely apolitical despite their participation in anti-German violence, were by midsummer growing more restive and more resentful toward the government, while apparently often remaining ill disposed toward foreigners. On 13 July the Police Department enjoined security policemen "to work closely with factory and mine inspectors; to use informants to ascertain the mood of workers and report thereon to governors and the Police Department; to arrest all agitators; to seek to mediate strikes; and to make clear that all disturbances of order will bring arrest and exile. Workers called for military service should be left to work on important military orders, but should be sent to the front if they participate in strikes." In practice, the authorities rarely applied such harsh methods. Strike leaders in Petrograd were arrested and exiled in only 9 cases out of 167; their exemption from the draft was also seldom revoked.[50]

The government's hesitancy to apply harsh repression may have stemmed in part from fear of popular reaction. In the first half of July, Bolshevik activists set up a regional committee in Ivanovo-Voznesensk, 150 miles northeast of Moscow. In early August they sent a representative, V. N. Naumov, to Moscow. Naumov was to invite a delegate from Moscow to take part in the committee and was to inform midlevel Bolsheviks of the committee's intention to launch an armed uprising on 8 or 9 August. Naumov's contact in Moscow was an informant, however, so no delegate was dispatched. Instead, on 10 August the gendarme chief in Vladimir arrested Naumov and several of his confederates. The arrests brought thousands of protesters into the streets. Troops issued a warning then fired, killing thirty and wounding fifty-three.[51]

Throughout this period senior officials often felt impotent. Shcherbatov admitted to his fellow ministers that their powerlessness in provinces under military jurisdiction was causing police and administrative officials to retire or seek transfer to the interior provinces. Worst of all, the public constantly blamed the interior minister for policies implemented or imposed by military authorities, who, as A. N. Iakhontov later wrote, "spoke with the government as with the administration of a defeated nation."[52]

At their meeting on 4 August, the Council of Ministers discussed the military authorities' mass expulsion of Jews from the frontal areas. "Even the anti-Semites," noted Iakhontov, "were appalled." Since the military authorities refused to halt the expulsions, the ministers agreed temporarily— and not without trepidation—to abolish the Pale of Settlement. Two days later, Polivanov dropped a bombshell: the emperor had resolved to assume supreme command at the front. The news devastated the ministers, who thought nothing could potentially undermine the emperor's prestige more than his association with eventual military failures. On the 9th Shcherbatov exclaimed, "I cannot . . . remain interior minister." On the 11th he warned of increasing unrest throughout the country, including anti-German and anti-Jewish violence. Most serious of all, the garrison troops were thought not to be fully reliable. Yet there was little his ministry could do to maintain order. Almost half of European Russia was under military rule. "How do you expect me to fight the revolutionary movement," Shcherbatov argued, "if they will not give me the use of troops, explaining that they are not reliable. With lower-ranked policemen [gorodovye] alone one cannot pacify all of Russia, especially when the police ranks are being thinned out not by the day but by the hour. And the population is stirred up by speeches in the Duma, lies in the newspapers, continuous reversals at the front, and rumors of disorders in the rear."[53]

The creation of several official and public organizations for coping with the war effort, though not opposed by the Council of Ministers and intended to improve relations between state and society, further weakened the government. Five special councils (for defense, food, transportation, fuel, and refugees) comprising both civil servants and public figures were accountable to the emperor alone. War industries committees drew worker-delegates into their deliberations. Finally, the national unions of zemstvos and town dumas won the right to create Zemgor, a committee for coordinating military supply that Globachev and Iakhontov both termed a "state within a state." Martynov fielded a few informants among the committees. Globachev almost seemed to throw up his hands. The security police force, he wrote, was well equipped "for combat with the revolutionary movement but was utterly powerless to combat the growing public revolutionary mood of the activist *[budiruiushii]* intelligentsia, which required other measures of a general political nature."[54]

While the ministers fretted over social disorder and public mistrust, the emperor fired Dzhunkovskii. On August 15 Shcherbatov summoned Dzhunkovskii to his summer quarters on Apteka Island and, with some embarrassment, supplied him Nicholas's handwritten order. "I insist," he wrote, "on the immediate dismissal of Dzhunkovskii from his post while keeping him a member of my suite." Dzhunkovskii was taken aback. "The empress," he thought, "must be behind it." The next day he wrote an anguished letter to Nicholas expressing his deep sadness at having lost the emperor's trust and requesting dismissal from his suite and permission to serve at the front. Nicholas denied his first request and granted the second, but refused to justify the dismissal. Dzhunkovskii, who went on to command various military units, later claimed it had been a "great misfortune, not to know why."[55]

What had caused Dzhunkovskii's fall? On 17 August, Shcherbatov told his fellow ministers that the news had come as a "complete surprise," a claim he persisted in as late as 1917. Krivoshein seemed to consider Dzhunkovskii's departure voluntary. "He had no moral right," argued Krivoshein, "to abandon his post because of his personal dissatisfaction." Others proffered cogent explanations. A. I. Spiridovich emphasized Dzhunkovskii's failure to warn Nicholas about an alleged plan for a palace coup involving Nikolai Nikolaevich. Martynov pointed to Dzhunkovskii's supposedly lenient treatment of German prisoners of war. N. P. Tikhmenev, a rightist editor, testified in 1917 that such rumors were rampant in rightist circles. On 3 August in the Duma, A. N. Khvostov, a nephew of A. A. Khvostov, denounced Dzhunkovskii's failure to effectively combat "German dominance."[56]

Others traced Dzhunkovskii's political demise to a secret report he delivered to Nicholas regarding Rasputin's scandalous behavior. Yet V. I. Gurko, a rightist state counselor, recalled that Dzhunkovskii's report had provoked Nicholas's ire against Rasputin, and Dzhunkovskii remarked that for two months the emperor had treated Dzhunkovskii most kindly. Even so, it is clear that Alexandra had had it in for him. On 16 June she reminded Nicholas that "Our first Friend," Philippe, had given her an icon with a little bell, "to warn me against those that are not right." It "would ring," she wrote on 9 September, "if they came with bad intentions. These [V. N.] Orlov, Dzhunkovskii, and [A. A.] Drentel'n who have that 'strange' fright of me are those to have a special eye upon." A powerful coalition apparently joined Alexandra, including A. A. Vyrubova, A. N. Khvostov, S. P. Beletskii, and V. N. Voeikov, as well perhaps as P. N. Durnovo, V. P. Meshcherskii, and the rightist activist V. G. Orlov, who complained to A. V. Krivoshein that the "gendarme corps is still terrorized by Dzhunkovskii. He destroyed the regional bureaus, removed informants from the military. . . . Thus the Interior Ministry suffers and will continue to from being completely uninformed."[57]

The final meetings of the Council of Ministers in August were full of anguish. On 24 August A. A. Khvostov blurted out that upon Nicholas's departure to the front "P. N. Miliukov will press a button and disorders will commence." Shcherbatov warned that the security police predicted widespread disorders within days of a dissolution of the Duma. On 2 September, the day Nicholas prorogued the Duma, Shcherbatov again warned of probable unrest. The situation in Moscow was "explosive. . . . The entire population is seized by some kind of insanity and has taken the form of so much combustible material." Sazonov warned ominously that "blood will flow tomorrow." Petrograd remained largely placid, but on the 4th strikes and street unrest broke out in Moscow. It continued till 14–15 September, when crowds clashed with the police. Martynov, describing the unrest, referred to its "antigovernment character" and to the "profound animosity of the hooliganizing *[khuliganstvuiushchei]* mob."[58]

Nicholas wrote optimistically to Alexandra on 9 September, "The ministers know extremely little of what goes on in the whole country." He was alienated from both his ministers and the government's sources of police intelligence, to say nothing of much of the educated public. The right-liberal Kadet V. A. Maklakov, in an infamous newspaper article of 27 September, described a car out of control, the driver apparently mad and the passengers despairingly helpless. The public understood that he meant Nicholas at the helm of Russia, yet the censors had no basis on which to punish either author or editor.[59]

REIGN OF ADVENTURERS

The immediate cause of V. A. Maklakov's outburst was the dismissal on 26 September of Shcherbatov and his replacement the next day by A. N. Khvostov, a rightist member of the Duma—the first Duma deputy ever to receive so high a position in the government. (In the weeks before the appointment Alexandra had maligned Shcherbatov and praised Khvostov.)[60] His deputy for police affairs was the indefatigable but unpopular S. P. Beletskii. The range of schemes and intrigues in which both officials involved themselves was unprecedented in the annals of the Russian police, as were their efforts to organize and mobilize right-wing support for the government. None of these efforts bore much fruit in the directions hoped for, but they unquestionably undermined public trust in the government and caused the decline of both officials in short order.

Aleksei Nikolaevich Khvostov was born in 1872 in Orel, where his family had large landholdings. Trained in law at the prestigious Alexander Lycée, he served as an assistant prosecutor in Moscow, then as vice-governor in Tula before his appointment as governor of Vologda (1906–1910) and Nizhegorod (1910–1912) provinces. As governor he apparently acquired the moniker Solovei-Razboinik, the name of a legendary Russian bandit. In 1912 he was elected from Orel to the fourth Duma, in which he chaired the rightists' fraction. S. E. Kryzhanovskii described him as "quite intelligent, talented, and cunning, but somehow frenzied, almost primitive in his instincts and moreover completely amoral, capable for the sake of personal interests or goals to embark on any actions whatever." Spiridovich recalled that Khvostov had told him in 1916 that "I am a person without limiting centers; it's all the same to me: go to a brothel with Rasputin or throw him under a train." Spiridovich thought that "this jovial, fat, rosy-cheeked, quick-tempered man was not a minister but a gangster."[61]

Khvostov immediately jettisoned Dzhunkovskii's thrifty control of the ministry's funding. Beletskii, appointed on 28 September, recalled that Khvostov had hoped to boost public support for the government by improving relations with the press, distributing patriotic imprints emphasizing the compassion of the imperial family, alleviating the plight of refugees, and providing foodstuffs to the poor in major urban centers. He also wanted to strengthen surveillance over revolutionary organizations, public activists, and prominent people of German origin, but discreetly and without a heavy hand. In reality, however, he zealously institutionalized the campaign against German "dominance" that he had led in the Duma. Within the interior ministry Khvostov set up "an entirely new office" to watch immigrants and foreigners and "created a special committee for the war on German dominance." On 25 November 1915 he urged governors to combat rumors of treason in high places with a struggle against "real cases of German dominance." The pursuit of this policy was like "pouring gasoline on a fire," remarked one historian. In January 1916 the Police Department also set up a separate division to handle such matters; by summer control over them resided with the prime minister.[62]

Khvostov had greater regard for the security police than had his predecessor. During a stop in Moscow on his way from Orel to Petrograd, Khvostov summoned senior officials of the interior ministry and singled out the gendarme officers among them for special praise.[63] Nevertheless, he left the running of security police affairs to Beletskii, a real expert.

G. I. Shavel'skii, the chief military chaplain, who had met Beletskii in 1911, found in him "interior nobility and decency, wonderfully combined with hard work and seriousness." In the intervening years, however, "he had radically changed in the other direction." V. P. Nikol'skii, head of the gendarme directorate, wrote to Shavel'skii that "While Beletskii ascended the bureaucratic hierarchy, he descended morally." His bad qualities gradually overshadowed the positive ones. His "immense ambition" drove him to support Khvostov's candidacy in the hope that he could supplant him, and his lustfulness led him to "organize drinking binges with dancing girls in his office" and to waste large amounts of money. By 1915, wrote Shavel'skii, Beletskii had become "much fatter," his voice more hoarse, and his "face, bluish and so puffy that one could not even see his eyes," leaving one with "the impression of a morally degraded drunkard."[64]

Khvostov and Beletskii both disliked Mollov, the police director, and they soon replaced him with K. D. Kafafov. A vice-director of the Police Department since 1912, Kafafov was a good administrator, but Beletskii must have especially relished his indifference to security policing, for which, according to Kafafov, Beletskii assumed full responsibility. To aid in the exercise of that responsibility, Beletskii selected as a vice-director of the Police Department I. K. Smirnov, until then a prosecutor in Petrograd. Beletskii also retained Vissarionov, whom he trusted fully, as an advisor and inspector. Finally, after consulting with Vissarionov, Beletskii tapped a few gendarme officers and prosecutors for slots in the Special Section.[65]

Beletskii needed Kafafov and the others for their administrative and policing abilities, but for the darker side of the police business and for his intrigues, he relied on some different, unsavory figures. One was M. S. Kommisarov. From 1912 to June 1915 Kommisarov had headed the gendarme station in Saratov. Then Dzhunkovskii had transferred him to Viatka, in the Russian hinterland. Vissarionov and A. M. Eremin warned Beletskii not to trust Kommisarov, so he sought another opinion from N. P. Zuev, "a living chronicle of the Police Department," who described how Kommisarov had taken the entire blame for the production of anti-Semitic leaflets in 1905, thus shielding his superiors. Beletskii needed an utterly loyal, highly trained, unscrupulous security officer like Kommisarov to watch one of the most powerful men in Petrograd—Grigorii Rasputin. Once Beletskii discovered that Kommisarov's wife enjoyed friendly relations with Rasputin, he named Kommisarov chief of the evacuated gendarme station in Warsaw that had fallen to the Germans in August, an appointment that kept him in Petrograd. If one is to believe Beletskii's story, Rasputin must have been the most closely observed person in Russia.[66]

Two other disreputable and highly colorful figures Beletskii drew into his orbit were I. F. Manasevich-Manuilov and M. M. Andronnikov. The former was born in 1869 in Kovno, the illegitimate son of P. L. Meshcherskii (the father also of the rightist V. P. Meshcherskii). He was adopted by F. S. Manasevich-Manuilov, who was sent for mail fraud to Siberia, where he became wealthy from gold mining. After attending high school in Petrograd, in 1888 Ivan made the acquaintance of V. P. Meshcherskii, who became his patron. In the same year he became an informant for the security bureau.[67]

I. F. Manasevich-Manuilov entered state service in 1892, reporting to the interior ministry and the St. Petersburg security bureau. In the 1890s he wrote for centrist and rightist newspapers in Petrograd, lived frequently in Paris, where he wrote for the newspaper *Gil Blas,* interviewed journalists and writers including Paul Verlaine, translated novels and plays, and adapted several plays for the Russian stage. In 1899 the interior ministry sent him to Rome to report on the Congregation for the Propagation of the Faith and, starting in 1901, on Russian radicals living abroad as well. Beginning in 1902, armed with tens of thousands of rubles, he promoted favorable coverage of Russia in several newspapers across Europe. During the war with Japan, he conducted foreign espionage. Removed from the government payroll in September 1906, Manasevich-Manuilov bilked several people out of money, but the cases against him were dropped at the insistence of Stolypin, who feared the shady revelations a trial might elicit. He returned to full-time journalism. Beletskii knew a resourceful person when he saw one, so when Manasevich-Manuilov asked him to temporarily detain someone who was competing for the affections of his lover, Beletskii was only too happy to oblige. In return, Manasevich-Manuilov informed Beletskii of trends in high society and officialdom. (Manasevich-Manuilov was happy to talk to anyone: he also furnished police secrets to Burtsev.)[68]

In comparison, Andronnikov, a descendant of an ancient Georgian clan, was utterly straightforward. He had served first in the interior ministry from 1897 to 1914, when he was dismissed for nonattendance, then in the Holy Synod. On the side he interceded with the high and mighty on behalf of various supplicants. A. F. Rediger recalled entertaining such intercessions in 1901 and again in 1915. In late 1915 Khvostov allegedly used him to spy on the imperial family and to influence the empress.[69]

Beletskii claimed that Andronnikov had introduced him to Rasputin, which may be true, though the encounter almost certainly took place earlier than late 1915, the time Beletskii indicated. Beletskii intervened frequently on behalf of Rasputin's followers and acquaintances, but mostly in order to curry favor with the empress. Khvostov and Beletskii "conspired to domesticate" Rasputin, according to Beletskii. They gave him money so he would not take it from others, and they kept compromising information on him.[70] Yet controlling the clever, resourceful man was difficult—as they both would discover early in 1916.

Beletskii and Khvostov adopted two main policies; one negative, one positive. First, they laid out plans to control popular agitation and to crush potential unrest. Second, they labored to increase public support for the government. The former policy had two aspects: surveillance and repression. The surveillance was extensive and varied. Beletskii worked with the Gendarme Corps to revise the officer training curriculum, placing more emphasis on ferreting out and combating military espionage. In the second half of October 1915 the Police Department ordered security police officers to make detailed reports at least monthly about the social and public life of everyone from the peasants to the nobility, from the members of wartime public organizations to religious sectarians, from the press to industrial workers. The department began to compile periodic surveys of the Russian revolutionary press abroad and then to distribute them in order "to provide gendarme officers with . . . the views of the leaders of the revolution." It also reproached provincial gendarme chiefs about being uninformed about Kadet activities and directed them to acquire informants within Kadet circles.[71]

In mid-November, Beletskii directed the security police "to establish careful surveillance over the mood of the lower military ranks in the rear and to report on any breach of discipline among them." It seems he did so in part because of police reports pointing to discontent among soldiers serving under officers of German origin. Even so, an interministerial commission weighted toward the armed forces apparently voted against reinstating informants in the military. Later in November, Kafafov urged officials at the Paris security bureau to provide more detailed coverage of Socialist-Revolutionary activists. Finally, Beletskii had a Zubatovite's concern for the welfare of informants. In late December he chided Globachev: "We have information that some of your officers treat their informants impolitely. This is unacceptable: one must treat them with mutual trust, kindness, and consideration."[72] A similar statement from Dzhunkovskii or Brune would have been inconceivable.

The application of repression neither increased nor diminished, yet senior officials grew more concerned about the potential for unrest. In early October M. A. Sofronov, the acting Special Section chief since June, urged forbidding the Kadets from holding their upcoming party congress. Later in the month, Mollov, who was still police director, pointed to the party's immense influence "on all layers of society and on those organizations that have sprung up during the war" and to "the marked antidynastic sentiment and extreme . . . nervousness of the popular mood." On 6 November Beletskii directed security policemen to prevent the Kadets from convening the congress. It nevertheless met three months later.[73]

A report of 22 October detailed the inability of administrative officials to regulate or limit the activities of the unions of zemstvos and town dumas, in part because the Council of Ministers had refused Maklakov's proposal to fire "unreliable" employees of the unions. It seems that the report bore no fruit. On 9 November Khvostov warned Goremykin that public activists were listing leftward and were planning to launch radical antigovernment actions at war's end, but he also assured him that the interior ministry was taking "necessary measures to reorganize security policing, in order to paralyze these trends." For the most part, however, although the security police maintained surveillance over public activists and sometimes sought to thwart their public activities, they rarely infringed on their personal liberty. One authority has noted that not a single Kadet was arrested during the World War.[74]

Still, serious preparations for confronting popular unrest were laid in Moscow, and perhaps in other major cities as well. Officials in the ancient capital defined three stages of emergency preparedness. In each case, the city was divided into sectors, and special units of police and military forces bore responsibility for maintaining order in each of them. In December the Police Department enjoined governors to prepare their police to use the force of arms to suppress popular unrest.[75]

More positively, Beletskii and Khvostov sought to win support for the government by both organizing rightists and reaching out to the broader public. In neither case did they enjoy much success. They apparently helped to organize congresses of right-wing activists, notably in late November in Nizhnii Novgorod. Beletskii also personally reconciled two rightist leaders, A. I. Dubrovin and N. E. Markov, and disbursed subsidies broadly among rightist activists amounting to as much as two million rubles during his half-year in office. The public clearly knew that the administration was now more favorable to rightists. The Academic Club of Moscow, a student association that had received subsidies from the interior ministry since 1911, mentioned its rightist affiliation for the first time in January 1916 in its yearly appeal for funding.[76]

For all his efforts, however, Beletskii was enough of a realist to admit their failure. He enjoined security policemen to provide "a true assessment of the [rightists'] activities and members." Summing up these reports, Kafafov acknowledged "the utter weakness in numbers and ideas of the rightists." I. G. Shcheglovitov, devotedly involved in right-wing activism since his retirement from his position as justice minister, saw little cause for optimism. "How strange everything is with us," he wrote. "In our monarchy there is only a handful of monarchists." Beletskii had to admit that rightist organizations could not "serve as a support for government efforts to stave off revolution."[77]

The rightists' weakness might have been a good thing from the perspective of senior officials, given their often seditious nature or simply given the tensions between the bureaucratic and populist varieties of monarchism. Globachev reported to Beletskii in late November 1915 that many rightist leaders were harshly criticizing government officials. The populist tendencies of some right-wing organizations went extremely far. In Saratov in May 1916, for example, the Union of Russian People defended the interests of local peasants against landlords. "The local administration is worried," wrote the gendarme chief, "that in case of agrarian disorders, the Union of Russian People cannot be considered a fully reliable organization." About the most the government could expect in the way of popular support, it seems, was sporadic violence against antigovernment agitation. The gendarme chief in Riazan, for example, entertained such hopes. Opposing such populist monarchism, Beletskii funded the publication and distribution to monarchist leaders of one thousand copies of a brochure explaining that true monarchism consisted in obedience to established authority. By spring 1916 senior officialdom's concern for preserving public tranquility trumped its desire to promote right-wing politics.[78]

Khvostov had begun to seek to expand public support for the government at a press conference soon after assuming office. Although he admitted to being a partisan of strong government, he expressed willingness to entertain the possibility of "certain concessions." His program received its initial fleshing out in an unsigned police report, variously dated 20 December 1915 and 26 February 1916 and entitled "What Is to Be Done?" The document warned of "extreme tension in all of society" and counseled "stimulating positive feelings in the people." Society would not tolerate an openly repressive course; therefore, "some minimal concessions must be granted, but their propaganda value must be maximized." The report's author advocated the immediate convocation of the Duma ("a lightning rod, not dangerous in itself"); releasing a few well-known political prisoners, such as E. K. Breshko-Breshkovskaia; reconvening the committee on the future of Poland; allowing the publication of one newspaper in Ukrainian; involving government officials more with the work of Zemgor; and prosecuting "big speculators" in order to appear to be doing something about inflation, among other measures. Breshko was not released, though a directive of February 1916 ordered the release of political detainees liable for military service and against whom incriminating evidence was weak. More important, Nicholas dismissed Goremykin and personally opened the Duma on 9 February 1916—his first visit in ten years.[79]

Beletskii and Khvostov were also attempting to win public support by reaching out to moderate and even radical journalists. I. V. Gessen recalled that Beletskii repeatedly satisfied his requests to secure the release of people arrested by the security police, including Gessen's nephew on several occasions. In February 1916, Gessen and M. A. Suvorin met with Khvostov, who complained of Rasputin's influence; Gessen thought that he did so with the hope that his complaint would reach and win the favor of the broader public. Khvostov also hoped to solidify public support by undertaking several measures aimed at fighting inflation and solving food- and fuel-supply problems. Decrees of 20 October and 19 December 1915 authorized the interior ministry to coordinate anti-inflation and food-supply efforts, respectively.[80]

It seems that the decrees served only to bog down Khvostov and his ministry in troubles largely unrelated to their primary task of maintaining order, and perhaps undermined their ability to do so in a crisis. Within the context of this broader endeavor of keeping order, on 9 January 1916 the Police Department issued an unusual directive, later notorious, warning local administrators that "the revolutionaries and their inspirers the Jews, as well as secret partisans of Germany, intend to call forth general discontent and protests against the war by means of hunger and extreme inflation on vital foodstuffs. To this end, ill-intentioned merchants, undoubtedly, hide goods, slow down deliveries, and, as much as possible, delay the unloading of goods on railroad stations." The directive proclaimed that the Jews also sought to "inculcate in the population a distrust of Russian money and to devalue it" so as to drive up the price of precious metals, which agents of the Jews across the Russian Empire allegedly were buying up. The directive concluded by noting that no action was to be taken by local officials. Kafafov, who signed the directive, later testified that General Headquarters had supplied much of its content and that Khvostov had encouraged its distribution. Beletskii claimed Kafafov had signed the directive without reading it. The promulgation of the document probably stimulated an increase in anti-Jewish sentiment within the police apparatus, but it did not lead to any immediate action.[81]

Much of the liberal opposition feared that Khvostov's campaign to win public support was succeeding, and officialdom worried about liberals' plans to seize power. Most of the participants at a Petrograd meeting of the Progressive Bloc in late October noted a "radical fall" in the oppositional mood of the population and an increase in political apathy. The Kadet A. I. Shingarev believed that "Khvostov took into account the historical moment" and was "skillfully using it."

Yet Khvostov clearly failed to diminish the public's alienation from the government. Most delegates from Zemgor and the war industries committees meeting in Moscow in early December 1915 were convinced that the emperor and his entourage wished to sign a separate peace with Germany. This charge was probably false, but some liberals were prepared to take matters into their own hands. On 13 March leaders of the unions of zemstvos and town dumas gathered for a banquet at Moscow's Prague Restaurant. N. V. Nekrasov's impassioned plea for "an all-Russian coordinating center" resonated with most participants, some of whom, in private conversations, called the proposed organization a "union of unions," recalling the loose organization that coordinated much revolutionary unrest in 1905. Two weeks later, two thousand people attended a meeting of the academic group of the Kadet Party held at the town duma. F. I. Rodichev lectured on "France in 1870," but while he was "speaking overtly of France," in the words of a police informant, "all understood that he was really talking about Russia" in 1916. Some of these activists and organizers were Freemasons, and Nekrasov's "coordinating center" was probably part of a Masonic plan. Yet the Police Department, which had been moderately preoccupied with Freemasonry previously, paid scant attention to the matter in 1916 and 1917 when serious Masonic political activities were afoot.[82]

But perhaps senior police officials were too preoccupied with their own murky intrigues. Khvostov and Beletskii had sought to harness Rasputin for their own advancement yet had found him indomitable. From early February 1916, according to Spiridovich, they had quarreled.

There was a lot to fight about: money, power, scandal, murder. I. V. Gessen, who met with Khvostov at this time, described him as "horribly fat, with a kind face and burning eyes." Gessen asked about rumors that Khvostov had sent V. A. Rzhevskii, a shady journalist, to arrange the killing of Rasputin. (Rzhevskii had been arrested, apparently on orders from Beletskii.) Khvostov replied that he had only sent him to persuade the right-wing monk Iliodor, then a fugitive in Norway, to hand over a manuscript denouncing Rasputin so it could be suppressed. Gessen and Suvorin, who accompanied him, were horrified. Khvostov, noticing their confusion, remarked, "don't look at this tragically; it's really comical." One of them asked how he could joke when he, the interior minister, was under investigation for his alleged involvement in an assassination attempt. Spiridovich, commissioned to investigate the matter, concluded that Khvostov had indeed plotted murder. In mid-February Khvostov fired Beletskii. His new deputy for police affairs, A. I. Pil'ts, remained in office exactly one month. On March 2 Alexandra wrote Nicholas that "the devil got hold of" Khvostov. The next day he was dismissed.[83]

SHTIURMER AS INTERIOR MINISTER

To replace Khvostov, Nicholas tapped Boris Vladimirovich Shtiurmer, a rightist member of the State Council whom he had appointed chairman of the Council of Ministers on 20 January 1916. Polivanov described Shtiurmer as "a tall man, upright, without facial movements, with reddish hair and beard, [who] never spoke." Shtiurmer apparently sought an accommodation between government and society. In a speech at the interior ministry he recalled his work in Tver Province as having been "in complete unity with all local zemstvo activists without any distinction between parties and groups." In reality, he had been a harsh administrator, but he was now projecting a message of conciliation. Perhaps senior official N. V. Plehve was right to say he "had no political convictions."[84]

Foreign Minister S. D. Sazonov found Shtiurmer and A. A. Bobrinskii, the friend and fellow right-wing activist he had picked as his principal deputy, to be detached from the interior ministry's work. A. V. Stepanov, a vigorous administrator and until then an official of the justice ministry, took charge of police affairs as a second deputy. Shtiurmer apparently hated E. K. Klimovich, whom Khvostov had named director of the Police Department two weeks before, so he simply refused to give him any orders or directives. All these changes (along with the replacement of eighty-seven governors and vice-governors during the previous twelve months) must have weakened the administrative apparatus considerably. V. M. Volkonskii, the third deputy interior minister, quipped that near his office they should have hung a sign: "On Saturdays, new program."[85]

Klimovich, a man of great personal energy, was the first and only gendarme officer to head the Police Department. He took the reins as public discontent intensified. Martynov reported almost desperately from Moscow on 25 February 1916 that "It would be a grave mistake to judge the mood of Russian society by its surface manifestations." Four days later, he noted a "sharp popular disaffection toward both the government" and, what was far more serious, the dynasty. Many people blamed Russia's poor military fortunes directly on the tsar. Rumors about the influence of "the German"—Empress Aleksandra—and of Rasputin within the court were circulating everywhere. Only police intervention, Martynov added, had saved the empress's sister, Elizaveta Feodorovna, when a mob attacked her residence in Moscow. In late April Martynov reported that at an informal gathering of Kadets P. D. Dolgorukov had exclaimed, "We are now living on a volcano." The Kadets then discussed how to harness for political purposes the popular anger over inflation.[86]

Even so, during the first five months of the year the peasantry had been relatively content. In Moscow Province, for example, monthly reports from the *uezdy* indicated that despite antigovernment sentiment among the educated public and efforts by agitators to stir up discontent among the masses, most peasants and even workers remained apolitical and did not oppose the war. True, in the Bogorodskii *uezd* many ordinary folk were complaining about the length of the war. "How sick I am of this war," more and more were saying. Yet the same report, of 24 February, noted that the taking of Erzerum a week before had improved the population's mood.[87]

At the end of April, senior officials from the interior ministry and the governors of fifteen provinces, mostly in central Russia, met to discuss radical activism and popular discontent. They worried about peasant hopes for land grants after the war, the zemstvo union's ability to escape government control, radical agitators' infiltration of cooperatives and worker sickness funds, the immense popularity of highly critical mass-circulation newspapers (like *Russkoe slovo*), the terrible material conditions of regular police and administrative officials, the meddling of military officials in administrative and economic affairs, and the inefficiency but political untouchability of the war industries committees. Several governors also complained that each provincial gendarme station was a "state within a state" that withheld secret information from governors.[88]

The governors saw some positive trends, including the relative political conservatism of the Union of Town Dumas, of provincial nobles, and of zemstvo activists at the *uezd* level; the decreased restiveness of factory workers; improved material conditions among refugees; and the economic well-being of many peasants. The officials proposed increased funding for regular police officials, recruitment of informants in the military, an increased recruitment of informants in factories, the imposition of full military censorship across the empire and not just in the theaters of war, an increase in official power to punish recalcitrant prisoners of war, the banning of bootlegged spirits, the institution of systematic censorship of films, an increase in government control over cooperatives, and the establishment of government control over railroad newspaper kiosks.[89] Not a single item on this agenda materialized.

The public movement, especially Zemgor and the war industries committees, concerned Klimovich immensely. He feared the formation of an alliance between military commanders and public activists, a fear that was not entirely unreasonable given the close ties to senior officers of such political leaders as A. I. Guchkov. Indeed, M. K. Lemke, a senior military censor at General Headquarters, wrote in his diary on 1 April that many front commanders would willingly support an effort to remove Nicholas from the throne. In April Klimovich prepared at least three memoranda and saw to it that one of each was supplied to each cabinet minister, something Police Department directors never did. The memoranda described the leading public activists as politically subversive and contended that they were conspiring to overthrow the government.[90]

Klimovich recognized the immense value of A. P. Martynov's sources of intelligence about nonrevolutionary public activists. After 1917, Klimovich boasted to M. V. Chelnokov, the head of the Union of Town Dumas, that ten newspaper correspondents had reported to the security police on Russia's public organizations. Avrekh thought he was exaggerating, yet the continuous, detailed reports on the organizations' activities furnished by Martynov leave no doubt about the breadth of knowledge of Martynov's informants in these milieus. His report of 28 June 1916 on public activists, for example, drew upon data from seven different informants.[91]

The government adopted many practical measures to hinder the work of public activists. In April the Council of Ministers restricted public conferences and assemblies involving out-of-town participants in order to hinder cooperation between urban and provincial activists, proposed to pack the war industries committees with government officials, and limited the committees' intermediary role in the awarding of government military contracts. On 6 May Klimovich warned security policemen that revolutionary activists were using those committees to mask agitation among industrial workers. In late April the interior ministry urged governors to restrict the activities of the Union of Zemstvos. Deputy Interior Minister A. V. Stepanov was willing to go quite far in the latter regard: in an encoded cable of 24 May he reminded the governor-general of Irkutsk that he was accountable not to the interior ministry, but only to the Senate, so, he told the governor-general, "the application of the laws on associations and unions is up to you."[92]

In the first half of June Shtiurmer gathered first a kitchen cabinet of ministers then the full Council of Ministers to formulate policy on public organizations. They were especially concerned about the war industries committees, but their only major practical decision was to urge the authorities in Petrograd and Moscow to require that organizers of public meetings secure the approval of military district authorities. Then sometime within the next month or so Shtiurmer commissioned I. F. Manasevich-Manuilov and I. Ia. Gurliand to create a special surveillance office for political affairs that would employ informants drawn from among "people occupying prominent positions in various bureaucratic and public circles." This office, according to Beletskii, was to carry out surveillance over civil servants, the legislature, the military, foreign powers, and the Russian and foreign press, thus duplicating the functions of the Police Department, the court ministry's intelligence services, and, to a lesser extent, military intelligence. The multiplication of security services usually indicates official distrust of the established security apparatus and points to administrative and political instability, as for example in Napoleonic and Restoration France.[93] In this case, it probably also stemmed from Globachev's inability to use informants to penetrate the milieux of public activism.

In late July Klimovich revoked an order of 10 April 1915 requiring that the security police report every two months on the revolutionary and public movements in their jurisdictions. Henceforth, they were to report as they acquired important intelligence.[94] It seems that events were speeding up in general, and senior police officials were no longer willing to wait for periodic summaries of political intelligence.

Police assessments of the elite and lower-class mood varied over time. Martynov reported on 19 July that in the minds of many activists "what had seemed so close in March, now seems much harder to obtain." The activists cited four main reasons for the shift: successes at the front; the rightward movement of some public organizations; a progressive differentiation of social classes; and a press leak of excerpts from a Police Department report that laid bare the radical plans of certain public organizations, which made some people more reluctant to join them. A major Police Department analysis issued in July, on the other hand, offered a deeply pessimistic assessment of the social and political trends in Russia and concluded that a revolution was "unavoidable" even if the war ended soon and on favorable terms. This was the first in a series of astute and prophetic reports that fell on deaf ears. The report's author justified this conclusion by pointing to "unemployment and inflation, émigrés working with enemy governments to distribute propaganda to captured Russian soldiers, and revolutionary propaganda in the military and in the rear." Combating political agitation among military personnel was "next to impossible because government regulations forbid recruiting informants in the military." Worse, police analysts saw numerous parallels with the social and political trends of 1905. They believed that Zemgor would play the role of the Union of Unions; and the central workers' group of the Central War Industries Committee, that of the Soviet.[95]

Plots and intrigues destabilized the political landscape further. In mid-June, in the midst of A. A. Brusilov's disastrous military offensive, whose temporary successes buoyed the popular mood, M. V. Alekseev, the emperor's chief of staff at General Headquarters, urged Nicholas to establish a military dictatorship. The emperor seriously considered the proposal. Shtiurmer, by contrast, advocated creating a civilian-dominated military council. Nicholas rejected this proposal but in early July appointed Shtiurmer to replace Sazonov as foreign minister. (A. A. Khvostov, until then justice minister, took over at the interior ministry.) Reports from ten *uezdy* in Moscow province indicated widespread disapproval of the replacement of Sazonov with Shtiurmer, who was frequently referred to as a German.[96]

In August both Manasevich-Manuilov and D. L. Rubinshtein, a banker with close ties to Rasputin, were arrested in conjunction with a probe of alleged speculators by the N. S. Batiushin Commission. Klimovich had ordered Manasevich-Manuilov's arrest, which caused Shtiurmer to demand Klimovich's dismissal. Yet A. A. Khvostov, as interior minister, refused categorically to dismiss Klimovich. Shtiurmer remained at his post, while Khvostov lost his. (Klimovich was removed in mid-September.)[97] Although the new interior minister, A. D. Protopopov, was a leading Octobrist in the Duma, the public bristled at the appointment. Therefore he not only faced a disorganized ministry and gradually rising popular discontent, he also became a more despised interior minister than even Shtiurmer, if that were possible.

CHAPTER SEVEN

COLLAPSE OF

THE WATCHFUL

STATE

- The turning point toward revolution came in fall 1916. Although the country side remained relatively calm and much of the broader population was still committed to the war effort, inflation began to increase and certain foodstuffs and other necessary goods grew scarcer. Many opposition elites became more impatient. Rumors of treason in high places, of corrupt political machinations, and of governmental incompetence abounded. "Politically pornographic" utterances and imprints, while rather innocent in comparison to those riling the French population in 1789, undermined the prestige of the imperial house and dynasty. Conspiracies aimed at removing the "mad chauffeur" and at establishing a republic or a military dictatorship were hatched in half the salons in Petrograd. Although rumors of impending rebellion began to circulate in January 1917, T. Ardov could still write in the *Utro Rossii* issue of 12 February 1917, "we stand before the abyss; but browse through history: there has not been a day that this country has not stood before the abyss, and yet it stands."[1]

Fall 1916 was a turning point in Russian—and indeed world—history not because of failures by the imperial security police, who actually came quite close to foreseeing the revolutionary overthrow of the government and dynasty. The police report of July 1916 that concluded that a revolution was unavoidable and the repeated warnings by A. P. Martynov and K. I. Globachev starting in the fall show that the security police, who rarely sounded the clarion call for merely political reasons, were acutely aware of the intensifying popular animosity toward the political system and indeed toward the ruling house itself. The police devastated the revolutionary underground both before and during the war and gave an extremely accurate overall assessment of the security situation in the empire. If theirs was a voice of Cassandra in the imperial government, the drama that played out from September on bore the hallmarks of a classical Greek tragedy. The eyes and ears of the government knew that doom beckoned, but its brain was powerless to resist. Indeed, the security police failed to impress upon senior officials the moment's urgency, and they could not convince Nicholas to act decisively and effectively, but then who could have done so?

PROTOPOPOV

At one o'clock in the afternoon on Friday, 15 September 1916, A. D. Protopopov phoned the minister of trade and industry, V. N. Shakhovskoi, saying he wanted to reveal a great secret about himself. Shakhovskoi guessed
correctly that Protopopov would be the interior minister. Shakhovskoi rejected the rumor that Rasputin had engineered the new appointment. After
all, A. V. Krivoshein and M. V. Rodzianko esteemed Protopopov, who had
favorably impressed Sazonov as the head of a parliamentary delegation to
Italy, France, and England, and the English king had mentioned him very
positively in a letter to Nicholas. According to V. N. Voeikov, Nicholas
pointed to Rodzianko, England's George V, and Sazonov in explaining the
pick. Yet evidence of Rasputin's influence is unmistakable. On 7 September
Alexandra had written to Nicholas, "Grigorii begs you *earnestly* to name
Protopopov." Two days later Nicholas responded that Protopopov was a
good man, but "I must think over that question as it takes me quite unexpectedly." Rasputin's ideas "about men," he added, "are sometimes queer,
as you know." Although he worried that administrative officials were being
replaced too often, which he considered "not good for the interior of the
country," the appointment went through. On 14 September Alexandra
gushed, "Our Friend says you have done a very wise act in naming him."[2]

Aleksandr Dmitrievich Protopopov was born into a gentry family in
1866. He had large landholdings (4,500 desiatins, or 12,150 acres) and
owned a textile factory in Simbirsk Province, where he resided. An energetic businessman, he had implemented several innovative schemes at his
factory, first driving it to the brink of bankruptcy and finally transforming
it into a highly profitable enterprise. Protopopov was also an extraordinarily dynamic public activist. He had held several local elective posts, had
chaired the Union of Cloth Manufacturers, was a member of numerous political and benevolent associations, had authored technical works on textile
manufacturing and peasant farming, and from 1907 to 1917 was an Octobrist deputy of the Duma, where he had joined the Progressive Bloc and
was serving as associate chairman. He also enjoyed close ties to powerful
banking circles and had secretly developed connections to rightist activists,
as well as to Rasputin, to whom P. A. Badmaev, a doctor of Tibetan medi-
cine and a general schemer, had introduced him. One Soviet historian argued that these circles and activists had worked through Rasputin to win
Protopopov's appointment.[3]

In recent years, however, Protopopov had grown psychologically unstable. Interviews in 1917 with Protopopov's servants and colleagues indicated that the new interior minister had an erratic, even chaotic, but fertile
mind frequently smitten with something like manias for a wide variety of activities to which he would wholly abandon himself for months at a time: mu-
sic, photography, women, business. Most respondents called him talkative,

Aleksandr Dmitrievich Protopopov, the last interior minister
(September 1916 to February 1917).

"very kind," and "popular." They also noted his periodic nervous crises, the most recent having occurred in 1915. Several officials who had worked closely with him in 1916 recalled that he did not seem to read the reports they prepared for him. The commander of the Gendarme Corps, D. N. Tatishchev, said that "he spoke endlessly." One of Protopopov's deputies, V. A. Bal'ts, claimed that he had no knowledge of the work of the interior ministry, "jumped from topic to topic," and "could not concentrate." A. T. Vasil'ev, a staunch supporter, while not denying Protopopov's inability to concentrate, could only protest that "he possessed vision in a far higher degree than many of his colleagues in office, and was, above all, a personality of incorruptible uprightness and candor."[4]

Protopopov's choice of P. G. Kurlov, his personal friend from their regimental days, as deputy for police affairs caused a scandal. Aside from the rumors connected with Stolypin's assassination, in August 1915 Kurlov had been removed from the office of Baltic governor-general amid allegations of malfeasance and indulgence toward Germans. In his spare time he had joined with Badmaev and L. A. Mantashev, an oilman and banker, in founding a company to build a railroad to Mongolia. He had suffered a stroke and walked with difficulty, and he was also hobbled by a legalistic handicap: the Senate, because its members disapproved of him, did not confirm his appointment. A. I. Spiridovich blamed Protopopov's absentmindedness; Vasil'ev pointed to intriguers. In any event, Kurlov had to conduct his work of actively overseeing the functioning of the Police Department "as a private advisor, who had no right to sign officials documents or to speak in the highest government institutions." Yet the public knew—or guessed, which was worse—his true role, and this led to outcries in the press and an interpellation in the Duma.[5]

Kurlov apparently recommended his friend A. T. Vasil'ev, most recently a censor, to replace E. K. Klimovich, who was made a senator, as Police Department director. Vasil'ev told the liberal *Birzhevye vedomosti* in early October that he would place legality and the law *(pravo i zakon)* at the center of his work. In his memoirs Vasil'ev wrote that he had planned to carry out an "internal reorganization of the administrative machinery of the police," but Spiridovich exclaimed to Kurlov that Vasil'ev "only drinks and plays cards." "How can he be Police Department director in such troubled times?" Rasputin had probably helped him get the position. Vasil'ev admitted to having met with Rasputin "many a time" and having conversed with him "about a great variety of topics," but he described him as a sagacious peasant without political influence. A month after his appointment, Vasil'ev enjoyed an audience of a quarter-hour with the empress, an unusual event for a police chief.[6]

Protopopov's appointment was intended in part to create a bridge between the Duma and the government, and indeed the new interior minister proposed to Nicholas that the legislature be granted the right to impeach cabinet officials, an important step on the path of constitutionalism. As late as 6 October some liberals and moderates welcomed this "capitulation before the educated public." As one remarked, "we could only have hoped for a liberal bureaucrat, and here's an Octobrist." Soon, however, Protopopov's parliamentary colleagues came to view him as a traitor, especially when rumors about Rasputin's influence and Protopopov's sycophancy at court surfaced. When A. F. Kerenskii noticed a reproduction of Guido's portrait of Christ in his office, Protopopov remarked, "I never part with Him. And when it is necessary to make a decision, He shows me the right path." Kerenskii thought to himself, "Who is he, a madman or a charlatan slyly adapting himself to the musty atmosphere of the chambers of the empress and the 'little house' of Anna Vyrubova?"[7]

On 19 October Protopopov met informally with leading members of the Progressive Bloc. Two participants, V. V. Shul'gin and a police informant, wrote almost identical descriptions of the encounter. Protopopov pleaded, "Why not talk with me as comrades?" P. N. Miliukov snapped, "A man who has served with Shtiurmer, . . . who persecutes the press and public organizations, cannot be our comrade." A. I. Shingarev jumped in: "You come to us not in modest frock-coat but in a gendarme uniform; how are we to understand this?" When the Octobrist Count I. I. Kapnist tried to calm Protopopov, the interior minister lashed out: "It's easy for you to sit on your chair there, you have a count's title; you have wealth and connections. . . . I have nothing but the personal support of the tsar, but with that support I'll go to the end, whatever your attitude toward me." Soon Duma deputies were passing to each other satirical poems mocking Protopopov's affection for the gendarme's uniform.[8]

SOCIAL TURMOIL

A rise in popular discontent in Russia coincided with Protopopov's assumption of office. Strikes became larger and more frequent. As bread and other staples disappeared from shops periodically, some rioting occurred. Peasant attacks on the property of people with German surnames increased. Administrative authorities in Moscow, on 4–5 October, declared the first stage of emergency preparedness according to a plan elaborated a year before. The key worry of government officials was whether the troops would remain loyal. In this regard, disquieting signs were unmistakable. From late summer until January the military censors observed a sharp increase in apathy among military personnel, up to 82 percent in the Third Army on the western front. By October senior officials in Moscow were expressing concern about the reliability of local troops.[9]

For now, however, the main preoccupations of the security police were the remaining revolutionary activists, the broader population, and well-known public figures. Among revolutionaries, only the Social Democrats suffered repeated arrests, on 13 September and 3 November in Petrograd, for example, and on 28 September and 22 October in Moscow. Globachev's report for October, while warning of some persistent dangers, triumphantly described the Social Democrats as being "in a miserable state" and the Socialist-Revolutionaries as "totally disorganized." Many more arrests of Social Democrats occurred through the end of the year.[10]

Security police reports on the broader population were less sanguine. Although people in the countryside around Moscow seem to have remained calm and as content as can be imagined after more than two years of total war, the mood of city dwellers in Moscow and Petrograd worsened precipitously. By late October Martynov observed "such irritation and anger of the masses [as] we have not seen before. . . . Not a single social class is in sympathy with the government." People were talking about taking revenge against "the chauffeur" after the war. Martynov warned almost prophetically that "if the food crisis continues, then no patriotic sentiment will stop the people from spontaneous disorders."[11]

The situation in Petrograd was much worse. "The food question," wrote Globachev, "is the sole and terrible cause of popular bitterness and discontent." For the moment "the movement is economic, but as soon as it crystallizes it will become political." The mass of workers were ready to engage in the "most savage food riots." According to Martynov, rumors of administrative corruption, official malfeasance, the influence of "dark forces," and treason in high places "spread insidiously through countless press accounts." On 30 October Vasil'ev admitted to Protopopov that the mood in the imperial capitals was more oppositional than in 1905–1906 and that "major disorders can arise in many places." Yet his report struck an optimistic note overall. The countryside was "calm and indifferent," and history had shown that "no revolution is possible without the peasantry."[12] Here was a clear bifurcation between professional security officers, like Globachev and Martynov, with their objective understanding of the immense political and social dangers threatening the government, and senior officials, like Vasil'ev and Protopopov, who often either refused to face reality or sugarcoated it for the benefit of the emperor and empress, who preferred to believe that their subjects—especially the military—would remain docile and loyal no matter how harsh their lives became.

On 1 November P. N. Miliukov delivered his now famous oration insinuating that, in regard to poor policy decisions and military defeats, B. V. Shtiurmer either had acted as an agent of the German state or had been a fool, and that in either case he could not have done more to disorganize Russia had he been a German spy. Miliukov also made a less-noticed reference to intrigues allegedly conducted in Switzerland by two police officials, L. A. Rataev and V. I. Lebedev. Miliukov implied that they and other, unnamed, police officials were involved in secret negotiations with the Germans. No evidence corroborating this allegation has come to light. In late December a senior Russian military attaché in France, A. A. Ignat'ev, avowed that Rataev and Lebedev were his agents and that Miliukov had "brought harm" to Russia's intelligence operations.[13]

In retrospect Miliukov believed that his speech, given its immense impact and wide distribution despite a ban on its publication, was the beginning of the revolution. Certainly provincial gendarmes reported that the oration and other speeches and letters were being copied and passed from hand to hand and were playing a huge role in increasing social tension. To try to stem the tide of opposition, on 2 November Protopopov directed governors to forbid public congresses and to delegate competent administrative observers, such as deputy governors but not gendarme officers, to all private meetings of public organizations.[14]

On 9 November Nicholas dismissed Shtiurmer as a concession to the public and replaced him with A. F. Trepov, the minister of transportation. Trepov made overtures to the public. He told Rodzianko: "I want to work with the Duma, and I will overcome the influence of Rasputin." Rodzianko demanded that Trepov remove Protopopov. On 10 November Nicholas wrote to Alexandra that he planned to dismiss the interior minister. "He jumped fr. one idea to another," he wrote. "It is risky leaving the min. of Int. in such hands at such times!" Nicholas added: "Only please don't mix in our Friend." The next day, Alexandra entreated him not to remove Protopopov. He "is honestly *for us*," she wrote. Meanwhile, Alexandra urged A. A. Mosolov to assist Protopopov in his work. He shared with her his concerns about the minister's nervous imbalance *(rasstroistvo)*. She admitted that Protopopov needed at his side an efficient administrator, a "balanced *[uravnoveshnyi]* man." Mosolov refused, noting that he had "no understanding of police matters and not enough legal knowledge."[15] Of course, neither did Protopopov, who nevertheless remained at his post.

Even so, the police apparatus continued to function, perhaps, as G. I. Shavel'skii believed in regard to the entire state machine, "only because previously it was well set up." On the day of Trepov's appointment, Protopopov ordered security policemen and governors to brace for possible disorders. He also appointed A. P. Balk as city governor of Petrograd. Kurlov wrote of Balk, a senior police official in Warsaw and Moscow since 1903, that he "knew a great deal about police affairs and was very honest." He also had had experience suppressing popular rebellion; he had been in Warsaw in 1905–1906. Now, together with S. S. Khabalov, the commander of the Petrograd military district, he worked out plan for crushing potential unrest. Sometime in late fall, the special surveillance office Shtiurmer had proposed in the spring began operations. Under the supervision of Vasil'ev, it prepared detailed reports on all spheres of political life, from the royal court and high-society salons to guard officers, Duma circles, and groupings of government officials, such as the nationalist group of N. N. Balashov.[16]

Despite some police reports suggesting an upswing in the popular mood in mid-November, by the end of the month Globachev warned of a food crisis and that inflation would engender discontent. Special Section sources indicate that Moscow city and province were gripped by "energetic antidynastic propaganda—not only among workers but among peasants too." Even the State Council was dissatisfied with the government. In late November a large majority passed a resolution demanding the "immediate removal of irresponsible forces" from the government. Most reports sent from the districts of Moscow Province in the first two weeks of December revealed a grim popular mood and strong antigovernment sentiment exacerbated by wild rumors. People talked heatedly about the alleged suicide of General A. A. Brusilov and the influence of "dark forces," with Rasputin behind them all.[17]

Police officials worried about demoralization and unrest among the troops and about officers plotting with opposition leaders. In late 1916, A. P. Kublitskii-Piotukh, a gendarme officer dispatched by Vasil'ev, found that throughout the army soldiers commonly asserted that "the Tsarina was a traitor in alliance with the Germans and was trying to bring about the defeat of Russia." When Protopopov conveyed the investigation's results to Nicholas, the emperor "read through the document, waved his hand in hopeless resignation, and never said another word about the matter." In October or November Martynov learned that a senior commander, allegedly M. V. Alekseev, had assured leaders of the Progressive Bloc of his "full support." A. V. Gerasimov, in early December, heard from a senior officer about "two oppositional centers." One involved commanders of key military districts at the front. The other was a palace conspiracy supposedly led by Grand Duke Andrei Vladimirovich and embracing nearly all the grand dukes and the officers close to them either as participants or as sympathizers.[18]

Police agents watched A. I. Guchkov with especial care because of his close ties to the military. A report of 9 December noted: "He has tried to gather all the threads of military power in the country." His ultimate goal was supposedly to "to follow the example of the 'Young Turks.'" Rodzianko hosted a meeting in early January at his home in which General A. M. Krymov, back from the front, and several Duma deputies, state counselors, and members of the Special Council for Defense took part. Krymov assured the group that the army would support a coup. Brusilov, who was not there, was later quoted as saying, "if I have to choose between tsar and Russia, I'll choose the latter." However, it seems these plots never got beyond an "embryonic" stage.[19]

Right-wing efforts to shore up the government and the dynasty, also afoot, were less serious, even though they enjoyed some official support, especially financial assistance. Kurlov was enthusiastic about a new government-subsidized newspaper, *Russkaia volia*, but even it started criticizing Protopopov harshly. Rightist leaders with or without official support began to organize an empire-wide conference of rightist organizations and redoubled their efforts to create a conservative parliamentary bloc. Their efforts failed. M. Ia. Govorukho-Otrok, a member of the State Council, tried to submit to Nicholas a proposal for transforming the Duma into a consultative body, appointing more rightists to the State Council, declaring a state of siege in the major cities, and strengthening the garrisons and supplying them with machine guns and artillery. Nicholas never received the memorandum, presumably because its author was not well enough connected to court circles. In mid-January A. A. Rimskii-Korsakov, a right-wing senator and State Council member close to Shtiurmer, submitted to Protopopov a proposal to strengthen the government by means of stricter censorship, draconian punishments for libel, generous subsidies for conservative media outlets, the rigorous application of martial law, confiscation of the property of activists seeking to overturn or weaken the state order, wide bestowal of awards on loyal subjects (especially among the masses), and increased police funding.[20] This proposal languished.

The most sensational of all the plots, and the only one to bear fruit, was the conspiracy to murder Rasputin. Its success did not stem from police inattentiveness. Shtiurmer told one witness that "Rasputin is being protected almost more thoroughly than the tsar." At the head of his security detail stood the shady but experienced and competent M. S. Kommisarov. The assassins' membership in high-society and right-wing circles probably explains their success: Rasputin, otherwise a highly suspicious man, imagined himself secure in the company of the immensely wealthy Prince F. F. Iusupov, whom he knew and trusted. Iusupov and his accomplices, V. M. Purishkevich and Grand Duke Dmitrii Pavlovich, the emperor's cousin, hoped that if they made Rasputin disappear, they would cause Nicholas to turn to his nobility for support. (One commentator argues that Samuel Hoare, a British agent, actually killed Rasputin to prevent him from bringing about a separate peace between Russia and Germany.)[21]

Not only did educated society applaud the murder, so did Gerasimov and many members of the imperial family, which made the division between the imperial couple and Russia's elites widen into a yawning canyon. Key in this development was a cable sent by Grand Duchess Elizaveta Fedorovna but intercepted by the police, congratulating Dmitrii Pavlovich and Iusupov for their deed. After the murder, Protopopov gave Alexandra several other letters from grand dukes and duchesses that were critical of her. The emperor chose not to approve a formal investigation of his nephew Dmitrii Pavlovich and instead exiled Dmitrii to Persia and Iusupov to an estate in Kursk Province. The new premier, N. D. Golitsyn, a personal friend of the imperial family, vainly sought to remove Protopopov, who remained in office until the fall of the dynasty.[22]

The political climate became even worse. G. E. Botkin, the son of Nicholas's personal physician, recalled his father's words, "What Youssoupoff actually has done is to fire the first shot of the revolution. He has showed others the way—when a demand is not granted, take the law in your own hands and shoot." G. I. Shavel'skii thought, "We are living on a volcano. A month ago, it was possible to fix things. Now, it is too late to save us from catastrophe." The British agent Bruce Lockhart reported that the military no longer supported the emperor, and Globachev reported on 5 January that the "mood in the capital is exceptionally disturbing." Wild rumors were circulating, and broad segments of the population expected both government repression and major popular unrest, leftist outbursts and an aristocratic palace coup. Martynov reported on the same day that Kadets and Progressists had pledged to reject the emperor's right to prorogue the Duma.[23]

However, the mood of one important segment of the population, the military, improved from mid-November to the early days of January. The report's author, attempting to account for the upswing, pointed to improved supplies of warm clothing and food, better-outfitted dwellings, better-stocked military shops, and improved entertainment possibilities.[24] With a mostly loyal military, the government could presumably weather nearly any political crisis.

TOWARD REVOLUTION

The New Year came in under clouds of conflict between the government and society and between the emperor and his extended family. According to police intelligence, society gossiped about Nicholas's cold greetings to the guests at his official reception and about the fact that he had invited only his brother Mikhail Aleksandrovich to the dinner that followed. At the reception Rodzianko tore his own arm away from Protopopov, who was trying to make peace. Even Mikhail felt alienated. A week later, he admitted to Rodzianko that "the whole family recognizes how harmful she [Alexandra] is. My brother and she are surrounded solely by traitors." Martynov recalled that the city governor, V. N. Shebeko, a tall, courtly Anglophile, held a New Year's Eve party "to show the unity of government and society, but society did not come. The food was excellent, but society was not there."[25]

Police officials were deeply concerned about popular unrest. The number of worker days lost to strikes increased nearly tenfold from November to December. On 20 December Protopopov ordered governors to take energetic measures to mediate labor disputes and quash strikes and to summon troops in case of violence. A report of 2 January prepared for Protopopov warned of a unification of opposition and revolutionary forces that, "as demonstrated by a study of the revolutionary movement in Russia, will occur only at the moment of a final, decisive 'assault' on the lawful authority, realized in the form of a series of mass disorders and, finally, a general armed insurrection." The report then pointed to numerous repressive actions designed to thwart both movements: in Moscow during 9–11 December the authorities shut down congresses of the unions of zemstvos and town dumas and banned several other meetings, and in Petrograd in the period of 9–18 December the police seized three illegal presses operated by revolutionaries.[26]

Several arrests aimed largely at Social Democratic organizers and activists ensued in early January. Even so, up to three hundred thousand workers struck in Petrograd on 9 January, the anniversary of Bloody Sunday. Protopopov immediately proposed stationing more troops in Petrograd; one squadron of naval guards was sent to Tsarskoe Selo. In early February,

Protopopov also directed local authorities to create special detachments for suppressing disorder. In Moscow all security forces were placed again on the first stage of alert.[27]

The political imagination of more and more elites and ordinary people grew feverish. Rumors of threats to senior officials and the imperial family abounded. The political circles of Petrograd, according to a police report of 13 January, excitedly discussed an alleged attempt on the life of the empress by either Prince S. V. Gagarin or Prince V. N. Obolenskii, two courtiers. On 14 January an informant related conversations with V. M. Zenzinov and A. F. Kerenskii, who both considered a revolution inevitable. On 16 January War Minister M. A. Beliaev warned "that revolutionary elements are organizing in the army."[28]

An informant report prepared on 19 January described deep and widespread popular disgruntlement. Everywhere one encountered harsh criticism of the government and of the dynasty: "in the streets, in trams, in stores, in theaters." People anxiously predicted a coming coup. Rumormongers "savored the details" of the inevitable atrocities in the coming conflagration. In conversation on politics, people would say "he should be shot" or "he should be stabbed." On 19 January, Globachev worried that "the working masses have come to believe in the necessity and feasibility of a general strike and a subsequent revolution," while "the educated elite circles have come to believe in the salutariness of political murder and terror." Overall, in the words of A. V. Amfiteatrov, "the man in the street has awoken from his ten-year slumber and is preparing to arise."[29]

Reports prepared for Protopopov on 16 and 19 January pointed to deep divisions among the Kadet leaders. They agreed only on the need to fight the war to a victorious end. On 19 January, however, Martynov presented to Vasil'ev a bleaker picture: V. A. Maklakov argued that "even the most moderate liberals, after a hard struggle, have come to the conclusion that *the revolutionary path of struggle is unavoidable. It is only a question of when precisely the struggle will begin.*" Globachev concurred, though less charitably, in a report of 26 January. The liberal and moderate opposition leaders, he wrote, awaited the overthrow of the government by the vanguard fighters, who would "clear off with their bodies the path to a bright future." Then the liberals and moderates would offer their services to the country in the role of "experienced and knowledgeable statesmen." On the same day Vasil'ev warned Protopopov that Rodzianko and the Progressive Bloc would soon deny the government's authority to dissolve the Duma; he also warned that Guchkov, G. E. L'vov, and A. I. Konovalov, supported by industrialists and military units, expected to seize power in a palace coup.[30]

Numerous contemporaries saw in Protopopov a simplistic villain. Kurlov and Globachev described Protopopov as incompetent, overwhelmed, and unwilling to impress upon Nicholas the gravity of the political situation. Kurlov wrote that by early January the interior ministry was in "total chaos." According to another source, Protopopov often failed to attend cabinet meetings. But other witnesses considered Protopopov ruthless and clever. Miliukov believed that he planned to draw huge crowds out into the streets on 14 February in order "to shoot them with machine guns." M. P. Chubinskii, a moderate journalist, noted that the public, sharing these fears, began to hoard water and candles. Even A. A. Mosolov recalled that Protopopov expected that "the dissolution of the state Duma would call forth better than any provocation the revolution into the street, where he vowed immediately to crush it with one massive shooting."[31]

Protopopov's major repressive initiative was the arrest of the central workers' group of the Central War Industries Committee. On the night of 26–27 January, Globachev's forces raided the section's offices, arresting nine members. On 17 February the Duma overwhelmingly adopted an interpellation challenging the government's action. Records seized by the police indicated that the workers' group had planned to spearhead a demonstration aimed at provoking Duma deputies to seize power. Indeed, on 29 November, K. A. Gvozdev, the chairman of the workers' group, had stated at a meeting held to elect representatives to the Central War Industries Committee, "it is vital to organize all dynamic social forces of Russia to fight against . . . our dreadful internal enemy—the autocratic order." Of the workers' section Tsuyoshi Hasegawa judged that "Protopopov and his police were justified in concluding that it was ultimately revolutionary, with the goal of overthrowing the government."[32]

Protopopov authorized no further repressive measures. He refused Globachev's request to arrest the leaders of the Central War Industries Committee, the unions of zemstvos and town dumas, and the Progressive Bloc. "These measures," Globachev wrote, "undoubtedly would have averted for a long time the possibility of a coup." Meanwhile, S. S. Khabalov laid plans for deploying police and troops armed with machine guns. Although he and N. V. General Ruzskii, the commander of the northwestern and northern fronts, refused to remove reserve units from Petrograd—perhaps the gravest error of the moment—they agreed to requisition four regiments of cavalry guards, but then Ruzskii ignored the order, according to Vasil'ev; or headquarters countermanded it to please the Duma, according to Grand Duke Aleksandr Mikhailovich; or Alekseev, preparing for a major offensive in the spring, refused to give up his guard regiments. The situation seemed grave, in any event. General Ruzskii apparently warned Khabalov of "terrible propaganda among the troops," because of which "we should never use weapons during disorders."[33]

Back in the fall Martynov, and to a lesser extent Globachev, had alerted Vasil'ev to strong antigovernment and antidynastic sentiments gripping the population. They had pointed to ominous rumors, popular disgruntlement, and discussions and plans for palace coups and other conspiratorial actions. But they had also provided reassuring accounts of the weakness of revolutionary activists and organizations. In the new year their reports more and more insistently sounded the alarm. On 28 January Globachev reported that the population was living in a world of rumors, lending credence to the wildest and most preposterous allegations, stories, and interpretations. The whole of society, he wrote, awaited "extremely important events," which were supposed to occur on "9 or 12 or 24 January, or perhaps on 1, 8, or 14 February, and so on." A week later Globachev warned that the "economic crisis is now affecting the entire population." The disintegration of the food-supply system, he cautioned, "combined with political sedition threatens Russia with a collapse never before experienced in Russian history." In a separate version of the same report, prepared for the emperor's information bureau, Globachev added in his own hand, "if no hunger rebellion has yet broken out, this does not mean that none is in the offing; and there is no doubt that that sort of outburst of the hungry masses—especially in the capital—will be the first step on the path of the most senseless and [indecipherable word] excesses of the most horrible kind of anarchistic revolution."[34]

On 6 February Martynov described the almost apocalyptic anxiety expressed at a Kadet central committee meeting two days before. Miliukov urged that the party persist in its intransigence. The historian A. A Kizevetter likened the political situation to that in "France at the end of the 18th century, or in Europe in 1848, . . . As an astronomer with mathematical tables can predict an eclipse of the sun or the approach of a comet, an historian of our time can predict the outcome of the struggle of the government with society. The government has step by step severed all its supports and now hangs by a single thread."[35]

The next day Globachev warned that revolutionary activists still planned to organize demonstrations at the Taurida Palace on 10 and 14 February. They would probably enjoy success, he wrote, given the sour mood of the working masses. Indeed, with high inflation and the periodic disappearance from shops of bread and meat, "one must expect . . . large-scale strikes, an attempt to organize a demonstration and to carry it to open confrontation . . . with the police and troops, in order to create a bloody incident, which would push the country to revolution."[36]

Worried about rallies scheduled for mid-February, on the 13th Martynov ordered the search of fifteen Moscow addresses associated with revolutionary activists; seven people were arrested. The next day, only modest disorders occurred. In Pegrograd, in contrast, Globachev ordered no arrests, and on the 14th over eighty thousand workers struck. According to Globachev's account, crowds of up to five hundred people walked down streets chanting "down with the war," "down with the police," and "beat the looters." Bread stores, having coincidentally run out of wares, shut their doors. People called for the removal of Protopopov. Rumors circulated of impending pogroms. Officers, most of them ensigns, also took part, taunting the police.[37]

Vasil'ev apparently did not take the ominous security police intelligence entirely seriously. The few of his reports to Protopopov still extant reflect only dimly the alarming nature of the conjuncture. Spiridovich returned from Yalta on 20 February, and "the helpless, miserable Vasil'ev" rebuffed his concerns. "'Everything is fine,' he said; 'the minister is a fine man and easy to work with.'" Spiridovich then visited the security bureau, where "they viewed the situation as hopeless." It surely did not help that on 2 February a new official, I. P. Vasil'ev, a minor gendarme officer of no relation to A. T. Vasil'ev, took the reins at the Special Section.[38]

On 21 February Spiridovich observed Protopopov consulting with V. N. Voeikov, the court commandant, about travel arrangements for the emperor. "Protopopov spoke merrily," recalled Spiridovich: "There is full order and calm in the capital; the emperor may depart with a quiet conscience." Voeikov confirmed that Protopopov "always assured me that there was nothing to worry about." The special surveillance office nevertheless was providing Protopopov with information starkly contradicting such optimism. According to a report of 23 February, for example, galloping inflation, the closing of small enterprises for want of raw materials, and scarcities of essential consumer goods were driving many people to argue that if the existing government could not alleviate their hardships, "power should be given to others." Later in the year Protopopov admitted to an investigating commission that he knew full well the dangers facing the country, but, as he put it, "I wished to calm the emperor and empress."[39]

THE FEBRUARY DAYS

When the Duma opened on 14 February, Rodzianko felt a sense of doom. Rumors had persisted of Protopopov's alleged plan, which was never substantiated by any concrete evidence, to provoke, then crush, violent demonstrations that day. Sometime around 20 February, amid fears that bread would soon be rationed, consumers bought up the entire supply, despite long lines and frigid temperatures of -14.5°C (6°F). Major factories shut down for want of fuel, and tens of thousands of laborers suddenly became idle. Oblivious to the gathering storm, Nicholas departed for Mogilev on 22 February. The next day, International Women's Day, it became much warmer (5–6°C, 41–43°F), and the sun shone. A large procession of students and women, chanting "Bread, bread," made its way down Nevskii Prospekt amid Cossack patrols. Major demonstrations took place outside the city center, about one hundred thousand workers struck, and protesters clashed with police thirteen times, but the forces of order remained in firm control.[40]

Spiridovich recalled that Globachev kept saying "Revolution is imminent" but then missed its beginning. Spiridovich esteemed Petrograd's security chief, "but he had neither the ability to undertake all the necessary measures, nor a broader vision. He was realistic, saw things rather clearly, but could not deal with them well." That evening, Globachev told Balk that he had no idea why crowds had massed in the streets during the day. Balk thought perhaps the good weather had drawn people out. The bread that day, though rationed, had been especially tasty too. Yet Balk knew danger was lurking. The city needed forty wagons of flour daily, but less was being delivered due to rail congestion. Protopopov confided to his diary that he was relying on military authorities to maintain order in the capital. His personal intelligence service cautioned that the attempts of revolutionary organizations "to spark a 'hunger rebellion' are not entirely unrealistic." The population of Petrograd, the service's report continued, "is stirred by the rise in prices, and a rebellion can be expected at any moment." More food and consumer goods had to be provided.[41] It seems Protopopov undertook no steps toward this end.

On the 24 February street demonstrations began at eight o'clock in the morning. By nine o'clock some forty thousand people were gathered on Liteinyi Prospekt, a main thoroughfare leading from Nevskii Prospekt, Petrograd's main artery, to Shpalernaia Street, where the Taurida Palace is situated. Police captains in the affected areas drafted reports right away but phoned them in to Balk only after eleven o'clock, as the number of demonstrators continued to swell. The police tried to control the crowds but could only nudge them up and down the Nevskii.[42]

What had started as a bread rally turned into an antigovernment protest with loud cries of "Down with the autocracy!" An eyewitness described the crowds as composed mostly of students, teenagers, women, and officers. In the afternoon, despite a request from Balk, Khabalov refused to station troops near policemen in isolated areas. Workers crossed the Neva River during the day, prompting War Minister M. A. Beliaev to propose that Khabalov order police to shoot at them in such a way that the bullets would fall before them. Khabalov issued no such order, though apparently a few police did shoot. By this point, only a few policemen had been wounded; none had been killed.[43]

When Balk read the police reports that evening, he realized that the situation was far graver than he had thought. He contacted Khabalov, who told him that the military authorities had decided not to use the force of arms. Court protocol thwarted Balk's effort to report urgently to Nicholas. His report, by tradition drafted in a lovely hand and signed at midnight, ran through various set topics, including "misfortunate incidents with military personnel," and allowed for only a few lines at the end on "incidents in the capital." It vexed the clerk that Balk wished to expand on this subject.[44]

That evening, Globachev warned Balk, Khabalov, and Protopopov that revolutionary activists hoped to incite demonstrators the next day to more resolute antigovernment protests. He added that some of the troops stationed in the city were not reliable. Khabalov authorized Globachev to arrest revolutionary leaders, then from his office in the general staff building Khabalov assumed full control over the city, dividing it into sectors and concentrating policemen near the headquarters of each sector. Globachev later argued that it would still have been possible to contain the disorders using only regular policemen and guards from the gendarme division.[45]

The public apparently saw a controlling hand behind all the events of the day. Iu. V. Lomonosov, a senior railroad official under both the emperor and the Bolsheviks, described a mocking look on policemen's faces. "I don't like this look: it smells of provocation; the police is up to something. . . . Strange: a rally is allowed, people walk freely, as though lured into a trap." By this time, however, the government was in reality losing control. Protopopov agreed to "sacrifice himself" and retire, since his very name "irritated the crowd."[46] He nevertheless remained at his post.

The newspapers of Saturday morning, 25 February, made little of the events of the previous day. N. V. Savich, an Octobrist, walked throughout almost all of Petrograd and did not notice anything out of the ordinary. "The streets were almost empty. The Nevskii was not busy. Policemen were peacefully standing at their posts. In other words, everything as usual." After visiting General Beliaev, he headed home.[47]

"When I approached the Nevskii," he wrote, "I was astonished at how quickly the appearance of the avenue had changed." The sidewalks were suddenly full of people heading toward Kazanskii Cathedral or the city duma. He wrote that it was "as if according to a secret signal people started flocking to some point in the city." Protesters grew bolder: students attacked and disarmed police. Professionals, artisans, and civil servants joined ordinary laborers in protests. Officially 201,248 workers laid down their tools. Balk recalled that in the afternoon and evening the crowd was dominated by "young punks [podonki] and students, many of whom were Jewish." Orators appeared, calling for the overthrow of the government and accusing senior officials of treason. Yet Spiridovich visited Protopopov that day and found him "happy and charming as usual." That evening, Protopopov finally reported to General Headquarters on the disorders, though without breathing a word about their political character.[48]

Because of reports warning that Social Democrats planned to cut electric power and other services and to undertake diverse measures aimed at launching an armed uprising, and that anarchists intended to blow up the headquarters of the security bureau and gendarme station, Globachev proposed that night to arrest up to two hundred revolutionary activists, as well as the reconstituted workers' group. Recent, rather tenuous evidence suggests that the alleged Social Democratic plot may have been proposed by a police informant.[49]

At midnight Prime Minister Golitsyn conferred with senior officials. Khabalov promised to resort to force of arms if necessary, though Balk thought he lacked conviction. Beliaev, wrote Balk, "spoke weakly, like a person fearing responsibility." Protopopov, like a university professor, "started enumerating political parties with influence on the events: 'imagine a circle with different segments, larger and smaller, colored in political colors—red, orange, black.'" Balk, with considerable understatement, remarked that he did not "think that those present were interested in political segments; time was of the essence." At the end of his discourse, Protopopov advocated taking decisive measures. The minister of agriculture A. A. Rittikh went further. Blood had to be shed. "If we wait," he warned, it would take "a sea of blood" to restore order. He spoke "with such an unswerving tone and with such passion, that everyone quieted down." Still, about all they could agree on, it seems, was to allow the workers' group to meet the next day. Telegrams to General Headquarters from Khabalov and Beliaev, while admitting that disorders had been occurring, gave the impression that everything was under control. Nevertheless, Nicholas issued his infamous order to open fire should the next day bring more turmoil.[50]

On Sunday the 26th Globachev reported that during the previous night his bureau had arrested one hundred members of revolutionary organizations, including five members of the Social Democratic Petrograd Committee, as well as two more members of the workers' group. Although the security bureau continued to function actively, it received less and less support from the regular police: that day only six phone reports from district police stations came in. Five informants reported as well. One, V. E. Shurkanov, spoke prophetically. If the troops remained loyal the revolutionary movement would collapse, he argued, but if not, "nothing will save the country from revolutionary overthrow."[51]

At around ten o'clock in the morning Balk learned that on the city's outskirts troops had started to fire on crowds. At noon detachments of the Volynskii Guards Regiment opened fire at the eastern end of the Nevskii. Troops soon began firing upon crowds south of the Nevskii and near the Taurida Palace. At six o'clock in the evening Globachev warned Khabalov that the crowds had refused to disperse even when fired upon and that he could no longer vouch for the reliability of the soldiers stationed in Petrograd. Khabalov supposedly refused to believe it. Later, Vasil'ev invited Protopopov to dinner. They chatted idly "for a long time." Afterward, Vasil'ev summoned Spiridovich and Globachev for coffee. Globachev wondered why on earth they had called him from his desk "at such a serious moment for a cup of coffee." Spiridovich recalled that Globachev had realized that "revolution was upon them," yet despite being a good officer, "He could not captivate the minister and compel him to act."[52]

At ten o'clock that night Protopopov departed to meet with the Council of Ministers, which agreed to suspend the Duma's session and to place a stronger, more popular man, such as General Alekseev, at the head of the government. Reports to Balk that night suggested that order had been restored but that the troops were tired and hungry. That day, Balk reckoned, some fifty people, mostly bystanders, had been killed. Globachev phoned him at three o'clock in the morning to report on a mutiny in the Second Fleet.[53]

By nine o'clock in the morning on Monday, 27 February, soldiers of four regiments had mutinied. Workers and soldiers began looting and setting fire to apartment buildings. At around ten o'clock the gendarme division joined the rebels, and the district court was in flames. Vasil'ev noted that gradually most troops mutinied, the telephone connections went down, and crowds attacked prisons and released inmates. Hasegawa argues that the soldiers' mutinies were decisive: one disciplined division could have suppressed the rebellion. But now there was no turning back. P. N. Vrangel' recalled that "thousands of criminals stormed out of the prisons and looted nearby clothing stores, leaving the streets littered with prison garb." Police stations in outlying quarters of the city were besieged and policemen were savagely killed. At noon the security bureau received its final recorded report from a regular police station. Many policemen donned civilian clothes and fled. The mob searched for them and tortured and killed some. The Taurida Palace became their refuge. "The Duma" wrote V. V. Shul'gin, "became a big district police station, only now policemen were brought in under arrest." The arrestees included eighty-three gendarme officers. The memory of the person, whoever it was, who thought to offer them shelter, wrote Balk, "should forever remain in our hearts."[54]

Heeding a warning about machine gun fire on Liteinyi Prospekt, Vasil'ev stayed at home that morning and gave orders to dismiss Police Department employees. When he received word of mobs attacking police headquarters, he directed the remaining officials to burn the addresses of police officials and lists of informants. When looters soon broke in, however, they were after another set of documents—regular criminal records: files, photographs, and fingerprints, to which they set fire. At five o'clock Globachev learned that a huge armed crowd, having sacked an alcohol purifying factory southeast of the city, was making its way toward the security bureau. He therefore dismissed all his men and locked up the building. Crowds soon pillaged and burned the security bureau and the gendarme station, destroying most of the archives of both institutions. In the words of a contemporary, so fell "the last pillar of the Old Regime."[55]

At ten o'clock in the evening the Council of Ministers agreed to remove Protopopov and to name in his stead A. S. Makarenko, until then the chief military prosecutor. Orders of his appointment were printed at naval headquarters, but no one was available to post them around the city. The ministers also placed Petrograd under a state of siege *(osadnoe polozhenie);* then the Council of Ministers ceased to function.[56]

By Tuesday morning, the 28th, a crowd stormed the back entrance of the security brigade headquarters, where Globachev had sought refuge, and he exited onto Morskaia Street and set off for Tsarskoe Selo, hoping to take part in any possible assault against the rebellion. Globachev's wife recalled that he and his assistants contemplated suicide. In the Admiralty Balk and Khabalov held out alone against the revolution. Khabalov confessed by telegram to General N. I. Ivanov, whom Nicholas had appointed during the night as military dictator in Petrograd, that he was in control of neither police nor military forces. Soon afterward a crowd burst in on Balk and his subordinates. They were searching for Khabalov, who had only just disappeared. Balk told them, "I am the city governor. Arrest me and take me to the Duma." A bit later a crowd came looking for Kurlov, and he turned himself in to them.[57]

Baron Raden, the commander of the Eight-Second Dagestan Regiment, arrived at the Baltic station at midday. In front of the station he witnessed shooting and saw a dead policeman lying in the street. Cars were moving around the city carrying armed soldiers with machine guns. In the afternoon the military commission of the provisional committee of the Duma ordered the disarming of all police stations. Atrocities were perpetrated against policemen. Globachev wrote that some were torn to pieces, cut in half, quartered between cars, shot, and burned alive. On 1 March he thought it the better part of prudence to return from Tsarskoe Selo and to turn himself in at the Taurida Palace.[58]

Moscow had remained relatively calm. The authorities declared the second level of alert only on the morning of 28 February, but the third level of alert was declared in the city center later in the day. Crowds sporting red flags gathered and a majority of workers struck, but no serious clashes took place. That evening representatives of the liberal opposition visited the chief of security operations for Moscow, General Vogak, and convinced him to observe neutrality the following day. Thus, although City Governor V. N. Shebeko declared martial law on the morning of 1 March and ordered troops to fire on unruly demonstrators, most of them refused. At 2:30 in the afternoon, the military district commander, General I. I. Mrozovskii, cabled to military headquarters: "Total revolution in Moscow. Military units are going over to the revolutionaries."[59] The government fell almost without a struggle in the ancient capital. Crowds looted and burned police stations here too.

Back in Petrograd liberal and socialist leaders worked both separately and together to found a new government. Military commanders urged Nicholas to yield to their demands and then to abdicate.[60] He did so late on 2 March.

DISMANTLING THE POLICE APPARATUS

Before word of the abdication could reach him at his home on Piatnitskaia Street in Moscow, Sergei Vasil'evich Zubatov shot himself in the right temple and died instantly. His son stated that for several days he had been extremely dejected as he had watched the systematic destruction of the Russian monarchy.[61]

A Moscow police station burned by revolutionaries in late February or early March 1917.

On the other side of the barricades the February Revolution brought a euphoric sense of liberation from political repression. The celebrated criminologist and crusader against repression M. N. Gernet, writing immediately after the fall of the monarchy, hailed it as a "political revolution unparalleled in human history," which had "raised us to an immeasurable moral height. Throwing open the doors of the fortified cells where our fighters had been buried alive, discovering them rotting away in distant exile, seeing their bodies still trembling on the gallows, the victorious people abolished capital punishment. And abolished it without any limitations and forever."[62] Indeed, the new government immediately began to dismantle the police apparatus, to rescind politically repressive laws, and to free political prisoners. In short, the new authorities effectively deprived themselves of nearly all means of repression.

On 1 March the almost entirely apolitical criminal investigation bureau in Petrograd announced its complete disbandment and referred victims of grave crime to the Duma. On 2 March, S. D. Urusov, again deputy interior minister after a twelve-year hiatus, declared to a journalist of the liberal *Birzhevye vedomosti* that the Police Department had been abolished. Urusov's task would be to "create a new central agency in charge of maintaining public order and tranquility in the country. The police will be public in Russia." He admitted that there would always be "malcontents, yet we will not prosecute anyone for political beliefs. . . . Security policing as such will be abolished."[63]

The next day the Provisional Government issued an official declaration on the creation of a popular militia that would have elected directors and would be subordinated to local elective government. Also on 3 March the Provisional Government dismissed all senior and middle-level interior ministry officials, "who by their former activities did not correspond to the conditions of the new order." On the 4th the remaining security bureaus, the Gendarme Corps, and the censorship apparatus were declared abolished. A decree published on 7 March effected a political amnesty and rescinded all extralegal punishments. On 10 March a decree formally abolished the Police Department and created a "temporary administration for regular police affairs."[64]

Around the same time, the Provisional Government closed down the Paris security bureau and "temporarily" removed all governors and vice-governors, appointing as their replacements "commissars" who were usually chosen from among local political activists. A decree ordering the dismantling of the Gendarme Corps but leaving in place the relatively apolitical fortress and railroad gendarme stations was issued on 30 March. The dismantling of the security police apparatus severely weakened military intelligence. S. M. Ustinov, the deputy head of counterintelligence for the Black Sea Fleet, called the dismissal of gendarme officers "a huge blow" to his operations.[65]

Directives to commissars of 15 and 24 March had approved the hiring of former police and gendarmes who had had nothing to do with security policing. The new militia began to emerge only in April, and in some places the imperial regular police continued to function, and in practice the Gendarme Corps was apparently not fully dismantled even at the end of May, though any gendarmes who were still active must have been fulfilling regular police duties along railroad lines. According to I. G. Tsereteli, a leading Menshevik, former political exiles everywhere "ended up at the head of the new administration institutions." To their credit, the new authorities were loath to exact an eye for an eye. Former police employees, including gendarmes, would receive pensions, and gendarmes were not to suffer arrest except by court order. Still, from September on all former police personnel were purged from government institutions, save regular policemen and low-level clerks.[66]

The new government, in its zeal to dismantle the police apparatus, opened the floodgates to a tide of criminality. The apparatus had, after all, combated regular crime more than it had political crime. Specific decrees eased the fate of regular criminals. On 25 March, for example, regular criminal punishments were reduced by half. V. D. Nabokov, a leading Kadet and legal counsel to the Provisional Government, recalled a "strange faith that everything would somehow work out fine by itself, become orderly and effective." Just as the revolution was idealized as great and bloodless, he wrote, "so also the populace was idealized." Some people were naive enough to imagine, continued Nabokov, that the great capital with all its criminal elements could function without a police force, that an improvised, inefficient, but well-paid militia could function with professional thieves and escaped convicts entering its ranks.[67]

Hasegawa found that until February 1917 Russian cities in general and Petrograd in particular had seen little violent crime. Then prisoners were freed and those who remained behind bars ruled their prisons. Criminality luxuriated. Citizens banded together to effect summary justice, including the lynching of pickpockets. In July criminals declared they would murder indiscriminately if mob justice did not cease. According to Hasegawa, "on the eve of the October Revolution, St. Petersburg was on the verge of collapse, threatened by waves of crime." Ethnically based violence grew endemic, with hundreds of pogroms launched across the country against Russian Germans and Jews and against various aliens.[68]

On 11 March the Provisional Government created what it called the Extraordinary Investigating Commission to lay bare the bankruptcy and corruption of the Old Regime by proving that senior officials had violated their own government's laws, had mercilessly repressed peaceable people, and had used egregious methods of operation. Evidence proving any of these allegations would help legitimize the new government and affirm legal continuity, since with a few important exceptions the laws of the Russian Empire remained in force. Already on 3 March scholars had begun removing police records from the buildings at 14 and 16 Fontanka Quay, and specialized commissions were soon established to hunt down police informants and to write the history of the security police.[69]

The direct participation in its work by one of Russia's greatest poets, Alexander Blok, made the commission truly extraordinary. Blok himself wrote descriptions of several police officials, including S. P. Beletskii, in whom he perceived "something kindly, animalistic." He's "having nightmares," wrote Blok, "dreaming of Rasputin." He called Spiridovich "a general who resembles a captain. Absurdly boorish, big and young. Always spoke in a businesslike fashion. Requested nothing, except for walks. And suddenly he turned his back to the soldiers, and, silently heaving, he wept." Blok was to supervise the writing of a massive, multiauthor study of the repressive politics and institutions of the imperial government, though only his book, *Last Days of the Old Regime,* was actually published. Another commission, to investigate the security police archives of Moscow and Warsaw, was set up in Moscow at the Historical Museum.[70]

The Extraordinary Commission interrogated many former officials. They concentrated on senior officials of the interior ministry, whom they intended to try for, among other things, their deployment of secret informants, but convicting them of any crime would have been next to impossible because, according to V. K. Agafonov, "the whole system supported the practice. Even the tsar knew about it and he was unaccountable." It is not surprising, therefore, that A. T. Vasil'ev had the impression that the examiners did not know what they were seeking; they were almost desperately grasping at the flimsiest incriminating material and pursuing "the object of constructing 'crimes' at any cost."[71]

Police officials adopted a variety of responses to the commission's efforts, from evasive to effusive, defiant to contrite, legalistic to commonsensical. Few erstwhile officials proudly asserted their loyalty and devotion to the Old Regime or avowed confidence in its security police. A. N. Khvostov, for example, flatly denied involvement with security policing. S. E. Vissarionov exclaimed, "I want the opportunity to repent before the whole Russian people." A. V. Gerasimov claimed he had only followed the orders of the interior ministry and was "now ashamed of my service." A. P. Martynov, testifying before the Commissariat of Public Accusations, stated that "In the last days of February I gave orders for no more arrests and released prisoners listed with the city governor. Even before the revolution I wished to go to the front. And now, along with my men, I hope we will not be deprived of the honor to shed our blood for the cause of the defense of the homeland and the Provisional Government." S. P. Beletskii was the commission's "best client."[72] No other official came close to his volubility, though his comprehensive written statements were aimed at justifying himself more than the system he had served.

In several cases investigators played cat and mouse with their legally trained opponents. On 4 May, for example, an examiner said to M. I. Trusevich, "We are both lawyers. You know that the motive for a crime in our law does not weaken its criminality; thus, an informant who takes part in an illegal organization is breaking the law." The former Police Department director argued the necessity of defending the system. "Should we give a green light to terrorism," he inquired, "or should we fight against it with long-standing methods? . . . One cannot fight an underground movement with above-board methods; one can only struggle against it by imitating its nature. . . . For any state order, it is a question of life and death." Trusevich asserted that all governments, even those of England and France, had security police forces that deployed informants. As A. Ia. Avrekh notes, even if the investigators could prove that using informants was illegal, and that was a big if, the fact that other European governments used them made it impossible to single out the imperial Russian government as especially odious.[73]

By October 1917 the commission had built up evidence for seven cases against former police officials. N. A. Maklakov, Beletskii, A. F. Shredel', and Spiridovich were held for official crimes connected with Beilis affair; Vasil'ev for patronizing and promoting provocation in general; Protopopov, Beletskii, Vasil'ev, and Globachev for patronizing provocation by

V. M. Abrosimov; Beletskii and I. M. Zolotarev for abetting R. V. Malinovskii's election to the Duma; Beletskii and K. D. Kafafov for issuing anti-Semitic directives; A. A. Makarov, Maklakov, A. N. Khvostov, Protopopov, Kurlov, Zolotarev, Beletskii, Zuev, V. A. Brune de St.-Hyppolite, Klimovich, and Vasil'ev for illegal actions related to perlustration; Protopopov for violating the law with his appointment of Kurlov; and Kurlov, Khvostov, Protopopov, and others for corruption and abuse of power. In the end several, including Protopopov, Kurlov, and Beletskii, were released on bail. None of these officials was ever tried, in part because the Provisional Government soon fell. Even informants could not be tried, since the Provisional Government's political amnesty had unintentionally covered all their crimes of association and involvement with revolutionaries. As Blok put it, the commission was "caught between the anvil of the law and the hammer of history."[74]

Many opponents of the Old Regime disapproved of the commission. V. L. Burtsev believed it held former security policemen in conditions worse than the revolutionaries had experienced under the tsar. N. P. Karabchevskii complained to N. K. Murav'e (then chairman of the commission but formerly, like Karabchevskii, a frequent legal defender of revolutionary activists) that many former officials were being kept in the Peter-Paul Fortress without charges. He recommended announcing a general amnesty for everyone except those guilty of specific crimes—for example, atrocities committed during and after the revolution. Taken aback, Murav'ev countered that the guards would not allow the release of "counterrevolutionaries." A. S. Zarudnyi, deputy justice minister, resigned his post in late March in protest, saying, "I cannot allow Makarov to be correct when he claimed, 'That is how it has always been and will be in the future.'" (Ironically, Zarudnyi became justice minister on 25 July.) M. V. Vishniak, a Socialist-Revolutionary activist and jurist, advised Murav'ev to hand all the cases to the prospective constituent assembly so it could decide what to do.[75]

The commission investigated several other matters but uncovered no conclusive evidence of egregious official malfeasance. S. G. Svatikov, a Social Democrat, went to Paris in early May to dismantle and investigate the Russian security police network abroad. He pursued allegations that P. I. Rachkovskii had fabricated the *Protocols of the Elders of Zion*. A Russian security police agent, Henri Bint, claimed that Matvei Golovinskii, an informant-journalist, had composed the document on orders from Rachkovskii. Although Burtsev and other commentators accepted this version of the document's origin, B. I. Nikolaevskii, a careful researcher, rejected it. He hesitated, however, to reveal his conviction on the matter until after the defeat of Hitler, and even then he divulged it only privately. Commission investigators also sought evidence that the Bolsheviks had received funds from the German government, but they found none.[76]

A. I. Galinovskii, a Moscow judge, concluded that the "grammar and logic" of the security law of 1881 had made it a permanent statute that only the supreme authority had the power to rescind and that therefore the government's recourse to the law had not constituted an abuse of power. (The law was annulled on 16 July 1917.) A major investigation into Protopopov's mental health, involving five doctors and dozens of interviews with people who knew him, found that during his tenure as interior minister he had been in "a state of clearly expressed maniacal excitation." M. N. Lebedev, a former judicial investigator, was charged with scrutinizing Police Department support of rightist organizations and activists. He concluded that senior police officials had to know that these organizations "incited people to a hostile attitude and disobedience toward the government authorities" and "fostered class and ethnic discord among the population of the empire," which "resulted in anti-Jewish pogroms . . . accompanied by murder and the pillaging of property."[77] This was, seemingly, a compelling argument, yet prosecutors did not take it up.

The commission also investigated what Hasegawa has called "one of the legends of the February Revolution": that Protopopov had ordered the installation of machine guns on rooftops and the preparation of policemen to use them against popular rebels. A huge number of contemporaries believed this legend, and most recently so does Orlando Figes. There were, he writes, "hundreds of police snipers hidden on the flat roofs of the buildings, some of them armed with machine-guns, who were firing at the crowds below." Figes refers to seven memoirs for this passage, and one can easily find many dozens more. A. V. Zavadskii, a former senator and associate chairman of the commission, himself admitted that in a state of nervous tension he apparently heard policemen shooting at crowds from machine guns on rooftops: "About such machine guns since then who has not spoken with a conviction that infects his listeners? At nearly every intersection, according to eyewitnesses, there were such machine guns. . . . Sometimes even I catch myself imagining them as truly existing." Yet, as Hasegawa notes, commission investigators concluded that although "scattered shooting incidents" did occur during the February events, "the police did not systematically use machine guns." Avrekh, who thoroughly read the commission's records, found no conclusive evidence for or against the legend, and in the end he rejected it too.[78]

The Extraordinary Investigating Commission had a hard time figuring out how many informants the police had deployed and who they were. Security policemen had destroyed many lists of informants during the February Days. Gerasimov claimed to have kept the names of his informants entirely secret in the period 1906–1909. Martynov had destroyed his lists. Commission investigators compiled lists of 420 pseudonyms and 235 actual names of informants employed in Moscow. Outside of Moscow and Petrograd investigators found the names of 830 informants who had worked in twelve provinces. Over the next several months forty lists of informants were published.[79]

Contemporaries grossly overestimated the actual number of police informants. Agafonov thought that thirty to forty thousand had been employed on the eve of the revolution, and he attributed the collapse of the imperial order in part to this "corps," this "ulcerous sore on the Russian body social." Another Socialist-Revolutionary, N. M. Osipovich, imagining a "whole gang" of informants for each revolutionary, suggested there might have been one hundred thousand. In the late 1920s, however, researchers employed by the Soviet security police compiled two lists of informants active from the 1880s to 1917 that totaled just 9,777 names. Drawing upon the research of other Soviet archivists and her own detailed analysis of the police files, Z. I. Peregudova reached the same result: in the course of forty years, the imperial Russian security police had employed roughly ten thousand informants, each for several years or only a few days, and on the eve of February 1917 there were just over 1,500 out of a population of 170 million. The East German Stasi, by contrast, deployed at the very least 174,000 informants (estimates range as high as two million) within a population of 17 million, in other words, proportionately at least one thousand times more.[80] The imperial Russian police targeted revolutionary activists almost exclusively, whereas the East German police—and all Soviet-style security police forces—targeted the whole of society.

■ ■ ■

After he had emigrated, V. D. Nabokov argued that the Bolshevik "coup itself was possible and so easily accomplished because the sense of existing authority had dissipated, an authority that was ready to defend and protect the civil order." Indeed, according to Globachev, P. N. Pereverzev, the justice minister from late April to early July, rejected the idea of deploying informants as "too undignified," even though he was seriously concerned about combating anarchism. When popular rebellion gripped Petrograd on 3–4 July, the director of the militia ordered Zigfrid Kel'son to assess the situation. Kel'son hopped on a motorcycle and drove up the Nevskii and another major street, then described what he had seen. His report was communicated to the premier. In most cases, he wrote, "the Provisional Government, the information bureau, and the militia in general derived their information from *newspapers*" on such topics. When the rebellion was drawing to a close, government officials apparently asked A. T. Vasil'ev to provide an analysis of the Bolshevik outlook and intentions, but once the officials thought "they had escaped disaster, then the Extraordinary Commission . . . resumed its activities," that is, it once again considered Vasil'ev a suspect in its ongoing investigations.[81]

The information bureau Kel'son referred to was created in reaction to the July Days. According to one historian, the bureau was similar to the

Special Section of the Police Department, but it clearly lacked the sources of covert intelligence available to the pre-February security police. The government essayed other measures to reassert its control amid the rapidly developing events. A decree of 12 July empowered the interior and war ministries to close press organs calling for insubordination to military authorities and inciting the public to civil war. On 2 August the government authorized administrative officials to search, arrest, imprison, and expel from Russia anyone "threatening the state defense, its internal security, and the liberty secured by the revolution." On 9 September a version of police supervision *(nadzor)* of criminals and suspected criminals was reinstated. None of these powers was used vigorously. Sometime in September, according to Kel'son, a Socialist-Revolutionary police institution was created (N. D. Avksent'ev, a Socialist-Revolutionary, was then interior minister). It does not seem to have been an effective force. On 25 October the chief of the Petrograd militia, N. V. Ivanov, received an order to arrest the members of the Bolshevik-dominated Military Revolutionary Committee. Ivanov put the order in his suitcase and proceeded to drink tea.[82] Russia's decade-long experiment with a burgeoning civil society was about to end with the coming to power of the Bolsheviks.

EPILOGUE

■   The heroes of this study, the security policemen and their informants, met with various fates, mostly unpleasant. Some were tracked down and brought to trial or summarily executed; a few killed themselves; the lucky ones managed to escape abroad but then generally lived in poverty, plying trades for which they had neither experience nor training.

According to the consensus of those who triumphed after February, police informants were the worst pariahs of the Old Regime. As V. L. Burtsev had written to the star informant Z. F. Zhuchenko back in 1909, "The future is ours. . . . There will be no place for you in Russia." The people despised informants, wrote G. G. Peretts, the commandant of the Taurida Palace. "Even Protopopov was considered human; they were not."[1]

The government immediately hunted down and imprisoned several suspected informants in March 1917. In prison M. E. Chernomazov committed suicide. An unnamed informant of the Moscow security bureau pleaded in his own defense, "We all began in the revolutionary movement with great idealism. We all became disillusioned when our ideals clashed with reality. Now we all feel deeply our errors. We hope the free people will be magnanimous toward us." Throughout the country, commissions and private citizens tracked down informants. Many people who had never informed fell under suspicion. Some provincial gendarme stations had "ghost informants" listed in their records, which complicated matters. In July a gendarme noncommissioned officer asked the Simbirsk investigating commission to attest that he had not been an informant—he wanted an attestation of his political reliability.[2] The system had made a half-circle: the officials who had formerly granted such attestations were seeking them from the very people on whom they had once passed such judgment.

The investigating commissions painstakingly ferreted out hundreds of names of informants. It is unclear how many were punished and to what extent. It is highly unlikely that any were legally put to death. The Provisional Government apparently exiled V. M. Abrosimov to Siberia. In April 1918 the Bolshevik regime created another commission, which started with all the Provisional Government's investigatory materials and then pursued investigations until 1941, leading to numerous trials and punishments of alleged informants of the Old Regime. Several hundred agents were uncovered after a careful study of archival materials. The prominent ones were shot in June 1918 as the civil war got under way. Many others were brought to trial and sentenced to prison. People with a lower-class background received somewhat lighter sentences. As late as 1925, A. V. Lunacharskii declared that "for all the people of our Union . . . tsarist provocateurs, tsarist spies are the most despised of beings."[3]

Numerous erstwhile informants sought to talk or scheme their way out of punishment or to face down their accusers. R. V. Malinovskii, imagining he could still count on Lenin's trust, returned to Russia in late October 1918. On 5 November he was tried, convicted, and executed. A. K. Sergeev-Serov ("Temnov"), called before the Revolutionary Tribunal in 1919, explained that the imperial security police had "tortured me: nearly every day called me to interrogation. A gendarme captain sat on a chair and put his feet on the table, always playing with his revolver." Apparently many accused of informing described just such a scenario; indeed, "some displayed real imagination," according to someone who studied such cases. The Bolshevik investigators knew full well, however, that the security police used promises of money far more than torture in recruiting informants. Sergeev-Serov was sentenced to execution.[4]

Some informants survived clandestinely within Soviet society for several years. M. N. Nikulin ("Iuzhnyi") informed from 1908 to 1917. In January 1918 he was named chairman of a *volost'* Soviet *ispolkom* (district executive committee). In May 1919 he was drafted into the army, and in 1920 he headed the First Army's commission for food seizures in Ukraine. In mid-October he was arrested for official crimes, but fled and assumed the surname Mikulin. By October 1923 he was chief accountant at a large enterprise. He was arrested again in 1925, and he was tried and executed in January 1926.[5]

A Bolshevik worker named D. S. Krut ("Zverev") had informed from summer 1915 to 1917 in Irkutsk and abroad, earning 150 rubles monthly. He had risen quickly among the émigré Social Democrats who "loved to see a worker-Marxist." After October 1917 he worked for both the Bolsheviks and Admiral A. V. Kolchak. He managed uniform-sewing shops for the Red Army, engaged in commodity speculation, and worked as a special agent of the Foreign Ministry of the Far-Eastern Republic and as a trade union organizer. Arrested four times, he was freed thrice, but the fourth time, in 1923, he was purged from the Communist Party, and in 1926, executed.[6]

V. F. Gabel', a minor informant in 1911–1913, served under the Bolsheviks in various financial institutions and in 1923 or 1924 managed a bank in Krasnoiarsk. Arrested in 1924 or 1925 then brought to trial, he was sentenced to death because as an educated man "he had not needed the money."[7] Surely many others met with a similar fate.

E. F. Azef died of natural causes in Germany in April 1918. Others, such as I. V. Dobroskok ("Nikolai-Golden-Glasses"), simply disappeared without a trace. He may have died, been killed, or just blended into Soviet society. Ia. A. Zhitomirskii, after interrogation in Paris, also disappeared. Many other informants must have done the same. Some people who had never informed were hounded or had their careers ruined because in police files their names were indicated as the source of agent *(agenturnye)* information, which sometimes referred to texts copied from intercepted letters.[8]

The security policemen of this story also suffered many fates after the fall of the tsar. The mood against them was hostile. Burtsev probably spoke for many when he wrote, "When there will no longer be censorship or a Police Department in Russia . . . the names Rachkovskii, Garting, and Gerasimov will be spoken of with more horror than Azef's." No sooner had the monarchy collapsed than soldiers in Kronstadt (or perhaps Finland) shot M. F. von Koten. Although the Provisional Government was highly suspicious of gendarme officers, it was not as hostile to them as was the broader population. In late March the Simbirsk administration had three former gendarme officers arrested "in the interest of public tranquility and order," another piquant reversal of roles. Most officers and NCOs of the former provincial and railroad gendarme stations in Simbirsk testified that they had had little involvement with security policing, had only verified "political reliability" of people, and despite continuous encouragement by their superiors in St. Petersburg had never or only rarely recruited informants.[9]

Ironically, the Bolsheviks' coming to power improved the lot of some gendarme officers for a brief time: several prominent officers fled when crowds emptied the prisons in October. The outbreak of civil war, however, spelled doom for many of them. Petr Pavlovich Martynov, Aleksandr Pavlovich's brother, was arrested along with several other officers and shot in summer 1918. Soon after the declaration of the Red Terror in September 1918, the government threatened to shoot gendarmes and to seize their property if they failed to register with the local authorities within four days, and after the civil war they had to notify the new security police of their movements. Bolshevik activists were encouraged to ridicule former security policemen like S. V. Zubatov in mock trials. More seriously, the criminal codes of 1924 and 1926 made it a crime to have worked for the imperial Russian security police. Between 1927 and 1940 lists of gendarmes and other security policemen compiled by Soviet archivists were printed and distributed to security police officials across the country, presumably to assist in hunting the imperial officers down. P. P. Zavarzin and A. P. Martynov both claimed that the Bolshevik government killed most former gendarme officers.[10]

The government also killed numerous former senior officials involved with policing or government repression. On 5 September, right after the declaration of the Red Terror, the Cheka shot N. A. Maklakov, I. G. Shcheglovitov, A. N. Khvostov, M. A. Beliaev, and S. P. Beletskii, and eighty or ninety other "counterrevolutionaries," in Khodynka Field outside Moscow. When Shcheglovitov was called forward to be shot, a Chekist declared: "here is a tsarist minister who shed the blood of workers and peasants all his life." Beletskii apparently tried to escape, but Chinese guards brought him back to be executed. The Cheka also executed A. D. Protopopov on 27 October 1918, A. A. Makarov around February 1919, and S. E. Vissarionov on an unspecified date.[11]

Few former police officials served the new government in sensitive positions. True, it seems likely that most of those who remained inside the country sought jobs with the only employer in Bolshevik territory during the civil war—Soviet government agencies. Thus, the Cheka of the Turkestan Republic claimed to have found many gendarmes, police, and agents of the imperial Russian security police working for Soviet agencies. Widespread rumors to the contrary, the reading of dozens of memoirs written by opponents of the Bolsheviks yielded allegations of only two former gendarme officers working for the Cheka. A similar accusation was lodged publicly against one well-known former gendarme officer—M. S. Kommisarov. Although hard evidence is wanting and he vehemently denied the accusation, several sources suggest he served with the Cheka during the civil war, then as a spy in Europe. He emigrated to the United States, perhaps in 1925, and died in a traffic accident in Chicago on 23 October 1933.[12] The only other security policeman who is known to have gone over to the other side after 1917 was the French citizen Henri Bint, a longtime detective of the Paris security bureau who served the Cheka with the Soviet diplomatic representation in Paris beginning in 1925. At least three perlustrators and the Special Section's master code breaker, I. A. Zybin, worked for the Bolshevik security police.[13]

Only one senior official involved with policing served the Bolsheviks: V. F. Dzhunkovskii. In December 1917 he retired from the army, and he was arrested in September 1918. In December over one hundred actors from four Moscow theaters appealed for his release. In 1919 he was sentenced to five years in prison for "counterrevolutionary activity," and while in prison he apparently assisted the Cheka. In the late 1920s he avoided being imprisoned again, allegedly thanks to his expertise in passport systems, which the government needed. By the late 1930s he had nothing to teach Stalin's security police, however. They shot him on 21 February 1938.[14]

Numerous imperial Russian security policemen managed to escape abroad, perhaps two to three hundred of them, according to A. P. Martynov, himself an emigrant. Arrested during the February Days, Martynov spent several months in the Kremlin's palace guardhouse while his wife tried to raise the fifty thousand rubles the Provisional Government demanded as bond for his release. Meanwhile the Extraordinary Investigating Commission examined his disbursal of funds but found nothing amiss.[15] After he was released in October 1917, he, his wife, and their sixteen-year-old son hid with various friends before heading south. In spring 1919 Martynov refused—then was refused—the role of director of security policing for the Volunteer Army, but he worked in counterespionage for a year in the general staff of the Whites' Black Sea fleet until the general evacuation in 1920.[16] He and A. F. Koshko, the last director of imperial Russia's criminal detection police, opened a detective agency in Constantinople. They fled in 1923: Koshko to Paris, where he died in 1928, and Martynov to the United States. Martynov lived in New York until 1948, when his wife died, then moved to San Francisco, where he soon died of a stroke. His older brother, Nikolai, also a gendarme officer, made it to France, where he died in 1936.[17]

A. V. Gerasimov was arrested on 7 March 1917, released at the insistence of Burtsev, who wanted to interrogate him personally, then arrested again two weeks later and placed in the Trubetskoi Bastion of the Peter-Paul Fortress. The guards, he recalled, discussed loudly whether it might be simpler to kill the prisoners. The Investigating Commission's N. K. Murav'ev planned to try Gerasimov for his alleged role in A. A. Petrov's assassination of S. G. Karpov, but testimony by Socialist-Revolutionary terrorists saved him. Fifteen days after the October coup, a commissar released Gerasimov, by then in a debtors prison. By May, as the civil war was beginning, Gerasimov declared himself a Ukrainian national since he had grown up there, and he fled south.[18] He died in Paris in the 1930s.

Another inmate of the Peter-Paul Fortress was A. I. Spiridovich, who had retired as the head of the emperor's security in August 1916 and been named Yalta city governor so he could secure the right to a state pension, which he had lost upon leaving the Gendarme Corps. There he met V. L. Burtsev, who had been arrested by the Bolsheviks on the day of their coup. He confided to Burtsev many details about security policing under the monarchy, and the two men played cards with the Socialist-Revolutionaries S. P. Mel'gunov and N. D. Avksent'ev, as well as with the Kadet N. M. Kishkin. In gratitude Burtsev, who was released in February 1918, may have helped Spiridovich to escape from Russia.[19]

In emigration, Spiridovich was by far the most prolific former security policeman. He published an account of his service under Zubatov and in Kiev; a study of Rasputin and his role in late imperial Russia; a two-volume history of the period when he bore responsibility for the emperor's personal security, which presents a detailed view of life at the imperial court; and a three-volume study of Russia in war and revolution.[20] All of these works, especially the latter two, are invaluable sources for the history of imperial Russia's last decade. An avid photographer, Spiridovich took hundreds of pictures of the imperial family, and he included dozens in his reminiscences of the court. Spiridovich also collected hundreds of newspaper clippings and bound them into a dozen scrapbooks on Russian politics and society.[21] Spiridovich lived, wrote, and lectured in Paris for many years, then moved to New York in 1950, where he continued to lecture on Russian history. He died in 1952.

P. P. Zavarzin was taken to the Peter-Paul Fortress after the February Revolution, but he was freed in the summer by Kerenskii in consideration for rendering advice to the government. He emigrated and wrote two books of memoirs in France, where he died, probably in the 1930s. I. K. Globachev conducted intelligence operations against the Bolsheviks in Petrograd, where he had sources of information close to M. S. Uritskii, the Cheka director in Petrograd, according to V. P. Nikol'skii, the last commander of the gendarme directorate. He escaped south during the Red Terror, directed security police operations in Odessa, then worked as a consular officer in the Russian embassy in Constantinople and wrote his memoirs. In July 1923 he departed for the United States, where he worked as a commercial artist in New York City. There he remained, except for a stint as deputy head of the Russian Paramilitary Union *(Russkii obshchevoinskii soiuz)* in Paris in 1930–1934. He died in 1941.[22]

Historians have unearthed some details about the fates of other security policemen. In 1919 A. M. Eremin served in the headquarters of the Orenburg Army, perhaps in charge of intelligence. E. K. Klimovich emigrated to Serbia. A. V. Krivoshein, the head of P. N. Wrangel's government in the Crimea in summer and fall 1920, wanted to invite a Professor Bilimovich to organize counterintelligence operations for the government. By mistake the invitation was forwarded to Klimovich, who nevertheless accepted the offer and, according to Krivoshein, acquitted himself very well. He died in Yugoslavia in 1930. P. I. Rachkovskii had died in 1911. L. A. Rataev died in 1917, but plays he had written under the nom de plume Bernikov were staged in Soviet Russia as late as 1923 in Iaroslavl and 1924 in Khar'kov. A. A. Krasil'nikov worked in a bank in Belgium. A. M. Garting, who served French counterintelligence during World War I, also lived in Belgium after the revolution.[23]

Among senior administrative officials in charge of police affairs, P. G. Kurlov departed Russia in August 1918, wrote his memoirs, and died in 1923. A. A. Lopukhin was involved with the Bolshevik government's nationalization of banks; in 1922 he emigrated to Paris and served on the board of directors of the Petrograd International Commercial Bank. He died in Paris in 1928. A. T. Vasil'ev spent several months in prison, lived in Petrograd until July 1918, then declared Ukrainian citizenship and found a job at the judicial tribunal in Kiev. War with the Bolshevik government forced him to flee to Hungary, thence to Prague, where his brother taught at the university, and on to Berlin and Munich. In Berlin an agent of the Cheka offered him a "quite considerable" sum to spy for the Bolsheviks. "I have seldom in my life experienced such satisfaction," wrote Vasil'ev, "as I felt the moment when I had the privilege of throwing that gentleman downstairs." When inflation struck, he and his wife moved to Paris. Vasil'ev found a lucrative job as a porter at the St. Lazare train station but lost it when it became known that he was not a French citizen. His wife got a job as a bottle washer at a perfume factory. Penniless, he found refuge in the Russian Homes kept by a kind Englishwoman in Sainte-Geneviève-des-Bois. He died on 31 December 1928 in the hospital of Houdon.[24]

Finally, L. P. Men'shchikov and M. E. Bakai, two former security policemen who had joined the opposition during and after the 1905 revolution, ended up in emigration. Bakai found work as an engineer in the French Congo and was still alive in 1931. Men'shchikov wrote a three-volume history of the confrontation between the Russian security police and the revolutionaries up to 1905, which was published in the Soviet Union in 1925–1932, as well as a biographical compendium of security policemen and informants, which is still unpublished. On 12 September 1932, at the age of sixty-two, he died in Paris at the Broussais Hospital for the poor.[25]

The descendants of two senior officials involved with policing had illustrious careers in art and letters. G. P. Sudeikin's son, born less than two years before the father's death in 1883, went on to become the important painter S. Iu. Sudeikin (he changed his patronymic to distance himself from his father). Almost completely apolitical, he emigrated in 1920 and settled in New York, where he died in 1946. P. D. Sviatopolk-Mirskii's son Dmitrii became one of the "most important Russian literary critics of the 20th century." He was a guard officer, served in the First World War and in Russia's civil war, emigrated to Britain, then returned to Soviet Russia in 1932 at Gorky's urging. He was exiled to Siberia in 1937, where he died in 1939.[26]

TOWARD A NEW POLICE STATE

An important recent debate among Anglo-American historians concerns the nature of society in late imperial Russia. Following Leopold Haimson and Richard Pipes, many scholars have argued that to some extent Russia's various social categories were underdeveloped and "fragmented," that Russia lacked strong "middling" social formations, and that the constitutional government lacked sufficiently developed and articulated social bases.[27] Other historians have suggested that late imperial Russia was developing into a pluralistic society with diverse centers of political power and variegated social forces—that is, a civil society in the modern European meaning of the term, with a flourishing press and publishing industry, educational establishments, philanthropic organizations, institutions of local self-government, a parliament, and multifarious nongovernmental organizations and associations. A civil society exists, most concretely, when legal constraints on state power shelter individuals and social groupings from arbitrary authority and coercion. As Peter Gatrell has argued, the failure of constitutionalism, "which was in any case a tender plant throughout much of Europe before (and after) 1914," was perhaps less surprising in Russia than the failure of anticonstutionalism.[28] Without any doubt, in Russia anticonstitutionalism failed—and civil society grew steadily—until the Bolsheviks seized power in 1917. Then why did constitutionalism also fail in Russia?

Recently Jörg Baberowski, in a powerful argument for late imperial Russian social incoherence and governmental weakness, has shown that the very development of civil society widened the gap between the propertied and educated elites, between the "European island," on the one hand, and the premodern peasant mass of the multiethnic empire, on the other, and weakened the already unstable imperial state system. Even the reformed legal system, the most Europeanized institution in pre-1917 Russia, seemed to the peasantry "not a defense before arbitrary power but an instrument of force of the authorities," which therefore delegitimized the government in the eyes of the rural masses.[29]

At the same time, the government's failure to further rein in administrative arbitrariness discredited it in the eyes of the educated public. As noted in chapter 2, V. M. Gessen argued in 1908 that the security law of 1881, which he called evidence of the government's "principled lawlessness," had helped to trigger the 1905 revolution by undermining the prestige of the government and deepening the resentment of the population. In 1912 the public activist S. Ordynskii, quoting from M. E. Saltykov-Shchedrin, asserted that "Everything is so wonderful in our country; we have only one wish: that the courts would not be supernatural *(sverkh"estestvennye)* but ordinary, as they are for thieves." For years after 1906–1908 the opposition press continued to reproach the government for its conduct in suppressing the revolution, even though the level of political repression declined markedly beginning in 1909.[30]

Since violent political unrest greatly diminished also in that period, it seems the government, despite the memory of the thousands of officials who had fallen victim to terrorists' bullets and bombs, could have abolished the security law of 1881 or at the very least administrative political exile. Either reform would have won considerable good will from Russia's educated elites. One can argue that by failing to guarantee full civil rights, to draw educated elites into the government, and to curtail recourse to harsh repressive measures, the imperial regime drove the elites toward the radical opposition, thus helping to polarize Russian state and society, which was a key prerequisite for a seizure of power by extremists.

The refusal of the liberal and moderate opposition to countenance any but liberal methods of governance, however, made it next to impossible for the government to share power with them. One thinks of P. A. Geiden's assertion in 1906 that were he interior minister, he would resign his post in the event of massive ethnic violence rather than declare martial law.[31] Given Russia's potential for major ethnic, agrarian, and labor unrest, one wonders whether the broadening of political participation and strengthening of the rule of law could have staved off revolution.

Ironically, or rather in keeping with the principle of the rule of law and the limits imposed on the executive branch by the Fundamental Laws of 1906, the security police eschewed the application of repressive measures against liberal and moderate political activists. Within the Duma, the publishing industry, the zemstvos and town dumas, and, during the World War, the war industries committees, liberals and moderates were left to engage in activities ranging from loyal opposition to overt and covert attacks on the entire order, so long as they were careful not to break the law or to give the appearance of doing so. The war prompted the government to open more venues for public activism and to cooperate with the public to some extent. When on the eve of the February Revolution liberals plotted to overthrow the government and planned to accuse Prime Minister Shtiurmer of treason, the security police, fully aware of many of these machinations, merely reported on them and took no concrete actions. The autocracy became more and more a watchful state, a political "meteorological office," as one historian called the French Third Republic's security police.[32]

The Menshevik O. A. Ermanskii found that the more sophisticated security police officials gave broad latitude to revolutionary activists, hoping that they would compromise themselves further and provide more grounds for incrimination. When he gained access to police files in 1917, Ermanskii discovered that the Special Section's painstaking analysis of detailed surveillance data had made the Police Department a "master of the situation" in the sense that "at any moment" it could "decide the fate if not of the revolution, then of the revolutionaries." Ermanskii continued with a question:

> Who gained more from this policy, the government or the revolutionaries? Of course, the Police Department was right that if the police arrested revolutionaries each time they were discovered, this would have cut the threads leading to the unmasking of further, related revolutionaries. . . . But the other side of the coin is that thanks to this system, we enjoyed relatively wide latitude. Our period of revolutionary activity was prolonged. While the Police Department carefully gathered material and then subjected it to scientific analysis, we were permitted to place a mine beneath the very edifice of autocracy and capitalism whose safeguard and perpetuation that clever system had been designed to ensure.[33]

Ermanskii's "mine" was the decades of assiduous propaganda work within all layers of society, and the phalanx of propagandists to which he referred were not senior party members, who continuously fell victim to police repression, but lower- and middle-level activists. Indeed, the monarchy collapsed not because of coordinated efforts by professional or other revolutionary activists, but thanks to incompetence at the highest levels of government and the delegitimation of the monarchy, combined with troop mutinies, elite disaffection, and popular war-weariness, all of which continuous revolutionary propaganda had exacerbated.

There were two other flaws in the system. First, the security police lacked an analytical center that was authorized to propose specific policy measures. The Special Section gathered masses of data and analyzed them competently and realistically yet could only report on the popular mood and the overall security situation in a matter-of-fact fashion. To make a difference in a crisis, the Special Section director needed to have the emperor's ear and his trust. He had neither. Second, when it really counted, during the First World War, the police fielded no informants in the military. This omission was huge. Nicholas believed deeply in the loyalty of the military forces and imagined them beyond the reach of propagandists. He and Dzhunkovskii both entertained premodern fantasies about the honor and dignity of the military, itself a highly corporatist institution whose leadership also insisted emphatically on its imperviousness to revolutionary contagion.

Nicholas deluded himself similarly in his general view of the Russian people. The revolution of 1905 might have led him to distrust their impulses and therefore firmly to embrace elite groups—the aristocracy, the bureaucracy, the educated public. Yet he did not. The war, with its genuine expressions of patriotism, its nationalist propaganda, and the sacrifices made by millions of soldiers, only reinforced his belief in the goodness of his people and his troops. Thus, the security police officers' warnings fell on deaf ears.

Years later, V. M. Molotov reflected on the sophistication of the imperial security police. "How many provocateurs—intelligent, capable, well-prepared!" he said. "The tsarist *okhranka* worked excellently." They had "smarter people than ours," he noted. He also admitted that he and Stalin had learned an important lesson from the relative leniency of the imperial apparatus of repression: theirs would be harsher and far more dogged. As the Stalin biographer Dmitrii Volkogonov noted, no political prisoner under Stalin would "ever manage five escapes, as he had." P. P. Zavarzin was right to argue that the new Bolshevik government took "security policing more seriously than any previous government."[34] It created a police state of a new type.

The Bolshevik repressive apparatus was far more brutal and cruel than its imperial predecessor, as numerous revolutionary activists with experience in Bolshevik jails remarked. S. P. Mel'gunov waxed positively lyrical about the prisons before 1917, which "the political prisoner now recalls almost with a joyful feeling." P. A. Sorokin, a founder of sociology in America, called the Bolshevik prisons "inhuman and deadly not only for the prisoner but also for his relatives, friends, and the groups to which he belonged. The Czarist prisons could be called a purgatory in comparison with the inferno of Communist prisons and camps." A. F. Kerenskii argued: "After having suffered through the totalitarian regimes in Europe and Russia, to call Stolypin a 'terrorist ruler' is just as ludicrous as to compare amateur singing to the perfect artistry of Shaliapin. . . . The number of innocent hostages shot in Russia in one day after [the Socialist-Revolutionary terrorist Fannie] Kaplan's attempt on Lenin's life [on 30 August 1918] significantly exceeded the number of those sentenced to hang by Stolypin's 'rapid-firing' military-field courts during the entire eight months of their existence." While this was probably an exaggeration, the official Soviet government daily, *Izvestiia*, reported that on 31 August 1918 the Cheka had executed 553 hostages in Nizhnii Novgorod and Petrograd alone.[35]

The Bolshevik leaders created an entirely new type of security police because they intended to fashion a new society and a new human being. According to Marxism-Leninism, all "nonproletarian" institutions and associations were counterrevolutionary by their very nature. This, coupled with the Bolsheviks' utopian ideal of unified political, economic, social, and cultural control, compelled them to destroy or bridle every element of Russia's incipient civil society and to root out the rule of law and all the liberal, modern, Europeanized institutions and procedures established over the course of more than fifty years. Only with the application of massive repression by means of a ruthless and obsessive security police could the Bolsheviks hope to bring about these changes.

As V. I. Lenin stated while he headed the fledgling Soviet government, the Cheka "was directly establishing the dictatorship of the proletariat" and every good Communist by definition was a "good chekist," or security policeman. In other words, the security police stood at the very center of Bolshevik governance and politics. And that police force wielded almost unlimited powers. M. Ia. Latsis, a senior Cheka official, told *chekisty:* "Everything is permitted to us, for we are the first in the world to raise a sword not for the sake of enserfment and oppression . . . but for the liberation from oppression and slavery of all. . . . Let there be blood as long as one can use it to paint in bright red the grey-white-black banner of the old plunderers' world."[36]

Under the imperial regime political activists were persecuted for their beliefs far longer than were their counterparts in western European countries, yet as in those countries they had generally received more lenient treatment than regular criminals. In Soviet Russia, the situation was reversed. Not only were political offenders often treated much worse than regular criminals, the scope of political criminality grew massively under the Bolshevik government, since engaging in all sorts of ordinary activities, including many economic transactions, was deemed politically criminal. The emphasis on political reeducation, the holding of families responsible for the deeds of their members, and the punishment of whole social categories also made the Soviet penal system harsher than its predecessor.[37]

More broadly, the imperial Russian government did not demand compliance with any well-defined program. The subjects of the tsar were required to be reliable—that is, "not to engage in activities harmful to the state's interests." But the government "did not expect them to lend active support to the state. They were free to hold opinions at variance with those of the government, perhaps even to express those opinions in some veiled or moderate form, but were not supposed to utter them loudly or forcefully." In the constitutional period, they could criticize the government from a variety of rostrums without fear of recrimination. The Bolshevik government, by contrast, "expected—and in some cases demanded—trustworthiness, that is, not mere outward adherence to certain rituals, principles, and beliefs, but active support of them."[38]

M. V. Vishniak, a Socialist-Revolutionary, argued that the Old Regime in the constitutional period had not been "totalitarian, it had not tried to control all aspects of people's personal life from top to bottom. Insofar as individuals avoided politics, in which the autocracy saw a threat to its existence, they were of no interest to the government." The Kadet A. V. Tyrkova-Williams declared: "We assured ourselves and others that we were being strangled in the hands of the autocracy. In reality we were free in body and soul. . . . Nobody forced us to say things we did not believe."[39]

Russia's new autocratic rulers lacked the respect for private property, privacy, self-government, due process, and the rule of law that had made the imperial political system less an autocracy than a constitutional monarchy. In this sense late imperial Russia was fully within the ambit of European governmental practice. Its Bolshevik successor set out on a different path.

GLOSSARY OF RUSSIAN TERMS

■ *Accent marks have been added as an aid to pronunciation.*
The accented syllable should be stressed.

agentúrnye	having to do with informants (collectively)
Cheká	early secret police
chásti	city districts (wards)
délo	case; record
doznániia	formal gendarme inquests
dvórnik(i)	residential superintendent(s)
filër(y)	surveillance agent(s)
gorodovyé	low-ranked urban policemen
Inspéktorskii otdél	personnel control department
kátorga	hard labor
nadziráteli	regular police inspectors
nadzór	surveillance
okhrána	security force; bodyguard; security police
okhránnik(i)	security policeman (policemen)
otdél(y)	section(s)
otdelénie (otdeléniia)	bureau(s); department(s); section(s)
pogróm	collective beating and looting, usually of Jews
prístavy	urban police captains
rozysknyé púnkty	political investigation offices (usually attached to minor gendarme stations)
strázhniki	rural guards
uchástki	precincts
uézd	small rural administrative unit
vólost'	smallest rural administrative unit
zaprós	Duma interpellation
zémstvo (zémstva)	organ(s) of provincial self-government

ABBREVIATIONS

ch.	chast' (file subdivision)
d. or dd.	delo/a (file/s)
f.	fond (collection)
GARF	Gosudarstvennyi arkhiv Rossiiskoi federatsii (State Archive of the Russian Federation)
GDSO	*Gosudarstvennaia Duma: Stenograficheskie otchety* (St. Petersburg, 1906–1916)
Gos.	Gosudarstvennoe (adjective meaning "state")
Izd.	Izdatel'stvo (publisher)
KEK	Jean Bronskaia and Vladimir Chuguev, eds., *Kto est' kto v Rossii i byvshem SSSR: Vydaiushchiesia lichnosti byvshego Sovetskogo Soiuza, Rossii i emigratsii* (Moscow: Terra, 1994)
l. or ll.	list/y (sheet/s)
lit.	litera (further file subdivision)
MGIAI	Moskovskii gosudarstvennyi istoriko-arkhivnyi institut
ob.	obratnaia storona (reverse side of sheet)
OI	*Otechestvennaia istoriia: Istoriia Rossii s drevneishikh vremen do 1917 goda: Entsiklopediia* (Moscow: Bol'shaia Rossiiskaia entsiklopediia, 1994)
op.	opis' (catalogue)
otd.	otdelenie (catalogue subdivision)
Padenie	P. E. Shchegolev, ed., *Padenie tsarskogo rezhima: Stenograficheskie otchety doprosov i pokazanii dannykh v 1917 g. v Chrezvychainoi Sledstvennoi Komissii Vremennogo Pravitel'stva*, 7 vols. (Leningrad: Gos. izd., 1925)
PPR	*Politicheskie partii Rossii. Konets XIX–pervaia tret' XX veka. Entsiklopediia* (Moscow: Rosspen, 1996)
RGIA	Rossiiskii gosudarstvennyi istoricheskii arkhiv (Russian State Historical Archive, St. Petersburg)

RGIAgM   Rossiiskii gosudarstvennyi istoricheskii arkhiv goroda Moskvy
          (Russian State Historical Archive of the City of Moscow)

RP   P. N. Nikolaev et al., eds., *Russkie pisateli, 1800–1917: Biografich
          eskii slovar'*, 4 vols. to date (Moscow: Sovet skaia entsiklopediia,
          1989–1999)

SM   *Sovet ministrov Rossiiskoi imperii, 1905–1906 gg.: Documenty i ma-
          terially* (Leningrad: Nauka, 1990)

SOS   *Spisok obshchego sostava chinov Otdel'nogo Korpusa Zhandarmov*
          (St. Petersburg: Tip. Shtaba Otdel'nogo Kor pusa Zhandarmov,
          1907–1911)

SU   *Sobranie uzakonenii i rasporiazhenii pravitel'stva, izdavaemoe pri
          Pravitel'stvuiushchem senate* (St. Petersburg: Senatskaia tip, 1906–1917)

t.   tom (volume)

Tip.   Tipografiia (Publisher)

VPR   *Vtoroi period revoliutsii: 1906–1907 gody*, pt. 3 of *Revoliutsiia 1905–1907
          gg. v Rossii: Dokumenty i materialy*, ed. A. M. Pankratov et al. (Moscow:
          Izd. Akademii nauk SSSR, 1957)

ZA   Zagranichnaia agentura (Paris Security Bureau Collection), Hoover
          Institution Archives

NOTES

PREFACE

1. Blok, "Poslednie," 13.
2. Volkogonov, *Stalin,* 9.
3. Fricke, *Bismarcks,* 12; Porter, *Origins,* xi.
4. Ruud and Stepanov, *Fontanka, 16;* Peregudova, *Politicheskii;* Lauchlan, *Russian Hide-and-Seek.* Frederic Zuckerman's *Tsarist Secret Police in Russian Society* is completely unreliable and therefore unusable. See my "Security." For a full and detailed inventory of all the book's errors and inaccuracies, see http://tigger.uic.edu/~daly/homepage/Research/zuckerman.html.

INTRODUCTION

1. There were three levels of security: the first covered the entire empire at all times; the second, reinforced security, was regularly imposed and covered at times over half the empire; the third, extraordinary security, was first imposed in 1905 and affected only a small territory.
2. Dvorianov, *V sibirskoi,* 154; Koshko, *Vospominaniia,* 155–57.
3. Tikhomirov, *Pochemu,* 24–25.
4. Pravilova, "Administrativnaia," 190–92 (Gessen); Payne, *Police State,* 32.
5. Chapman, *Police State,* 44 *(Justizstaat).*
6. Shipov, *Vospominaniia,* 396.
7. Gurko, *Tsar' i tsaritsa,* 14 (initiatives); Tolstaia, ed., *Vospominaniia,* 24 (ministers' influence), 202–204; Cross, "Geography," 706; Shvarts, *Moia perepiska,* 69 (rebuffed).
8. Pokrovskii, *Gosudarstvennyi,* 11, 27, 52 (budget data); Lauchlan, *Russian Hide-and-Seek,* 111.
9. Baberowski, *Autokratie,* 337.
10. Anfert'ev, ed., *Ot pervogo,* 445–47.
11. Kulikov, "Vysshaia," 51–52.
12. Krivoshein, *A. V. Krivoshein,* 7–16; Tolstaia, ed., *Vospominaniia,* 209.
13. Martynov, *Moia sluzhba,* 8.
14. On the outlook and views of gendarme officers, see Daly, *Autocracy under Siege,* 58–59.

15. On new rules regulating this practice, see Police Department to governors, 13 November 1907, GARF, f. 102, op. 260, d. 17, ll. 301–301 ob.

16. "Evno Azef," 195.

17. Bukhbinder, "Zubatovshchina," 96–97.

18. Spiridovich, "Pri tsarskom rezhime," 124.

19. Galvazin, *Okhrannye*, 133 (Broitman); Budnitskii, *Terrorizm*, 4 (Guchkov).

20. Daly, *Autocracy under Siege*, 117.

21. Stepun, *Byvshee*, 1:123; Mandel'shtam, *Shum*, 33, 40.

22. Margolis, Gerasimova, and Tikhonova, eds., "Zapisnye," 492, 496; Zenzinov, *Iz zhizni*, 56, 65–69; Parvus, *Po tiur'mam*, 56.

23. Piskarev, "Vospominaniia," 105; Galvazin, *Okhrannye*, 160.

24. Budnitskii, *Terrorizm*, 337–39.

25. Daly, *Autocracy under Siege*, 135.

26. Smirnov, *Kalendar' russkoi revoliutsii*, 52.

27. Piskarev, "Vospominaniia," 113–14 (sabotage).

28. Rediger, *Istoriia moei zhizni*, 1:476–77; Bushnell, *Mutiny*, 72–78.

29. Belokonskii, *V gody*, 155–56.

30. Miliukov, *Vospominaniia*, 232–33; Maklakov, *Vlast'*, 428. For an excellent analysis of the "Okhrana myth," see Lauchlan, *Russian Hide-and-Seek*, chapter 1.

1—POLICING THE CONSTITUTIONAL ORDER IN 1906

1. Gorodnitskii, *Boevaia*, 106–107; "Pokushenie na Dubasova."

2. Spiridovich, *Istoriia bol'shevizma*, 120.

3. Obninskii, *Novyi stroi*, 1:131.

4. Tagantsev, *Perezhitoe*, 71n (brother-in-law); Pokrovskii, ed., "Perepiska," 187 (Akimov), 186 (Witte).

5. Tkhorzhevskii, *Poslednii*, 65.

6. Krugliakov and Shilov, eds., "Dnevnik," 99 (diary entry, 12 January 1906).

7. Lieven, "Bureaucratic Authoritarianism," 391–402.

8. Dzhunkovskii to interior ministry, 17 October 1906, GARF, f. 102, OO (II), 1906, d. 828, ch. 18, l. 6; Reinbot to Garin, 19 January 1908, GARF, f. 826, op. 1, d. 107, l. 25 ob.; "Pravitel'stvennomu Senatu . . . donoshenie," 13 November 1908, 6–7; Dzhunkovskii, *Vospominaniia*, 1:141; Shatina, "Mestnyi," 144–46.

9. Dzhunkovskii, *Vospominaniia*, 1:213; Entin, ed., *Politicheskie*, 135 (Vilnius); Martynov, *Moia sluzhba*, 273–76; SOS (10 July 1911), 280.

10. Martynov, *Moia sluzhba*, 64 (description), 213 (brilliant); Gerasimov, *Na lezvii*, 56–58.

11. Mosolov, *Pri dvore*, 170 (trains), 202 (Trepov).

12. Spiridovich, *Dernières années*, 1:20–32.

13. Spiridovich testimony, in *Padenie*, 3:27–28; Agafonov, *Zagranichnaia*, 121; Spiridovich, *Dernières années*, 1:210 (photographs). On the force's security procedures, see Spiridovich testimony, 7–10 October 1911, GARF, f. 271, op. 1, d. 15, ll. 77–79 ob.

14. *SM*, 134–91; *VPR, Ianvar'–aprel' 1906 goda*, 1:83, 93–95, 99–103 (Nicholas's concerns); Thurston, *Liberal City*, 87–90 (cities); Moscow governor to Police Department, 17 October 1906, GARF, f. 102, OO, 1906, otd. II, d. 828, ch. 18, l. 12 ob. (province); Drezen, ed., *Tsarizm*, 66 (police salaries).

15. Drezen, ed., *Tsarizm*, 66 (police salaries), 48–49 (compensation); Police Department to governors, 18 August 1906, GARF, f. 102, OO (II), 1906, d. 4, ch. 19, lit. A, ll. 65–65 ob (compensation).

16. *VPR, Ianvar'–aprel' 1906 goda*, 1:141–42 (meetings); Lazarevskii, ed., *Zakonodatel'nye*, 232 (7 February), 251–53 (13 February); "Spravka," GARF, f. 102, OO, 1905, d. 2075, t. 1, l. 366 ob.–369 (orders, late February).

17. Lur'e, ed., "K istorii," 130 (damage); "Memoriia," in *SM*, 159–63 (6 January); *Polnoe sobranie*, ser. 3, vol. 26, pt. 1, no. 27371 (7 February); *VPR, Ianvar'–aprel' 1906 goda*, 1:144–48 (3 February), 151–52 (12 March).

18. *VPR, Ianvar'–aprel' 1906 goda*, 151 (April); Tolstaia, ed., *Vospominaniia*, 201; "Memoriia," in *SM*, 279–80 (24 February); Stepanov, *Chernaia*, 81–82 (sentences).

19. Daly, *Autocracy under Siege*, 181–82; Usherovich, *Smertnye*, 494–95 (total executions). S. S. Ostroumov, citing Usherovich, claims that 6,107 people were killed by the punitive expeditions ("Repressii," 41). According to Usherovich, however, in all 6,107 people were executed from 1905 to 1917 by the imperial Russian government: 4,738 by court sentence and 1,369 without trial (Usherovich, *Smertnye*, 493–94).

20. Ivanov, "Karatel'naia," 399, 410, 419.

21. Witte to Nicholas II, 10 February 1906, in *SM*, 238–39; "Tablitsy mestnostei Rossii"; Pushkareva, *Zheleznodorozhniki*, 226 (railroads).

22. Agafonov, *Zagranichnaia*, 259; Shcherbakov, "Iz istorii," 256 (Riga); Tiutiukin, *G. V. Plekhanov*, 227 (St. Petersburg).

23. *VPR, Ianvar'–aprel' 1906 goda*, 1:149–51, 213, 303, 306, 312, 315, 319–20.

24. Tiutchev, *V ssylke*, 95–96.

25. *VPR, Ianvar'–aprel' 1906 goda*, 1:192–93, 214, 223, 302, 312 (letter), 313, 315, 320, 701.

26. N. Erofeev, "Azef, E. F.," in *PPR*, 22; Gerasimov, *Na lezvii*, 68–71.

27. Gerasimov, *Na lezvii*, 68–71; Gorodnitskii, *Boevaia*, 107, 128; Spiridovich, *Dernières années*, 1:148; "Pokushenie na Dubasova."

28. Gerasimov, *Na lezvii*, 72–73; Gorodnitskii, *Boevaia*, 128. Azef apparently took part in Gapon's murder (Spiridovich, *Histoire du terrorisme russe*, 358–59).

29. Obninskii, *Polgoda*, 70–71.

30. *SM*, 178n2 (villages); Witte to Nicholas II, 23 January and 19 February 1906, in *SM*, 199–200, 263–64.

31. *VPR, Ianvar'–aprel' 1906 goda*, 1:260–62.

32. Shebalov, "Vopros," 169–97; Tolstaia, ed., *Vospominaniia*, 182.

33. Police Department to governors, gendarme chiefs, and security chiefs, 14 February 1906, "Sekretnye tsirkuliary i instruktsii," 132, Library of Congress, Rare Book Reading Room.

34. Council of Ministers, 17 February 1906, RGIA, f. 1276, op. 2, d. 6. ll. 1–2.

35. Volynia governor to Stolypin, 8 May 1906, GARF, f. 102, D-5, 1906, d. 3, ch. 181, l. 2; Police Department director to Stolypin, 22 May 1906, GARF, f. 102, D-5, 1906, d. 3, ch. 181, ll. 9, 10 (cable from father); report to committee, GARF, f. 102, D-5, 1906, d. 3, ch. 181, l. 11.

36. Tatarov, ed., "Bor'ba," 100.

37. *VPR, Ianvar'–aprel' 1906 goda*, 1:106; Bushnell, *Mutiny*, 154–60; Schapiro, *Communist Party*, 99; Spiridovich, *Histoire du terrorisme russe*, 329–44.

38. *VPR, Ianvar'–aprel' 1906 goda*, 1:157; *VPR, Oktiabr'–dekabr' 1906 goda*, 372.

39. Bogdanovich, *Tri poslednikh*, 376, 378.

40. Gessen, "V dvukh," 297; Shipov, *Vospominaniia*, 410, 417 ("outrageous"); Maklakov, *Iz vospominanii*, 297; Maklakov, *Vlast'*, 558; Galinovskii, "Zakliuchitel'noe postanovlenie," GARF, f. 1467, op. 1, d. 396, ll. 276–78 (commission); Vodovozov, ed., "Tsarskosel'skoe," 185–87, 219–22 (judges), 227–28 (coup).

41. See Daly, "Pravitel'stvo," 25–45.

42. Ibid., 29–34.

43. Stepanskii, *Samoderzhavie*, 3, 17–20, 31–32; McDaniel, *Autocracy*, 119–20 (Witte), 137 (regulation).

44. Stepanskii, *Samoderzhavie*, 31–32; Bradley, "Voluntary Associations," 132–48.

45. Stepanskii, *Samoderzhavie*, 70 (1899); Bonnell, *Roots of Rebellion*, 194–203, 266; Laverychev, *Tsarizm*, 207–9; Bulkin, "Soiuz," 252 (rubric); Bulkin, "Departament," 220–21 (approval).

46. Bonnell, *Roots of Rebellion*, 276–77; Schapiro, *Communist Party*, 98–99; Reinbot to Stolypin, 17 October 1906, GARF, f. 102, OO (II), 1906, d. 828, ch. 18, l. 1.

47. *VPR, Mai–sentiabr' 1906 goda*, 1:421–24 (18 May); Mstislavskii, "Iz istorii," 12–14.

48. Pushkareva, *Zheleznodorozhniki*, 256 (identification), 275 (arrests).

49. Grinevich, *Professional'noe*, 198.

50. Bradley, "Voluntary Associations," 132–48; Bradley, "Russia's Parliament," 212–36; Garvi, *Zapiski*, 39n.

51. Kornev, ed., "Dokumenty," 83–85; Emmons, *Formation of Political Parties*, 185–92 (repression), 193–205 (campaigning, Octobrists), 223–24; Kornev, "II Gosudarstvennaia," 144n32 (legal status).

52. Durnovo to governors, 19 April 1906, GARF, f. 102, OO, 1905, d. 2606, l. 7; *VPR, Ianvar'–aprel' 1906 goda*, 1:157, 337 and 340 (arrests), 341 and 345 (preparations).

53. Savinkov, *Vospominaniia*, 198–99; Gerasimov, *Na lezvii*, 68.

54. Pavlov, *Esery-maksimalisty*, 77; Geifman, *Thou Shalt Kill*, 57, 59; Zyrianov, *Petr Stolypin*, 35.

55. Leonov, *Partiia*, 129 (data); Morozov, *Partiia*, 332–42 (local units).

56. Zenzinov, *Iz zhizni*, 32 (official suspension); Gorodnitskii, *Boevaia*, 108 (uninformed); Spiridovich, *Dernières années*, 1:84 (continued terrorism).

57. Shipov, *Vospominaniia*, 431–32 (public perception); Kokovtsov, *Iz moego proshlogo*, 149 (Goremykin); Gerasimov, *Na lezvii*, 75 (apartment).

58. Levin, "Petr Arkad'evich Stolypin," 452, 458; Ascher, *P. A. Stolypin*, 43–59 (unrest), 120.

59. Gerasimov, *Na lezvii*, 75; Spiridovich, *Velikaia*, 1:183–84.

60. "Makarov, A. A.," in *Padenie*, 7:372; "Vospominaniia Kafafova," GARF, f. 5881, op. 2, d. 390, l. 89 (principle); Peregudova, *Nesostoiavshaiasia*, 6–7; Makarov testimony, in *Padenie*, 2:93; Weissman, *Reform in Tsarist Russia*, 207–17.

61. Borodin, *Gosudarstvennyi*, 166, 349n228; "Shcheglovitov, I. G.," in *Padenie*, 7:439.

62. Emmons, *Formation of Political Parties*, 359–60 (mandate); "Proekt," 18 April 1906, in *SM*, 459 (reforms); Vinaver, *Konflikty*, 49–50, 67–68.

63. Gerasimov, *Na lezvii*, 76; *SOS* (1 June 1907), pt. 2:562 (Bertgol'dt); Peretts, *V tsitadeli*, 92 (telephone); "V kontse 1916 g.," 148 (emperor); Lauchlan, *Russian Hide-and-Seek*, 320–21.

64. Likhomanov, *Bor'ba*, 62 (press); Kaminka, "Neprikosnovennost'," 1980–84.

65. Panina, "Gosudarstvennaia Duma," 1:264 (procedure of interpellation); RGIA, f. 1278, op. 1, dd. 355–650 (First Duma's interpellations of the interior ministry); Rabe, *Widerspruch,* 135 (administrative punishments).

66. Shipov, *Vospominaniia,* 455; Obninskii, *Novyi stroi,* 1:139–44; Petrunkevich, "Iz zapisok," 245; Police Department to governors, 22 June 1906, ZA, XIIId(1), 9 (permission to petition).

67. Vinaver, *Konflikty,* 74–75 (5 May); Obninskii, *Novyi stroi,* 1:70 (1 June); Makrinskii, "Smertnaia," 1989–92 *(Pravo);* Kuz'min-Karavaev, cited in M. I. Leonov, *Partiia,* 132.

68. Utevskii, *Vospominaniia,* 33 (Shcheglovitov); Vinaver, *Konflikty,* 142 ("furious"); Viktorskii, *Istoriia smertnoi,* 367–68 (Duma votes).

69. *Materialy k istorii,* xciii (Lopukhin); Harcave, ed., *Memoirs of Count Witte,* 516–17.

70. Lauchlan, *Russian Hide-and-Seek,* 270–74; Laporte, *Histoire de l'okhrana,* 163 (rumors); Shchegolev, "Russkii," 198 (denial); "Manasevich-Manuilov, I. F.," in *Padenie,* 7:375 (dismissal).

71. Lopukhin, *Otryvki,* 95; Gurko, *Features,* 446 (oversight of exile system); Emmons, *Formation of Political Parties,* 319 (election); GDSO, 2nd Duma, first session, sitting 23 (8 April 1906), 1129–32; Gessen, "V dvukh," 228.

72. Spiridovich, "Petr"; "Rachkovskii, P. I.," in *Padenie,* 7:403–4; *SOS* (10 July 1911), 2:318; Koz'min, ed., *S. V. Zubatov,* 123 (pension); Gessen, "V dvukh," 288.

73. Obninskii, *Devianosto,* pt. 1:66–68.

74. Ibid., pt. 1:68–69.

75. Trusevich testimony, in *Padenie,* 3:213 ("cleaning out"); Peregudova, "Departament politsii," 24–25, 177n (private police forces).

76. "Trusevich, M. I.," in *Padenie,* 7:426; Martynov, *Moia sluzhba,* 60; Gerasimov, *Na lezvii,* 90; Kurlov, *Gibel',* 79; Beletskii testimony, in *Padenie,* 3:264; Spiridovich, *Dernières années,* 1:106.

77. Stolypin to Council of Ministers, 29 May 1906, GARF, f. 1467, op. 1, d. 396, l. 178; Stolypin to governors, 29 May 1906, in *VPR, Mai–sentiabr' 1906 goda,* 1:74.

78. Tiutiukin, *Iul'skii,* 21 (terrorism), 47 (conservative voices); RGIA, f. 1276, op. 2, d. 172, ll. 10 ob.–14 (statistics); Bogdanovich, *Tri poslednikh,* 599 (Chukhnin); Koz'min, ed., *S. V. Zubatov,* 124n8 (Kozlov); Spiridovich, *Dernières années,* 1:89 (Kozlov).

79. Sidorov, ed., "Mobilizatsiia," 158–59. See also an entire police file on the empire-wide effort to combat the revolutionary movement (Police Department to gendarmes and security chiefs, 25 July 1906, GARF, f. 102, op. 316, 1906, d. 342, l. 1).

80. Tiutiukin, *Iul'skii,* 42 (convoking governors), 46–47 (early July); Police Department to railroad gendarmes, 1 July 1906, GARF, f. 102, OO (II), 1906, d. 100, ll. 1–2 ob.; Police Department to gendarme and security chiefs, 1 July 1906, GARF, f. 102, op. 260, d. 16, ll. 95 ob.–96; interior ministry to governors, 1 July 1906, GARF, f. 102, op. 260, d. 16, ll. 97–98 ob.; Sidorov, ed., "Mobilizatsiia," 160–61.

81. Tiutiukin, *Iul'skii,* 76; *Polnoe sobranie,* ser. 3, vol. 26, pt. 1, no. 28102.

82. Interior ministry directive, 11 July 1906, in "Spravka," GARF, f. 102, OO, 1905, d. 2075, t. 1, l. 369.

83. Izvol'skii, *Vospominaniia,* 129; Sidorovnin, ed., *Stolypin,* 197 (declaration), 201 (proposal for reforms); Ascher, *Revolution of 1905,* 2:223–26 (overtures to moderates); Tiutiukin, *Iul'skii,* 206–7 (promises); "Pis'mo kn.," 300–4 (Trubetskoi); Schapiro, *Communist Party,* 91–92 (Mensheviks).

84. Bushnell, *Mutiny*, 171–224 (soldiers' unrest); *VPR, Mai–sentiabr' 1906 goda*, 1:94 ("red guards"); Petrov, ed., "Kronshtadtskoe," 91–93; Nabokov, *Letters*, 6; Kritsman, ed., "Nikolai," 215–20.

85. *VPR, Mai–sentiabr' 1906 goda*, 1:268 (7 July), 275 (23 July in St. Petersburg), 466 (23 July in Moscow), 520 (18 July), 550 (30 June in Moscow); Klimovich to Trusevich, 14 August 1906, GARF, f. 102, OO (I), 1906, op. 234, d. 7, ch. 14, ll. 8–9.

86. "Khronika," *Pravo*, no. 22 (4 June 1906), 2023–24; no. 23 (11 June 1906), 2088–89; no. 24 (18 June 1906), 2189–90; no. 25 (25 June 1906), 2260–61; no. 26 (2 July 1906), 2300–2302; no. 27 (9 July 1906), 2346–48; no. 28 (16 July 1906), 2387–89; no. 29 (23 July 1906), 2427–30; no. 30 (30 July 1906), 2499–2501; no. 31 (6 August 1906), 2555–58; no. 32 (13 August 1906), 2603–2605; no. 33 (20 August 1906), 2660–62.

87. Leonov, *Partiia*, 275 (targets); Bogdanovich, *Tri poslednikh*, 394 (Pobedonostsev), 397 (Durnovo); Pavlov, *Esery-maksimalisty*, 174–75 (Apteka); Ol'-denburg, *Tsarstvovanie*, 1:363–64; Geifman, *Thou Shalt Kill*, 74, 170; Police Department to governors, 13 July 1906, GARF, f. 102, op. 316, 1906, d. 215, l. 33; Gorodnitskii, *Boevaia*, 108 (Stolypin); Rediger, *Istoriia moei zhizni*, 1:452.

88. Koshko, *Vospominaniia*, 83–88 (Blok).

89. Ibid., 98 (fear); Martynov, *Moia sluzhba*, 67, 71, 88–89, 94.

90. V. I. Lenin, "Partizanskaia voina," in Lenin, *Polnoe*, 15:5 (30 September 1906); Zavarzin, *Rabota*, 127–29.

91. Spiridovich, *Histoire du terrorisme russe*, 272–77; Leonov, *Partiia*, 128; Pavlov, *Esery-maksimalisty*, 81 (seizure), 169 (plan).

92. Pavlov, *Esery-maksimalisty*, 170–83 (Ryss); D. Pavlov, "Ryss, S. Ia.," in *PPR*, 537; Berlin, "Ob odnom," 95 (Ryss); Praisman, *Terroristy*, 224–27 (Ryss); Spiridovich, *Dernières années*, 1:106–7.

93. Geifman, *Thou Shalt Kill*, 45–58, 130–48, 154–59, 162–79; Spiridovich, *Istoriia bol'shevizma*, 354–55, 364–78.

94. Savinkov, *Vospominaniia*, 165; Krugliakov and Shilov, eds., "Dnevnik," 100 (Dediulin); Pozner, ed., *Pervaia*, 46 (Bolsheviks), 92 (law); Novikova, "Velikoe," 137 (election).

95. Spiridovich, *Dernières années*, 1:133 (half-million); *Novoe vremia*, cited in GARF, f. 102, OO, 1906 (I), d. 2, ch. 35, l. 39 ob. (watch shop); Vrangel', *Vospominaniia*, 194.

96. Morozov, *Partiia*, 334 (leaders); Kuz'min, *Moi vospominaniia*, 61 (unauthorized); Budnitskii, ed., *Istoriia terrorizma*, 415–19 (Lomidze); Mstislavskii, "Iz istorii," 14–16; Brazhe, ed., "'Krasnaia,'" 213 ("robber gang").

97. Pavlov, *Esery-maksimalisty*, 74–77 (incidence of robbery); Geifman, *Thou Shalt Kill*, 21–22 (numbers); Mikhailov, *Sovet*, 183 (liquor stores).

98. Schapiro, *Communist Party*, 88–9, 97, 104, 107–8; Spiridovich, *Istoriia bol'shevizma*, 388–97; Gerasimov, *Na lezvii*, 87, 91–3; Geifman, *Thou Shalt Kill*, 75–81, 112–22, 148–52; Williams, *Other Bolsheviks*, 103–24; Police Department to governors, gendarme chiefs, and security chiefs, 12 December 1906, GARF, f. 102, op. 260,.d. 16, l. 200.

99. Tarnovskii, "Dvizhenie,"66 (murders), 98 (other crime); Mikhailov, *Sovet*, 43 (property crime); Genkin, *Po tiur'mam*, 28 (blending); Gessen, "V dvukh," 213.

100. Lambroza, "Pogroms," 228–29; Rawson, *Russian Rightists*, 129; Miliukov, *Vospominaniia*, 268–69; Gessen "V dvukh," 237–38 (beating, Gertsenshtein); Narskii, "Gertsenshtein, M. Ia." in *OI*, 1:549; Stepanov, *Chernaia*, 154 (Polovnev); Lauchlan, *Russian Hide-and-Seek*, 281–83 (Polovnev).

101. Stepanov, *Chernaia,* 158.

102. Gerasimov, *Na lezvii,* 150–52; Reinbot testimony, in *Padenie,* 6:121–22, 127; correspondence, Moscow security bureau—Special Section, 31 July to 17 August 1906, GARF, f. 102, OO, 1906 (I), d. 2, ch. 35, ll. 22–23, 29; Ruud and Stepanov, *Fontanka,* 160–64 (assassins).

103. Lauchlan, *Russian Hide-and-Seek,* 275–81.

104. "A. F. Kerenskii: Posledniaia liubov'," televised broadcast on the channel "Kul'tura," Moscow, 3 July 2001, at 10:50 P.M., with host G. Borovik. My thanks to Leonid Trofimov for bringing this broadcast to my attention.

105. Geifman, *Thou Shalt Kill,* 59; N. Erofeev, "Konopliannikova, Z. V.," in *PPR,* 3:590; M. Iu. Katin-Iartsev, "Min, G. A.," in *OI,* 3:590; Spiridovich, *Dernières années,* 1:109–12; Bing, *Secret Letters,* 217; Pokrovskii, ed., "Perepiska," 198.

106. Rediger, *Istoriia moei zhizni,* 2:9 (training exercises), 2:81–82 (debilitating effect of repressive duties), 2:82n (numbers); Fuller, *Civil-Military Conflict,* 144–46.

107. Dan, "Obshchaia," 2:49n. On specific police operations, see *VPR,* 1:466–70, 478–82, 489–500, 622–23; Shatina, "Mestnyi," 152–54, 161–68; Spiridovich, *Istoriia bol'shevizma,* 326–28.

108. Liublinskii, "Prestupnost'," 36:653–54 (statistics); Justice Ministry to prosecutors, 14 July 1906, in Drezen, ed., *Tsarizm,* 79; directives to gendarme chiefs (31 July 1906) and railroad gendarme chiefs (28 July 1906), in Iarmysh, "Karatel'nye organy," 152, 164–65; Police Department directive, 8 August 1906, cited in Police Department to gendarme chiefs, 16 October 1906, GARF, f. 102, OO, 1902, d. 825, l. 31. The justice ministry would have preferred a curtailment, rather than an expansion, of the gendarmes' investigatory function. See "Kratkaia ob"iasnitel'naia zapiska k proektu Ministra Iustitsii," 1907, RGIA, f. 1276, op. 3, d. 121, l. 9.

109. Ordynskii, "Pechat' i sud," 129, 139–40.

110. Glazunov, "Sudebnyi," 14, 19–20; Baberowski, *Autokratie,* 752–54; Bonch-Bruevich, *Bol'shevistskie,* 5.

111. Gruzenberg, *Ocherki,* 111 (Gessen).

112. Ibid., 97–99; Volkogonov, *Trotskii,* 1:89.

113. N. Degkov, "Maklakov, V. A.," in *PPR* 336; Sokolinskii, "Fidlerovskoe," 24–25; Dzhunkovskii to Stolypin, 17 October 1906, GARF, f. 102, OO (II), 1906, d. 828, ch. 18, l. 14 ob. On Shcheglovitov's disciplining of officials of the judicial branch, see Iarmysh, "Karatel'nye organy," 239.

114. Daly, *Autocracy under Siege,* 34; Baberowski, *Autokratie,* 229; Liublinskii, "Prestupnost'," 654.

115. Fuller, *Civil-Military Conflict,* 115–27, 176–83; Baberowski, *Autokratie,* 759 (procedure), 761 (quitting).

116. Baberowski, *Autokratie,* 761 (mild punishments); Polianskii, *Tsarskie,* 35–36 (political crime percentages); Karpeev, "Voenno-okruzhnoi," 241 (harsh sentences); Filat'ev, "Dorevoliutsionnye," 141 (statistics); Liublinskii, "Prestupnost'," 654 (sentences); Rawson, "Death Penalty," 37.

117. "Perepiska N. A. Romanova," 104 (14 August); Fuller, *Civil-Military Conflict,* 173–76; Faleev, "Shest'," 43–70; *VPR, Oktiabr'–dekabr' 1906 goda,* 67 (9 October); M. A. Sinel'nikov, "Voenno-polevye sudy," in *OI,* 1:425 (numbers); Police Department to Makarov, 17 November 1906, GARF, f. 102, D-1, 1907, d. 10, ll. 1–1 ob (funds).

118. "Pravitel'stvennoe soobshchenie," 1.

119. Rediger, *Istoriia moei zhizni,* 1:475–77; Pokrovskii, ed., "Perepiska," 201.

120. Emmons, *Formation of Political Parties,* 358 (Guchkov); Baberowski, *Autokratie,* 765 *(Novoe vremia); Aleksandr Ivanovich Guchkov,* 44; Shipov, *Vospominaniia,* 492–93; O. Terebov, "Shipov, D. N.," in *PPR,* 700; Zverev, ed., "Iz zapisok A. F. Redigera,"* 126–27; Dzhunkovskii, *Vospominaniia,* 181–82; Drezen, ed., *Tsarizm,* 82 (Rediger); Maklakov, *Rechi,* 50.

121. Statistical reports, 1904–1909, GARF, f. 102, op. 304, d. 96, ll. 1–3. For a list of the places from which people were banished, see GARF, f. 102, op. 304, d. 116.

122. "Vospominaniia Kafafova," GARF, f. 5881, op. 2, d. 390, l. 99; "Iz otcheta Senatora," 928.

123. See directives of 8 September and 22 December 1906, which cite directives of 17 July and 31 October. In "Sekretnye tsirkuliary i instruktsii," 196, 215–15 ob.

124. Gernet, *Istoriia tsarskoi tiur'my,* 4:74–77 (statistics, borderlands); *Ezhegodnik,* 41 (1906–1913); Malinovskii, *Krovavaia,* 2:85 (Vladikavkaz), 115 (unevenly).

125. Polianskii, *Tsarskie,* 39. By sentence of the district military courts, five people were executed in 1905, thirty-seven in 1906, sixty-nine in 1907, and 184 in 1908, nearly all of them in Warsaw (GARF, f. 102, OO, 1909, d. 50, ch. 9, l. 82).

126. Gernet, *Istoriia tsarskoi tiur'my,* 4:115.

127. The total broke down as follows, 93 in 1905; 1,351 in 1906; 3,790 in 1907; and 4,770 in 1908 ("Obzor . . . za 1905–1908 gg.," GARF, f. 102, OO, 1909, d. 50, ch. 9, l. 82).

128. Zavarzin to Police Department, 20 August 1910, GARF, f. 102, op. 316, 1910, d. 315, ll. 41–41 ob.; Kantor, ed., "Kratkaia avtobiografiia M. E. Bakaia," 155; Men'shchikov to Burtsev, 20 December 1911, GARF, f. 5802, op. 2, d. 385a, l. 9.

129. Burtsev, *Bor'ba,* 1:167.

130. Levitskii, "Imenem," 144–51.

131. Spiridonova, "Iz zhizni," 14:192–93, 16:115.

132. Khaziakhmetov, "Polozhenie," 179 (local authorities); Genkin, *Po tiur'-mam,* 24, 41, 43; Koshko, *Vospominaniia,* 107; Gershuni, *Iz nedavnego,* 208–15 (conditions), 246 (noncommissioned officers); Mikhailov, *Chetvert',* 164.

133. Gruzenberg, *Ocherki,* 99; Sverdlov, "Massovaia," 34; "Deistviia pravitel'stva," *Pravo,* no. 33 (20 August 1906), 2647 (prosecution).

134. Nikitina, "Tornaia," 19.

135. "O merakh . . . ," 28 August 1906, RGIA, f. 1276, op. 2, d. 80, ll. 5–7ob.; Osobyi zhurnal Soveta ministrov, 9 September 1906, RGIA, f. 1276, op. 2, d. 80, ll. 8–11; Zavarzin, *Rabota,* 162.

136. Levin, "Petr Arkad'evich Stolypin," 453; Shipov, *Vospominaniia,* 481, 484; Ascher, *P. A. Stolypin,* 181 (Tverskoi).

137. Sidorov, ed., "Mobilizatsiia," 162–82.

138. *Spisok vysshykh chinov,* 51; "Vasil'ev, A. T.," in *Padenie,* 7:304; Martynov, *Moia sluzhba,* 47–48.

139. Peregudova, "Departament politsii," 23–24; "Raspredelenie . . .," GARF, f. 102, op. 308a, d. 55, ll. 1–3; inventory *(opis')* for GARF, f. 102, OO, part 2, 1906.

140. Laporte, *Histoire,* 29 (offices); Peregudova, "Departament politsii," 27.

141. "Zapiska dlia pamiati," November 1909, GARF, f. 102, op. 316, 1909, d. 361, ll. 4–5 ob.; Makarov to Stolypin, 20 October 1909, GARF, f. 102, OO, 1909, d. 50, ch. 2, ll. 91v-d; service records, GARF, f. 63, op. 53, d. 32, ll. 202 (Mednikov); Val-is'ev to gendarme and security chiefs, 27 September 1906, GARF, f. 280, op. 5, d. 5000, ch. 12 (photographs); Peregudova, "Sluzhba," 255–57; Romanov, *Na strazhe,*

76–78 (provinces); Peregudova, "Departament politsii," 89–91 (service status); Moscow city governor reports, 1907–1908, GARF, f. 102, OO, d. 101a, ll. 2–112 (enrolling of surveillants).

142. Gendarme Corps to gendarme chiefs, 6 October 1906, GARF, f. 102, op. 260, d. 17, ll. 382–83; Romanov, *Na strazhe,* 71–72 (revolvers); Moscow gendarme station to Police Department, 25 July 1906, GARF, f. 102, op. 316, 1906, d. 1040, ll. 2–3; Iarmysh, "Karatel'nye organy," 137 (Kiev).

143. Martynov, *Moia sluzhba,* 94–95 (Saratov), 128 ("fanatic"); Martynov to Trusevich, 27 October 1906, GARF, f. 102, OO, d. 825, ch. 14, l. 103; Martynov to Special Section, 5 November 1906, GARF, f. 102, op. 316, 1906, d. 1039, ll. 4; Special Section to Martynov, 26 November 1906, GARF, f. 102, OO, d. 825, ch. 14, l. 118.

144. On the gendarmes' self-perception and outlook, see Daly, *Autocracy under Siege,* 58–59, 62–63.

145. Pavlov, *Esery-maksimalisty,* 183–88; Gerasimov, *Na lezvii,* 91–93.

146. Agafonov, *Zagranichnaia,* 191 (Moscow); Klimovich-Garting-Trusevich, July-August 1906, GARF, f. 102, op. 316, 1906, d. 1287, ll. 1–13; Kukanov, "Gern-gross-Zhuchenko,'" 97–98; *VPR, Oktiabr'–dekabr' 1906 goda,* 102, 114–16, 121, 357 (mass arrests).

147. Viazmitinov, "Zhandarmy," 89 (Nicholas), 90 (military organizations), 92 (informal directives); Moscow security bureau to precinct captains, 28 November 1906, RGIAgM, f. 475, op. 19, d. 127, l. 115 (new recruits); Gernet, *Istoriia tsarskoi,* 5:121 (arrests); Zverev, ed., "Iz zapisok A. F. Redigera," 99.

148. Police Department report, 1 September 1906, RGIA, f. 1276, op. 2, d. 81, ll. 1–1 ob.; Moscow security bureau to Special Section, 23 September 1906, GARF, f. 102, OO, 1906, (I), d. 2, ch. 35, l. 95; Moscow security bureau to Special Section, 26 November 1906, GARF, f. 102, OO, 1906, (I), d. 2, ch. 35, l. 77; Moscow security bureau to police captains, 14 December 1906, RGIAgM, f. 475, op. 19, d. 127, ll. 129–129 ob.

149. Daly, *Autocracy under Siege,* 71; Obninskii, "Pechat' i administratsiia," 188; Bonch-Bruevich, *Bol'shevistskie,* 5–7, 50–51.

150. Nikolaevskii, *Istoriia odnogo predatelia,* 202 (Azef), 232–33 (Pavlov); Geif-man, *Thou Shalt Kill,* 69 (Dubasov); Bogdanovich, *Tri poslednikh,* 412 (vest); N. Erofeev, "Kudriavtsev, E. P.," in *PPR,* 288; Spiridovich, *Dernières années,* 1:146 (Launits), 147 (Pavlov); "Egorov, Nikolai," in *Bol'shaia,* 24:423.

151. *Aleksandr Ivanovich Guchkov,* 44.

2—REVOLUTION'S END

1. Uranov report, 13 September 1906, GARF, f. 102, OO (I), d. 1284, ll. 2 ob.–17; *SOS* (1 June 1907), pt. 2:228 (Uranov).

2. Correspondence of September and October 1906 in GARF, f. 102, op. 316, 1906, d. 1052 ll. 4–9 ob., 12–17 ob., 19–20 ob., 26–27 ob.; GARF, f. 102, op. 316, 1908, d. 540, ll. 68–75 ob.

3. Trusevich to Stolypin, November 1906, GARF, f. 102, op. 262, d. 18, ll. 1–4; Hildermeier, *Sozialrevolutionäre,* plate facing page 218 (network).

4. Kupritsyn, Mulukaev, and Koriakov, comps., *Istoriia politsii,* 69–71 (creation); Police Department to governors, 8 January 1907, GARF, f. 102, op. 260, d. 17,

ll. 1a–1a ob.; GARF, f. 280, op. 1, 1907, d. 3020, l. 38 (Moscow bureau); Hildermeier, *Sozialrevolutionäre*, 215–59; Martynov, *Moia sluzhba*, 187–88 (Saratov); Peregudova, "Departament politsii," 47; Romanov, *Na strazhe*, 27. For a list of the provinces in each region, see GARF, f. 102, op. 262, d. 16, l. 1.

5. Peregudova, "Departament politsii," 46 (number of bureaus); budget for 1907, GARF, f. 102, op. 316, 1908, d. 50, l. 1; Daly, *Autocracy under Siege*, 133 (1904); Pushkareva, "Rossiiskoe," 43 (terrorism); Pokrovskii, *Gosudarstvennyi*, 17, 19 (interior ministry budget), 52 (police budget).

6. See *SOS* (15 November 1912), 268, and (15 June 1913), 282; Reinbot to Stolypin, 19 June 1908, GARF, f. 63, 1913, op. 53, d. 308, l. 65 (4 April).

7. *SOS* (15 June 1913), 268, 282; Martynov, *Moia sluzhba*, 276; "Vospominaniia Kafafova," GARF, f. 5881, op. 2, d. 390, l. 98; Adrianov to Police Department, 26 May 1908, GARF, f. 63, op. 53, d. 308, l. 65–66 ob.; Spiridovich, *Dernières années*, 1:419; "Psikhologiia predatel'stva," 232 (unnamed informant).

8. Pribylev, *Zinaida Zhuchenko*, 30–33 (Bel'skii); Daly, *Autocracy under Siege*, 85–86 (Zubatov).

9. Shatina, "Mestnyi," 68 (Reinbot, Gershel'man); Peregudova, "Departament politsii," 50 (Trusevich letter; emphasis in original); Stolypin to governors, 8 January 1907, GARF, f. 102, op. 260, d. 17, ll. 1a–1a ob.

10. Vasil'ev to regional chiefs, 6 September 1907, GARF, f. 102, op. 260, d. 17, ll. 108–108 ob. (advisory); Vasil'ev to von Koten, 28 May 1907, GARF, f. 280, op. 1, d. 3008, l. 24; Kupritsyn, Mulukaev, and Koriakov, comps., *Istoriia politsii*, 69–71 (arrests); "K ubiistvu," 7 (wry comment).

11. Vasil'ev to regional chiefs, 13 April 1907, GARF, f. 280, op. 1, d. 3000, t. 2, l. 12; Kurlov to regional chiefs, 2 May 1907, GARF, f. 280, op. 5, d. 5000, ch. 1, ll. 4–4 ob.; Kurlov to regional chiefs, 3 September 1907, GARF, f. 102, op. 260, d. 17, ll. 108–108 ob. (sending of officers to police institutions).

12. "Kratkaia zapiska," December 1912, GARF, f. 102, OO, 1912, d. 248, l. 44 ob. (summer 1907); Martynov, *Moia sluzhba*, 179; von Koten to railroad gendarme posts, August 1907, GARF, f. 280, op. 1, d. 3008, ll. 53–55; monthly requests for information, 1907, GARF, f. 280, op. 1, d. 3008, ll. 212, 231, 252; Moscow security bureau to police captains, 25 November 1907, RGIA g. Moskvy, f. 475, op. 19, d. 21, l. 43 (robbery); Vasil'ev to regional chiefs, 5 August 1907, GARF, f. 280, op. 5, d. 5000, ch. 12, l. 23 (torpedoes).

13. Morozov, *Partiia*, 33 *(Znamia truda)*; Peregudova, "Departament politsii," 191n86 (more bureaus).

14. Correspondence, May–June 1907, GARF, f. 280, op. 1, d. 3020, ll. 3–48; directives to provincial chiefs, 3 and 19 October 1907, GARF, f. 102, op. 260, d. 17, ll. 187, 248–49.

15. Deputy interior minister report, 1909, GARF, f. 102, OO, 1909, d. 50, ch. 2, ll. 91e–zh (reform); "Shkola filerov," 44–49; Moscow city governor reports, 1907–1908, GARF, f. 102, OO, 1907, d. 101a, ll. 2–112; Trusevich to regional security chiefs, 15 May 1908, GARF, f. 280, op. 2, d. 5000, t. 2, l. 63; von Koten to provincial chiefs, 18 December 1907, GARF, f. 63, OO, 1907, d. 45, l. 384 (stories); "O grimirovanii," GARF, f. 102, op. 261, d. 205, ll. 1–2 ob. (disguises); Vasil'ev to gendarme chiefs, 2 March 1908, GARF, f. 102, op. 316, 1908, d. 50, l. 18; von Koten to Trusevich, March 1908, GARF, f. 280, op. 2, d. 5009, ll. 8, 13–14, 46, 53. l. 8.

16. Spiridovich, *Dernières années*, 1:135.

17. Vasil'ev report, 7 November 1907, GARF, f. 102, OO, 1907, d. 812, ll. 1–2 (Beklemishev and Eremin); Trusevich to Stolypin, November 1906, GARF, f. 102, op. 262, d. 18, l. 2 ob. (command center); A. P., "Departament," 22 (specialization).

18. Yearly archival inventories, GARF, f. 102, OO, 1898–1917; Peregudova, "Departament politsii," 26–30 (surveillance).

19. Police Department to governors, 14 January 1908, RGIAgM, f. 46, op. 17, d. 94, l. 1; Daly, *Autocracy under Siege*, 12, 16, 20 (Third Section).

20. GARF, f. 102, OO, 1907–1917 (records); chief of archive report, 24 September 1912, GARF, f. 102, D-5, 1912, d. 668, l. 112 (cards).

21. Special Section to gendarme and security chiefs, 5 November 1908, GARF, f. 102, OO, 1908, d. 433, l. 1; Special Section to Paris Security Bureau, 9 April 1909, GARF, f. 102, OO, 1908, d. 433, l. 6; Peregudova, "Prizhiznennye," 46n (total number of titles); Peregudova, "Biblioteka," 112–13 (librarian).

22. Peregudova, "Departament politsii," 38, 73–74 (inspections); Special Section to regional security chiefs, 10 February 1907, GARF, f. 102, op. 316, 1908, d. 540, l. 2; instructions, GARF, f. 102, op. 316, 1908, d. 540, ll. 1–53, 96–102; Vissarionov testimony, in *Padenie*, 3:449.

23. Klimovich testimony, in *Padenie*, 1:81; "Polozhenie . . ," 9 February 1907, GARF, f. 102, op. 262, 1907, d. 23, l. 8; informant lists, GARF, f. 503, op. 1, dd. 30, 31.

24. Vissarionov testimony, in *Padenie*, 3:450; Kurlov, *Gibel'*, 80. See also Daly, *Autocracy under Siege*, 95–96.

25. Ascher, *Revolution of 1905*, 2:274–77 (organizations) 278–80; Likhomanov, *Bor'ba*, 78–79, 107 (publications); Kir'ianov, ed., "Pravye," 80–82 (pitting rightists against each other); Levin, *Second Duma*, 63 (pressuring opponents); Shatina, "Mestnyi," 178 (arrests).

26. Special Section to governors and city police chiefs, 24 February 1907, GARF, f. 102, OO, d. 580, ll. 2–2 ob.; Moscow city governor to police captains, 9 January 1907, RGIAgM, f. 475, op. 19, d. 127, l. 9; *VPR, Oktiabr'–dekabr' 1906 goda*, 69, 78 (earlier directives); Police Department directive, 29 January 1907, RGIA, f. 1276, op. 3, d. 1, ll. 2–2 ob.

27. *VPR, Ianvar'–iiun' 1907 goda*, 1:70–72 (Stolypin).

28. Ascher, *Revolution of 1905*, 2:284 (election results); Stolypin to governors, 24 February 1907, GARF, f. 102, OO, d. 580, ll. 2–2 ob.

29. Stolypin, *Nam nuzhna*, 53–54; draft bill, RGIA, f. 1276, op. 3, d. 1, ll. 3–31; Petrunkevich, "Iz zapisok," 245; Pokrovskii, "Zapiski," 133–34 (visits).

30. Sidorovnin, ed., *Stolypin*, 217–28; A. I. Shingarev testimony, in *Padenie*, 7:3–4.

31. Chermenskii, *Burzhuaziia*, 378–80 (postponement); Viktorskii, *Istoriia smertnoi*, 368 (bills); Lazarevskii, ed., *Zakonodatel'nye*, 524–26 (praising criminal acts).

32. *Gosudarstvennaia duma: Ukazatel'*, 308–13; archival inventory, RGIA, f. 1278, op. 1, dd. 794–97, 806–8, 937, 1236–72. *GDSO*, 2nd Duma, second session, sitting 25 (10 April 1907), cols. 1180–1914; sitting 27 (13 April 1907), cols. 2009–82; and sitting 40 (17 May 1907), cols. 685–778; Levin, *Second Duma*, 245–54; Mitsit, "O pytkakh," 139–48; Lauchlan, *Russian Hide-and-Seek*, 207.

33. Rabe, *Widerspruch*, 117–19; Lopukhin, *Iz itogov*; Gessen, *Iskliuchitel'noe*, 72–73, 171, 177, 181, 264–65; Kurlov to gendarme and security officers, 27 June 1907, GARF, f. 102, op. 260, d. 17, l. 63; Levin, "Russian Bureaucratic Opinion," 9.

34. Coquin, *1905: La Révolution*, 131 (popular unrest); Moscow security bureau to district captains, 2 March 1907, TsGIAgM, f. 475, op. 19, d. 22, l. 49 (manuals); Pozner, ed., *Pervaia*, 24–25, 106–10, 179, 233–41, 247 (partisan warfare); Tagantsev, *Smertnaia kazn'*, 91n (terrorism statistics); Leonov, *Partiia*, 129; Rediger, *Istoriia moei zhizni*, 2:163 (warning), 169 (insurance).

35. Rediger, *Istoriia moei zhizni*, 1:544 (Apteka memorial); Gerasimov, *Na lezvii*, 102–7; Stolypin speech (7 May 1907), in Stolypin, *Nam nuzhna*, 83–85; Markelov, "Pokushenie," 133–176; Spiridovich, *Histoire du terrorisme russe*, 454–69, 473 (admission of complicity); Spiridovich, *Dernières années*, 1:149–73 (Maklakov: 170); A. B., ed., *Zakulisami*, 248–61.

36. Ascher, *Revolution of 1905*, 2:326–28 (threats); Prussakov, *Kto ubil*, 133 (Bulatsel'); Stolypin to governors, 16 April 1907, GARF, f. 271, op. 1, d. 15. l. 10a.

37. Rawson, *Russian Rightists*, 131–32 (list), 137, 257n49 (pogrom); Miliukov, *Vospominaniia*, 283; Gruzenberg, *Ocherki*, 155; *SOS* (February 1908), 2:484 (Dukel'skii).

38. L'vov, "Sem' let," 75–84 (Witte); Ruud and Stepanov, *Fontanka*, 111–14 (Fedorov and Kazantsev); Rawson, *Russian Rightists*, 134–35 (Iollos); Lauchlan, *Russian Hide-and-Seek*, 261–69, 285–88.

39. Gerasimov, *Na lezvii*, 152–53; Lauchlan, *Russian Hide-and-Seek*, 292–93 (Kommisarov).

40. *Padenie*, 2:43–44 (Manuilov), 6:120–22 (Reinbot); L'vov, "Sem' let," 70–71 (semiofficial security forces).

41. Burtsev testimony, in *Padenie*, 1:321–22; Harcave, ed., *Memoirs of Count Witte*, 629–39; Lauchlan, *Russian Hide-and-Seek*, 295–97.

42. Special Section to gendarme and security chiefs, 19 April 1907, GARF, f. 102, op. 260, d. 17, l. 17; Gerasimov, *Na lezvii*, 99–101; Laporte, *Histoire*, 204; Swain, *Russian Social Democracy*, 22–23 (trade unions); VPR, *Ianvar'–iiun' 1907 goda*, 233–35 (Klimovich); Shatina, "Mestnyi," 181–82 (press).

43. *Pervoe maia*, 307n238 (strikes); Coquin, *1905: La Révolution*, 131 (popular unrest); Bogdanovich, *Tri poslednikh*, 427 (Kurlov), 431 (Kleigel's); Kurlov, *Gibel'*, 7.

44. Voitinskii, "Delo," 99–120; Mikhailov, "V. S. Voitinskii," 88; VPR, *Ianvar'–iiun' 1907 goda*, 1:79 (Trusevich), 82 (indictment); Levin, *Second Duma*, 312–38; Levin, "Shornikova Affair," 2–4.

45. Glinka, *Odinnadtsat'*, 47 (guards); Lazarevskii, ed., *Zakonodatel'nye*, 557–58 (Nicholas); "Perepiska N. A. Romanova," 113 (police actions); Valk, "K istorii," 76–86 (trials); Voitinskii, "Delo," 103–4; Levin, *Second Duma*, 342–44.

46. Morozov, *Partiia*, 278–91 (plans for uprising), 292–300 (mutinies); Pushkareva, "Rossiiskoe," 43 (terrorists); Geifman, *Thou*, 113 (bank).

47. Tolstoi, "Obiazatel'nye," 88–89; city governor report, RGIAgM, f. 46, op. 14, t. 4, d. 3474, l. 7 (Dubasov); VPR, *Ianvar'–iiun' 1907 goda*, 1:85–89 (Stolypin).

48. VPR, *Ianvar'–iiun' 1907 goda*, 1:161 (Gerasimov); Gernet, *Istoriia tsarskoi*, 5:106 (Gerasimov); von Koten to Special Section, 10 September 1907, GARF, f. 280, op. 1, d. 3000, t. 2, ll. 76–76 ob.; "Rossiiskaia sotsial-demokraticheskaia rabochaia partiia," 1908, GARF, f. 102, op. 253, d. 272, l. 5 (Social Democratic ranks); McKean, *St. Petersburg*, 53, 59; Viazmitinov, "Zhandarmy," 92 (military); Iarmysh, "Karatel'nye organy," 209 (Ukraine); *Pervoe maia*, 308n250 (leaflets).

49. Hildermeier, *Sozialrevolutionäre*, 307–15; Spiridovich, *Histoire du terrorisme russe*, 496, 502–3; Morozov, *Partiia*, 32–38; Pavlov, *Esery-maksimalisty*, 193–96, 200; Sypchenko, *Narodno-sotsialisticheskaia*, 31–55 (antiterrorist wing).

50. Police Department directive, 7 September 1907, GARF, f. 102, OO, 1913, d. 281, l. 85 (jails); Special Section to regional security bureaus, 25 January 1908, GARF, f. 280, 1911, op. 5, d. 5000, ch. 12, l. 9 (schools); Vasil'ev to gendarme and security officers, 8 September 1907, GARF, f. 102, OO, 1914, d. 322, l. 15 (military); Police Department to security and gendarme chiefs, 16 May 1908, GARF, f. 102, op. 260, d. 20, ll. 181–84 (countryside); Vasil'ev to security bureaus, 4 October 1907, GARF, f. 102, op. 260, d. 17, ll. 189b–189v ob.; Gerasimov, *Na lezvii*, 99–100; Agafonov, *Zagranichnaia*, 204 (expression of radical views).

51. Von Koten to Police Department director, 20 December 1907, GARF, f. 280, op. 5, d. 5000, ch. 15, l. 12; Pushkareva, *Zheleznodorozhniki*, 281 (archive); Kudelli, "Iz zhizni," 220–23; Iu. Iu. Figatner, "Zinov'ev, G. E.," in *OI*, 2:276; Iu. Iu. Figatner, "Kamenev, L. B.," in *OI*, 2:469; Leonov, *Partiia*, 348–49 (Tamerfors); Nestroev, *Iz dnevnika*, 81; Klimovich to gendarme and security chiefs, 15 November 1908, GARF, f. 102, op. 260, d. 20, l. 341–341 ob.

52. Narskii, "Paradoks," 55, 58–59.

53. "Psikhologiia predatel'stva," 225–27.

54. Ibid., 227–28.

55. Ibid., 229–35.

56. Inspection reports, Moscow region, August 1907, GARF, f. 280, op. 1, d. 3008, ll. 53–56 (apartments); gendarme stations to Moscow regional bureau, December 1907, GARF, f. 280, op. 1 d. 3008, ll. 212, 231, 252 (informants); Moscow gendarme station to Special Section, 6 February 1908, GARF, f. 102, op. 316, 1908, d. 112, ch. 13, l. 2; Special Section to gendarme chiefs, 2 March 1908, GARF, f. 102, op. 316, 1908, d. 50, ll. 17–18.

57. *Kostromskoe*, 7; Daly, *Autocracy under Siege*, 61–62 (denunciations); Trusevich to governors and security police, 31 March 1908, GARF, f. 280, op. 5, d. 5000, ch. 11, l. 3.

58. *Polnoe sobranie*, 3rd ser., vol. 27, no. 29313 (27 June); Polianskii, *Tsarskie*, 32; Drezen, ed., *Tsarizm*, 89–90 (Rediger); Sadikov, "P. A. Stolypin," 215–21 (Gazenkampf).

59. Liublinskii, "Prestupnost'," 652–54; Ordynskii, "Pechat' i sud," 129 (seditious imprints).

60. Asin, "K statistike," 1–37 (conditions); Wheatcroft, "Crisis," 40–41 (number of prisons, mortality); *Annuaire statistique* (1911), 123; "Kurlov, P. G.," in *Padenie*, 7:364; Kurlov, *Gibel'*, 81; *Otchet po Glavnomu tiuremnomu*, 1:47 (escapes).

61. Karpeev, "Voenno-okruzhnoi," 241; Filat'ev, "Dorevoliutsionnye," 138 (1908 statistics); Usherovich, *Smertnye*, 10–11 (number executed); "Vedomost' o chisle lits," GARF, f. 102, D-2, 1910, d. 34, l. 32 (exiles); Shcherbakov, "Chislennost'," 213 (number of exiles on hand).

62. Bonch-Bruevich, *Bol'shevistskie*, 180; Williams, *Other Bolsheviks*, 114–22, 160–62; McKean, *St. Petersburg*, 48–49; Police Department directive, 3 September 1907, GARF, f. 102, op. 260, d. 17, ll. 99–105 ob; von Koten to Police Department, 10 September 1907, GARF, f. 280, op. 1, d. 3000, t. 2, ll. 76–83; Police Department directive, 4 October 1907, GARF, f. 102, op. 260, d. 17, ll. 189b–189b ob.

63. Kuprin, "Morskaia bolezn'," 59–83; I. A. Potliar, "Kuprin, A. I.," in *RP*, 3:233 (Gorky); Bonch-Bruevich, *Vospominaniia*, 60–61 (Iordanskii).

64. Melancon, "'Marching,'" 250–52.

65. Levin, *Third Duma*, 73–94 (meddling); Anan'ich, Ganelin, Paneiakh, et al., *Vlast'*, 554 (numbers); Police Department report, 22 December 1909, GARF, f. 102, D-1, 1909, d. 500, l. 33; Waldron, "States," 20 (Ignat'ev Commission); Conroy, *Peter Arkad'evich Stolypin*, 104–105.

66. "Khronika vnutrennei zhizni," 77–79 (Vilna); Kalmykov, "K voprosu,'" 79–80 (Belousov).

67. See correspondence, July 1907, GARF, f. 63, OO, 1907, d. 45, ll. 121–22; Police Department to governors, 29 November 1907, GARF, f. 102, op. 260, d. 17, ll. 323–23 ob.

68. Diakin, *Samoderzhavie*, 29; Rozenberg, "Neskol'ko," 237 (four thousand items confiscated); Kushakova, ed., "Doneseniia," 98–101 (plays); *Ezhegodnik*, 47 (fines); Tobolin, ed., "Iz arkhiva," 105 (Shcheglovitov); Daly, "Pravitel'stvo," 31 (inability to publish legally); Panchenko, *Leninskaia*, 194, 212.

69. Gorelov, *Bol'sheviki*, 54–55 (unions, membership); Antoshkin, *Professional'noe*, 158–59 (strikes), 164 (unions closed); McKean, "Bureaucracy," 230; Swain, "Freedom," 177 (front organizations).

70. Swain, "Freedom," 180–81 (reasons for decline); Police Department to gendarme and security officers, 27 July 1907, GARF, f. 102, op. 260, d. 17, ll. 69–69 ob.; Blazhchuk, "Zapiska," 1908, RGIA, f. 1282, op. 1, d. 722, ll. 1–2 (trade unions in Europe), 2–4 ob. (lawsuits); Grinevich, *Professional'noe*, 93 (meetings, entertainment); Pushkareva, *Rabochee*, 90 (reasons for closures); Peregudova, "Departament politsii," 159 (informants), 160 (police loath to close too many unions).

71. Bradley, "Voluntary Associations," 148 (aspiration to create democratic liberties); Bradley, "Russia's Parliament," 228–36 (congresses); Tagantsev, *Russkoe*, 2:378–79 (League); Riha, "Constitutional Developments," 91 (parties).

72. Police Department to governors, 29 September 1908, GARF, f. 102, OO, 1908, d. 537, l. 3; Kizevetter, *Na rubezhe*, 446–48; Stepun, *Byvshee*, 1:176–77, 187, 214 (Belyi).

73. Stolypin to Adrianov, March 1908, RGIA g. Moskvy, f. 475, op. 17, d. 94, ll. 4–7; von Koten report, 30 April 1908, GARF, f. 102, OO, 1908, d. 364, ch. 2, ll. 1–2 ob.

74. V. Kriven'kii, "Posse, V.A.," in *PPR*, 476–77; Cherniaev, "Zapadnoe," 185–86, 195 (congress, Zhedenov); Pushkareva, *Rabochee*, 98 (numbers).

75. "Vissarionov, S. E.," in *Padenie*, 7:317; "Kratkaia zapiska," December 1912, GARF, f. 102, OO, 1912, d. 248, ll. 41 (career), 43 ob. (work with Klimovich and von Koten); Martynov, *Moia sluzhba*, 54–55 (appearance and family background); Blok, *Zapisnye*, 343; S. E. Vissarionov testimony, in *Padenie*, 5:226 (inspection tours).

76. Spisok chinov, 1911, GARF, f. 102, op. 295, d. 4, l. 1 (Klimovich's service); Entin, ed., *Politicheskie*, 143–426 (surveys); Klimovich to gendarme and security officers, 19 October 1908, RGIA g. Moskvy, f. 475, op. 17, d. 94, l. 2.

77. Police Department report, 26 October 1908, RGIA, f. 1276, op. 4, d. 81, l. 10 ob.; Peregudova, "Departament politsii," 31–32.

78. "Otchet zasedanii," 185–201. See the original in GARF, f. 102, op. 316, 1908, d. 182.

79. Klimovich to Trusevich, 27 March 1908, GARF, f. 102, op. 316, 1908, d. 50, l. 59; Stolypin to governors, 15 May 1908, GARF, f. 102, op. 260, d. 20, ll. 174–76 ob.; Klimovich to gendarme and security chiefs, 30 December 1908, GARF, f. 102, op. 260, d. 20, l. 378; "Instruktsiia po organizatsii," GARF, f. 63, op. 47, d. 524, ll. 1–14; Lur'e and Peregudova, "Tsarskaia," 61–63 (instruction).

80. Von Koten to gendarme and security officers, 15 December 1908, GARF, f. 280, op. 2, d. 5000, t. 2, ll. 96–97; Klimovich to gendarme and security chiefs, 20 November 1908, GARF, f. 102, op. 260, d. 20, l. 346.

81. Neuberger, *Hooliganism;* Odessa District Court, 22 November 1907, RGIA, f. 1405, op. 531, 1907, d. 189, ll. 22–24 ob.

82. Vitenberg, "Vo glave," 197 (Europe); Weissman, *Reform in Tsarist Russia,* 134–35 *(Vestnik);* Trusevich to governors, 28 June 1908, RGIA, f. 1405, op. 531, d. 189, l. 53 ob. (school); *Polnoe sobranie,* ser. 3, vol. 28, pt. 1, no. 30672 (6 July 1908); Mulukaev, *Politsiia,* 76–79 (bureaus); Peregudova, "Departament politsii," 181n38 (funding).

83. Narbutov, "Proekt," 131–33; Peregudova, *Nesostoiavshaiasia,* 7–13.

84. Trusevich subcommission, RGIA, f. 1217, op. 1, d. 6, ll. 183–97, 332–33a; Dubrovskii, "Agrarnoe," 190 (governors' support).

85. Ansimov, "Okhrannye otdeleniia i mestnaia," 123 (commander); *Revoliutsionnaia mysl'; Pervoe maia,* 308–309; "Reinbot, A. A.," in *Padenie,* 7:404.

86. "Iz otcheta o perliustratsii," 141–45; O. Terebov, "Shipov, D. N.," in *PPR,* 700; Zyrianov, *Petr Stolypin,* 72–73 (Tolstoy).

87. "Eremin, A. M.," in *Padenie,* 7:339; Arkomed, "Krasnyi," 71–83; Fuks, "Bor'ba," 34:202–20, 35:128–41.

88. Morozov, *Partiia,* 381–82 (plots), 383 (Reval), 423–24 (airplane); Gerasimov, *Na lezvii,* 118–30; Gernet, *Istoriia tsarskoi,* 4:136–37; Spiridovich, *Dernières années,* 213 (airplane), 250–52 (Reval), 252 (quotation), 280–81 (Kronstadt); Gorodnitskii, *Boevaia,* 134–40 (plots), 141–46 (Reval).

3—WATERSHED: THE AZEF AFFAIR

1. Diakin, *Samoderzhavie,* 135–40 (rumors), 152 (proposal); Sapov, ed., *Vekhi,* 7–8.

2. Kurlov, *Gibel',* 5–8.

3. Spiridovich, *Dernières années,* 1:312; "Vospominaniia K. D. Kafafova," GARF, f. 5881, op. 2, d. 390, l. 100; Martynov, *Moia sluzhba,* 208; Gerasimov, *Na lezvii,* 171 (empress); Shidlovskii, *Vospominaniia,* 1:188.

4. Kurlov, *Gibel',* 8 (commander), 93 (formal role), 116 (training), 118 (security); Stolypin to Nicholas, 23 May 1909, RGIA, f. 1284, op. 250, d. 15, l. 34 (salary); Kulikov, "Vysshaia," 45 (title); interior ministry reports, 1909–1911, RGIA, f. 1284, op. 250, d. 15, l. 43, 65, 68, 74 (actual role); Beletskii testimony, in *Padenie,* 3:259 (inspections); reports on counterespionage bureaus, 1908–1910, GARF, f. 102, op. 316, 1909, d. 282, ll. 37–59, 148, 156–69.

5. Kurlov, *Gibel',* 90–94, 107; Beletskii testimony, in *Padenie,* 2:257–58 (dislike of Trusevich); "Vo glave . . . Zueva," 200–203; Martynov, *Moia sluzhba,* 175; Spiridovich, *Dernières années,* 1:313; A. P., "Departament," 23 (creature).

6. Z. I. Peregudova, "Beletskii, S. P.," in *OI,* 1:191–92; "Vo glave . . . Beletskogo," 184–201; Spiridovich, *Dernières années,* 2:176 (appearance).

7. Naumov, *Iz utselevshikh,* 189; Shavel'skii, *Vospominaniia,* 2:50 (Nikol'skii); Avrekh, *Tsarizm,* 111 (Kharlamov).

8. Gerasimov, *Na lezvii,* 171.

9. Morozov, *Partiia,* 444; Nikitinskii, *Zagranichnaia,* 32–33; von Koten to Klimovich, 10 January and mid-February 1909, GARF, f. 102, OO, 1909, d. 5, ch. 34, ll. 29, 60–61 ob.

10. Savinkov, *Vospominaniia*, 267 (Krest'ianinov), 268–69 (Saratov); Daly, *Autocracy under Siege*, 148 (Rubakin), 169–70 (Men'shchikov); "Iz vospominanii ob Azefe," in *Znamia truda*, nos. 23–24, cited in GARF, f. 102, op. 316, 1910, d. 315, l. 7 (Mednikov).

11. Argunov testimony, 1910, GARF, f. 1699, op. 1, d. 78, ll. 41 (lack of concern about police surveillance), 46 (habits).

12. Burtsev, *V pogone*, 67–69, 74, 87–88; Spiridovich, *Dernières années*, 1:305–6.

13. Zubatov to Burtsev, 21 March 1908, in Koz'min, ed., *Zubatov*, 91.

14. Pavlov, *Esery-maksimalisty*, 193; A. Kensitskii, 7 April 1908, "Otkrytoe pis'mo," ZA, XXIVc, 2; Garting to Police Department, 30 March and 25 September 1908, ZA, XXIVa, 5.

15. Burtsev, *V pogone*, 87–91; Gessen, "V dvukh," 288 (Kadet circles); Petrunkevich, "Iz zapisok," 350 (Kadet circles); Spiridovich, *Dernières années*, 1:311 (Stolypin); Baluev, "Delo," 134 (cousin), 139 (vain attempts to join Kadets).

16. Burtsev, *V pogone*, 136–39; Burtsev to Spiridovich, 4 January 1916, Spiridovich Papers, box 25, f. 1.

17. Gorodnitskii, *Boevaia*, 148–50; Morozov, *Partiia*, 190.

18. Gorodnitskii, *Boevaia*, 151–52; Gerasimov, *Na lezvii*, 133–34; Argunov, "Azef," 108, 112–14; Argunov testimony, 1910 GARF, f. 1699, op. 1, d. 78, ll. 57–59.

19. Argunov testimony, 1910 GARF, f. 1699, p. 1, d. 78, ll. 59–61; Praisman, *Terroristy*, 359–67.

20. Praisman, *Terroristy*, 367.

21. Argunov, "Azef," 120; Argunov testimony, 1910, GARF, f. 1699, op. 1, d. 78, ll. 61–63.

22. "Azef, E. F.," in *OI*, 1:34; Gerasimov, *Na lezvii*, 134–35; Gorodnitskii, *Boevaia*, 154 (proclamation), 168 (Chernov), 184–85, 199–203 (terrorist acts); Lur'e "Azef," 175 (address).

23. The two exceptions are Gerasimov, *Na lezvii* and Geifman, *Entangled*. See my *Security Services*, 965–66.

24. Daly, *Autocracy under Siege*, 90, 96, 148–49; Gorodnitskii, *Boevaia*, 127–29.

25. Gorodnitskii, *Boevaia*, 162–64 (Gerasimov's negligence); Praisman, *Terroristy*, 287–94 (failure to report 1907 plots); Morozov, *Partiia*, 383 (failure to report 1908 plots); Gerasimov, *Na lezvii*, 125.

26. Gorodnitskii, *Boevaia*, 171–74 (Natanson, Lopatin).

27. Geifman, *Entangled*, 160; Gorodnitskii, *Boevaia*, 169 (Levin).

28. Nikolaevskii, *Istoriia odnogo predatelia*, 128 (Chernov); Skalichev, "Azef," 132; Morozov, *Partiia*, 386–88 (Lazarkevich); Argunov, "Azef," 24.

29. Bakai, "Iz vospominanii," 100, 108.

30. "Delo Azefa"; Obninskii, *Novyi*, 2:201; "Odesskii Azef," *Birzhevye vedomosti*, 13 December 1911, excerpted in GARF, f. 102, op. 316, 1911, d. 1, ch. 57, lit. d, l. 39; Tagantsev, *Perezhitoe*, 70n.

31. Spiridovich, *Dernières années*, 1:309 (consultation of security policemen); Kurlov, *Gibel'*, 95–96; *Zapros ob Azefe*, 9–11, 14, 17, 26.

32. *Zapros ob Azefe*, 35–38 (Pergament), 41–58 (Stolypin).

33. *Zapros ob Azefe*, 77–86.

34. Ibid., 93–95.

35. Ibid., 114–15 (Sazonov), 129–39 (Shubinskoi).

36. Ibid., 147–51; Spiridovich, *Dernières années*, 1:310.

37. Payne, *Police State*, 265; Svatikov, *Russkii*, 28 (Chernov).

38. Burtsev to Spiridovich, 4 January 1916, Spiridovich Papers, box 25, folder 1; Schleifman, *Undercover*, 81–85 (continued unmasking), 91–113 (obsession with provocation), 191–92 (Figner); Sidorov and Tiutiunnik, "V. L. Burtsev," 58 (Chernov); N. M., "Delo," 6 (main party organ).

39. Zorin, *Potomki*, 3; Morozov, *Partiia*, 195 ("different eyes"), 228 ("apathy"); Geifman, *Thou Shalt Kill*, 53–54 (Savinkov), 235–37 (end to terror).

40. Schleifman, *Undercover*, 54 (distribution of informants by party), 114 (Social Democrats on the informant question); "Spisok sekretnykh sotrudnikov," April 1912, GARF, f. 102, op. 316, 1912, d. 202, t. 2, ll. 26–27 and, 1913, GARF, f. 102, op. 316, 1913, d. 200, ll. 16–17; Ansimov, *Bor'ba*, 59 (Dzerzhinskii).

41. Ansimov, *Bor'ba*, 65; Peregudova, "Departament politsii," 75–77 (Orlovskii).

42. Kurlov, *Gibel'*, 99, 111–12; Nikolaevskii, *Istoriia odnogo predatelia*, 275 (permission); Baluev, "Delo," 141 (Nicholas on hard labor).

43. Laporte, *Histoire*, 211; Kurlov, *Gibel'*, 99–100; Engel'ke and Ignatovich, eds., *Deistvuiushchaia*, 37–38.

44. *Delo A. A. Lopukhina*, 28, 86–87.

45. Ibid., 90 (quotation), 97, 116.

46. Tobolin, ed, "Iz arkhiva," 106 ("splendid"); "Lopukhin, A. A.," in *Padenie*, 7:369; "Reabilitatsiia," 1; Gurko, *Features*, 637n44.

47. Burtsev, "Moia bor'ba," 1–6.

48. Von Koten report, 8 May 1909, GARF, f. 102, op. 316, 1909, d. 189, ll. 85–88 ob.; Garting to Zuev, 25 April 1909, GARF, f. 102, op. 316, 1909, d. 189, l. 53; "Un drame mysterieux," *La Patrie* (9 May 1909), excerpted in GARF, f. 102, op. 316, 1909, d. 189, l. 55; *Le Matin* (14 May 1909), excerpted in GARF, f. 102, OO, 1909, d. 220, l. 21.

49. Garting to Zuev, 25 April 1909, GARF, f. 102, op. 316, 1909, d. 189, l. 53 ob. (pressing of charges); Special Section report, 18 February 1910, GARF, f. 102, OO, 1909, d. 220, l. 138 (Labori); Burtsev, "Moia bor'ba," 9–18.

50. Informant report of 29 November 1910, GARF, f. 102, op. 316, 1906, d. 1019, l. 122 (Urusov and Kovalenskii); "Iz pisem L. A. Rataeva," 146n4 (Kovalenskii); "Novyi razoblachitel'," 3.

51. Garting to Vissarionov, 11/24 April 1909, ZA, XXIVa, 5; GARF, f. 102, op. 316, 1909, d. 189, ll. 14–18 (report on Tsikhotskaia), 173–74 (Tsikhotskaia to prosecutor), 217–21 (report on Tsikhotskaia, 1913).

52. N. Erofeev, "Lapina, E. L. M.," *PPR*, 301–302; Gorodnitskii, *Boevaia*, 198; Morozov, *Partiia*, 409–12.

53. Morozov, *Partiia*, 202 (commission), 233 (money), 236 (conclusion), 408 ("gendarme station"), 485–86 (terror); Spiridovich, *Dernières années*, 1:415 (plan).

54. Men'shchikov, *Russkii*, 244–45; Koznov, "Metamorfozy," 118 (lists); Men'shchikov, letter to the editor, *Katorga i ssylka* 22 (1926), 285; police report on Men'shchikov, 1910, GARF, f. 102, op. 316, 1910, d. 88, ll. 73–76, 81 ob. (effectiveness); Special Section to border gendarmes, 15 February 1910, box 179, folder 1, Nicolaevsky Collection, Hoover Institution Archives (resentment); Volkov, *Petrogradskoe*, 10 (finding a job).

55. Nikolaevskii, "Pamiati"; Police Department report, June 1916, GARF, f. 102, op. 316, 1916, d. 25, ll. 5–5 ob.; A. N. Petrov, "Garting, A. M.," in *OI*, 1:516

(interpellation); Andreev to Police Department, 6 August 1909, ZA, IIIa(9), 2–8; Svatikov, *Russkii,* 29 (leaks).

56. Spiridovich, *Dernières années,* 1:313 (charming man, same regiment); Beletskii testimony, in *Padenie,* 3:298.

57. Brachev, *Mastera,* 98 (Bittard-Monin); Nikitinskii, *Zagranichnaia,* 16 (Ergardt), 119–20 (private agency); Krasil'nikov to Zuev, 24 January 1911, GARF, f. 102, op. 316, 1911, d. 1, ch. 1, lit. d, ll. 17–22; Police Department, June 1916, GARF, f. 102, op. 316, 1916, d. 25, ll. 5–5 ob. (Bint and Sambain).

58. Pribylev, *Zinaida Zhuchenko,* 4–6 (description); Burtsev and Zhuchenko, August 1909, GARF, f. 102, op. 316, 1906, d. 1019, ll. 17–17 ob. (threats, Bakai).

59. Pavlov, *Agenty,* 35–36 (meeting in Germany), 43 (acid), 45 (guess regarding source of Burtsev's information); Burtsev and Zhuchenko, August 1909, GARF, f. 102, op. 316, 1906, d. 1019, ll. 20–20 ob. ("sacred institution"); Police Department directive, 15 February 1910, GARF, f. 102, op. 316, 1910, d. 88, l. 14 (pension); "Nabolevshie voprosy," 10.

60. GARF, f. 102, op. 316, 1906, d. 1019, ll. 79 (request), 103 (pension), 104 (Berlin police), 125 (praise for Zhuchenko), 133 (Liebknecht), 162 (arrest); report on Men'shchikov, 4 September 1910, GARF, f. 102, op. 316, 1910, d. 88, l. 39 (pension); A. N. Petrov, "Gengross [sic]-Zhuchenko, Z. F.," in *OI,* 1:526 (Belgium).

61. Burtsev, "V bor'be," 17:21–22.

62. Zavarzin to Zuev, 3 January 1910, GARF, f. 102, op. 316, 1907, d. 694, ll. 27–27 ob. (husband); Alekseev, *Provokator,* 37–41 (newspapers), 4 (Soviet court), 53 (lawsuit); Stolypin to Nicholas II, 31 January 1911, GARF, f. 102, op. 316, 1907, d. 694, l. 35 (pension).

63. "Bundovskii Azef," in Serebrennikov, ed., *Soblazn,* 392–95.

64. Burtsev, "V bor'be," 26:20–21.

65. Ibid., 26:21–22.

66. Koz'min, "K istorii," 103 (Burtsev and Kropotkin); Andreev to Zuev, 4/17 September 1909, ZA, XXIVa, 5; "Tsirkuliar," 125; Police Department report, 1910, GARF, f. 102, op. 316, 1910, d. 329; Sidorov and Tiutiunnik, "V. L. Burtsev," 59 (rumors); arrest order, 31 March 1910, ZA, XXIVb, 6; Gorev, "Leonid Men'shchikov," 139 (shunning of Men'shchikov).

67. Cherkunov, "K voprosu," 97–100 (Serov); *Pravda,* no. 204 (30 December 1912), excerpted in GARF, f. 102, OO, 1912, d. 378, l. 85; Elenskii to Zuev, 10 August 1912, GARF, f. 102, OO, 1912, d. 378, ll. 24–25 (plea); von Koten to Zuev, 28 August 1912, GARF, f. 102, OO, 1912, d. 378, ll. 32–34 (plea, sums of money, children); Globachev to Police Department, 18 March 1915, GARF, f. 102, OO, 1912, d. 378, ll. 170–171 ob. (work, plea).

68. Morozov, *Partiia,* 416–22; D. Pavlov, "Klimova, N. S.," in *PPR,* 254; Gorodnitskii, *Boevaia,* 218–24.

69. Offers of services, 1908–1910, GARF, f. 102, op. 316, 1908, d. 59; recruitment files, GARF, f. 4888, op. 5; recruitment file, GARF, f. 4888, op. 5, d. 635 (Moscow recruitment); list of informants, 1913, GARF, f. 102, op. 316, 1911, d. 1, ch. 57, lit. d, ll. 168–69 (St. Petersburg recruitment); Selivanov, "Provokatorsha," 145–46 (Romanova); Police Department to gendarme and security chiefs, January 1909, GARF, f. 102, op. 316, 1907, d. 721, ll. 56–57.

70. Gerasimov report, 17 July 1909, GARF, f. 102, op. 316, 1909, d. 194, ll. 6–17; von Koten report, 20 January 1909, GARF, f. 102, OO, 1909, d. 50, ch. 2, l. 2; Zuev to gendarme and security chiefs, 3 October 1912, GARF, f. 102, op. 308a, 1913, d. 34, l. 2 ob.

71. Replies to Police Department, December 1909, GARF, f. 102, op. 267, d. 35, ll. 28–32; Police Department to security chiefs, 20 March 1909, GARF, f. 102, op. 308a, 1909, d. 20, ll. 1–1 ob.; Daly, *Autocracy under Siege,* 42 (numbers); Peregudova, "Vazhnyi," 379 (numbers); Zuev to Stolypin, 18 February 1910, GARF, f. 102, op. 316, 1910, d. 333, l. 8 ob.; Vissarionov to Kurlov, 3 April 1910, GARF, f. 102, op. 316, 1910, d. 333, ll. 26–38 (31–32: Moscow and Warsaw; 32 ob.–33: equipment); Police Department reports, February 1911, GARF, f. 102, op. 267, d. 35, ll. 70, 74–75 ob. (new bureaus).

72. "Karpov, S. G.," in *Padenie,* 7:351; Gerasimov, *Na lezvii,* 147; Spiridovich, *Dernières années,* 1:313; Vissarionov testimony, in *Padenie,* 3:481; Martynov, *Moia sluzhba,* 175, 186.

73. Schleifman, *Undercover,* 119–20, 128–29; N. Erofeev, "Minor, O. S.," in *PPR,* 366 (arrest of Petrov).

74. Morozov, *Partiia,* 446; Gorodnitskii, *Boevaia,* 207–11; "Iz zapisok A. A. Petrova," 136; Gerasimov, *Na lezvii,* 169–70.

75. Morozov, *Partiia,* 449; Gerasimov, *Na lezvii,* 174–75; Spiridovich, *Dernières années,* 1:417 (seizure of Petrov).

76. "Iz zapisok A. A. Petrova," 82–94; Gerasimov, *Na lezvii,* 166–68; Martynov, *Moia sluzhba,* 183–84; Schleifman, *Undercover,* 120–24; Gerasimov testimony, in *Padenie,* 3:13; Kurlov, *Gibel',* 112.

77. Morozov, "B. V. Savinkov," 252 (investigating commission), 454–62 (three versions).

78. Morozov, *Partiia,* 465; Gerasimov, *Na lezvii,* 172–78; Morozov, "B. V. Savinkov," 251 (investigation, report); Agafonov, *Zagranichnaia,* 194 (report).

79. Morozov, *Partiia,* 467–68, 471; N. M., "Delo," 3–6; "K ubiistvu polkovnika Karpova," 9.

80. Von Koten, service records, GARF, f. 63, op. 53, d. 308, ll. 268–69; Stepanov to Shtiurmer, 10 May 1916, GARF, f. 102, op. 316, 1916, d. 25, l. 4; "Zavarzin, P. P.," in *Padenie,* 7:340; Zavarzin to Zuev, 11 April 1911, GARF, f. 102, op. 316, 1911, d. 1, ch. 46, lit. a, ll. 61 ob.–62; Martynov, *Moia sluzhba,* 219–20.

81. Police Department to gendarme and security officers, 18 December 1909, GARF, f. 102, op. 308a, d. 19, l. 1; Police Department to gendarme and security officers, 19 December 1910, GARF, f. 102, op. 316, 1911, d. 124, lit. b, t. 2, l. 19 ob.; Kurlov, *Gibel',* 112–13; Police Department internal directive, 12 January 1910, GARF, f. 102, op. 316, 1910, d. 188, ll. 1–2 (limiting access to director); Police Department internal directive, 19 January 1910, GARF, f. 102, op. 310, d. 6, l. 1 (Special Section); Police Department to gendarme and security officers, 17 January 1910, GARF, f.102, op. 260, d. 396, ll. 8–9 (prison informants); Police Department to gendarme and security officers, 25 January 1910, GARF, f. 102, OO, 1911, d. 124, lit. v, l. 12 (infiltration); "Tsirkuliar," 125; Police Department to gendarme and security officers, 31 March 1910, GARF, f. 102, op. 260, d. 396, l. 105 (unreliable informants). See the lists of unreliable informants compiled by police officials in GARF, f. 503, op. 1, d. 30 (1909–1913) and 31 (1907–1915). The lists contain 457 and 444 persons, respectively, the largest numbers relating to 1909–1910.

82. "Iz zapisok A. A. Petrova," 138.

83. *Zapros ob Azefe,* 77–86.

4—THE APOGEE OF THE WATCHFUL STATE

1. Sidorov, "Iz zapisok," 94 (Gershel'man); Avrekh, *Stolypin,* 287 (orders to governors); "Spiski mestnostei," GARF, f. 102, op. 302, d. 4, ll. 31 ob., 58–59, 71; "Perechen'," 1911–1913, GARF, f. 102, op. 302, d. 8, ll. 1–10 ob, 21–28; "Nastol'nye reestry," 1908–1910, GARF, f. 102, op. 270, dd. 80–82 (state-crime cases).

2. Zavarzin reports, GARF, f. 102, OO, 1910, d. 9, ch. 46, lit. b, l. 31; GARF, f. 102, OO, 1911, d. 9, ch. 46, ll. 151–151 ob.; GARF, f. 102, OO, 1910, d. 235, ll. 97, 141, 213–13 ob.; GARF, f. 280, op. 4, 1910, d. 5010, ll. 26–29; GARF, f. 102, op. 316, 1911, d. 1, ch. 46, lit. a, l. 47 ob.

3. McKean, *St. Petersburg,* 84; Morozov, *Partiia,* 31 (collapse of party committees), 274 (coffers); Spiridovich, *Istoriia bol'shevizma,* 273 (quotation), 274 (seizure of presses); Koznov, "Bor'ba," 64–65 (smuggling operation); "Vospominaniia Podvoiskogo o rabote v Pravde," RGASPI, f. 146, op. 1, d. 142, l. 48.

4. Beletskii testimony, in *Padenie,* 3:259 (description), 4:430 (systematization); "Broetskii, M. E.," "Eremin, A. M.," "Zaitsov, N. V. [sic]," and "Peshkov, N. A.," in *Padenie,* 7:311, 339, 341, 396; "Kratkaia zapiska," December 1912, GARF, f. 102, OO, 1912, d. 248, ll. 40–43 ob. (systematization, Vissarionov); Martynov, *Moia sluzhba,* 277 (systematization).

5. Personnel list, March 1911, GARF, f. 102, OO, 1911, d. 46, ll. 47–49; Special Section report, 10 May 1910, GARF, f. 102, OO, 1910, d. 48, l. 144 (typewriters); Daly, *Autocracy under Siege,* 42 (teasing out data); Special Section report, 1913, GARF, f. 102, OO, 1913, d. 9, t. 1, l. 4 (Savitskii).

6. Statistical table on directives, December 1912, GARF, f. 102, OO, 1912, d. 248, l. 48; Peregudova, "Departament politsii," 35 (breakdown).

7. Special Section directives, 8 March 1910, GARF, f. 102, op. 260, d. 396, ll. 74–74 ob. (camouflaging sources); 1 September 1913, GARF, f. 280, op. 5, d. 5000, ch. 12, ll. 111–111 ob. (not supplying documents to third parties); 1912, GARF, f. 102, OO, d. 248, l. 16 (safeguarding secret documentation); 1910, GARF, f. 280, op. 5, d. 5000, ch. 3, t. 1, l. 7 (using tact); 9 January 1910, GARF, f. 280, op. 5, d. 5000, ch. 12, l. 29 (reporting to governors); 18 October 1910, ZA, XIIId(1), 10 (requesting information from detective police); 5 March 1910, GARF, f. 102, op. 260, d. 257, l. 17–17 ob. (searching suspects); 27 March and 2 and 19 July 1911, GARF, f. 280, op. 5, d. 5000, ch. 12, ll. 67–68 (exile, treatment of suspects), 75 (interrogation), 78 (detention); 5 February 1911, GARF, f. 280, op. 5, d. 5000, ch. 12, l. 62 ("not a formal endeavor").

8. Special Section directive, 12 May 1910, GARF, f. 280, op. 5, d. 5000, ch. 12, l. 37; Special Section directive, 23 June 1910, GARF, f. 280, op. 5, d. 5000, ch. 12, l. 40.

9. "Kratkaia zapiska," December 1912, GARF, f. 102, OO, 1912, d. 248, l. 44.

10. Vissarionov to Zavarzin, 14 April 1910, f. 63, op. 53, d. 518, l. 52–52 ob.; Special Section report, 31 March 1911, GARF, f. 102, op. 316, 1911, d. 202 (Warsaw); Kurlov, *Gibel',* 115–16; Special Section report, February 1911, GARF, f. 102, op. 316, 1911, d. 150, ll. 1–2, 35–41, 54–57.

11. Vissarionov to Zuev, 10 November 1911, GARF, f. 102, op. 316, 1911, d. 148, l. 1 ob.; Peregudova, "Departament politsii," 41–42, 189n63–64 (dismissals, probation); draft report, April 1912, GARF, f. 102, OO, 1912, d. 248, ll. 6 ob.–7 (inspection teams), 14 ob.–23 ob. (lists).

12. Kurlov to security chiefs, 3 April and 3 October 1910, ZA, XIIId(1), 10 (sta-

tioning of officers at regional bureaus); "Instruktsiia," GARF, f. 102, OO, 1912, d. 309, ll. 2-4 (sample exam), 6-7 (structure), 35-45 (course offerings).

13. "Konspekt lektsii," GARF, f. 102, op. 253, d. 243, ll. 1-146 (course outline); Sergeev, "Zhandarmy-istoriki," 376-77 (Thun); "Politicheskii rozysk i ego osushch-estvlenie" (lecture on security policing); Spiridovich, *Dernières années*, 1:427-37. Jeremiah Schneiderman has translated the outline from Spiridovich's lectures on security policing as "From the Files."

14. Entin, ed., *Politicheskie* (treatises); Peregudova, "Departament politsii," 40 (textbooks); Sidorova, "Istoriki," 40-47 (textbooks); Skhemy, GARF, f. 102, op. 253, d. 387 (diagrams); "Revoliutsionnoe dvizhenie v Rossii," 280 (chart); Arapava, "Tsarskie," 40-49 (chart).

15. Spiridovich, *Dernières années*, 1:427 (Gendarme Corps); Vissarionov to Zuev, 10 November 1911, GARF, f. 102, op. 360, 1911, d. 148, l. 2-4 ob.; Zuev to gendarme and security officers, 3 October 1912, GARF, f. 102, op. 308a, 1913, d. 34, l. 2 (enticements); "Polozhenie," 24 December 1913, GARF, f. 102, OO, 1914, d. 130, ll. 29-36 ob. (criteria).

16. Correspondence, 16 and 25 April 1910, GARF, f. 102, op. 316, 1910, d. 50, ch. 46, lit. a, ll. 148, 153 (Zavarzin); Spiridovich testimony, in *Padenie*, 3:38 (Kuliabko's studies with Spiridovich); Stepanov, *Zagadki*, 216 (Kuliabko's marriage to Spiridovich's sister); "Kuliabko, N. N.," in *Padenie*, 7:363.

17. Moscow security bureau report, 27 April 1912, GARF, f. 102, op. 316, 1911, d. 1, ch. 46, lit. a, l. 153 ob. (three thousand under surveillance); "Spisok," GARF, d. 102, op. 316, 1916, d. 186, ll. 45-45 ob. (Zavarzin's staff); Zavarzin to Vissarionov, 20 April 1912, GARF, f. 102, op. 316, 1912, d. 202, t. 2, ll. 20-27 (number of informants), 29-30 (number of surveillants).

18. Moscow security bureau to Second Precinct of Meshchanskaia Ward, 2 July 1915, RGIAgM, f. 475, op. 19, d. 61, l. 57 (specific requests for information); Zavarzin to regular police, 24 December 1910, RGIAgM, f. 475, op. 17, d. 611, ll. 95-95 ob.; Stolypin to governors, 7 November 1911, GARF, f. 280, op. 5, d. 5000, ch. 12, ll. 86-86 ob. (countryside); Stolypin to governors, 27 November 1910, GARF, f. 102, op. 260, d. 396, l. 367 (tearooms); Stolypin to governors, 9 November 1911, GARF, f. 102, OO, 1911, d. 120, t. 1, l. 42 (commemoration of Napoleon's defeat).

19. "Spisok," April 1912, GARF, f. 102, op. 316, 1912, d. 202, t. 2, ll. 26-27; Schleifman, *Undercover*, 64.

20. "Spisok," 1913, GARF, f. 102, op. 316, 1913, d. 200, ll. 16-17.

21. "Spisok," 1913, GARF, f. 102, op. 316, 1913, d. 200, ll. 16-17; "Instruktsiia," 1914, GARF, f. 102, op. 261, d. 240, l. 1; Martynov, *Moia sluzhba*, 226.

22. Blinova, "Delo,'" 202-204 (conference); Zuev directives, October 1910 and June 1911, GARF, f. 102, op. 308a, d. 26, ll. 3-3 ob., 6-7; Zavarzin report, 1912, GARF, f. 102, op. 316, 1912, d. 202, t. 3, ll. 79, 81-82 ob. (inventory); Drezen, "Baltiiskii," 132, 147-48.

23. Koznov, "Bor'ba," 63-65 ("informant problem," party activists who were informants); Lenin testimony, in Lenin, *Polnoe*, 32:511n125; "Zhitomirskii, Is. A.," in *Bol'shaia sovetskaia entsiklopediia*, 25:550; Agafonov, *Zagranichnaia*, 129 (suspicions of Zhitomirskii), 130 (Lenin on Zhitomirskii).

24. Koznov, "Bor'ba," 68-71 (Malinovskii); "Spisok," April 1912, GARF, f. 102, op. 316, 1912, d. 202, t. 2, l. 26 (Malinovskii's salary).

25. Tsiavlovskii, ed., *Bol'sheviki,* 272, 328n25 (nicknames), 327n19 (central committee), 327n20 (Plekhanov), 331n35 (Zimmerwald); Morozov, *Partiia;* Gorodnitskii, *Boevaia;* Leonov, *Partiia,* 21 (quotation).

26. Special Section to gendarme and security chiefs, 22 December 1910, GARF, f. 102, op. 260, d. 396, l. 410 (reasons for dissatisfaction); Bulkin, "Departament," 233 (union members not arrested); city governor order, 25 April 1910, RGIAgM, f. 475, op. 19, d. 47, l. 151 (regular policemen).

27. Blondinka reports, 20 October 1910 to February 1912, GARF, f. 102, op. 316, 1912, d. 202, t. 3, ll. 70–75 ob.; "'Blondinka,'" 208–209; Martynov, *Moia sluzhba,* 227–29.

28. Avrekh, "Dokumenty," 40–48.

29. Avrekh, "Dokumenty," 43–44 (L'vov), 46–48 (Grave); *Protokoly,* 3:91, 153–55, 157, 166, 183 (16 September).

30. A. I. Serkov, "Masonstvo," in *OI,* 3:503–507.

31. Beletskii to interior minister, 19 March 1913, GARF, f. 102, op. 316, 1905, d. 12, ch. 2, ll. 164–66 ob. (inconclusive reports); Avrekh, *Masony,* 237–38 (Kedrin), 238 (Mets), 265 (Vissarionov), 276–87 (Alekseev); GARF, f. 102, op. 316, 1905, d. 12, ch. 2, ll. 45–136 (bibliography), 185–94 ob. (Mets); Startsev, *Russkoe,* 78 (Orthodox).

32. Avrekh, *Masony,* 244 (Mets), 276–87 (Alekseev), 314–17 (Rataev); Platonov, *Ternovyi,* 720–21 and 746–69 (Rataev).

33. Kozlova and Startsev, "Nikolai Vissarionovich Nekrasov," 86–87, 93; Startsev, *Russkoe,* 105–13 (supreme council); Andreev, "Evoliutsiia," 3.

34. Startsev, *Russkoe,* 71 (NKVD), 96 (interpellations), 120 (pledge); Nikolaevskii, *Russkie,* 78.

35. Gerasimov, *Na lezvii,* 161–65; Gerasimov testimony, in *Padenie,* 3:11–12; Mosolov, *Pri dvore,* 245 (censorship); Sidorov, "Iz zapisok," 98–99 (Novoselov, Nicholas); N. A. Panov and S. M. Polovinkin, "Novoselov, M. A.," in *RP,* 4:230–31.

36. GARF, f. 102, D-1, 1910, d. 7, d. 8, d. 9, t. 2, d. 68, ch. 33 (security arrangements); financial report, September 1916, GARF, f. 102, D-1, 1916, d. 10, l. 1 ob.; RGIA, f. 1284, op. 250, d. 15 (security measures); Kurlov, *Gibel',* 118; "Proekt polozheniia," 7 December 1910, and "Instruktsiia chinam," GARF, f. 102, op. 316, 1909, d. 361, ll. 31, 191–97; Special Section to gendarme and security chiefs, 2 June 1911, GARF, f. 280, op. 5, d. 5000, ch. 12, ll. 70–71.

37. Gerasimov, *Na lezvii,* 179–81; Alexander, *Always,* 293–98.

38. Special Section to gendarme and security chiefs, 22 December 1910, GARF, f. 102, op. 260, d. 396, l. 414 (gendarme chiefs supposed to report to Police Department); Derevianko, "Shpionov," 51–53 (war with Japan); GARF, f. 102, op. 316, 1908, d. 390, ll. 148, 156–169 (commission, budget); Karpeev, "Kontrrazvedyvatel'-noe," 2:422–23; "Vedomost'," January 1910, GARF, f. 102, D-1, 1908, d. 70, t. 1, ll. 5–7 ob. (von Koten's bureau); GARF, f. 102, op. 308a, 1910, d. 25, ll. 3–5 (directives); Grekov, *Russkaia,* 210–12 (weak counterespionage capabilities).

39. GARF, f. 102, op. 267, d. 40, ll. 50–53 (Katkov), 60–61 (police report).

40. S. A. Stepanov, "Illiodor," in *OI,* 2:338; Stepanov, *Chernaia,* 203–204; S. A. Stepanov, "Vostorgov, I. I.," in *OI,* 1:466; Zavarzin to Zuev, 3 March 1911, GARF, f. 63, OO, 1911, d. 250, l. 3 (Vostorgov's speech); Martynov, *Moia sluzhba,* 34; Gurko, *Tsar' i tsaritsa,* 95–97 (friends at court).

41. Avrekh, *Stolypin,* 278–82 (budget), 294 *(Rossiia);* Zuev to regional chiefs, 22 June 1911, GARF, f. 280, op. 5, d. 5000, ch. 12, l. 73 (complaints).

42. GARF, f. 102, OO, 1911, d. 27, t. 1, ll. 4–5 ob. (letter), 10–11 (Zuev).

43. Dzhunkovskii, *Vospominaniia*, 1:598; Spiridovich, *Dernières années*, 2:93–98.

44. Kurlov, *Gibel'*, 121–24; Gan, "Ubiistvo," 986 (Bogrov).

45. Sidorovnin, ed., *Stolypin*, 133 (Rein); Spiridovich, *Dernières années*, 2:108 (Kuliabko), 112–13 (security in theater); GARF, f. 271, op. 1, d. 15, ll. 84–88 (conflicts between security forces).

46. Spiridovich, *Dernières années*, 2:118 (Stolypin's exclamation); GARF, f. 271, op. 1, d. 16, ll. 43–45 (Kuliabko testimony); GARF, f. 271, op. 1, d. 25, l. 354 (tickets), 409 (police intervention to protect Bogrov), 410 (Bogrov's entrance unbeknownst to officials), 415 (shooting); Kurlov, *Gibel'*, 125–31; Geifman, *Thou Shalt Kill*, 237–40 (Bogrov hanged).

47. Samokhvalov testimony, 22 September 1911, GARF, f. 271, op. 1, d. 15, ll. 140–41 ob.; Spiridovich, *Dernières années*, 2:126 (convert).

48. Spiridovich, *Dernières années*, 2:129 (first target, rightists), 156 (suspicion); Sidorovnin, ed., *Stolypin*, 147 (Bogrov's admission), 152–53 (Bogrov's testimony); Gan, "Ubiistvo," 995 (bandits, targets); N. V. Brandorf testimony, 29 September 1911, GARF, f. 271, op. 1, d. 25, l. 414 (Bogrov threatened by comrades); V. V. Kriven'kii, "Bogrov, M. G.," in *OI*, 1:258; RGIA, f. 1284, op. 250, d. 15, l. 75 (Kurlov's resignation).

49. Kokovtsov, *Iz moego*, 1:409–11; Sidorovnin, ed., *Stolypin*, 164–66 (order to governors); Spiridovich, *Dernières années*, 2:127 (thanks from Nicholas).

50. V. N. Kokovtsov testimony, in *Padenie*, 7:93.

51. Kuliabko testimony, GARF, f. 271, op. 1, d. 16, ll. 70–71.

52. Kuliabko testimony, GARF, f. 271, op. 1, d. 16, l. 71; Spiridovich, *Dernières années*, 2:93; Spiridovich testimony, GARF, f. 271, op. 1, d. 2, ll. 62–62 ob., GARF, f. 271, op. 1, d. 25, ll. 436–40, and GARF, f. 271, op. 1, d. 15, l. 70 ob.

53. Kurlov testimony, 25 September 1911, GARF, f. 271, op. 1, d. 25, ll. 397–98; Kurlov testimony, 14–19 October 1911, GARF, f. 271, op. 1, d. 2, ll. 123 ob., 126 ob., 134.

54. Stepanov, *Zagadki*, 214–16 (inspections), 243–302 (full report; for inspections see 255–60), 278–79 (rivalry); GARF, f. 271, op. 1, d. 25, ll. 349–51, 363–66 (inspections).

55. Zaitsev to Zuev, 15 December 1911, GARF, f. 102, op. 316, 1911, d. 167, l. 59 (Kuliabko); State Council to interior ministry, 5 January 1913, RGIA, f. 1284, op. 250, d. 15, l. 87; Kurlov, *Gibel'*, 135 (pension); Martynov, *Moia sluzhba*, 204 (photographer); Spiridovich, *Dernières années*, 2:308; Sidorovnin, ed., *Stolypin*, 158–60 (Kokovtsov).

56. Dzhunkovskii, *Vospominaniia*, 1:599; Gerasimov, *Na lezvii*, 178–79; Avrekh, *Stolypin*, 390–99; Avrekh, *Tsarizm*, 138.

57. Stepanov, *Zagadki*, 166 (duty to protect Stolypin), 190 (Petrov), 219 (accusations), 222 (conclusion).

58. Spiridovich, *Dernières années*, 2:160–62; GARF, f. 102, op. 316, 1911, d. 167, ll. 5 (Kuliabko challenged), 31–41 (newspaper); *Grazhdanin*, no. 36 (18 September 1911): 14–16.

59. Gredeskul, *Terror*, 23, 28–33.

60. "Makarov, A. A.," in *Padenie*, 7:372; "Vospominaniia K. D. Kafafova," GARF, f. 5881, op. 2, d. 390, l. 109; Spiridovich, *Dernières années*, 2:175–79.

61. "Zolotarev, I. M.," in *Padenie*, 7:342–43; Dzhunkovskii, *Vospominaniia*, 1:613–14.

62. Dzhunkovskii, *Vospominaniia*, 1:649, 675; Spiridovich, *Dernières années*, 2:182–84; Vissarionov to Makarov, 25 April 1912, GARF, f. 102, op. 316, 1912, d. 314, ll. 22–30 ob.; Vissarionov to Makarov, April 1912, GARF, f. 102, op. 316, 1912, d. 202, t. 1, l. 83.

63. Vissarionov to Beletskii, April 1912, GARF, f. 102, op. 316, 1912, d. 202, t. 2, ll. 49–53; Beletskii testimony, in *Padenie*, 4:341–43.

64. Martynov, *Moia sluzhba*, 216–17, 264–65; comparative budgetary data, GARF, f. 102, D-1, 1910, d. 70, t. 1, ll. 5–7 ob.

65. Shatsillo, "Lenskii," 384–85; Melancon, "Ninth Circle," 785–92; "Treshchenkov, N. V." in *SOS* (13 June 1913), 2:570. Treshchenkov's case went to court in April 1914; in October Nicholas decreed that he be allowed to serve in the army until the war's end (Shatsillo, "Lenskii," 387–88).

66. Costello, *"Novoe,"* 41–42 *(Rossiia);* McReynolds, *News*, 237–38 *(Kopeika);* GDSO, 3rd Duma, session 5, sitting 102 (11 April 1912): 1953.

67. *Grazhdanin*, no. 24 (17 June 1912): 13–15.

68. Elwood, *Russian*, 219–22; Arutiunov, *Rabochee*, 259 (Bolsheviks), 311; McKean, "Bureaucracy," 231.

69. Police Department to gendarme and security chiefs, 19 May 1912, cited in GARF, f. 102, OO, 1916, d. 341, ll. 5–6 ob.; "Svodka mer," 12 October 1912, GARF, f. 102, OO, 1905, d. 2606, ll. 40–47 ob.; Bulkin, "Departament," 128–31 (surveillance); Peregudova, "Departament politsii," 159 (September meeting); Arutiunov, *Rabochee*, 311 (November meeting).

70. Korbut, ed., "Uchet," 219 (agitation); Egorov, *Baltflot*, 33 ("mushrooms"); Drezen, "Baltiiskii," 144–46 (July mutiny); Dybenko, *Iz nedr*, 16–21; "Dybenko, P. E.," in *KEK*, 180–81; "Zapiska," 2 August 1912, GARF, f. 102, D-5, 1912, d. 668, ll. 77–78.

71. "Zapiska," 2 August 1912, GARF, f. 102, D-5, 1912, d. 668, ll. 78–79; Lerkhe to Makarov, 29 November 1912, GARF, f. 102, D-5, 1912, d. 668, l. 136 (Makarov's approval of recommendations).

72. Zuev, "Politicheskii," 181 (unreliability of sailors); Korbut, ed., "Uchet," 219 (coups); "Zapiska," 2 August 1912, GARF, f. 102, D-5, 1912, d. 668, l. 77–80 ob.; Borodin, *Gosudarstvennyi*, 205–206 (commentators); Beletskii to gendarme and security chiefs, 18 November 1912, ZA, XIIId(1), 11.

73. Spiridovich, *Istoriia bol'shevizma*, 235–36; Koznov, "Bor'ba," 60–63 (accusations); reports on arrests in Moscow, 21–29 April 1912, GARF, f. 102, op. 316, 1912, d. 202, t. 3, ll. 107–15; Lenin, *Polnoe*, 48:84, cited in Elwood, *Russian*, 237; Arutiunov, *Rabochee*, 213–14 (Armand); McKean, *St. Petersburg*, 88–97.

74. Golubeva, *V. D. Bonch-Bruevich*, 61 *(Pravda);* Maksimova, "Luch," 325; N. Erofeev, "Trudovoi golos," in *PPR*, 627; Arutiunov, *Rabochee*, 225; Andronov, *Boevoe*, 60.

75. Andronov, *Boevoe*, 71–76.

76. Andronov, *Boevoe*, 71; Badaev, *Bol'sheviki*, 316–17.

77. Berezhnoi, *Tsarskaia*, 220 *(Pravda);* Kaptelov, Rozental', and Shelokhaev, eds., *Delo*, 115–16 (Beletskii); Badaev, *Bol'sheviki*, 314.

78. Koznov, "Bor'ba" 69–70; Spiridovich, *Istoriia bol'shevizma*, 243–44; Tsiavlovskii, ed., *Bol'sheviki*, 27–28 (obstacles).

79. Elwood, *Roman Malinovskii*, 23–54 (Lenin: 28); Kaptelov, Rozental', and Shelokhaev, eds., *Delo*, 11 (havoc), 14 (Beletskii's editing of speeches), 109–10 (wedge), 114 (Beletskii's softening of speeches); Vissarionov testimony, in *Padenie*, 5:220 (wedge); Beletskii testimony, in *Padenie*, 2:286.

80. Beletskii directive, 3 October 1912, GARF, f. 102, op. 308a, 1913, d. 34, ll. 2–2 ob.; Vissarionov to Beletskii, 21 October 1912, GARF, f. 102, OO, 1912, d. 309, ll. 76–77 ob.; Peregudova, *Politicheskii sysk*, 100–102.

81. "Sravnitel'nyi perechen'...," 11 December 1912, GARF, f. 102, op. 261, d. 21, ll. 2–11; "Kratkaia zapiska," 22 December 1912, GARF, f. 102, OO, 1915, d. 100, ll. 11–24.

82. Beletskii report, February 1913, GARF, f. 102, OO, 1905, d. 2606, ll. 94–97.

5—A MORALIST RUNNING THE POLICE APPARATUS

1. Laporte, *Histoire*, 231.

2. "Maklakov, N. A.," in *Padenie*, 7:373; Gurko, *Features*, 521; "Vospominaniia K. D. Kafafova," GARF, f. 5881, op. 2, d. 390, l. 111; Spiridovich, *Dernières années*, 2:125 (Chernigov).

3. Iakhontov, "Pervyi," 335–36 (views and attitude, vulnerability); Krivoshein, *A. V. Krivoshein*, 221; Avrekh, *Tsarizm*, 111–13 (program).

4. Kurlov, *Gibel'*, 142 (friend); Dzhunkovskii, *Vospominaniia*, 2:97 (quotations).

5. Avrekh, *Tsarizm*, 259–60 (rightists), 283n121 (*Utro Rossii*).

6. "Prikaz," 4; Dzhunkovskii, *Vospominaniia*, 2:125 (Lopatin).

7. Dzhunkovskii, *Vospominaniia*, 2:105 ("unpleasant"), 219 (campaign).

8. Dzhunkovskii, *Vospominaniia*, 2:98 (assembly), 138 (15 February), 275 (commissions).

9. Ia. D. Baum, "Departament," 55–56; Rabe, *Widerspruch*, 154 (thousands released); Dzhunkovskii, *Vospominaniia*, 2:150–51 (St. Petersburg), 290–91 (exile); Gruzenberg, *Ocherki*, 114 (articles of the criminal code); GARF, f. 102, D-5, 1913, d. 46, ch. 2, ll. 2–2 ob. (number freed); GARF, f. 102, D-5, 1913, d. 178, ch. 1, l. 150 (number in exile); Special Section to fifth division, 31 January 1914, GARF, f. 102, OO, d. 130, l. 27 (escapees).

10. Dzhunkovskii, *Vospominaniia*, 2:147; Wortman, *Scenarios*, 2:459 (bomb threats).

11. Dzhunkovskii, in *Padenie*, 5:74 (unfamiliar); Dzhunkovskii, *Vospominaniia*, 2:122 ("unlimited trust"); GARF, f. 102, OO, 1915, d. 100, l. 24 (summer 1912); GARF, f. 102, op. 261, d. 21, ll. 5–6 ob. (conferees); Zavarzin, *Rabota*, 243; GARF, f. 280, op. 5, d. 5000, ch. 12, l. 103 (deployment of informants banned); Beletskii testimony, in *Padenie*, 3:328–29 (Dzhunkovskii's initiative).

12. "K arestam"; Dzhunkovskii, *Vospominaniia*, 2:177–78; Dzhunkovskii to gendarme and security chiefs, 1 May 1913, ZA, XIIId(1), 11.

13. Special Section to regional security bureaus, 25 January 1908, GARF, f. 280, 1911, op. 5, d. 5000, ch. 12, 1. 9.

14. Dzhunkovskii, *Vospominaniia*, 2:217–19; "Kratkaia," GARF, f. 102, OO, 1915, d. 100, l. 23 (fifteen bureaus); Special Section report, 9 January 1913, GARF, f. 102, OO, 1912, d. 234, t. 1, ll. 110–16 (six more); "Khronika," *Pravo*, no. 7 (17 February 1913): 420–22.

15. Dzhunkovskii to several gendarme chiefs, 15 May 1913, GARF, f. 102, OO, 1913, d. 119, ll.185–88; Beletskii to gendarme and security chiefs, 15 May 1913, ZA, XIIId(1), 11.

16. Dzhunkovskii testimony in *Padenie*, 5:72; Vissarionov to Zuev, 11 July 1911, GARF, f. 102, op. 316, 1909, d. 61 ll. 26–26 ob.; Kratkaia zapiska, December 1912, ibid., f. 102, OO, 1912, d. 248, l. 40 ob.; Beletskii to Maklakov, 15 November 1913, GARF, f. 102, op. 316, 1914, d. 366, ll. 1–7 ob.; GARF, f. 280, op. 5, d. 5000, ch. 10, ll. 19–20 ob. (directive).

17. Dzhunkovskii, *Vospominaniia*, 2:273–74.

18. GARF, f. 102, op. 267, d. 40, ll. 60–61 (tampering), 69–73 (investigation); GARF, f. 102, op. 316, 1910, d. 333, ll. 52–53 (commission).

19. Izmozik and Vitenberg, "Kto Vy," 168 (exposé); Zaslavskii, ed., "Iz perepiski," 183 (sausage).

20. Dzhunkovskii, *Vospominaniia*, 2:231–34 (budget data); Dzhunkovskii testimony, in *Padenie*, 5:79; draft of instruction, July 1913, ZA, VIf, 2; P. K. Lerkhe to M. E. Broetskii, 3 April 1914, GARF, f. 102, OO, d. 130, l. 80 (telegrams).

21. Dzhunkovskii testimony, in *Padenie*, 5:74; Dzhunkovskii, *Vospominaniia*, 2:128.

22. Dzhunkovskii testimony, in *Padenie*, 5:75; Dzhunkovskii, *Vospominaniia*, 2:139.

23. Rozental', "Stranitsy," 96 (Koshko); Z. I. Peregudova, "Beletskii, S. P." in *OI*, 1:192 (funds); Dzhunkovskii, *Vospominaniia*, 2:128 (capacity for work).

24. Dzhunkovskii testimony, in *Padenie*, 5:70; Dzhunkovskii, *Vospominaniia*, 2:283–84 (senator); Beletskii testimony, in *Padenie*, 2:266.

25. "Vo glave . . . Briun-de-Sent-Ippolita," 234–36; Martynov, *Moia sluzhba*, 48–49; Dzhunkovskii, *Vospominaniia*, 2:74, 284–85; "Vospominaniia K. D. Kafafova," GARF, f. 5881, op. 2, d. 390, l. 121; Globachev, "Pravda," 52.

26. Dzhunkovskii, *Vospominaniia*, 2:183–85.

27. Dzhunkovskii, *Vospominaniia*, 2:169 (Strekalovskii), 170 (Petr), 242 (Aleksandr); Vissarionov to Dzhunkovksii, 22 May 1913, GARF, f. 102, op. 316, 1911, d. 1, ch. 57, lit. d, ll. 113–116 ob.; Martynov, *Moia sluzhba*, 250–51; Dzhunkovskii to Martynov, 2 August 1913, GARF, f. 102, op. 316, 1911, d. 1, ch. 46, lit. d, t. 3, l. 82.

28. GARF, f. 102, op. 316, 1911, d. 1, ch. 57, lit. d, ll. 116–16 ob. (monthlong wait) ; 147–47 ob. ("inadmissible" inaction), 149–54 (explanation).

29. Inspection report, November 1913, GARF, f. 102, op. 261, d. 65, ll. 1–37 (esp. 9 ob.–10); Kurlov to Shtiurmer, 10 May 1916, GARF, f. 102, op. 316, 1916, d. 25, ll. 2–4 ob. (promotion); *Golos Moskvy*, 8 February 1914, excerpted in GARF, f. 102, OO, 1913, d. 50, ch. 57, l. 128 (retirement); "Popov, P. K.," in *Padenie*, 7:399; Dzhunkovskii, *Vospominaniia*, 2:289; Dzhunkovskii testimony, in *Padenie*, 5:113.

30. *Golos Moskvy*, 3 February 1914, excerpted in GARF, f. 102, OO, 1913, d. 50, ch. 57, l. 118 (dismissed); Dzhunkovskii, *Vospominaniia*, 2:219 (uniform), 285 ("provocateur").

31. Dzhunkovskii, *Vospominaniia*, 2:156–57; Daly, *Autocracy under Siege*, 13 (Nicholas I); Beletskii testimony, in *Padenie*, 2:350 (supervision of security police), 3:280 (Broetskii); "Broetskii, M. E.," in *Padenie*, 7:311; Peregudova, *Politicheskii*, 211 (warning to Beletskii).

32. Miroliubov, "Politicheskii," 30–31 (unification of structure, continued importance); GARF, f. 102, OO, 1914, d. 130, ll. 55–59 (duties), 76–77 (roster).

33. GARF, f. 102, op. 316, 1914, d. 366, ll. 33–34, 41 (Engbrekht); GARF, f. 102, op. 316, 1914, d. 366, t. 1, ll. 102–336 (materials); GARF, f. 102, op. 261, d. 240, ll. 1–46 (informants).

34. GARF, f. 102, op. 308a, d. 51, ll. 1–8 and 9–14 ob. (versions); Peregudova, *Politicheskii*, 211–14.

35. Dzhunkovskii, *Vospominaniia*, 2:288; GARF, f. 102, OO, 1914, d. 130, ll. 29–36 ob. (hiring); Dzhunkovskii testimony, in *Padenie*, 5:69; Police Department to gendarme and security officers, 28 May 1914, GARF, f. 102, OO, 1914, d. 130, ll. 198 ob.–202.

36. Martynov, *Moia sluzhba*, 233, 242; Spiridovich, *Velikaia*, 1:181; Platonov, *Ternovyi*, 215 (Florinskii); *SOS* (15 June 1913), 3:319 (Perm); Iarmysh, "Karatel'nye organy," 228 (counterreforms).

37. GARF, f. 102, D-5, 1913, d. 178, ch. 1, ll. 112–14, 143 (exile); GARF, f. 102, D-5, 1913, d. 178, ch. 1, l. 143 (exiles); Shcherbakov, "Chislennost'," 219 *(katorzhniki)*.

38. Most of these reports are found in GARF, f. 102, OO, 1913 and 1914, dd. 5 and 9; GARF, f. 102, OO, 1913 and 1914, dd. 5 and 9, ch. 46 and 57.

39. Vissarionov to Dzhunkovskii, 22 May 1913, GARF, f. 102, op. 316, 1911, d. 1, ch. 57, lit. d, l. 113–116 ob.; Martynov to Beletskii, 3 December 1913, GARF, f. 102, OO, 1913, d. 5, ch. 46, ll. 76–76 ob.; Lipkin, "Nakanune," 57, 62 (provincial towns); Martynov to Beletskii, 21 December 1913, GARF, f. 63, 1913, d. 1325, ll. 1–4; "Otchet," GARF, f. 102, op. 255, d. 57 (calm in St. Petersburg); Maksakov, "1912–1913 g.g.," 441 (Bolsheviks closer to workers), 446–48 (letter); Spiridovich, *Istoriia bol'shevizma*, 250–51 (impact of arrests).

40. Iurenev, "'Mezhraionka,'" 109–19, 136; "Novyi pod"em," 242–43, 212 (illegal presses); Panchenko, *Leninskaia*, 227–28 (hectographs); Loginov, "Lenin," 152–57 (fines, fund-raising); Maksimova, "Luch," in *PPR*, 325 (fines, fund-raising); I. Rozental', "Pravda," in *PPR*, 481 (44,000 rubles); Lur'e, Polianskaia, and Bystrianskii, eds., *Bol'shevistskaia*, 103–4, 152–53.

41. Avrekh, *Tsarizm*, 111–13; Anan'ich et al., *Krizis*, 525 (colleagues); Berezhnoi, *Tsarskaia*, 234–35.

42. Korbut, ed., "Uchet," 220 (Maklakov), 219–27 (reports, special file); Daly, *Autocracy under Siege*, 76, 92 (Zubatov); Arutiunov, *Rabochee*, 312 (arbitration chambers); McKean, "Bureaucracy," 230 ("political coloring").

43. Valk, "K istorii," 77, 86–90.

44. Dzhunkovskii, *Vospominaniia*, 1:228–29 (Shcheglovitov); Kokovtsov, *Iz moego*, 2:158–61; Voitinskii, "Delo," 122–24; Levin, "Shornikova Affair," 5–17.

45. Correspondence on draft bill, December 1912–February 1913, RGIA, f. 1276, op. 3, d. 1, ll. 53, 93–96; Riha, "Constitutional Developments," 109.

46. "Novyi pod"em," 238–39 (Petrovskii); Solodkov, *Bol'shevistskaia*, 121 (curia); Moscow gendarme station to Special Section, 10 April 1913, GARF, f. 102, OO, 1913, d. 5, ch. 47, ll. 2–5 ob. (curia); Koznov, "Bor'ba," 71 (Bolshevik fraction).

47. Semennikov, *Monarkhiia*, 91–95; Anan'ich, Ganelin, and Paneiakh, eds., *Vlast'*, 558; Shcheglovitov testimony, in *Padenie*, 2:437–38; Maklakov testimony, in *Padenie*, 3:133–34; Krivoshein, *A. V. Krivoshein*, 217–18.

48. Iakhontov, "Pervyi," 336 (Maklakov's isolation); Florinskii, *Krizis*, 37 (Maklakov's isolation).

49. Dzhunkovskii, *Vospominaniia*, 2:78–79; Dzhunkovskii testimony, in *Padenie*, 5:84; Martynov, *Moia sluzhba*, 232–35; Beletskii testimony, *Padenie*, 2:280.

50. Tsiavlovskii, ed., *Bol'sheviki*, 30–31; I. Rozental', "Malinovskii, R. V.," in *PPR*, 339–40.

51. Beletskii testimony, in *Padenie*, 3:283, 286; Koznov, "Bor'ba," 68–73 (report); Spiridovich, *Istoriia bol'shevizma*, 265.

52. Ansimov, *Bor'ba*, 30, 102 (suspicions); Bukharin, "Kopiia," 117 (suspicions); Elwood, *Roman Malinovskii*, 6–10; Robbins, "Vladimir Dzhunkovskii," 635–54.

53. Shub, *Lenin*, 151–53 (Poronino); Elwood, "Malinovskii Affair," 8–12 (investigation, upon returning to Russia); Elwood, *Roman Malinovskii*, 48–56; Ponomarev, ed., *Partiia*, 411 (numbers).

54. Dzhunkovskii, *Vospominaniia*, 2:336–80 (Baku); Arutiunov, *Rabochee*, 361–68; Loginov, "Lenin," 233 (number of strikers), 234 (newspapers as centers of unrest); Voinova, "Iiul'skie," 215–23.

55. Lur'e, ed., "Pod"em," 137–38 (1913 and 1914 strike data); Haimson, "Problem of Social Stability," 348, 356; McKean, *St. Petersburg*, 192 (labor unrest as endemic), 226–27 (Russian stability); Pipes, *Russian Revolution*, 192 (labor rest as endemic); Brainerd, "Octobrists," 173 (harvest); Popov reports, 13–25 July 1914, GARF, f. 270, op. 1, d. 99, ll. 1, 8, 13–20, 38–41.

56. Wortman, *Scenarios*, 2:439, 455, 466; Vissarionov to Dzhunkovskii, 22 May 1913, GARF, f. 102, op. 316, 1911, d. 1, ch. 57, lit. d, l. 116; Drachevskii to Beletskii, 7 November 1913, GARF, f. 102, OO, 1913, d. 147, l. 74 ob. (Fontanka); Brainerd, "Octobrists," 160–64.

57. Von Koten to Beletskii, 26 May 1913, GARF, f. 102, OO, 1913, d. 27, ch. 57, ll. 11–12 ob.; Costello, "Novoe," 49.

58. Police reports, 10, 17, and 18 October 1913, GARF, f. 102, OO, 1913, d. 147, ll. 5–7, 16, 21–22; Vishnevskii, *Liberal'naia*, 168–78 (Progressists).

59. Bradley, "Russia's Parliament," 228–36.

60. Beletskii to Maklakov, 19 March 1913, GARF, f. 102, op. 316, 1905, d. 12, ch. 2, ll. 164–68 ob.; Avrekh, *Masony*, 325–29 (Beletskii report), 331–35 (responses to the directive); Platonov, *Ternovyi*, 691 (Popov), 773–801 (Rataev); Brune to gendarme and security officers, 24 May 1914, ZA, XIIId(1), 11.

61. Andreev, "Evoliutsiia," 7–9.

62. Ostrovskii, "Ostorozhno," 172–73.

63. Stepanov, *Chernaia*, 267, 277, 284–85.

64. Stepanov, *Chernaia*, 302; Utevskii, *Vospominaniia*, 65–66; Baberowski, *Autokratie*, 609–11.

65. Maklakov and Beletskii to governors, 27 September to 9 October 1913, GARF, f. 102, OO, 1911, d. 157, t. 2, ll. 100–2, 141, 151, 167, 213–15 ob.; Maklakov testimony, in *Padenie*, 3:124; Beletskii testimony, in *Padenie*, 3:360, 373.

66. *Ezhegodnik*, 44 (press persecution); Sidorov, "Iz zapisok," 100 (V. A. Maklakov); Korbut, ed., "Uchet," 224 (strikes); Beletskii report, 15 October 1913, GARF, f. 102, op. 236 (II), 1906, d. 175, t. 7, ll. 25–28, 130–31 ob.

67. Rogger, "Russia in 1914," 96 (public image); Avrekh, *Tsarizm*, 274; Zaslavskii, ed., "Iz perepiski," 182–83 (coalition); Anan'ich et al., *Krizis*, 517 (manipulate); Krivoshein, *A. V. Krivoshein*, 148 ("us and them"), 186–87.

68. Gruzenberg, *Ocherki*, 123; Arutiunov, *Rabochee*, 322 (Lenin).

69. Dzhunkovskii, *Vospominaniia*, 2:293–95; Bel'chikov, "Zapreshchenie," 226 (official correspondence).

70. Dzhunkovskii, *Vospominaniia*, 2:294–96; Bel'chikov, "Zapreshchenie," 229 (arrests).

6—THE SECURITY POLICE IN THE FIRST WORLD WAR

1. Rogger, "Russia in 1914," 107 (Lukomskii), 110 (Maklakov, Duma), 111–14 (civil society); Pares, *Fall of the Russian Monarchy*, 191 (St. Petersburg); McKean, *St. Petersburg*, 368.

2. *SU*, 12 July 1914, GARF, f. 270, op. 1, d. 99, l. 3; *SU*, 20 July 1914, no. 189, art. 2053; "Deistviia pravitel'stva," 2289–91 (commanders empowered); Izmozik, "Pervye," 156 (censorship).

3. Petrograd military censorship committee, 15 September 1914, 16 and 28 April 1915, and 9 May GARF, f. 116, op. 1, d. 632, ll. 3, 19, 21, 22 (prohibitions); Lemke, *250 dnei*, 364–67, 374–77, 381–87 (more prohibitions).

4. Maklakov to governors, 21 July 1914, GARF, f. 215, op. 1, d. 174, l. 28; *SU*, 25 July 1914, no. 199, art. 2075.

5. "Pamiatnyi listok," 16 May 1914, GARF, f. 102, OO, d. 130, l. 102 *(intsident)*; Police Department report, RGIA, f. 1284, op. 250, d. 44, ll. 97–99; Police Department to governors, 14 October 1914, GARF, f. 102, D-2, 1914, d. 71, l. 222 and passim (railroad passes); "Plan evakuatsii," GARF, f. 215, op. 1, d. 174, ll. 27–28, 31–32 (evacuation); Martynov to police captains, 28 May 1915, RGIAgM, f. 475, op. 19, d. 61, l. 30.

6. Miroliubov, "Dokumenty," 82 (staff); "Soveshchanie gubernatorov," 148 (two-thirds), 165 (land captains); *Kostromskoe*, 7 ("epidemic"); Iarmysh, "Karatel'nye organy," 227 (rehiring retired officers); GARF, f. 102, OO, 1914, d. 325, ll. 5–5 ob. (training new officers), 10 (appeal), 15 (little success).

7. Nikol'skii to Dzhunkovskii, 22 July 1914, GARF, f. 270, op. 1, d. 99, l. 27 (Vedeniapin); *SOS* (15 June 1913), pt. 3:326; "Obshchee polozhenie," 30 (counterespionage); Miroliubov, "Politicheskii," 43, 207 (numbers); *SOS* (1 June 1907), 639; V. B. Frederiks testimony, in *Padenie*, 5:41 (emperor's security service).

8. Znamenskii to Vissarionov, December 1915, GARF, f. 102, op. 316, 1916, d. 186, l. 57 (twelve informants); Klimovich testimony, in *Padenie*, 1:110 (resistance); Klimovich to gendarme and security chiefs, 24 March 1916, GARF, f. 102, op. 316, 1916, d. 310, l. 1 (agreed); GARF, f. 503, op. 1, d. 204, ll. 23–50 (lists).

9. Miroliubov, "Dokumenty," 81 (budget); "Spravka po proektu smety," RGIA, f. 1282, op. 6, d. 705. l. 22 (regular police); "Smeta na 1915 god," GARF, f. 102, D-1, 1915, d. 16, ch. 8, ll. 2–3 (3.3 million); Pavlov, *Agenty*, 10–13 (Shchegolev).

10. Police Department to gendarme and security chiefs, 10 April 1915, GARF, f. 102, OO, 1915, d. 175, l. 1; GARF, f. 97, op. 4, d. 1, ll. 5 (creation of clearinghouse), 11 (Ratko); Spiridovich testimony, *Padenie*, 3:47–48; Spiridovich, *Dernières années*, 2:397, 404–5.

11. Agafonov, *Zagranichnaia*, 176–77, 182–64 (Paris bureau); Grekov, *Russkaia*, 219–21 (decree), 247–48 (frontal areas), 295–96 (Ergardt); Special Section report, 30 July 1916, GARF, f. 102, op. 267, d. 43, ll. 47–49 (cryptographers); list of suspected spies, 1914, GARF, f. 102, op. 302, d. 438, ll. 1–71; Vassiliyev, *Ochrana*, 114–16

(allegations of espionage); Kurlov, *Gibel'*, 188–92 (allegations of espionage); Lemke, *250 dnei*, 730–40 (three orders); Shliapnikov, *Kanun*, 154.

12. Iakovlev, "Kontrrazvedka," 33 (offices, conclusion); Vassiliyev, *Ochrana*, 117–19 (harassment), 125 (quotation); Grekov, *Russkaia*, 280 (overstepping bounds), 331 (conclusion); Kurlov, *Gibel'*, 162–63 (overstepping bounds, Batiushin); "Batiushin, N. S.," in *Padenie*, 7:306; Lemke, *250 dnei*, 734 (plot).

13. Iakhontov, "Tiazhelye," 10–11 (theater), 17–19 (quotation: 19); Kurlov, *Gibel'*, 164.

14. Miroliubov, "Politicheskii," 84–93, 117–21 (repression), 208–14; Mints, "Revoliutsionnaia," 60–61 (number arrested); Leiberov, "V. I. Lenin," 78 (slates).

15. Koznov, "A fakty," 153 (membership); Miroliubov, "Politicheskii," 105–106 (arrests in various localities), 122–31 (Socialist-Revolutionaries); Agafonov, *Zagranichnaia*, 205 (Brune); Spiridovich, *Istoriia bol'shevizma*, 298.

16. Martynov report, late December 1915, GARF, f. 102, op. 316, 1916, d. 186, ll. 157–58; St. Petersburg security bureau report, March 1916, GARF, f. 102, op. 316, 1915, d. 1, ch. 57, lit. d, l. 60; Krasil'nikov to Kafafov, 24 December 1915, GARF, f. 102, OO, 1915, d. 9, ll. 36–36 ob.

17. Badaev, ed., "Arest," 35–36 (periodical, protests); Badaev, *Bol'sheviki*, 325 (periodical), 376 (Romanov), 381–85 (arrests); Tsvetkov-Prosveshchenskii, "Rabochie," 178 (Shurkanov); Gal'perina et al., eds., *Sovet ministrov*, 381n151 (Krivoshein).

18. Badaev, ed., "Arest," 35–36 (periodical, protests), 37 (break), 42–43 (Popov); Badaev, *Bol'sheviki*, 325 (periodical), 376 (Romanov), 381–85 (arrests); Tsvetkov-Prosveshchenskii, "Rabochie," 178 (Shurkanov); Gal'perina et al., eds., *Sovet ministrov*, 381n151 (Krivoshein), 385n175 (Shcheglovitov).

19. Badaev, ed., "Arest,'" 44–45 (Popov), 47 (Shcheglovitov), 48–51 (military court); Badaev, *Bol'sheviki*, 325 (deprivation), 400–403 (argument), 416 (sentence); Spiridovich, *Velikaia*, 1:41; Dzhunkovskii, *Vospominaniia*, 2:523–25.

20. Shliapnikov, *Kanun*, 188–189 (methods), 346–347 (three months), 348 (methods), 349–351 (surveillants); A. Chernobaev, "Shliapnikov, A. G.," in *PPR*, 702.

21. Shliapnikov, *Kanun*, 46–47 (passport); Kerenskii, *Rossiia*, 107 (railway stations); Zelikson-Bobrovskaia, *Zapiski*, 193–94.

22. Krasil'nikov to Brune, 12 September 1914, ZA, XXIVd; Nikitinskii and Markov, eds., *Zagranichnaia*, 62 (August 1914); Shchegolev, *Okhranniki*, 69 (taking chances); O. V. Budnitskii, "Burtsev, V. L.," in *OI*, 1:314; Burtsev, "Moi otnosheniia," box 1, folder 52; Burtsev, *Bor'ba*, 377, 379–82; Globachev, "Pravda," 111.

23. Iaroslavskii, "Nakanune," 26–28.

24. Papernikov, "Fevral'skaia," 93; Sosnovskaia, "Uchastie," 92–93.

25. Martynov to Brune, 6 August 1914, GARF, f. 102, OO, otd. 1, 1906, op. 234, d. 7, ch. 14, ll. 8–9 ("red cross"); Stasova, "Partiinaia," 90.

26. GARF, f. 102, OO, 1914, d. 5 ch. 46 lit. b, t. 2, ll. 249–59, 264–69 ob., 270–275 ob. (December); Menitskii, *Revoliutsionnoe*, 1:392–400 (Brune survey).

27. Tsiavlovskii, ed., "Moskovskaia," 258–63, 273–76 (Martynov); St. Petersburg security bureau report, March 1916, GARF, f. 102, op. 316, 1915, d. 1, ch. 57, lit. d, l. 60.

28. *SOS* (10 July 1911), 2:318 (Globachev's service record); *SOS* (15 June 1913), 2:282 (von Koten); "Globachev, K. I.," and "Popov, P. K.," in *Padenie*, 7:326, 399; Vissarionov to Zuev, 31 March 1911, GARF, f. 102, op. 316, 1911, d. 202, ll. 62–63; Dzhunkovskii, *Vospominaniia*, 2:169.

29. Globachev report, 18 August 1916 in GARF, f. 102, OO, 1916, d. 27, ch. 57, ll. 17–21; Spiridovich, *Velikaia,* 1:184.

30. Kuz'min-Karavaev, "Voprosy," 384–87; *Pervoe maia,* 266–268 (strikers); Menitskii, *Revoliutsionnoe,* 1:233–35.

31. Lohr, "Enemy Alien Politics," 1–18.

32. Ibid., 37–78.

33. Maklakov to Warsaw governor-general, 12 August 1914, GARF, f. 215, op. 1, d. 432, l. 14; Lohr, "Enemy Alien Politics," 112–14 (police per exile); GARF, f. 102, D-2, 1914, d. 102, l. 127 (number of exiles).

34. GARF, f. 102, OO, 1914, d. 105, ll. 87–87 ob. (Dzhunkovskii); Grekov, *Russkaia,* 233 (Petrograd and Moscow); RGIAgM, f. 475, op. 19, d. 91, ll. 3 (sectarians), 8 (Jews released from German camps); GARF, f. 102, OO, 1915, d. 116, t. 1, ll. 7–8 (Germanism); Nelipovich, "V poiskakh," 59–60 (hostages).

35. Eletskii, ed., "Ssylka," 209–12, 227–41; S. I. Mikhail'chenko, "Grushevskii, M. S.," in *OI,* 1:647.

36. Brune to gendarme and security chiefs, 28 March and 16 May 1915, ZA, XIIId(1), folder 12.

37. Popov, ed., "Pervye," 6 (Sazonov); Lohr, "Enemy Alien Politics," 320–21 (Maklakov); Kafafov to governors and security policemen, 21 May 1915, ZA, XI-IId(1), folder 12.

38. Lohr, "Enemy Alien Politics," 312, 325–31; Kir'ianov, "'Maiskie," 144 (as if the German army had bombarded the city).

39. Lohr, "Enemy Alien Politics," 331–33.

40. Ibid., 335.

41. Kir'ianov, "'Maiskie," 141–42 (report).

42. Lohr, "Enemy Alien Politics," 323n30, 334–41, 358–61; Figes, *People's Tragedy,* 285.

43. Maklakov to governors, 31 May 1915, GARF, f. 102, OO, 1915, d. 246, ll. 45a–45a ob.; Anan'ich et al., *Krizis,* 551 (Kostroma); Martynov, cited in Lohr, "Enemy Alien Politics," 149 (4 June), 342 (5 June).

44. Lohr, "Enemy Alien Politics," 353–60 (workers and soldiers); police reports, GARF, f. 102, OO, 1915, d. 246, ll. 62–62 ob., 80–83, 88–89, 141–141 ob., 154–154 ob. (rumors); Kuz'min-Karavaev, "Voprosy," 384.

45. Anan'ich et al., *Krizis,* 554–55; Kulikova, "Iz istorii," 149–50 (configurations), 163; Krivoshein, *A. V. Krivoshein,* 222–23 (devotion), 230–31; "Maklakov, N. A.," in *Padenie,* 7:373; Tobolin, ed., "Iz arkhiva," 113 (bitterness).

46. Shakhovskoi, *"Sic transit,"* 92 (protégé); Krivoshein, *A. V. Krivoshein,* 230n (stables); Kuz'min-Karavaev, "Voprosy," 378–80 (public opinion).

47. Dzhunkovskii, *Vospominaniia,* 2:572–74; Shcherbatov testimony, in *Padenie,* 7: 223–24, 235.

48. "Vo glave . . . Mollova," 237–40; "Mollov, R. G.," in *Padenie,* 7:382; Globachev, "Pravda," 53–54; Iakhontov, "Pervyi," 338; Avrekh, *Tsarizm,* 162 (Muratov).

49. Diakin, *Russkaia,* 78 (Sukhomlinov); Shavel'skii, *Vospominaniia,* 2:286, 289 (Khvostov's reputation); A. A. Khvostov testimony, in *Padenie,* 5:471; "Za nedeliu," June 1915, p. 1 (optimism and caution).

50. Grave, comp., *Burzhuaziia,* 37 (midsummer); GARF, f. 102, OO, 1915, d. 116, t. 1, ll. 27–28 ob. (13 July); McKean, "Bureaucracy," 241 (St. Petersburg).

51. Inozemtsev, "Rasstrel," 97–118.

52. Iakhontov, "Tiazhelye," 17–19 (powerlessness); Iakhontov to V. I. Gurko, 19 December 1925, in Gal'perina et al., eds., *Sovet ministrov,* 486 ("defeated nation").

53. Iakhontov, "Tiazhelye," 42 (Iakhontov), 43–46 (Pale), 53–56 (Polivanov's bombshell), 57–59 (9th; Pale), 63–66 (11th).

54. Krupina, "Politicheskii," 62; V. Guterts, "Voenno-promyshlennye," in *OI,* 1:425–26; A. S. Senin, "Zemgor," in *OI,* 2:244; Globachev, "Pravda," 14, 50; Iakhontov, "Pervyi," 301; Martynov, *Moia sluzhba,* 53, 289–90.

55. Dzhunkovskii, *Vospominaniia,* 2:633 (order), 635 (letter).

56. Gal'perina et al., eds., *Sovet ministrov,* 224 (Shcherbatov); Iakhontov, "Tiazhelye," 77 (Krivoshein); Spiridovich, *Velikaia,* 1:181; Martynov, *Moia sluzhba,* 258; Kir'ianov, ed., "Perepiska," 10:137 (Tikhmenev); Dzhunkovskii, *Vospominaniia,* 616 (Khvostov).

57. Gurko, *Tsar' i tsaritsa,* 80; Dzhunkovskii, *Vospominaniia,* 2:117–19 (Meshcherskii), 568–71, (report on Rasputin); Vassiliyev, *Ochrana,* 151 (Rasputin); Rozental', "Stranitsy," 97 (Rasputin); Fuhrmann, *Complete Wartime Correspondence,* 149 (June), 221 (September); Shavel'skii, *Vospominaniia,* 2:23n7 (coalition); Orlov to Krivoshein, RGIA, f. 1276, op. 11, d. 167, l. 308.

58. Iakhontov, "Tiazhelye," 102–104 (24 August), 128 and 131–36 (2 September); Grave, comp., *Burzhuaziia,* 37, 40 (unrest).

59. Fuhrmann, *Complete Wartime Correspondence,* 223 (9 September); *Russkie vedomosti,* no. 221 (27 September 1915), excerpted in Grave, comp., *Burzhuaziia,* 65; N. Dedkov, "Maklakov, V. A.," in *PPR,* 336.

60. Fuhrmann, *Complete Wartime Correspondence,* 242 (maligning of Shcherbatov); Gurko, *Tsar' i tsaritsa,* 24 (praise for Khvostov).

61. "Khvostov, A. N.," in *Padenie,* 7:432; Lin'kov, Nikitin, and Khodenkov, eds., *Gosudarstvennye,* 192 (service record); Avrekh, *Tsarizm,* 109 (moniker), 110 (Spiridovich); Kryzhanovskii, *Vospominaniia,* 148.

62. Kurlov, *Gibel',* 144 (jettisoning of Dzhunkovskii's control); Miroliubov, "Politicheskii," 31 ("new office'); "Vospominaniia S. P. Beletskogo," 6; Vassiliyev, *Ochrana,* 113 (Duma); Lohr, "Enemy Alien Politics," 57–58 ("special committee"), 232 ("German dominance"); Grekov, *Russkaia,* 277 ("pouring gasoline"); *Programma kursa,* 26 (separate division).

63. Sidorov, "Iz zapisok," 106–107.

64. Shavel'skii, *Vospominaniia,* 2:50–52.

65. Beletskii testimony, in *Padenie,* 4:130–31; Kafafov testimony, in *Padenie,* 2:136; "Vo glave . . . Kafafova," 241–43; "Vospominaniia K. D. Kafafova," GARF, f. 5881, op. 2, d. 390, l. 99.

66. Beletskii testimony, in *Padenie,* 4:338–39 (Zuev), 344 (Viatka), 345 (Kommisarov's wife); "Kommisarov, M. S.," in *Padenie,* 7:357; "Vospominaniia S. P. Beletskogo," 53 (surveillance of Rasputin).

67. A. I. Reitblat, "Manasevich-Manuilov, I. F.," in *RP,* 3:504.

68. "Manasevich-Manuilov, I. F.," in *Padenie,* 7:374–75; Beletskii testimony, in *Padenie,* 4:375–379; "Vospominaniia S. P. Beletskogo," 65–67; Burtsev, "Moi otnosheniia," 16–20.

69. "Andronnikov, M. M.," in *Padenie,* 7:301–2; Rediger, *Istoriia moei zhizni,* 1:332, 2:405; A. N. Khvostov testimony, in *Padenie,* 1:51 (spying); Avrekh, *Tsarizm,* 116 (influencing the empress).

70. "Vospominaniia S. P. Beletskogo," 12 (Andronnikov), 21 (domesticating Rasputin); Shavel'skii, *Vospominaniia*, 2:52 (intervening); Z. I. Peregudova, "Beletskii, S. P.," in *OI*, 1:192 (empress); Spiridovich, *Velikaia*, 1:268 (compromising information); Gessen, "V dvukh," 342.

71. Beletskii testimony, in *Padenie*, 4:132 (curriculum), 2:292 (orders to security police officers); "Kratkii obzor," 27 October 1915, GARF, f. 102, op. 253, d. 42 (press); Police Department to gendarme chiefs, 30 October 1915, GARF, f. 102, OO, 1915, d. 27, l. 94 (Kadets).

72. Beletskii to security police, 15 November 1915, ZA, XIIId(1), folder 12; Raskol'nikov, "Volneniia," 94–103 (soldiers); Globachev, "Pravda," 52 (informants); Miroliubov, "Politicheskii," 126 (Kafafov); Beletskii to Globachev, 31 December 1915, GARF, f. 102, op. 316, 1915, d. 1, ch. 57, lit. d, l. 45.

73. Miroliubov, "Politicheskii," 135 (Sofronov), 136 (Kadet congress); Mollov to Beletskii, 30 October 1915, GARF, f. 102, OO, 1915, d. 27, ll. 69–70; GARF, f. 102, OO, 1915, d. 27, l. 112 (Beletskii).

74. GARF, f. 1467, op. 1, d. 581, ll. 2–5 ob. (report); RGIA, f. 1276, op. 11, d. 167, ll. 54 ob.–56 (Khvostov); Miroliubov, "Politicheskii," 137 (no Kadet arrested).

75. Livchak, "Krakh," 117–18 (Moscow); Police Department to governors, 10 December 1915, GARF, f. 1467, op. 1, d. 879, l. 14.

76. Kir'ianov, ed., "Pravye v 1915," 147, 176 (Shcheglovitov); Kir'ianov, ed., "Perepiska," 10:125, 138; correspondence, 1911–1916, GARF, f. 102, D-1, 1913, d. 150, ll. 3–17 (Academic Club).

77. Avrekh, "Dokumenty," 49 (Beletskii enjoins police officers); Kafafov to Beletskii, 28 November 1915, GARF, f. 102, OO, 1915, d. 310, ll. 144–46; Kir'ianov, ed., "Pravye," 85 (Beletskii); Kir'ianov, ed., "Pravye v 1915," 176 (Shcheglovitov).

78. Kir'ianov, ed., "Perepiska," 3:146–47 (Globachev), 7:115 (Riazan); Report of Saratov gendarme chief, 17 May 1916, GARF, f. 102, OO, 1916, d. 291, ll. 5–15 ob.; GARF, f. 102, OO, 1916, d. 244, l. 29 (funding); Kir'ianov, ed., "Pravye v 1915," 147 (desire to promote right-wing politics trumped).

79. Anan'ich et al., *Krizis*, 577–78; GARF, f. 102, OO, 1916, d. 307, lit. a, t. 1, ll. 57–60 ob. (initial fleshing out); GARF, f. 102, OO, d. 77, l. 99 (release); Avrekh, *Tsarizm*, 166 (visit).

80. Gessen, "V dvukh," 339; Gessen, "Iz nedavnego," 61; Anan'ich et al., *Krizis*, 578–79.

81. ZA, XIIId(1), folder 12 (directive); Kafafov testimony, in *Padenie*, 2:135–41 (quotations: 135); Blok, *Zapisnye*, 329 (Beletskii).

82. Lapin, "Progressivnyi blok," 143–57 (Shingarev: 145–46); Grave, comp., *Burzhuaziia*, 13–15 (December), 93 (Prague Restaurant); Globachev report, 25 March 1916, GARF, f. 102, OO, 1916, d. 27, ch. 57, ll. 4–5 ob. (Rodichev); Avrekh, *Masony*, 337.

83. Spiridovich, *Velikaia*, 2:45; Gessen, "Beseda," 76–82; S. A. Stepanov, "Iliodor," in *OI*, 2:338; Z. I. Peregudova, "Beletskii, S. P.," in *OI*, 1:192; Fuhrmann, *Complete Wartime Correspondence*, 393; "Pil'ts, A. I.," in *Padenie*, 7:396.

84. Polivanov, "Deviat'," 9:130–33, 140n11; Lapin, "Progressivnyi," 185 (Plehve).

85. Sazonov, *Vospominaniia*, 380; Anan'ich et al., *Krizis*, 637 (refusal to issue directives); "Stepanov, A. V.," in *Padenie*, 7:309; Avrekh, *Tsarizm*, 169 (replacement of governors); Anan'ich, Ganelin, and Paneiakh, eds., *Vlast'*, 625 (Volkonskii).

86. Grave, comp., *Burzhuaziia*, 75–78 (February); Martynov to Klimovich, 29 April 1916, GARF, f. 102, op. 316, 1916, d. 160, ll. 59–59 ob.

87. Monthly province gendarme reports, January to May 1916, GARF, f. 58, op. 5, d. 399, ll. 1–84; assistant for Bogorodskii *uezd* to gendarme chief, 24 February 1916, GARF, f. 58, op. 5, d. 399, ll. 35–35 ob.

88. "Soveshchanie gubernatorov," 150–69.

89. Ibid., 145–69; Anan'ich et al., *Krizis*, 592.

90. Lemke, *250 dnei*, 701; "Obzor . . . ," 16 April 1916, RGIA, f. 1276, op. 11, d. 167, ll. 313–23 ob.; Diakin, *Russkaia*, 184 (memoranda).

91. Avrekh, "Dokumenty," 39 (Chelnokov); Grave, comp., *Burzhuaziia*, passim; Martynov, *Moia sluzhba*, 289–90; Martynov report, 28 June 1916, GARF, f. 102, 1916, d. 48, ch. 46, ll. 13–17 ob.

92. Anan'ich et al., *Krizis*, 591–93 (Council of Ministers); Klimovich to gendarme and security chiefs, 6 May 1916, GARF, f. 102, OO, 1916, d. 341, ll. 8–8 ob.; Grave, comp., *Burzhuaziia*, 105 (Stepanov).

93. Anan'ich et al., *Krizis*, 602 (special surveillance office); Grave, comp., *Burzhuaziia*, 107 (approval); Beletskii testimony, in *Padenie*, 4:514; Daly, *Autocracy under Siege*, 12 (France).

94. Klimovich to gendarme and security chiefs, 29 July 1916, ZA, XIIId(2), folder 62.

95. Grave, comp., *Burzhuaziia*, 101–103 (Martynov); "Obshchee polozhenie," 24–30.

96. GARF, f. 58, op. 5, d. 399, ll. 109 (mood), 123–28 (disapproval); Diakin, *Russkaia*, 216–19 (Alekseev); Naumov, *Iz utselevshikh*, 2:526–28 (Nicholas's consideration of dictatorship proposal); Florinskii, *Krizis*, 189–91 (military council).

97. "Rubinshtein, D. L.," in *Padenie*, 7:412; Spiridovich, *Dernières années*, 2:419–21; Beliaev, "Peterburgskie,"12–13 (Manasevich-Manuilov); Avrekh, *Tsarizm*, 131–32.

7—COLLAPSE OF THE WATCHFUL STATE

1. Kolonitskii, "'Politicheskaia,'" 76 ("pornographic"); Diakin, *Russkaia*, 317 (Ardov).

2. Shakhovskoi, *"Sic transit"*, 83; Voeikov, *S tsarem*, 187; Fuhrmann, *Complete Wartime Correspondence*, 574, 577, 582.

3. M. Golostenov and I. Narskii, "Protopopov, A. D.," in *PPR*, 490; "Badmaev, P. A.," in *Padenie*, 7:304; Anan'ich et al., *Krizis*, 605–606.

4. Testimony on Protopopov, GARF, f. 1467, op. 1, d. 453, ll. 3, 7, 17 ob.–45, 68–71 ob.; d. 447, ll. 10 ob–13, 16 ob.–17, 38 (Tatishchev); d. 446, l. 2 (Bal'ts); Vassiliyev, *Ochrana*, 202–203.

5. Kurlov, *Gibel'*, 8 (appointment), 210–11 (Senate, outcries); "Kurlov, P. G.," in *Padenie*, 7:364; "Mantashev, L. A.," in *Padenie*, 7:376; Spiridovich, *Velikaia*, 2:127 (stroke), 3:40 (absentminded, Duma); Vassiliyev, *Ochrana*, 195; Anan'ich et al., *Krizis*, 638 (acting as a private advisor); Rodzianko, "Krushenie," 156 (Senate).

6. Vassiliyev, *Ochrana*, 130–36 (Rasputin), 191–92 (appointment), 198 (empress); "Klimovich, E. K.," in *Padenie*, 7:354; Spiridovich, *Velikaia*, 2:126 (Kurlov's friend, drinking); *Birzhevye vedomosti* (2 October 1916, evening edition), GARF, f. 102, op. 295, d. 43, l. 4.

7. Avrekh, *Tsarizm*, 165 (right to impeach cabinet officials); Grave, comp., *Burzhuaziia*, 141 ("capitulation"); Diakin, *Russkaia*, 32 ("here's an Octobrist"); Anan'ich, Ganelin, and Paneiakh, eds., *Vlast'*, 629 (traitor); Kerenskii, *Rossiia*, 120–21.

8. Shul'gin, *Gody-Dni-1920*, 314–19; Martynov to Vasil'ev, 31 October 1916, GARF, f. 102, op. 316, 1916, d. 160, ll. 168–72 ob.; "V kontse 1916 g.," 152, 154 (mocking Protopopov).

9. Hasegawa, *February*, 99–101; Lohr, "Enemy Alien Politics," 361 (attacks); Livchak, "Krakh," 119 (plan for emergency preparedness), 120 (reliability of troops); D'iachkov, "Velikaia," 63.

10. Martynov reports, 28 October and 3 December 1916, GARF, f. 102, OO, 1916, d. 5, ch. 46, ll. 27–28; Miroliubov, "Politicheskii," 210, 213–14; Pokrovskii, ed., "Politicheskoe," 28–30; Globachev to Vasil'ev, 2 January 1917, GARF, f. 102, OO, 1917, d. 5, ch. 57, l. 1.

11. GARF, f. 58, op. 5, d. 399, ll. 20–72, 157–61, 175–82, 183–84 (Moscow countryside); Anfimov, ed., "Tsarskaia," 204–7 (Martynov).

12. Pokrovskii, ed., "Politicheskoe," 5–6, 24–25 (Globachev); Martynov to Vasil'ev, 30 September 1916, GARF, f. 102, OO, 1916, d. 48, ch. 46, ll. 58–59 (rumors); Grave, comp., *Burzhuaziia*, 136–39 (Vasil'ev).

13. Pavlov and Sholokhaev, eds., *Rossiiskie*, 182 (speech); Brachev, *Mastera*, 61 (attaché).

14. Iskhakov, ed., *Strana*, 12 (retrospect); McReynolds, *News*, 266 (ban); Grave, comp., *Burzhuaziia*, 152 (public congresses forbidden); Pskov, Kazan, and Odessa gendarme stations to Police Department, November 1916, GARF, 102, OO, 1916, d. 307, lit. A, t. 1, ll. 191, 197, 207–207 ob.; Moscow gendarme station to Police Department, 19 November 1916, GARF, f. 58, op. 5, d. 399, l. 255.

15. Rodzianko, "Krushenie," 149; Fuhrmann, *Complete Wartime Correspondence*, 649, 651; "Trepov, A. F.," in Lin'kov, Nikitin, and Khodenkov, eds., *Gosudarstvennye*, 186; Mosolov, "Iz moikh," 15.

16. Shavel'skii, *Vospominaniia*, 2:224; GARF, 102, OO, 1916, d. 307, lit. A, t. 1, ll. 97, 102 (bracing for disaster); Kurlov, *Gibel'*, 208; "Balk, A. P.," in *Padenie*, 7:305; Anan'ich et al., *Krizis*, 634 (Balk and Khabalov); "V ianvare," 91 (special surveillance office); Blok, "Poslednie," 20 (special surveillance office).

17. GARF, f. 58, op. 5, d. 399, ll. 255 (upswing), 303 (Special Section), 305–10 (Moscow districts); Globachev report, 26 November 1916, GARF, f. 97, op. 4, d. 117, ll. 93–95; Borodin, *Gosudarstvennyi*, 159 (State Council).

18. Vassiliev, *Ochrana*, 206; Martynov, *Moia sluzhba*, 290–91; Gerasimov, *Na lezvii*, 187.

19. Report on Guchkov, 9 December 1916, GARF, f. 102, OO, 1917, d. 307. lit. A, ll. 121–31 ob.; Rodzianko, "Krushenie," 157–58; Anan'ich et al., *Krizis*, 643 ("embryonic").

20. Kir'ianov, ed., "Perepiska," 8:88 (financial assistance); Kurlov, *Gibel'*, 215; Kir'ianov, ed., "Pravye v 1915," 147–48 (conference); Anan'ich et al., *Krizis*, 618–19 (Govorukho-Otrok); Diakin, *Russkaia*, 23–24 (Shtiurmer); Tatarov, "Programma," 242–44 (Rimskii-Korsakov).

21. Shavel'skii, *Vospominaniia*, 2:224 (protection of Rasputin); Pipes, *Russian Revolution*, 262–63; Shishkin, *Ubit'*, 89, 91, 147–48, 154, 173.

22. Bulgakov, *Avtobiograficheskie*, 88 (applauding of the murder); Gerasimov, *Na lezvii*, 187; Iusupov, *Konets*, 201 (cable); Protopopov testimony, in *Padenie*,

4:111–12; Gessen, "V dvukh," 353; Avrekh, *Tsarizm,* 144 (power struggle); A. M. Golitsyn, "Golitsyn, N. D.," in *OI,* 1:579.

23. Botkin, *Real Romanovs,* 127; Shavel'skii, *Vospominaniia,* 2:224; Hughes, "'Revolution Was in the Air," 92–93 (Lockhart); GARF, f. 102, OO, 1917, d. 20, ch. 57, ll. 1–3 (Globachev); GARF, f. 102, OO, 1917, d. 307–A, ll. 6–8 (Martynov).

24. "Revoliutsionnoe dvizhenie v voiskakh," 417–19 (mood in the military).

25. Vasil'ev to Protopopov, 18 January 1917, GARF, f. 102, OO, 1917, d. 307–A, l. 51; Glinka, *Odinnadtsat',* 173 (reception); Rodzianko, "Krushenie," 160 (Mikhail); Martynov, *Moia sluzhba,* 286–88.

26. GARF, f. 97, op. 4, d. 117, l. 117 (strikes); Protopopov to governors, 20 December 1916, GARF, f. 102, OO, 1916, d. 341, ll. 71–73; "V ianvare," 92–95 (2 January).

27. "Spisok . . . ," GARF, f. 102, OO, 1917, d. 169, ll. 1–20 (arrests); Miroliubov, "Politicheskii," 91 (9 January); Anan'ich et al., *Krizis,* 634 (troops); Livchak, "Krakh," 121 (first stage of alert).

28. Vasil'ev to Protopopov, 13 January 1917, GARF, f. 102, OO, 1917, d. 205, l. 2; informant report, 14 January 1917, GARF, f. 102, OO, 1917, d. 9, ch. 46, lit. b, l. 1; Gelis, "Revoliutsionnaia," 44–45 (Beliaev).

29. Informant report, 19 January 1917, GARF, f. 102, OO, 1917, d. 20, ch. 57, ll. 6–10 ob. (Amfiteatrov: 6); Globachev report, 19 January 1917, GARF, f. 97, op. 4, d. 117, ll. 113 ob.–114 ob.

30. "V ianvare," 96–97 (16 January), 101–2 (19 January); Martynov to Vasil'ev, 19 January 1917, GARF, f. 102, OO, 1917, d. 27, ch. 46, l. 3 (emphasis in the original); Anan'ich et al., *Krizis,* 644 (Globachev); Vasil'ev report, 26 January 1917, GARF, f. 97, op. 4, d. 117, ll. 118–19.

31. Kurlov, *Gibel',* 214; Florinskii, *Krizis,* 62 (failure to attend meetings); Globachev, "Pravda," 70–72; Miliukov testimony, in *Padenie,* 6:350–52; Miliukov, *Vospominaniia,* 450; Chubinskii, "God revoliutsii," 235; Mosolov, "Iz moikh," 14–15.

32. Protopopov testimony, in *Padenie,* 4:87–88;. Avdeev, "Pervye dni," 16–18 (Duma); Miroliubov, "Politicheskii," 118 (records); Globachev report, January 1917, GARF, f. 102, OO, 1917, d. 347, l. 34; Menitskii, ed., "K istorii," 45 (Gvozdev); Hasegawa, *February,* 132.

33. Globachev, "Pravda," 25; Vassiliyev, *Ochrana,* 207–8; Romanov, *Kniga,* 224; Bubnov, *V tsarskoi,* 321 (Alekseev); "Iz dnevnika A. V. Romanova," 203 ("propaganda").

34. Grave, comp., *Burzhuaziia,* 125 (28 January); Globachev to Vasil'ev, 5 February 1917, GARF, f. 102, OO, 1917, d. 20, ch. 57, ll. 23–32 ob.; Globachev report, GARF, f. 97, op. 4, d. 117, l. 124 ob.

35. Martynov to Vasil'ev, 6 February 1917, GARF, f. 102, OO, 1917, d. 27, ch. 46, lit. b, ll. 1–6.

36. Globachev to Vasil'ev, 7 February 1917, GARF, f. 1467, op. 1, d. 582, ll. 44–45 ob.

37. Martynov to Vasil'ev, 14 February 1917, GARF, f. 102, OO, 1917, d. 5, ch. 46, ll. 1–1 ob.; Livchak, "Krakh," 122; Hasegawa, *February,* 208 (14th); Grave, comp., *Burzhuaziia,* 186–88 (crowds).

38. Grave, comp., *Burzhuaziia,* 179 (report to Protopopov); Spiridovich, *Velikaia,* 3:63; *SOS* (15 June 1913), 2:437; "Vasil'ev, I. P.," in *Padenie,* 7:314.

39. Spiridovich, *Velikaia,* 3:69; Voeikov, *S tsarem,* 202; "V ianvare," 121–22 (23 February); Avrekh, *Tsarizm,* 167 (commission).

40. Rodzianko, "Krushenie," 168; Miliukov, *Vospominaniia,* 450 (rumors); Pipes, *Russian Revolution,* 272–73 (20 February temperature); Balk, "Poslednie," 1 (22 February); B. G. "Fevral'skaia revoliutsiia," 162–64 (procession); McKean, *St. Petersburg,* 461–65 (demonstrations).

41. Spiridovich, *Velikaia,* 3:79; Balk, "Poslednie," 2–3; Dobolin, ed., "Iz dnevnika A. D. Protopopova," 176–77; "V ianvare," 122–23 (intelligence service).

42. Ganelin, "24 fevralia," 76–77.

43. Ibid., 76–79; Lomonosov, *Vospominaniia,* 221 (eyewitness).

44. Balk, "Poslednie," 4v.

45. Ibid.; Khabalov testimony, in *Padenie,* 1:188; Globachev, "Pravda," 78–79.

46. Lomonosov, *Vospominaniia,* 221; "Iz dnevnika A. D. Protopopova," 178.

47. Ganelin, "24 Fevralia," 81 (newspapers); Savich, *Vospominaniia,* 193–94.

48. Savich, *Vospominaniia,* 194–95; McKean, *St. Petersburg,* 460–62, 474–75; "Vedomost'," RGIA, f. 1282, op. 1, d. 741, l. 173 (strikes); Balk, "Poslednie," 5a-5v; Spiridovich, *Velikaia,* 3:98–99 (Protopopov).

49. Globachev report, 25 February 1917, GARF, f. 102, OO, 1917, d. 341, ch. 57, ll. 42–43; Barshtein and Shalaginova, eds., "Departament," 112 (Social Democrats); Ganelin, "Diskussia," 222 (informant).

50. Balk, "Poslednie" (25 February), 5v-7; Hasegawa, *February,* 264–65 (telegrams).

51. Globachev report, 26 February 1917, GARF, f. 102, OO, 1917, d. 341, ch. 57, l. 45; B. G., "Fevral'skaia revoliutsiia," 170–75 (quotation: 175).

52. Balk, "Poslednie," 7–8; Globachev report, 26 February 1917, GARF, f. 102, OO, 1917, d. 341, ch. 57, l. 45 ob.–46; Globachev, "Pravda," 80–81; Vassiliyev, *Ochrana,* 214; Spiridovich, *Velikaia,* 3:115.

53. Shakhovskoi, *"Sic transit,"* 199 (Council); Balk, "Poslednie," 7–8.

54. Balk, "Poslednie," 9 (four regiments mutinied, looting), 11 (memory); Vassiliyev, *Ochrana,* 217; Khasegava, "Fevral'skaia," 100; Vrangel', *Vospominaniia,* 219; B. G., "Fevral'skaia revoliutsiia," 176 (policemen); Shul'gin, *Gody-Dni-1920,* 463; Peretts, *V tsitadeli,* 77 (eighty-three gendarme officers);.

55. Vassiliyev, *Ochrana,* 219–20; Miroliubov, "Politicheskii," 146 (records); Globachev, "Pravda," 84; Peregudova, "Deiatel'nost'," 13 (archives); B. G., "Fevral'skaia revoliutsiia," 170 ("last pillar").

56. Shakhovskoi, *"Sic transit",* 200–1; Balk, "Poslednie," 14; Raskin et al., eds., *Vysshie,* 1:198 (Council of Ministers).

57. Globachev, "Pravda," 87–88, 90–91; Globacheva, "Preliudiia," 17; Blok, "Poslednie," 41–42; Peretts, *V tsitadeli,* 32; Balk, "Poslednie," 17; Kurlov, *Gibel',* 219.

58. "Fevral'skaia revoliutsiia 1917 goda," 3 (Raden); Jones, *Russia in Revolution,* 264–68 (atrocities); F. D., "Fevral'skaia revoliutsiia v Petrograde," 69 (police stations ordered to disarm).

59. Livchak, "Krakh," 116–24.

60. Danilov, "Moi vospominaniia," 228.

61. "Samoubiistvo."

62. Gernet cited in Karelin, *Smertnaia,* 3.

63. F. D., "Fevral'skaia revoliutsiia v Petrograde," 70 (1 March); Kel'son, "Militsiia," 220–21 (Urusov).

64. *Rech'* (7 March 1917): 7; *SU,* 7 March 1917, no. 55, art. 346; Vlasov, "Sozdanie," 46–47 (10 March).

65. Provisional Government sessions, 4 and 10 March 1917, GARF, f. 1779, op. 2, d. 3, ll. 2, 25; Romanov and Romanova, *Zakat*, 89 (30 March), 95 (military intelligence); Zdanovich, "Organizatsiia," 14 (Ustinov).

66. Interior ministry to commissars, 15 and 24 March 1917, GARF, f. 1791, op. 1, d. 116, ll. 2, 9; Vlasov, "Sozdanie," 47 (in practice); Tsereteli, *Vospominaniia*, 1:19; Miroliubov, "Politicheskii," 155 (pensions), 157 (gendarmes not to suffer arrest); interior ministry directive, September 1917, GARF, f. 1779, op. 2, d. 423, ll. 8–9.

67. *SU* (25 March 19), no. 68, art. 386; Iskhakov, ed., *Strana*, 395–96 (Nabokov).

68. Hasegawa, "Crime," 249–65 (quotation: 249); Figes, *People's Tragedy*, 400 (lynching); Lohr, "Enemy Alien Politics," 362–63 (pogroms).

69. Provisional Government meeting, 11 March 1917, GARF, f. 1779, op. 2, d. 3, l. 33 ob.; *SU* (11 March 19), no. 61, art. 363; Avrekh, "Chrezvychainaia," 76, 87 (lay bare the bankruptcy); Peregudova, *Politicheskii*, 216–20 (commissions); Peregudova, "Deiatel'nost'," 14 (removing police records).

70. Blok, *Zapisnye*, 334, 352; Medvedev, ed., *Dnevnik*, 2:18; "Proekt . . . ," GARF, f. 1467, op. 1, d. 222, ll. 35 ob.–38, 53–61 (multiauthor study); GARF, f. 1779, op. 2, d. 3, l. 123–123 ob. (Moscow).

71. Agafonov, *Zagranichnaia*, 216; Vassiliyev, *Ochrana*, 243–45.

72. A. N. Khvostov testimony, in *Padenie*, 6:74; Vissarionov testimony, in *Padenie*, 5:213; Gerasimov testimony, in *Padenie*, 3:8, 17; Martynov testimony, GARF, f. 504, op. 1, d. 413, l. 114; Avrekh, *Masony*, 219 ("best client").

73. Trusevich testimony, in *Padenie*, 3:212–15, 218; Avrekh, "Chrezvychainaia," 89 (imperial Russian government as odious).

74. Miroliubov, "Politicheskii," 163–64; Avrekh, "Chrezvychainaia," 94–96; Blok, *Zapisnye*, 321.

75. Burtsev, *Bor'ba*, 1:361; Karabchevskii, *Chto glaza*, 132; Varfolomeeva, ed., "Eto chisto politseiskaia mera," 81 (Zarudnyi); Vishniak, *Dan'*, 294–95.

76. Svatikov, *Russkii*, 68; Svatikov, "Sozdanie", 163–67; Budnitskii, ed., *Evrei*, 223–27 (Nikolaevskii); Blok, *Dnevnik*, 227 (funds).

77. Galinovskii, "Zakliuchitel'noe . . . ," GARF, f. 1467, op. 1, d. 396, ll. 268–300 (quotations: 293, 300); testimony on Protopopov, GARF, f. 1467, op. 1, d. 453, ll. 1–104 ob. (quotation: 104 ob.); Kir'ianov, ed., "Perepiska," 10:138–42 (Lebedev).

78. Hasegawa, *February*, 296; Figes, *People's Tragedy*, 316; Zavadskii, "Na velikom," 7; Avrekh, "Chrezvychainaia," 87–88.

79. Gerasimov, *Na lezvii*, 58; "Spisok," July 1917, GARF, f. 5802, op. 2, d. 263, l. 1 (Martynov, pseudonyms); GARF, f. 4888, op. 5, d. 638, ll. 1–241 (names); Miroliubov, "Politicheskii," 166; "Spiski," GARF, f. 503, op. 1, d. 204, ll. 2–31 (830 informants); Peregudova, *Politicheskii*, 228 (forty lists).

80. Agafonov, *Zagranichnaia*, 212, 216; Osipovich, *Shpiony*, 13; Peregudova, *Politicheskii*, 232–38; Koehler, *Stasi*, 8, 18.

81. Iskhakov, ed., *Strana*, 396 (Nabokov); Globachev, "Pravda," 123–24; Kel'son, "Militsiia," 225 (emphasis in original); Vassiliyev, *Ochrana*, 253–54.

82. Vlasov, "Sozdanie," 47 (bureau); Galinovskii, "Zakliuchitel'noe," GARF, f. 1467, op. 1, d. 396, ll. 288 ob.–289; Kel'son, "Militsiia," 226–27; Kel'son, "Padenie," 198.

EPILOGUE

1. Burtsev to Zhuchenko, August 1909, GARF, f. 102, op. 316, 1906, d. 1019, ll. 20 ob.; Peretts, *V tsitadeli*, 86.

2. Koznov, "Bor'ba," 68 (Chernomazov); defense appeal, 29 March 1917, GARF, f. 504, op. 1, d. 507, ll. 1–2; Romanov and Romanova, *Zakat*, 184 (attestation).

3. Vassiliyev, *Ochrana*, 207 (Ambrosimov, here spelled "Ambrozilov"); Kaptelov and Peregudova, "Byl li Stalin," 91; Kaptelov, Rozental', and Shelokhaev, eds., *Delo*, 154; Bonnell, *Roots*, 422n117, 422n118, 423n123, 424n127; GARF, f. 1005, op. 1a (lighter sentences); Alekseev, *Istoriia*, vi (Lunacharskii).

4. I. S. Rozental', "Malinovskii, R. V.," in *OI*, 3:460; Lipkin, "Nakanune," 61–62.

5. Lipkin, "Provokator Nikulin-Mikulin," 98–119.

6. Lipkin, "Provokator D. S. Krut," 88–114.

7. Cherkunov, "Provokator," 195–206.

8. Levitskii, "Provokator," 105; "Zhitomirskii, Ia. A.," in *Bol'shaia* 25:550; Peregudova, *Politicheskii*, 232, 281.

9. Burtsev to Spiridovich, 4 January 1916, box 25, folder 1, Spiridovich Papers, Yale University Archives; "Vospominaniia Kafafova," GARF, f. 5881, op. 2, d. 390, l. 98 (von Koten); Zavarzin, *Rabota*, 162 (von Koten); Romanov and Romanova, *Zakat*, 123 (officers arrested), 156–76 (testimony of officers).

10. Martynov, *Moia sluzhba*, viii (brother), 74; Romanov and Romanova, *Zakat*, 25 (notification, criminal codes), 188 (government threats against gendarmes); Pletnev, *Instsenirovka* (trials); *Spisok byv. chinov; Spisok b. unter-ofitserov; Spravochnik-spisok;* Zavarzin, *Rabota*, 62.

11. Shilov, *Gosudarstvennye deiateli*, 70, 391, 550, 708, 767; Z. I. Peregudova, "Beletskii, S. P.," *OI*, 1:192; Leggett, *Cheka*, 111–12; Lur'e, *Politseiskie i provokatory,* 365; Kobiakov, "Krasnyi sud," 275.

12. Burtsev, "Moi otnosheniia," 35; Laporte, *Histoire*, 145; Spiridovich, "Pri tsarskom rezhime," 201; "Konets M. S. Komissarova"; Golinkov, *Krushenie*, 2:56; Brunovskii, "Delo bylo v S.S.S.R.," 31; Krasnov, "Iz vospominanii," 107.

13. Budnitskii, ed., *Evrei*, 215n10 (Bint); Mironenko and Freeze, eds., *Putevoditel'*, 1:324 (Bint); Izmozik, "Rossiiskie," 224 (purlustrators, Zybin); Laporte, *Histoire*, 30 (Zybin).

14. Rozental', "Stranitsy," 91, 100–103 (Dzhunkovskii).

15. Martynov, *Moia sluzhba*, 74; Investigating Commission reports, GARF, f. 1467, op. 1, d. 92, ll. 1–9; report on wife's visits, GARF, f. 504, op. 1, d. 413, l. 37; Commissariat of Public Accusation report, 1917, GARF, f. 504, op. 1, d. 413, l. 23.

16. Scruples about involvement with security (or even regular) police institutions persisted among former opposition activists, even during the civil war. The Kadet V. N. Pepeliaev was willing to take charge of the Police Department under Kolchak only because it would not deploy a security police force and because he intended to "reform the police institutions, make them less abusive." See Elachich, "Obryvki," 56. I am grateful to Scott Smith for bringing this source to my attention.

17. Richard Wraga, "Introduction," in Martynov, *Moia sluzhba*, viii; Martynov, *Moia sluzhba*, 53; Dmitrii Koshko, "Russkii Sherlok Kholms," in Koshko, *Ocherki*, end of volume.

18. Gerasimov, *Na lezvii*, 189–92.

19. RGIA, f. 1284, op. 250, d. 25, ll. 2, 7, 9, 19 (Yalta); Mel'gunov, *Vospominaniia*, 1:141; O. V. Budnitskii, "Burtsev, V. L.," in *OI*, 1:314; Spiridovich, *Dernières années*, 1:16.

20. Spiridovich, "Pri tsarskom rezhime"; Spiridovich, *Raspoutine;* Spiridovich, *Dernières années;* Spiridovich, *Velikaia*.

21. See them in the Widener Library at Harvard University.

22. Zavarzin, *Rabota*, 170–74; Zavarzin, *Zhandarmy;* Globachev, "Pravda," 100–103; report on Globachev by V. P. Nikol'skii, 30 June 1919 (copy kindly given to the author by Globachev's grandson, Vladimir Marinich); private conversation with Vladimir Marinich.

23. Peregudova, *Politicheskii*, 71 (Rataev), 92 (Klimovich), 103 (Eremin); Krivoshein, *A. V. Krivoshein*, 335; "Krivoshein, A. V.," in Shilov, *Gosudarstvennye*, 332; Brachev, *Mastera*, 105 (Krasil'nikov); A. N. Petrov, "Garting, A. M.," in *OI*, 1:516.

24. Kurlov, *Gibel'*, 220–23; Z. I. Peregudova, "Kurlov, P. G.," in *OI*, 3: 227; L. G. Aronov, "Lopukhin, A. A.," in *OI*, 391–92; Vassiliyev, *Ochrana*, 22, 259–65; Bostunich, "A. T. Vasil'ev."

25. Nikolaevskii, *Istoriia odnogo predatelia*, 221 (Bakai); Gorev, "Leonid Men'shchikov," 140n; Z. I. Peregudova, "Men'shchikov, L. P.," in *OI*, 3:555; Men'shchikov, *Okhrana;* L. P. Men'shchikov, "Chernaia kniga," GARF, f. 1723, op. 1, d. 375; "L. P. Men'shchikov."

26. I. Gofman, "Sudeikin, S. Iu.," in *Russkoe zarubezh'e*, 615–17; Ascherson, "Baleful Smile," 9–10.

27. See Haimson, "Problem of Social Stability"; Haimson, "'Problem' . . . Revisited"; Pipes, *Russian Revolution;* McKean, "Constitutional Russia"; Roosa, *Russian Industrialists*.

28. Among recent studies, see Clowes, Kassow, and West, eds., *Between Tsar and People;* McReynolds, *News;* Gatrell, "'Constitutional Russia': A Reponse"; Ruud, *Russian Entrepreneur*.

29. Baberowski, *Autokratie*, 783–89.

30. Gessen, *Iskliuchitel'noe*, 171, 177; Ordynskii, "Pechat' i sud," 152; Rabe, *Widerspruch*, 120 (press).

31. *Aleksandr Ivanovich Guchkov*, 45.

32. Berlieu, "Professionalization," 37.

33. Ermanskii, *Iz perezhitogo*, 47–49.

34. Chuev, *Sto*, 145, 150, 314, 408; Volkogonov, *Stalin*, 4; Zavarzin, *Rabota*, 60.

35. Zenzinov, *Iz zhizni*, 102; Argunov, "Bez svobody," 88–89; Mel'gunov, *Vospominaniia*, 1:139; Sorokin, *Long Journey*, 85; Kerenskii, *Rossiia*, 70; Pipes, *Russian Revolution*, 819 *(Izvestiia)*.

36. Tsvigun et al., ed., *V. I. Lenin*, 6, 363; Fel'shtinskii, *VchK-GPU*, 72 (Latsis).

37. Papadatos, *Le délit*, x, 105–6, 110; Kimerling, "Civil Rights."

38. Daly, *Autocracy under Siege*, 68.

39. Vishniak, *Dan'*, 147; Tyrkova-Villiams, *Na putiakh*, 115.

WORKS CITED

PRIMARY SOURCES

Archival Material

Gosudarstvennyi arkhiv Rossiiskoi federatsii (GARF, Moscow)
fond 58 Moskovskoe zhandarmskoe upravlenie
fond 63 Moskovskoe okhrannoe otdelenie
fond 102 Departament politsii
fond 271 Deloproizvodstvo Senatorov M. I. Trusevicha l N. V. Shul'gina
fond 280 Moskovskoe raionnoe okhrannoe otdelenie
fond 503   Osobaia komissiia po obsledovaniiu deiatel'nosti b. Departamenta
    politsii
fond 504 Komissiia po obespecheniiu novogo stroia
fond 826 Dzhunkovskii, V. F.
fond 1005 Sud RSFSR
fond 1467 Chrezvychainaia sledstvennaia komissiia
fond 1699 Sudebno-sledstvennaia komissiia tsentral'nogo komiteta partii sotsial-
    istov-revoliutsionerov po delu Azefa
fond 1723 Men'shchikov, L. P.
fond 1779 Kantseliariia Vremennogo pravitel'stva
fond 1791 Glavnoe upravlenie po delam militsii . . . Vremennogo pravitel'stva
fond 5802 Burtsev, V. L.
fond 5881 Prague Archive

Hoover Institution Archives (Stanford, California)
    Collection Balk, A.
    Collection Burtsev, V. L.
    Collection Elachich, S. L.
    Collection Nicolaevsky, B. I.
    Collection Okhrana (ZA)

Rossiiskii gosudarstvennyi arkhiv sotsial'no-politicheskoi istorii (RGASPI, Moscow)
    fond 146 Podvoiskii, N. I.

Rossiiskii gosudarstvennyi istoricheskii arkhiv (RGIA, St. Petersburg)
    fond 1276 Sovet ministrov

fond 1278 Gosudarstvennaia duma
fond 1282 Kantseliariia Ministerstva vnutrennikh del
fond 1284 Departament obshchikh del Ministerstva vnutrennikh del
fond 1405 Ministerstvo iustitsii

Rossiiskii gosudarstvennyi istoricheskii arkhiv g. Moskvy (RGIAgM, Moscow)
fond 46 Gradonachal'stvo
fond 475 Uchastkovye pristava

Yale University Archives (New Haven, Conn.)
Collection Spiridovich, Alexander Ivanovich

Unpublished Works

Balk, A. "Poslednie piat' dnei tsarskogo Petrograda (23–28 fevralia 1917 g.): Dnevnik poslednego Petrogradskogo Gradonachal'nika." A. Balk Collection, Hoover Institution.
Burtsev, V. L. "Moe znakomstvo s gen. Spiridovichem." In Burtsev Papers, box 1, folder 52, Hoover Institution Archives.
———. "Moi otnosheniia s okhrannikami, 1915-1916." In Burtsev Papers, box 1, folder 52, Hoover Institution Archives.
———. "Moia bor'ba s russkimi provokatorami." In Burtsev Papers, box 2, folder 2. Hoover Institution Archives.
Elachich, S. A. "Obryvki vospominanii" (1934). S. A. Elachich Collection, Hoover Institution.
Globachev, Konstantin I. "Pravda o russkoi revoliutsii. Vospominaniia byvshego nachal'nika Petrogradskogo okhrannogo otdeleniia." Bakhmetev Archive, Columbia University Library.
Globacheva, Sofiia. "Preliudiia proiskhodiashshikh v mire sobytii." Unpublished manuscript kindly given to the author by Vladimir Marinich, Globacheva's grandson.
Iarmysh, A. N. "Karatel'nye organy tsarizma na Ukraine v kontse XIX–nachale XX v." Doktorskaia diss., Khar'kovskii iuridicheskii institut, 1990.
Karpeev, I. V. "Voenno-okruzhnoi apparat tsarskoi Rossii na sluzhbe vnutrennei politiki samoderzhaviia (iiun' 1907–iiul' 1910 gg.)." Kandidat. diss., MGIAI, 1987.
Lohr, Eric. "Enemy Alien Politics within the Russian Empire during World War I." Ph.D. diss., Harvard University, 1999.
"L. P. Men'shchikov." Box 179, folder 2. Nicolaevsky Collection, Hoover Institution Archives.
Miroliubov, A. A. "Politicheskii sysk Rossii v 1914–1917 gg." Kandidat. diss., MGIAI, 1988.
Nikolaevskii, B. "Pamiati L. P. Men'shchikova." Box 179, folder 2, B. I. Nicolaevsky Collection, Hoover Institution.
Peregudova, Z. I. "Departament politsii v bor'be s revoliutsionnym dvizheniem: Gody reaktsii i revoliutsionnogo pod"ema." Kandidat. diss., MGIAI, 1988.
"Politicheskii rozysk i ego osushchestvlenie." Box 27, folder 1. Spiridovich Papers, Yale University Archives.
"Sekretnye tsirkuliary i instruktsii." N.p., n.d. Library of Congress Rare Book Reading Room.

Shatina, Natalia V., "Mestnyi gosudarstvennyi apparat samoderzhaviia v bor'be s pervoi rossiiskoi revoliutsiei (na primere Moskvy)." Kandidat. diss., MGIAI, 1989.

Spiridovich, A. I. "Petr Ivanovich Rachkovskii." Box 26, envelope. Spiridovich Papers, Yale University Archives.

Published Works

A. B., ed. *Za kulisami okhrannogo otdeleniia: S dnevnikom provokatora, pis'mami okhrannikov, tainymi instruktsiiami.* Berlin: Heinrich Caspari, 1910.

A. P. "Departament politsii v 1892–1908 gg.: Iz vospominanii chinovnika." *Byloe* 27–28 (November–December 1917): 17–24.

Agafonov, V. K. *Zagranichnaia okhranka: Sostavleno po sekretnym dokumentam Zagranichnoi Agentury i Departamenta Politsii.* Moscow: Kniga, 1918.

Aleksandr Ivanovich Guchkov rasskazyvaet: Vospominaniia predsedatelia Gosudarstvennoi dumy i voennogo ministra Vremennogo pravitel'stva. Moscow: Voprosy istorii, 1993.

Alekseev, I. V. *Istoriia odnogo provokatora: Obvinitel'noe zakliuchenie i materialy k protsessu A. E. Serebriakova.* Ed. S. N. Sheverdin. Moscow: Izd. Moskovskogo Gubsuda, 1925.

———. *Provokator Anna Serebriakova.* Moscow: Izd. Politkatorzhan, 1932.

Alexander, Grand Duke of Russia. *Always a Grand Duke.* Garden City, N.Y.: Garden City Publishing, 1933.

Anfert'ev, I. A., ed. *Ot pervogo litsa.* Moscow: Patriot, 1990.

Anfimov, A. M., ed., "Tsarskaia okhranka o politicheskom polozhenii v strane v kontse 1916 g." *Istoricheskii arkhiv* 1 (January–February 1960): 203–209.

Ansimov, N. N. "Okhrannye otdeleniia i mestnaia vlast' tsarskoi Rossii v nachale XX v." *Sovetskoe gosudarstvo i pravo,* no. 5 (1991): 119–25.

Antoshkin, D. *Professional'noe dvizhenie v Rossii: Posobie dlia samoobrazovaniia i kursov po professional'nomu dvizheniiu.* 3rd ed. Moscow: VTsSPS, 1925.

Arapova, L. I. "Tsarskie okhranniki v roli istorikov: Skhema istorii revoliutsionnogo dvizheniia v Rossii." In *Golosa istorii: Sbornik nauchnykh trudov,* vol. 23, no. 2. Moscow: Muzei revoliutsii, 1992.

Argunov, A. "Azef—sotsialist-revoliutsioner." In *Provokator: Vospominaniia i dokumenty o razoblachenii Azefa,* ed. P. E. Shchegolev. Moscow: Priboi, 1929.

———. "Bez svobody." *Golos minuvshego na chuzhoi storone* 13 (1925): 86–130.

Arkomed, S. T. "Krasnyi terror na Kavkaze i okhrannoe otdelenie." *Katorga i ssylka* 13 (1924): 71–83.

Asin, T. "K statistike arestovannykh i ssylnykh." *Russkoe bogatstvo,* no. 10 (1906): 1–37.

Avdeev, N. "Pervye dni Fevral'skoi revoliutsii: Khronika sobytii: Neskol'ko slov o prichinakh revoliutsii." *Proletarskaia revoliutsiia,* no. 13 (1923): 3–49.

B. G. "Fevral'skaia revoliutsiia i okhrannoe otdelenie." *Byloe* 29 (January 1919): 158–76.

Badaev, A. *Bol'sheviki v Gosudarstvennoi dume: Vospominaniia.* 8th ed. Moscow: Gos. izd. politicheskoi literatury, 1954.

———, ed. "Arest dumskoi 'piaterki' v 1914 g." *Krasnyi arkhiv* 64 (1934): 31–51.

Bakai, M. E. "Iz vospominanii M. E. Bakaia. Provokatory i provokatsiia." *Byloe* 8 (1908): 99–136.

Barshtein, E. K., and L. M. Shalaginova, eds. "Departament politisii o plane petro-gradskikh bol'shevikov v fevrale 1917 goda." *Voprosy arkhivovedeniia* 1 (1962): 111–12.

Baum, Ia. D. "Departament politsii i vopros ob amnistii v 1913 godu." *Katorga i ssylka* 89 (1932): 54–61.

Bel'chikov, N., ed. "Zapreshchenie chestvovaniia pamiati T. Shevchenko." *Krasnyi arkhiv* 76 (1936): 226–30.

Belokonskii, I. P. *V gody bespraviia, 1880–1890 g*. Moscow: Izd. Politkatorzhan, 1930.

Berlin, P. "Ob odnom poveshennom." *Katorga i ssylka* 59 (1929): 92–100.

Bing, Edward J. *The Secret Letters of the Last Tsar, Being the Confidential Correspondence between Nicholas II and His Mother, Dowager Empress Maria Feodorovna*. Preface by R. H. Bruce Lockhart. New York: Longmans, Green, and Co., 1938.

Blinova, Natalia. "Delo 'o revoliutsionnom dvizhenii v armii.'" In *Sbornik materialov i statei*. Moscow: Gos. izd., 1921.

Blok, Aleksandr. *Dnevnik*. Moscow: Sovetskaia Rossiia, 1989.

———. "Poslednie dni starogo rezhima." In *Arkhiv russkoi revoliutsii*, vol. 4., ed. I. V. Gessen. 1926. Reprint, Moscow: Terra, 1993.

———. *Zapisnye knizhki, 1901–1920*. Moscow: Khudozhestvennaia literatura, 1965.

"'Blondinka'—v Iasnoi poliane v 1910 godu," *Byloe* 25 (September 1917): 196–209.

Bogdanovich, A. *Tri poslednikh samoderzhtsa*. Moscow: Novosti, 1990.

Bonch-Bruevich, V. *Bol'shevistskie izdatel'skie dela v 1905–1907 gg.: Moi vospominaniia*. Leningrad: LOIZ, 1933.

———. *Vospominaniia*. Moscow: Khudozhestvennaia literatura, 1968.

Bostunich, Grigorii. "A. T. Vasil'ev," *Novoe vremia* (9 February 1929).

Botkin, Gleb. *The Real Romanovs, as Revealed by the Late Czar's Physician and His Son*. New York: Fleming H. Revell, 1931.

Brazhe, L., ed. "'Krasnaia gvardia' v Rige 1906 g." *Krasnyi arkhiv* 41–42 (1930): 213–15.

Brunovskii, V. "Delo bylo v S.S.S.R. (Stranichka iz vospominanii byvshego 'smert-nika')." In *Arkhiv russkoi revoliutsii*, vol. 19, ed. I. V. Gessen. 1928. Reprint, Moscow: Terra, 1993.

Bubnov, A. *V tsarskoi stavke: Vospominaiia admirala Bubnova*. New York: Izd. imeni Chekhova, 1955.

Budnitskii, O. V., ed. *Istoriia terrorizma v Rossii v dokumentakh, biografiiakh, issle-dovaniiakh*. 2nd rev. ed. Rostov-na-Donu: Feniks, 1996.

Bukharin, N. "Kopiia pis'ma N. Bukharina V. Leninu." *Voprosy istorii*, no. 9 (1993): 117.

Bukhbinder, N. A. "Zubatovshchina v Moskve." *Katorga i ssylka* 1 (1925): 96-133.

Bulgakov, Sergei. *Avtobiograficheskie zametki*. 2nd ed. 1946. Reprint, Paris: YMCA Press, 1991.

Bulkin, F. "Soiuz metallistov i Departament politsii." *Krasnaia letopis'* 5 (1922): 252–67.

Bulkin [Semenov], Fedor. "Departament politsii i soiuz metallistov." *Krasnaia letopis'* 9 (1924): 125–62; and 8 (1923): 220–33.

Burtsev, V. L. *Bor'ba za svobodnuiu Rossiiu: Moi vospominaniia, 1882–1924 gg*. 2 vols. Berlin: Gamaiun, 1924.

———. "V bor'be s provokatorami: Vospominaniia V. L. Burtseva: Provokatorsha Putiata." *Illiustrirovannaia Rossiia*, no. 16 (8 April 1939): 20–22.

———. "V bor'be s provokatorami: Vospominaniia V. L. Burtseva: Provokatorsha Serebriakova." *Illiustrirovannaia Rossiia,* no. 17 (15 April 1939): 21–22.

———. *V pogone za provokatorami.* Moscow: Molodaia gvardiia, 1928.

Cherkunov, A. N. "K voprosu o provokatsii Iulii Serovoi." *Katorga i ssylka* 20 (1925): 95–101.

———. "Provokator Vladislav Feliksovich Gabel': Iz vospominanii smolenskogo katorzhnika." *Katorga i ssylka* 22 (1926): 195–206.

Chuev, F. *Sto sorok besed s Molotovym: Iz dnevnika F. Chueva.* Moscow: Terra, 1991.

Dan, F. "Obshchaia politika pravitel'stva i izmeneniia v gosudarstvennoi organizatsii v period 1905-1907 gg." In *Chast' pervaia i vtoraia. Izmeneniia v techenii 1904-7 gg. ekonomicheskogo i politicheskogo stroia.* Vol. 4 of *Obshchestvennoe dvizhenie v Rossii v nachale XX-go veka,* ed. L. Martov, P. Maslov, and A. Potresov. St. Petersburg: "Obshchestvennaia Pol'za," 1912.

Danilov, Iu. N. "Moi vospominaniia ob Imperatore Nikolae II-om i Vel. Kniaze Mikhaile Aleksandroviche." In *Arkhiv russkoi revoliutsii,* vol. 19, ed. I. V. Gessen. 1926. Reprint, Moscow: Terra, 1993.

"Deistviia pravitel'stva—imennye vysochaishie ukazy." *Pravo,* no. 30 (1914): 2289–91.

Delo A. A. Lopukhina v osobom prisutstvii pravitel'stvuiushchego senata. Stenograficheskii otchet. St. Petersburg: Tip. P. I. Artsivi, 1910.

"Delo Azefa," *Rech',* no. 19 (20 January 1909): 1.

Derevianko, I. V. "Shpionov lovit' bylo nekomu: Kontrrazvedyvatel'naia sluzhba Rossii v period russko-iaponskoi voiny, 1904–1905." *Voenno-istoricheskii zhurnal,* no. 12 (1993): 51–53.

Dobolin, Iv., ed. "Iz dnevnika A. D. Protopopova." *Krasnyi arkhiv* 10 (1925): 175–83.

Drezen, A. "Baltiiskii flot v gody pod"ema, 1910–1913 g.g." *Krasnaia letopis'* 36 (1930): 126–63; and 37 (1930): 123–56.

———, ed. *Tsarizm v bor'be s revoliutsiei 1905-1907 gg.: Sbornik dokumentov.* Moscow: Gos. sotsial'no-ekonomicheskoe izd., 1936.

Dubrovskii, S., ed. "Agrarnoe dvizhenie v 1905 g. po otchetam Dubasova i Panteleeva." *Krasnyi arkhiv* 11–12 (1925): 182–92.

Dybenko, P. E. *Iz nedr tsarskogo flota k velikomu oktiabriu.* Moscow: Voennoe izd. Ministerstva oborony Soiuza SSR, 1958.

Dzhunkovskii, V. F. *Vospominaniia.* 2 vols. Ed. A. L. Lapina. Moscow: Izd. imeni Sabashnikovykh, 1997.

Egorov, Al. *Baltflot v gody reaktsii, 1909–1913.* Moscow: Izd. Politkatorzhan, 1928.

Eletskii, Pavel, ed. "Ssylka M. S. Grushevskogo." *Minuvshee* 23 (1998): 207–62.

Engel'ke, A. P., and N. E. Ignatovich, eds. *Deistvuiushchaia chast' Ugolovnogo ulozheniia, Vysochaishe utverzhdennogo 22 Marta 1904 g.* St. Petersburg: Tip. t-va A. F. Marks, 1908.

Entin, E. M., ed. *Politicheskie partii i politicheskaia politsiia: Dokumental'noe issledovanie v trekh chastiakh.* Moscow: Minsk-Gomel', 1996.

Ermanskii, O. A. *Iz perezhitogo, 1887–1921.* Preface by P. Lepeshinskii. Moscow: Gos. izd., 1927.

Ezhegodnik gazety "Rech'" na 1914 god. St. Petersburg: Izd. redaktsii gazety "Rech'," 1914.

F. D. "Fevral'skaia revoliutsiia v Petrograde." *Krasnyi arkhiv* 41–42 (1930): 62–102.

Faleev, N. I. "Shest' mesiatsev voenno-polevoi iustitsii." *Byloe* 2 (February 1907): 43–81.

Fel'shtinskii, Iu. G., ed., *VChK-GPU: Dokumenty i materialy*. Moscow: Izd. Gumanitarnoi literatury, 1995.

"Fevral'skaia revoliutsiia 1917 goda: Dokumenty stavki verkhovnogo glavnokomanduiushchego i shtaba glavnokomanduiushchego armiami severnogo fronta." *Krasnyi arkhiv* 22 (1927): 3–70.

Filat'ev, G. "Dorevoliutsionnye voennye sudy v tsifrakh." *Katorga i ssylka* 68 (1930): 138–67.

Fuhrmann, Joseph T., ed. *The Complete Wartime Correspondence of Tsar Nicholas II and the Empress Alexandra, April 1914–March 1917*. Westport, Conn.: Greenwood, 1999.

Fuks, S., ed. "Bor'ba s revoliutsionnym dvizheniem na Kavkaze v epokhu stolypinshchiny: Iz perepiski P. A. Stolypina s gr. I. I. Vorontsovym-Dashkovym." *Krasnyi arkhiv* 34 (1929): 184–221; and 35 (1929): 128–50.

Gal'perina, B. D., et al., ed. *Sovet ministrov Rossiiskoi imperii v gody pervoi mirovoi voiny: Bumagi A. N. Iakhontova (Zapisi zasedanii i perepiska)*. St. Petersburg: Dmitrii Bulanin, 1999.

Gan, L. "Ubiistvo P. A. Stolypina." *Istoricheskii vestnik*, no. 135 (1914): 960–97.

Garvi, Peter A. *Zapiski sotsial-demokrata, 1906–1921*. Newtonville, Mass.: Oriental Research Partners, 1982.

Gelis, Iosif, ed. "Revoliutsionnaia propaganda v armii v 1916–1917 g.g." *Krasnyi arkhiv* 17 (1926): 36–50.

Genkin, [I.]. *Po tiur'mam i etapam*. St. Petersburg: Gos. izd., 1922.

Gerasimov, A. V. *Na lezvii s terroristami*. Paris: YMCA Press, 1985.

Gernet. M. N. *Istoriia tsarskoi tiur'my*. 3rd ed. 5 vols. Moscow: Gos. izd. iuridicheskoi literatury, 1961–1963.

Gershuni, Grigorii. *Iz nedavnego proshlogo*. Paris: Tribune russe, 1908.

Gessen, I. V. "Beseda s A. N. Khvostovym v fevrale 1916 g." In *Arkhiv russkoi revoliutsii*, vol. 11, ed. I. V. Gessen. 1926. Reprint, Moscow: Terra, 1993.

———. "Iz nedavnego proshlogo: Beseda s ministrov vnutrennikh del A. N. Khvostovym." *Byloe* 23 (July 1917): 56–63.

———. "V dvukh vekakh: Zhiznennyi otchet." In *Arkhiv russkoi revoliutsii*, vol. 22, ed. I. V. Gessen. 1937. Reprint, Moscow: Terra, 1993.

Gessen, Vladimir M. *Iskliuchitel'noe polozhenie*. St. Petersburg: Pravo, 1908.

Glinka, Ia. V. *Odinnadtsat' let v gosudarstvennoi dume, 1906–1917: Dnevnik i vospominaniia*. Ed. B. Vitenberg. Moscow: Novoe literaturnoe obozrenie, 2001.

Globachev, K. I. "Pravda o russkoi revoliutsii: Vospominaniia byvshego nachal'nika Petrogradskogo okhrannogo otdeleniia." Ed. Jonathan Daly and Z. I. Peregudova. *Voprosy istorii*, nos. 7–10 (2002).

Gorev, B. "Leonid Men'shchikov: Iz istorii politicheskoi politsii i provokatsii (po lichnym vospominaniiam)." *Katorga i ssylka* 10 (1924): 130–40.

Gosudarstvennaia duma: Ukazatel' k stenograficheskim otchetam. Second convocation, 1907. St. Petersburg: Gos. tip., 1907.

Gosudarstvennaia duma: Stenograficheskie otchety. St. Petersburg: Gos. tip., 1906–1916.

Grave, B. B., comp. *Burzhuaziia nakanune fevral'skoi revoliutsii*. Moscow: Gos. izd., 1927.

Gredeskul, N. A. *Terror i okhrana*. St. Petersburg: Obshchestvennaia pol'za, 1912.

Grinevich, V. *Professional'noe dvizhenie rabochikh v Rossii*. St. Petersburg: Slovo, 1908.

Gruzenberg, O. O. *Ocherki i rechi*. New York: N. Grusenberg Pregel, 1944.

Gurko, V. I. *Features and Figures of the Past: Government and Opinion in the Reign of Nicholas II.* Trans. Laura Matveev. Stanford, Calif.: Stanford University Press, 1939.

——. *Tsar' i tsaritsa.* Paris: Vozrozhdenie, 1929.

Harcave, Sydney, ed. *The Memoirs of Count Witte.* Armonk, N.Y.: M. E. Sharpe, 1990.

Iakhontov, A. "Pervyi god voiny (iiul' 1914–iiul' 1915 g.): Zapiski, zametki, materialy i vospominaniia byvshego pomoshchnika upravliaiushchego delami Soveta ministrov." Ed. R. Sh Ganelin and M. F. Florinskii. *Russkoe proshloe* 7 (1996): 245–348.

——. "Tiazhelye dni: Sekretnye zasedaniia Soveta Ministrov, 16 iiulia–2 sentiabria 1915 goda." In *Arkhiv russkoi revoliutsii,* vol. 18, ed. I. V. Gessen. 1926. Reprint, Moscow: Terra, 1993.

Iaroslavskii, E. M. "Nakanune Fevral'skoi revoliutsii v Iakutske." In *V iakutskoi nevole: Iz istorii politicheskoi ssylki v iakutskoi oblasti: Sbornik materialov i vospominanii,* ed. M. A. Braginskii et al. N.p., 1927.

Inozemtsev, M., ed. "Rasstrel ivanovo-voznesenskikh rabochikh v 1915 g." *Krasnyi arkhiv* 68 (1935): 97–118.

Iskhakov, S. M., ed. *Strana gibnet segodnia: Vospominaniia o Fevral'skoi revoliutsii 1917 goda.* Moscow: Kniga, 1991.

Iurenev, I. "'Mezhraionka,' 1911–1917 g.g.: Vospominaniia." *Proletarskaia revoliutsiia,* no. 1–2 (1924): 109–39.

Iusupov, F. F. *Konets Rasputina: Vospominaniia.* 1927. Reprint, Moscow: Otechestvo, 1990.

Ivanov, S. "Karatel'naia ekspeditsiia polk. Rimana." *Krasnyi arkhiv* 11–12 (1925): 398–420.

"Iz dnevnika A. V. Romanova za 1916–1917 gg." *Krasnyi arkhiv* 26 (1928): 186–210.

"Iz otcheta o perliustratsii dep. politsii ot 1908 g." *Krasnyi arkhiv* 27 (1928): 138–59.

"Iz otcheta Senatora Kuz'minskogo." *Pravo,* no. 10 (12 March 1906): 917–29; and no. 11: 1030–35.

"Iz pisem L. A. Rataeva." *Byloe* 23 (1917): 144–48.

"Iz zapisok A. A. Petrova." *Byloe* 13 (1910): 82–138.

Izvol'skii, A. P. *Vospominaniia.* Moscow: Mezhdunarodnye otnosheniia, 1989.

Jones, Stinton. *Russia in Revolution.* London: Herbert Jenkins, 1917.

"K arestam sredi uchashchikhsia: Ot Departamenta politsii." *Rech',* no. 109 (23 April 1913): 3.

"K ubiistvu polkovnika Karpova." *Znamia truda,* no. 25 (January 1910): 6–10.

Kaminka, A. "Neprikosnovennost' deputatov." *Pravo,* no. 22 (4 July 1906): 1980–84.

Kantor, R. M., ed. "Kratkaia avtobiografiia M. E. Bakaia." *Russkoe proshloe* 5 (1923): 153–57.

Kaptelov, B. I., I. S. Rozental', and V. V. Shelokhaev, eds. *Delo provokatora Malinovskogo.* Moscow: Respublika, 1992.

Karabchevskii, N. *Chto glaza moi videli.* 2 vols. Berlin: Izd. Ol'gi D'iakovoi, 1921.

Karelin, A. *Smertnaia kazn'.* Detroit: Izd. progressivnogo soiuza, 1923.

Kel'son, Zigfrid. "Militsiia Fevral'skoi Revoliutsii: Vozrozhdenie okhranki." *Byloe* 33 (1925): 220–35.

——. "Padenie Vremennogo Pravitel'stva." *Byloe* 34 (1925): 191–205.

Kerenskii, A. F. *Rossiia na istoricheskom povorote: Memuary.* Moscow: Respublika, 1993.

"Khronika," *Pravo,* nos. 22–33 (4 June–20 August 1906).

"Khronika vnutrennei zhizni." *Russkoe bogatstvo,* no. 12 (1908): 77–83.

Kir'ianov, Iu. I. "'Maiskie besporiadki' 1915 g. v Moskve." *Voprosy istorii,* no. 12 (1994): 137–50.

———, ed. "Perepiska pravykh i drugie materialy ob ikh deiatel'nosti v 1914–1917 godakh." *Voprosy istorii* (1996), no. 3, 142–65; no. 7, 106–29; no. 8, 78–100; no. 10, 119–43.

Kizevetter, A. *Na rubezhe dvukh stoletii: Vospominaniia, 1881–1914*. Introduction by Richard G. Robbins Jr. 1929. Reprint, Cambridge, U.K.: Oriental Research Partners, 1974.

Kobiakov, Sergei. "Krasnyi sud: Vpechatleniia zashchitnika v revoliutsionnykh tribunalakh." In *Arkhiv russkoi revoliutsii*, vol. 7, ed. I. V. Gessen. 1922. Reprint, Moscow: Terra, 1993.

Kokovtsov, Vladimir Nikolaevich. *Iz moego proshlogo: Vospominaniia 1903–1991 gg.* 2 vols. Moscow: Nauka, 1992.

"Konets M. S. Komissarova." *Vozrozhdenie* (16 November 1933), no. 3089.

Korbut, Mikhail, ed. "Uchet departamentom politsii opyta 1905 goda." *Krasnyi arkhiv* 18 (1926): 219–27.

Kornev, V. V., ed. "Dokumenty o bor'be s kadetami pri vyborakh v Gosudarstvennuiu dumu v period pervoi russkoi revoliutsii." *Sovetskie arkhivy*, no. 4 (1976): 82–86.

Koshko, A. F. *Ocherki ugolovnogo mira tsarskoi Rossii: Vospominaniia byvshego nachal'nika Moskovskoi sysknoi politsii i zaveduiushchego vsem ugolovnym rozyskom Imperii*. Moscow: Stolitsa, 1992.

Koshko, I. F. *Vospominaniia gubernatora (1905–1914 g.): Novgorod, Samara, Penza*. Petrograd: Sodruzhestvo, 1916.

Kostromskoe Okhrannoe Otdelenie: Zapiski zhandarmskogo ofitsera. Kostroma: Izd. Br. S. V. i V. V. Lbovskikh, 1917.

Koz'min, B. "K istorii razoblacheniia Azefa." *Katorga i ssylka* 32 (1927): 102–7.

———, ed. *S. V. Zubatov i ego korrespondenty: Sredi okhrannikov, zhandarmov i provokatorov*. Moscow: Gos. izd., 1928.

Krasnov, V. M. "Iz vospominanii o 1917–1920 g.g.: Prodolzhenie." In *Arkhiv russkoi revoliutsii*, vol. 11, ed. I. V. Gessen. 1923. Reprint, Moscow: Terra, 1993.

Kritsman, L. E., ed. "Nikolai Romanov o revoliutsionnom dvizhenii v armii v 1905–1906 gg." *Krasnyi arkhiv* 41–42 (1930): 215–20.

Krugliakov, B., and A. A. Shilov, eds. "Dnevnik G. O. Raukha." *Krasnyi arkhiv* 19 (1926): 83–109.

Kryzhanovskii, S. E. *Vospominaniia: Iz bumag S. E. Kryzhanovskogo, poslednego gosudarstvennogo sekretariia Rossiiskoi imperii*. Berlin, Petropolis, 1938.

Kudelli, P. "Iz zhizni peterburgskoi organizatsii RS-DRP (b.) v period reaktsii." *Krasnaia letopis'* 14 (1925): 220–23.

Kukanov, A. V. "Gerngross-Zhuchenko A. F.: 'Sotrudniki est' i budut.'" In *Politicheskii sysk v Rossii: Istoriia i sovremennost'*. St. Petersburg: Izd. Sankt-Peterburgskogo universiteta ekonomiki i finansov, 1997.

Kulikova, S. V., ed. "Iz istorii bor'by v verkhakh nakanune Fevral'skoi revoliutsii: Novye dokumenty." *Russkoe proshloe* 6 (1996): 148–80.

Kuprin, A. I. "Morskaia bolezn'." In *Sobranie sochinenii v deviati tomakh*, vol. 5. Moscow: Pravda, 1964.

Kupritsyn, V. M., R. S. Mulukaev, and V. P. Koriakov, comps. *Istoriia politsii dorevoliutsionnoi Rossii*. Moscow: Moskovskaia vysshaia shkola militsii, 1981.

Kurlov, P. G. *Gibel' imperatorskoi Rossii*. Berlin: Otto Kirchner, 1923.

Kushakova, O. A., ed. "Doneseniia tsenzorov o zapreshchenii postanovki p'es v gody stolypinskoi reaktsii." *Sovetskie arkhivy*, no. 3 (1972): 98–101.

Kuz'min, I. *Moi vospominaniia o podpol'e.* Moscow: Staryi bol'shevik, 1934.

Kuz'min-Karavaev, V. "Voprosy vnutrennei zhizni." *Vestnik Evropy* (July 1915): 375–87.

Lapin, N., ed. "Progressivnyi blok v 1915–1917 gg." *Krasnyi arkhiv* 52 (1932): 143–96.

Lazarevskii, N. I., ed. *Zakonodatel'nye akty perekhodnogo vremeni, 1904–1908 gg.: Sbornik zakonov, manifestov, ukazov.* 3rd rev. ed. St. Petersburg: Pravo, 1909.

Lemke, Mikh. *250 dnei v tsarskoi stavke: 25 sent. 1915–2 iulia 1916.* Peterburg: Gos. izd., 1920.

Lenin, Vladimir Il'ich. *Polnoe sobranie sochinenii.* 5th ed. 55 vols. Moscow: Gos. izd. Politicheskoi literatury, 1967–1970.

Levin, Alfred. *The Third Duma: Election and Profile.* Hamden, Conn.: Archon, 1973.

Levitskii, V. "Imenem Trusevicha." *Katorga i ssylka* 54 (1929): 144–51.

Levitskii, V [Vl. Tsederbaum]. "Provokator 'Nikolai-Zolotye ochki': Iz vospominanii." *Byloe* 35 (1926): 81–105.

Lipkin, A. "Nakanune protsessa bol'shevistkoi fraktsii IV Gosudarstvennoi Dumy: K istorii provokatsii v Rossii." *Katorga i ssylka* 30 (1927): 49–67.

———. "Provokator D. S. Krut: Po materialam proizvodstva Moskovskogo gubernskogo suda." *Katorga i ssylka* 27 (1269): 88–114.

———. "Provokator Nikulin-Mikulin." *Katorga i ssylka* 23 (1926): 98–119.

Liublinskii, P. "Prestupnost' i ugolovnaia statistika." In *Entsiklopedicheskii slovar' russkogo bibliograficheskogo instituta Granata,* vol. 36. Moscow: Izd. Russkogo bibliograficheskogo instituta Granata, n.d.

Livchak, B. F. "Krakh planov 'okhrany' Moskvy ot revoliutsii." *Voprosy istorii,* no. 4 (1972): 116–25.

Lomonosov, Iu. V. *Vospominaniia o martovskoi revoliutsii 1917 goda.* Moscow: Rossiiskii gosudarstvennyi gumanitarnyi universitet, 1994.

Lopukhin, A. A. *Otryvki iz vospominanii (po povodu "Vospominanii" S. Iu. Witte).* Moscow: Gos. izd, 1923.

———. *Iz itogov sluzhebnogo opyta: Nastoiashchee i budushchee russkoi politsii.* Moscow: Tip. V. M. Sablina, 1907.

Lur'e, M. L., ed. "K istorii bor'by samoderzhaviia s agrarnym dvizheniem v 1905–1907 gg." *Krasnyi arkhiv* 78 (1933): 128–60.

———. "Pod"em rabochego dvizheniia pered pervoi imperialisticheskoi voinoi." *Krasnyi arkhiv* 82 (1937): 136–63.

Lur'e, M. L., L. I. Polianskaia, and V.A. Bystrianskii, eds. *Bol'shevistskaia pechat' v tiskakh tsarskoi tsenzury, 1910–1914: Gazety "Zvezda," "Pravda": Sbornik dokumentov.* Leningrad: Gazetno-zhurnal'noe i knizhnoe izd., 1939.

L'vov, L. "Sem' let nazad: Pokusheniia na zhizn' gr. Vitte." *Russkaia mysl',* no. 2 (1914): 48–84.

Maklakov. V. A. *Iz vospominanii.* New York: Izd. imeni Chekhova, 1954.

———. *Rechi, sudebnye, dumskie i publichnye lektsii, 1904–1926.* Paris: Izd. iubileinogo komiteta, 1949.

———. *Vlast' i obshchestvennost' na zakate staroi Rossii (Vospominaniia).* Paris: n.p., 1936.

Makrinskii, S. P. "Smertnaia kazn' i bor'ba s politicheskimi prestupleniiami." *Pravo,* no. 22 (4 July 1906): 1984–92.

Maksakov, V., ed. "1912–1913 g.g.," *Proletarskaia revoliutsiia,* no. 3 (1923): 435–53.

Malinovskii, I. *Krovavaia mest' i smertnye kazni.* 2 vols. Tomsk: Tip. Sibirskogo T-va Pechatn. Dela, 1908–1909.

Mandel'shtam, O. *Shum vremeni.* Leningrad: Vremia, 1925.

Margolis, A. D., N. K. Gerasimova, and N. S. Tikhonova, eds. "Zapisnye knizhki Polkovnika G. A. Ivanishina." *Minvushee* 17 (1994): 477–572.

Markelov, K. "Pokushenie na tsareubiistvo v 1907 g. (Protsess Nikitenko, Siniavskogo, Naumova, Prokof'evoi i dr.)." *Byloe* 31 (1925): 133–76.

Martynov, Aleksandr P. *Moia sluzhba v Otdel'nom korpuse zhandarmov: Vospominaniia.* Ed. Richard Wraga. Stanford, Calif.: Stanford University Press, 1973.

Materialy k istorii russkoi kontr-revoliutsii. Vol. 1 of *Pogromy po ofitsial'nym dokumentam.* St. Peterburg: Obshchestvennaia pol'za, 1908.

Medvedev, P. N., ed. *Dnevnik Al. Bloka.* 2 vols. Leningrad: Izd. Pisatelei Leningrada, 1928.

Mel'gunov, S. P. *Vospominaniia i dnevniki.* 2 vols. Paris: Les éditeurs réunis, 1964.

Menitskii, Iv. *Revoliutsionnoe dvizhenie voennykh godov (1914–1917): Ocherki i materialy.* 2 vols. Moscow: Izd. Kommunisticheskoi akademii, 1924–1925.

———, ed. "K istorii 'Rabochei gruppy' pri Tsentral'nom voenno-promyshlennom komitete." *Krasnyi arkhiv* 57 (1933): 43–84.

Men'shchikov, Leonid. *Okhrana i revoliutsiia. K istorii tainykh politicheskikh organizatsii v Rossii.* 3 vols. Moscow: Izd. politkatorzhan, 1925–28.

———. *Russkii politicheskii sysk za granitsei.* Part 1. Paris: n. p., 1914.

Mikhailov, I. K. *Chetvert' veka podpol'shchika.* Moscow: Gos. izd. politicheskoi literatury, 1957.

Miliukov, P. N. *Vospominaniia.* Moscow: Politizdat, 1991.

Mitsit ("Martyn"), Karl. "O pytkakh v Rizhskom sysknom otdelenii." *Byloe* 13 (1910): 139–48.

Morozov, K. N., ed. "B. V. Savinkov i boevaia organizatsiia PSR v 1909–1911." *Minuvshee* 18 (1995): 243–314.

Mosolov, A. A. "Iz moikh vospominanii v Rumynii." *Illiustrirovannaia Rossiia,* no. 16 (8 April 1939): 14–15.

———. *Pri dvore poslednego Rossiiskogo imperatora: Zapiski nachal'nika kantseliarii Ministerstva Imperatorskogo Dvora.* Moscow: Ankor, 1993.

Mstislavskii, S. "Iz istorii voennogo dvizheniia: Po lichnym vospominaniiam: 'Ofitserskii' i 'Boevoi' Soiuzy 1906–1908 g.g." *Katorga i ssylka* 55 (1929): 7–31.

N. M. "Delo Petrova." *Znamia truda,* no. 25 (January 1910): 3–6.

Nabokov, Constantine. *Letters of a Russian Diplomat to an American Friend, 1906–1922.* Ed. John F. Melby and W. W. Straka. Lewiston, N.Y.: Edwin Mellen Press, 1989.

"Nabolevshie voprosy: Pis'mo k tovarishcham." *Znamia truda,* no. 25 (January 1910): 10.

Naumov, A. N. *Iz utselevshikh vospominanii, 1868–1917.* 2 vols. New York: Izd. A. K. Naumovoi i O. A. Kusevitskoi, 1954.

Nestroev, Gr. *Iz dnevnika maksimalista.* Paris: Russkoe knigoizdatel'stvo, 1910.

Nikitina, Ek. "Tornaia doroga: Tiur'ma i katorga 1905–1913 godov: Materialy k istorii." In *Deviatyi val: K desiatiletiiu osvobozhdeniia iz tsarskoi katorgi i ssylki,* ed. V. Vilenskii et al. Moscow: Izd. Politkatorzhan, 1927.

Nikitinskii, I., and S. Markov, eds. *Zagranichnaia agentura Departamenta politsii: Zapiski S. Svatikova i dokumenty zagranichnoi agentury.* Moscow: Glavnoe arkhivnoe upravlenie NKVD SSSR, 1941.

Nikolaevskii, B. *Istoriia odnogo predatelia: Terroristy i politicheskaia politsiia.* Moscow: Izd. politicheskoi literatury, 1991.

―――. *Russkie masony i revoliutsiia*. Ed. Iu. Fel'shtinskii. Moscow: Terra, 1990.

Nikol'skaia, G., ed. "Iz rezoliutsii Nikolaia Romanova." *Krasnyi arkhiv* 63 (1934): 130–32.

Notovich, F., ed. "Iz perepiski Nikolaia i Marii Romanovykh v 1907–1910 gg." *Krasnyi arkhiv* 50–51 (1932): 161–93.

"Novyi pod"em rabochego dvizheniia, 1910–1914." *Krasnyi arkhiv* 62 (1934): 223–48.

"Novyi razoblachitel'—Leonid Men'shchikov," *Russkoe slovo*, no. 201 (1 September 1910).

Obninskii, Viktor. *Devianosto dnei v odinochnom zakliuchenii: Tiuremnye zametki*. 2 parts. Moscow: n.p., 1917.

―――. *Novyi stroi*. 2 parts. Moscow: Tip. Russkogo Tovarishchestva, 1911.

―――. "Pechat' i administratsiia." In *Svoboda pechati pri obnovlennom stroe*. St. Petersburg: Obshchestvennaia pol'za, 1912.

―――. *Polgoda russkoi revoliutsii: Sbornik materialov k istorii russkoi revoliutsii (oktiabr' 1905–aprel 1906 gg.)*. Vol. 1. Moscow: Tip. I. N. Kholchev, 1906.

"Obshchee polozhenie k iuliu 1916 g. Zapiska departamenta politsii." *Byloe* 31 (1918): 24–30.

Ol'denburg, S. S. *Tsarstvovanie Imperatora Nikolaia II*. 2 vols. Munich: Izd. Obshchestva Rasprostraneniia Russkoi Natsional'noi i Patrioticheskoi Literatury, 1949.

Ordynskii, Sergei. "Pechat' i sud." In *Svoboda pechati pri obnovlennom stroe*. St. Petersburg: Obshchestvennaia pol'za, 1912.

Osipovich, N. M. *Shpiony: Rasskazy o sekretnykh sotrudnikakh*. Khar'kov: Kul'tura i trud, 1932.

"Otchet o zasedanii pervogo s"ezda Nachal'nikov Raionnykh okhrannykh otdelenii." In *Sbornik materialov i statei*, vol. 1. Moscow: Gos. izd., 1921.

Otchet po Glavnomu tiuremnomu upravleniiu za 1910 god. 2 parts. St. Petersburg: Tip. S.-Peterburgskoi tiur'my, 1912.

Panchenko, V. S. *Leninskaia nelegal'naia pechat' (1910–1914 gg.)*. Rostov-na-Donu: Izd. Rostovskogo universiteta, 1970.

Panina, A.L. "Gosudarstvennaia Duma." In *Gosudarstvennost' Rossii: Slovar'-Spravochnik*. 4 vols. to date. Moscow: Nauka, 1996–2001, 1:262–65.

Papernikov, Ia. "Fevral'skaia revoliutsiia v Irkutske." *Katorga i ssylka* 30 (1927): 93–98.

Pares, Bernard. *The Fall of the Russian Monarchy: A Study of the Evidence*. New York: Alfred A. Knopf, 1939.

Parvus [A. L. Gel'fand]. *Po tiur'mam vo vremia revoliutsii: Pobeg iz Sibiri*. St. Petersburg: Shipovnik, 1908.

Pavlov, D. B., and V. V. Shelokhaev, eds. *Rossiiskie liberaly: Kadety i oktiabristy (Dokumenty, vospominaniia, publitsistika)*. Moscow: Rosspen, 1996.

Pavlov, P. *Agenty, zhandarmy, palachi*. Petrograd: Izd. Byloe, 1922.

"Perepiska N. A. Romanova i P. A. Stolypina." *Krasnyi arkhiv* 5 (1924): 102–28.

Peretts, G. G. *V tsitadeli russkoi revoliutsii: Zapiski komendanta Tavricheskogo dvortsa, 27 fevralia—23 marta 1917 g.* 1917. Reprint, St. Petersburg: VIRD, 1997.

Pervoe maia v tsarskoi Rossii, 1890–1916 gg. Sbornik dokumentov. Moscow: Gos. izd. politicheskoi literatury, 1939.

Petrov, F., ed. "Kronshtadtskoe vosstanie 1906 g." *Krasnyi arkhiv* 77 (1936): 91–116.

Petrunkevich, Ivan Il'ich. "Iz zapisok obshchestvennogo deiatelia. Vospominaniia," ed. A. A. Kizevetter. In *Arkhiv russkoi revoliutsii*, vol. 21, ed. I. V. Gessen. 1926. Reprint, Moscow: Terra, 1993.

Piskarev, Aleksei. "Vospominaniia chlena peterburgskogo soveta rabochikh deputatov, 1905 goda." *Krasnaia letopis'* 4, no. 15 (1925): 102–15.

"Pis'ma kn. V. P. Meshcherskogo, P. A. Stolypina i N. A. Maklakova k P. G. Kurlovu." *Byloe* 21 (1918): 128–31.

"Pis'mo kn. E. N. Trubetskogo Nikolaiu Romanovu po povodu rospuska Gosudarstvennoi Dumy." *Krasnyi arkhiv* 10 (1925): 300–304.

Pletnev, V. F. *Instsenirovka: Sud nad Zubatovym i Gaponom.* Moscow: Vserossiiskii proletariat, 1925.

Pokrovskii, I. P. *Gosudarstvennyi biudzhet Rossii za poslednie desiat' let (1901–1910).* St. Petersburg: B.M. Vol'fa, 1911.

Pokrovskii, M., ed. "Perepiska Nikolaia II i Marii Fedorovny, 1905–1906 gg." *Krasnyi arkhiv* 22 (1927): 153–209.

———. "Politicheskoe polozhenie Rossii nakanune Fevral'skoi revoliutsii v zhandarmskom osveshchenii." *Krasnyi arkhiv* 17 (1926): 3–35.

———. "Zapiski F. A. Golovina." *Krasnyi arkhiv* 19 (1926): 110–49.

"Pokushenie na Dubasova: Iz neizdannykh vospominanii B. V. Savinkova." *Utro Rossii,* no. 282 (1917).

Polivanov, A. A. "Deviat' mesiatsev vo glave voennogo ministerstva (13 iunia 1915 g.—13 marta 1916 g." Parts 1–11. *Voprosy istorii* 9:123–40; 10:135–59; and 11:120–44 (1994).

Polnoe sobranie zakonov Rossiiskoi imperii. 3rd series. St. Petersburg: Gos. tip., 1906–1917.

Popov, A., ed. "Pervye dni mirovoi voiny." *Krasnyi arkhiv* 65–66 (1934): 3–68.

Pozner, S. M., ed. *Pervaia boevaia organizatsiia bol'shevikov, 1905–1907 gg.* Moscow: Staryi Bol'shevik, 1934.

"Pravitel'stvennoe soobshchenie." *Rossiia,* no. 218 (24 August 1906).

"Pravitel'stvuiushchemu senatu, po pervomu dempartamentu, Senatora, revizuiushchego po VYSOCHAISHEMU poveleniiu Moskovskoe Gradonachal'stvo, Donoshenie, 13 November 1908." N.p., n.d.

Pribylev, A. V. *Zinaida Zhuchenko: Iz vospominanii A. V.Pribyleva.* Moscow: Byloe, 1919.

"Prikaz g.-m. Dzhunkovskogo." *Rech',* no. 58 (1 March 1913).

Programma kursa "Istoriia politicheskogo rozyska, razvedki i kontrrazvedki v Rossii do 1917 g." Moscow: Glavnoe arkhivnoe upravlenie NKVD SSSR, 1946.

Protokoly tsentral'nogo komiteta Konstitutsionno-demokraticheskoi partii, 1915–1920. 6 vols. Moscow: Rosspen, 1998.

Prussakov, A. I. *Kto ubil Gertsenshteina?* St. Petersburg: n.p., 1909.

"Psikhologiia predatel'stva: Iz vospominanii 'sotrudnika.'" *Byloe* 27–28 (1924): 225–37.

Raskol'nikov, F., ed. "Volneniia vo flote v 1915 godu." *Krasnyi arkhiv* 9 (1925): 94–103.

"Reabilitatsiia," *Rech',* no. 57 (28 February 1913): 1.

Rediger, Aleksandr. *Istoriia moei zhizni: Vospominaniia voennogo ministra.* 2 vols. Moscow: Kanon-Press-Ts.—Kuchkovo pole, 1999.

Revoliutsionnaia mysl' 1 (April 1908): 1.

"Revoliutsionnoe dvizhenie v Rossii, 1772–1913 g.g. v skhematicheskom izobrazhenii po dannym departamenta politsii: Skhema istoricheskogo razvitiia partii S.-R. i S.-D. v Rossii." *Krasnaia letopis'* 1 (1924): 280.

"Revoliutsionnoe dvizhenie v voiskakh vo vremia mirovoi voiny." *Krasnyi arkhiv* 4 (1923): 417–21.

Rodzianko, M. V. "Krushenie Imperii: Zapiski predsedatelia Russkoi Gosudarstvennoi Dumy." In *Arkhiv russkoi revoliutsii*, vol. 17, ed. I. V. Gessen. 1926. Reprint, Moscow: Terra, 1993.

Romanov, Aleksandr Mikhailovich, Velikii kniaz'. *Kniga vospominanii.* Moscow: Sovremennik, 1991.

Rozenberg, Vladimir. "Neskol'ko tsifrovykh itogov." In *Svoboda pechati pri obnovlennom stroe.* St. Petersburg: Obshchestvennaia pol'za, 1912.

Sadikov, P., ed. "P. A. Stolypin i smertnaia kazn' v 1908 g." *Krasnyi arkhiv* 12 (1926): 215–21.

"Samoubiistvo S. V. Zubatova." *Utro Rossii*, no. 62 (5 March 1917): 7.

Sapov, V. V., ed. *Vekhi: Pro i contra.* St. Petersburg: Izd. Russkogo Khristianskogo gumanitarnogo instituta, 1998.

Savich, N. V. *Vospominaniia.* St. Peterburg: Logos, 1993.

Savinkov, Boris. "Vospominaniia terrorista." In *Izbrannoe.* Moscow: Politizdat, 1990.

Sazonov, S. D. *Vospominaniia.* Paris: Knigoizd. E. Sial'skoi, 1927.

Schneiderman, Jeremiah. "From the Files of the Moscow [sic] Gendarme Corps: A Lecture on Combating Revolution." *Canadian Slavic Studies*, 2, no. 1 (Spring 1968): 86–99.

Selivanov, A. "Provokatorsha A. M. Romanova: Iz vpechatlenii vstrechi." *Katorga i ssylka*, 23 (1926): 145–48.

Semennikov, V. P. *Monarkhiia pered krusheniem, 1914–1917: Bumagi Nikolaia II i drugie dokumenty. Stat'i V. P. Semennikova.* Moscow: Gos. izd., 1927.

Serebrennikov, A., ed. *Soblazn sotsializma: Revoliutsiia v Rossii i evrei.* Paris: YMCA Press–Russkii put', 1995.

Sergeev, A. A. "Zhandarmy-istoriki: Bibliograficheskaia zametka." *Golos minuvshego* 9–10 (1917): 365–80.

Shakhovskoi, V. N. *"Sic transit gloria mundi" (Tak prokhodit mirskaia slava), 1893–1917 gg.* Paris: IMPR. de Navarre, 1952.

Shavel'skii, Georgii. *Vospominaniia poslednego protopresvitera russkoi armii i flota.* 2 vols. 1954. Reprint, Moscow: Krutitskoe patriarshee podvor'e, 1996.

Shchegolev, P. E. *Okhranniki, agenty, palachi.* Moscow: Prosvet, 1992.

———. "Russkii Rokambol': I. F. Manasevich-Manuilov po arkhivnym materialam." In *Okhranniki, agenty, palachi*, ed. P. E. Shchegolev. Moscow: Prosvet, 1992.

———, ed. *Padenie tsarskogo rezhima: Stenograficheskie otchety doprosov i pokazanii dannykh v 1917 g. v Chrezvychainoi Sledstvennoi Komissii Vremennogo Pravitel'stva.* 7 vols. Leningrad: Gos. izd., 1925.

Shebalov, A., ed. "Vopros o smertnoi kazni za politicheskie prestupleniia nakanune pervoi Dumy: Arkhivnye materialy po istorii 1905–1906 g.g." *Katorga i ssylka* 17 (1925): 169–97.

Shidlovskii, S. I. *Vospominaniia.* 2 vols. Berlin: Otto Kirchner, 1923.

Shipov, D. N. *Vospominaniia i dumy o perezhitom.* Moscow: Izd. M. i S. Sabashnikovykh, 1918.

"Shkola filerov." *Byloe* 25 (September 1917): 44–49.

Shliapnikov, A. G. *Kanun semnadtsatogo goda. Semnadtsatyi god.* 2 vols. Moscow: Izd. politicheskoi literatury, 1992.

Shul'gin, V. *Gody-Dni-1920.* Moscow: Novosti, 1990.

Shvarts, A. N. *Moia perepiska so Stolypinym. Moi vospominaniia o Gosudare*. Ed. K. A. Bakh. Moscow: Greko-latinskii kabinet, 1994.

Sidorov, A. A. "Iz zapisok moskovskogo tsenzora: 1909–1917." *Golos minuvshego* 1/3 (January–March 1918): 93–114.

Sidorov, N. A., and L. I. Tiutiunnik. "V. L. Burtsev i rossiiskoe osvoboditel'noe dvizhenie (po materialam TsGAOR SSSR i TsPA IML pri TsK KPSS)." *Sovetskie arkhivy* no. 2 (1989): 56–62.

Sidorov, N. I., ed. "Mobilizatsiia reaktsii v 1906 g." *Krasnyi arkhiv* 32 (1929): 158–82.

Sidorovnin, Gennadii, ed. *Stolypin: Zhizn' i smert': Sbornik*. 2nd ed. Saratov: Sootechestvennik, 1997.

Skalichev, I. "Azef v roli kontrabandista." *Katorga i ssylka* 17 (1925): 131–34.

Smirnov, E. *Kalendar' russkoi revoliutsii*. Ed. V. L. Burtsev. Petrograd: Shipovnik, 1917.

Sobranie uzakonenii i rasporiazhenii pravitel'stva, izdavaemoe pri Pravitel'stvuiushchem senate. St. Petersburg: Senatskaia tip., 1906–1917.

Sokolinskii, A. V. "Fidlerovskoe delo: Vospominaniia uchastnika." *Katorga i ssylka*, 31 (1927): 7–25.

Sorokin, Pitirim A. *A Long Journey: The Autobiography of Pitirim A. Sorokin*. New Haven, Conn.: College and University Press, 1963.

Sosnovskaia, L. P. "Uchastie politicheskikh ssyl'nykh v izdanii 'Sibirskogo zhurnala' i 'Sibirskogo obozreniia.'" In *Ssylka i obshchestvenno-politicheskaia zhizn' v Sibiri (XVIII—nachalo XX v.)*, ed. L. M. Goriushkin. Novosibirsk: Nauka, 1978.

"Soveshchanie gubernatorov v 1916 g." *Krasnyi arkhiv* 33 (1929): 145–69.

Sovet ministrov Rossiiskoi imperii, 1905–1906 gg.: Dokumenty i materialy. Leningrad: Nauka, 1990.

Spiridonova, M. A. "Iz zhizni na Nerchinskoi katorge." *Katorga i ssylka* 14 (1925): 185–204; and 16 (1925): 115–33.

Spiridovitch, A. I. *Histoire du terrorisme russe, 1886–1917*. Trans. Vladimir Lazarevski. Paris: Payot, 1930.

———. *Istoriia bol'shevizma v Rossii ot vozniknoveniia do zakhvata vlasti, 1883–1903–1917*. Paris: Franko-Russkaia Pechat', 1922.

———. *Les dernières années de la cour de Tsarskoïe-Selo*. 2 vols. Trans. M. Jeanson. Paris: Payot, 1928.

———. "Pri tsarskom rezhime." In *Arkhiv russkoi revoliutsii*, vol. 15, ed. I. V. Gessen. 1926. Reprint, Moscow: Terra, 1993.

———. *Raspoutine, 1863–1916, d'après les documents russes et les archives privés de l'auteur*. Paris: Payot, 1935.

———. *Velikaia voina i fevral'skaia revoliutsiia, 1914–1917 g.g.* 3 vols. New York: Vseslavianskoe izd., 1960.

———. *Zapiski zhandarma*. 1930. Reprint, Moscow: Khudozhestvennaia literatura, 1991.

Spisok b. unter-ofitserov i ofitserov zhandarmskikh uchrezhdenii i okhrannykh otdelenii, chinov b. Departamenta politsii. Chast. 1–aia. Sostavlen po dannym Arkhiva revoliutsii RSFSR i mestnykh arkhivov. Moscow: OGPU, 1929.

Spisok byv. chinov Otdel'nogo Korpusa zhandarmov. Sostavlen po dannym Arkhiva revoliutsii RSFSR. Moscow: OGPU, 1927.

Spisok obshchego sostava chinov Otdel'nogo Korpusa Zhandarmov. St. Petersburg: Tip. Shtaba Otdel'nogo Korpusa Zhandarmov, 1907–1911.

Spisok vysshykh chinov tsentral'nykh ustanovlenii Ministerstva vnutrennikh del. Part 1. St. Petersburg: Tip. Ministerstva vnutrennikh del, 1914.

Spravochnik-spisok ofitserskogo i riadovogo sostava zhandarmskikh uchrezhdenii, Okhran-nykh otdelenii, agentov okhrannoi agentury dvortsovogo komendanta i chinov Departamenta politsii MVD tsarskoi Rossii. Moscow: GAU NKVD SSSR, 1940.

Stasova, E. D. "Partiinaia rabota v ssylke i v Petrograde." In *V gody podpol'ia: Sbornik vospominanii, 1910 g.-fevral' 1917 g.* Moscow: Izd. politicheskoi literatury, 1964.

Stepun, Fedor. *Byvshee i nesbyvsheesia.* 2nd ed. 2 vols. St. Petersburg: Aleteia, 2000.

Stolypin, Petr Arkad'evich. *Nam nuzhna velikaia Rossiia: Polnoe sobranie rechei v Gosudarstvennoi dume i Gosudarstvennom sovete, 1906–1911.* Moscow: Molodaia gvardiia, 1991.

Svatikov, S. *Russkii politicheskii sysk za-granitsei: Po dokumentam Parizhskogo Arkhiva Zagranichnoi Agentury Departamenta Politsii.* Rostov-na-Donu: n.p., 1918.

Sverdlov, Ia. M. "Massovaia ssylka: 1908–1916." In *Izbrannye proizvedeniia: Stat'i, rechi, pis'ma.* Moscow: Politizdat, 1976.

"Tablitsy mestnostei Rossii, nakhodiashchikhsia na iskliuchitel'nom polozhenii." *Pravo,* no. 10 (12 March 1906): 909–16.

Tagantsev, N. S. *Perezhitoe: Uchrezhdenie Gosudarstvennoi Dumy v 1905–1906 gg.* Petrograd: Gos. tip., 1919.

———. *Russkoe ugolovnoe pravo: Letktsii: Chast' obshchaia.* 2 vols. 1902. Reprint, Moscow: Nauka, 1994.

———. *Smertnaia kazn': Sbornik statei N. S. Tagantseva.* St. Petersburg: Gos. Tip., 1913.

Tarnovskii, E. N. "Dvizhenie prestupnosti v rossiiskoi imperii za 1899–1908 g.g." *Zhurnal Ministerstva iustitsii* 15, no. 9 (1909): 52–99.

Tatarov, I., ed. "Bor'ba S. Iu. Vitte s agrarnoi revoliutsiei." *Krasnyi arkhiv* 31 (1928): 81–102.

———, ed. "Programma soiuza russkogo naroda pered Fevral'skoi revoliutsiei." *Krasnyi arkhiv* 20 (1927): 242–44.

Tikhomirov, Lev. *Pochemu ia perestal byt' revoliutsionerom.* Rev. ed. Moscow: Tip. vil'de, 1895.

Tiutchev, N. S. *V ssylke i drugie vospominaniia.* Ed. A. V. Pribyleva. Leningrad: Priboi, 1925.

Tkhorzhevskii, I. I. *Poslednii Peterburg: Vospominaniia kamergera.* Ed. S. S. Tkhorzhevskii. St. Petersburg: Aleteia, 1999.

Tobolin, ed. "Iz arkhiva Shcheglovitova." *Krasnyi arkhiv* 15 (1926): 104–17.

Tolstaia, L. I., ed., *Vospominaniia ministra narodnogo prosveshcheniia Grafa I. I. Tolstogo, 31 oktiabria 1905 g.—24 aprelia 1906 g.* Moscow: Greko-latinskii kabinet, 1997.

Tolstoi, Pavel. "Obiazatel'nye postanovleniia o pechati v poriadke okhrany." In *Svoboda pechati pri obnovlennom stroe.* St. Petersburg: Obshchestvennaia pol'za, 1912.

Tsereteli, I. G. *Vospominaniia o fevral'skoi revoliutsii.* 2 vols. Paris: Mouton, 1963.

Tsiavlovskii, M., ed. *Bol'sheviki: Dokumenty po istorii bol'shevizma s 1903 po 1916 god byvshego Moskovskogo Okhrannogo Otdeleniia.* Ed. I. E. Gorelov. 3rd ed. Moscow: Izd. politicheskoi literatury, 1990.

———. "Moskovskaia okhranka v 1915 g. (Doklad S. E. Vissarionova o proizvedennoi im v dekabre 1915 g. revizii b. Mosk. Okhrannogo Otdeleniia tovarishchu ministra vnutr. del S. P. Beletskomu)." *Golos minuvshego* 1–3 (January-March 1918): 252–87.

"Tsirkuliar o V. L. Burtseve." *Byloe* 27–28 (November-December 1917): 125.

Tsvetkov-Prosveshchenskii, A. K. "Rabochie vnov' podnialis' na bor'bu." In *V gody podpol'ia: Sbornik vospominanii, 1910 g.-fevral' 1917 g.* Moscow: Izd. politicheskoi literatury, 1964.

Tsvigun, S. K., et al., eds. *V. I. Lenin i VChK: Sbornik dokumentov (1917–1922 gg.)*. Moscow: Izd. Politicheskoi literatury, 1975.

Tyrkova-Villiams, A. *Na putiakh k svobode*. New York: Izd. imeni Chekhova, 1952.

Utevskii, B. S. *Vospominaniia iurista*. Moscow: Iuridicheskaia literatura, 1989.

"V ianvare i fevrale 1917 g.: Iz donesenii sekretnykh agentov A. D. Protopopova." *Byloe* 13 (1918): 91–123.

"V kontse 1916 g." *Byloe* 30 (1918): 148–56.

Valk, S. "K istorii aresta i suda nad sotsial-demokraticheskoi fraktsiei II Gosudarstvennoi Dumy." *Krasnyi arkhiv* 16 (1926): 76–86.

Varfolomeeva, Iu. V., ed. "Eto chisto politseiskaia mera ne dolzhna iskhodit' ot ministra pravosudiia . . . : Pis'mo A. S. Zarudnogo A. F. Kerenskomu." *Otechestvennye arkhivy*, no. 5 (1999): 81–84.

Vassiliyev, A. T. *The Ochrana: The Russian Secret Police*. Ed. Rene Füllöp-Miller. Philadelphia: J. B. Lippincott, 1930.

Viazmitinov, M. N. "Zhandarmy i armiia: Politicheskii sysk i vooruzhennye sily Rossii v revoliutsii 1905–1907 gg." *Voenno-istoricheskii zhurnal*, no. 1 (1995): 89–93.

Viktorskii, S. N. *Istoriia smertnoi kazni v Rossii i sovremennoe ee sostoianie*. Moscow: Tip. Imperatorskogo Moskovskogo Universiteta, 1912.

Vinaver, M. *Konflikty v pervoi dume*. St. Petersburg: M. Ia. Minkov, 1907.

Vishniak, Mark. *Dan' proshlomu*. New York: Izd. imeni Chekhova, 1954.

Vitenberg, V. M., A. V. Ostrovskii, and Z. I. Peregudova, eds. "Vo glave Departamenta politsii: Formuliarnyi spisok o sluzhbe K. D. Kafafova." *Iz glubiny vremen*, no. 11 (1999): 241–43.

———. "Vo glave Departamenta politsii: Formuliarnyi spisok o sluzhbe M. I. Trusevicha." *Iz glubiny vremen*, no. 8 (1997): 195–98.

———. "Vo glave Departamenta politsii: Formuliarnyi spisok o sluzhbe N. P. Zueva." *Iz glubiny vremen*, no. 8 (1997): 199–206.

———. "Vo glave Departamenta politsii: Formuliarnyi spisok o sluzhbe R. G. Mollova." *Iz glubiny vremen*, no. 11 (1999): 237–40.

———. "Vo glave Departamenta politsii: Formuliarnyi spisok o sluzhbe S. P. Beletskogo." *Iz glubiny vremen*, no. 9 (1997): 184–201.

———. "Vo glave Departamenta politsii: Formuliarnyi spisok o sluzhbe V. A. Briunde-Sent-Ippolita." *Iz glubiny vremen*, no. 11 (1999): 234–36.

Vodovozov, V., ed. "Tsarskosel'skoe soveshchanie." *Byloe* 26 (October 1917): 183–245.

Voeikov, V. N. *S tsarem i bez tsaria: Vospominaniia poslednego Dvortsovogo Komendanta Gosudaria Imperatora Nikolaia II*. 1936. Reprint, Moscow: Voennoe izd., 1995.

Voinova, K. "Iiul'skie dni 1914 goda v Moskve: Khronika sobytii," *Proletarskaia revoliutsiia* 30 (July 1924): 215–23.

Voitinskii, Vladimir. "Delo sotsial-demokraticheskoi fraktsii 2-oi Gosudarstvennoi Dumy i voennaia organizatsiia." *Letopis' revoliutsii* 1 (1923): 99–124.

Volkov, A. *Petrogradskoe okhrannoe otdelenie*. Petrograd: Znanie-sila, 1917.

"Vospominaniia S. P. Beletskogo." In *Arkhiv russkoi revoliutsii*, vol. 12. 1923. Reprint, Moscow: Terra, 1993.

Vrangel', Baron P. N. *Vospominaniia: Ot krepostnogo prava do bol'shevikov*. Berlin: Slovo, 1924.

Witte, S. Iu. *Vospominaniia*. 3 vols. Tallinn: Skif-Aleks, 1994.

"Za nedeliu," *Rech'* (15 June 1915): 1.

Zapros ob Azefe v Gosudarstvennoi dume (Zasedaniia 50 i 51–oe, po stenograficheskomu otchetu). St. Petersburg: Ekaterinskoe pechatnoe delo, 1909.

Zaslavskii, D. "Iz perepiski tsarskikh sanovnikov nakanune voiny i revoliutsii." *Krasnyi arkhiv* 61 (1933): 179–85.

Zavadskii, S. V. "Na velikom izlome: Otchet grazhdanina o perezhitom v 1916–1917 godakh." *Arkhiv russkoi revoliutsii,* vol. 11, ed. I. V. Gessen. 1926. Reprint, Moscow: Terra, 1993.

Zavarzin, P. P. *Rabota tainoi politsii.* Paris: Izd. avtora, 1924.

———. *Zhandarmy i revoliutsionery: Vospominaniia.* Paris: Izd. avtora, 1930.

Zelikson-Bobrovskaia, Ts. [S.]. *Zapiski riadovogo podpol'shchika (1894–1914).* 2 parts. Moscow: Gos. izd., 1922.

Zenzinov, Vladimir. *Iz zhizni revoliutsionera.* Paris: n.p., 1919.

Zorin, S. *Potomki provokatora Azefa.* Petrograd: Gos. izd., 1921.

Zverev, R., ed. "Iz zapisok A. F. Redigera." *Krasnyi arkhiv* 60 (1933): 92–133.

SECONDARY SOURCES

Anan'ich, B. V., et al. *Krizis samoderzhaviia v Rossii, 1895–1917.* Leningrad: Nauka, 1984.

Anan'ich, B. V., R. Sh. Ganelin, and V. M. Paneiakh, eds. *Vlast' i reformy: Ot samoderzhavnoi k sovetskoi Rossii.* St. Petersburg: Dmitrii Bulanin, 1996.

Andreev, D. A. "Evoliutsiia politicheskoi doktriny russkogo masonstva, 1906–1917 gg." *Vestnik moskovskogo universiteta. Istoriia,* series 8, no. 4 (1993): 3–12.

Andronov, S. A. *Boevoe oruzhie partii: Gazeta "Pravda" v 1912–1917 godakh.* Leningrad: Lenizdat, 1984.

Ansimov, N. N. *Bor'ba bolshevikov protiv tainoi politicheskoi politsii samoderzhaviia, 1903–1917.* Sverdlovsk: Izd. Ural'skogo universiteta, 1989.

Arutiunov, G. A. *Rabochee dvizhenie v Rossii v period novogo revoliutsionnogo pod"ema 1910–1914.* Moscow: Nauka, 1975.

Ascher, Abraham. *P. A. Stolypin: The Search for Stability in Late Imperial Russia.* Stanford, Calif.: Stanford University Press, 2001.

Ascher, Abraham. *The Revolution of 1905: Authority Restored.* Stanford, Calif.: Stanford University Press, 1992.

Ascherson, Neal. "Baleful Smile of the Crocodile." *London Review of Books* (8 March 2001).

Avrekh, A. Ia. "Chrezvychainaia sledstvennaia komissiia Vremennogo pravitel'stva: Zamysel i ispolnenie." *Istoricheskie zapiski* 118 (1990): 72–101.

———. "Dokumenty Departamenta politsii kak istochnik po izucheniiu liberal'no-oppozitsionnogo dvizheniia v gody pervoi mirovoi voiny." *Istoriia SSSR,* no. 6 (1987): 32–49.

———. *Masony i revoliutsiia.* Moscow: Izd. politicheskoi literatury, 1990.

———. *Stolypin i Tret'ia duma.* Moscow: Nauka, 1968.

———. *Tsarizm nakanune sverzheniia.* Moscow: Nauka, 1989.

Baberowski, Jörg. *Autokratie und Justiz. Zum Verhältnis von Rechsstaatlichkeit und Rückständigkeit im ausgehenden Zarenreich, 1864–1914.* Frankfurt am Main: Vittorio Klostermann, 1996.

Bakhturina, A. Iu. "Gosudarstvennoe upravlenie okrainami Rossiiskoi Imperii v gody pervoi mirovoi voiny." In *1917 god v sud'bakh Rossii i mira: Fevral'skaia revoliutsiia ot novykh istochnikov k novomu osmysleniiu,* ed. P. V. Volobuev et al. Moscow: Institut rossiiskoi istorii RAN, 1997.

Baluev, B. P. "Delo A. A. Lopukhina." *Voprosy istorii,* no. 1 (1996): 134–43.

Beliaev, S. G. "Peterburgskie bankiry v nachale XX v." *Iz glubiny vremen,* no. 6 (1996): 3–22.

Berezhnoi, A. F. *Tsarskaia tsenzura i bor'ba bol'shevikov za svobodu pechati (1985–1914).* Leningrad: Izd. Leningradskogo universiteta, 1967.

Berlieu, Jean-Marc. "The Professionalization of the Police under the Third Republic in France, 1875–1914." In *Policing Western Europe: Politics, Professionalization and Public Order, 1850–1940,* ed. Clive Emsley and Barbara Weinberger. New York, Greenwood, 1991.

Bol'shaia sovetskaia entsiklopediia. 66 vols. Moscow: Izd. Sovetskaia entsiklopediia, 1926–1947.

Bonnell, Victoria E. *Roots of Rebellion: Workers' Politics and Organizations in St. Petersburg and Moscow, 1900–1914.* Berkeley: University of California Press, 1983.

Borodin, A. P. *Gosudarstvennyi sovet Rossii (1906–1917).* Kirov: Viatka, 1999.

Brachev, V. S. *Mastera politicheskogo syska dorevoliutsionnoi Rossii.* St. Petersburg: Nestor, 1998.

Bradley, Joseph. "Russia's Parliament of Public Opinion: Association, Assembly, and the Autocracy, 1906–1914." In *Reform in Modern Russia: Progress or Cycle?* ed. Theodore Taranovski. Washington, D.C.: Woodrow Wilson Center Press, 1995.

———. "Voluntary Associations, Civil Culture, and *Obshchestvennost'* in Moscow." In *Between Tsar and People: Educated Society and the Quest for Public Identity in Late Imperial Russia,* ed. Edith W. Clowes, Samuel D. Kassow, and James L. West. Princeton, N.J.: Princeton University Press, 1991.

Brainerd, Michael C. "The Octobrists and the Gentry in the Russian Social Crisis of 1913–14." *Russian Review* 38 (April 1979): 160–79.

Bronskaia, Jean, and Vladimir Chuguev, eds. *Kto est' kto v Rossii i byvshem SSSR: Vydaiushchiesia lichnosti byvshego Sovetskogo Soiuza, Rossii i emigratsii.* Moscow: Terra, 1994.

Budnitskii, O. V. *Terrorizm v rossiiskom osvoboditel'nom divizhenii: Ideologiia, etika, psikhologiia (vtoraia polovina XIX–nachalo XX v.)* Moscow: Rosspen, 2000.

———, ed. *Evrei i russkaia revoliutsiia: Materialy i issledovaniia.* Moscow: Gesharim, 1999.

Bushnell, John. *Mutiny amid Repression: Russian Soldiers in the Revolution of 1905–1906.* Bloomington, Ind.: Indiana University Press, 1985.

Chapman, Brian. *Police State.* New York: Praeger, 1970.

Chermenskii, E. D. *Burzhuaziia i tsarizm v pervoi russkoi revoliutsii.* Moscow: Mysl', 1970.

Cherniaev, V. Iu. "Zapadnoe semia na russkom pole: Eticheskii kommunizm perioda revoliutsii i grazhdanskoi voiny." In *Russkaia emigratsiia do 1917 goda—laboratoriia liberal'noi i revoliutsionnoi mysli.* St. Petersburg: Evropeiskii Dom, 1997.

Chubinskii, M. P. "God revoliutsii, 1917: Iz dnevnika." In *1917 god v sud'bakh Rossii i mira: Fevral'skaia revoliutsiia ot novykh istochnikov k novomu osmysleniiu,* ed. P. V. Volobuev et al. Moscow: Institut rossiiskoi istorii RAN, 1997.

Clowes, Edith W., Samuel D. Kassow, and James L. West, eds. *Between Tsar and People: Society and the Quest for Public Identity in Late Imperial Russia.* Princeton, N.J.: Princeton University Press, 1991.

Conroy, Mary Schaeffer. *Peter Arkad'evich Stolypin: Practical Politics in Late Tsarist Russia.* Boulder, Colo.: Westview, 1976.

Coquin, F. X. *1905: La Révolution russe manquée*. Brussels: Editions complexe, 1985.

Costello, David R. "*Novoe vremia* and the Conservative Dilemma, 1911–1914." *Russian Review* 37 (January 1978): 30–50.

Cross, Truman B. "Geography and Arbitrariness: Factors in Russian Revolutionism." *Slavic Review* 24 (December 1965): 706–708.

Daly, Jonathan W. *Autocracy under Siege: Security Police and Opposition in Russia, 1866–1905*. DeKalb: Northern Illinois University Press, 1998.

———. "Pravitel'stvo, pressa i antigosudarstvennaia deiatel'nost' v Rossii, 1906–1917 gg." *Voprosy istorii*, no. 10 (2001): 25–45.

———. "Security Services in Imperial and Soviet Russia," *Kritika* (Fall 2003): 955–73.

D'iachkov, V. L., and L. G. Protasov. "Velikaia voina i obshchestvennoe soznanie: Prevratnosti indoktrinatsii i vospriiatiia." In *Rossiia i pervaia mirovaia voina: Materialy mezhdunarodnogo nauchnogo kollokviuma*, ed. N. N. Smirnov et al. St. Petersburg: Dmitrii Bulanin, 1999.

Diakin, V. S. *Russkaia burzhuaziia i tsarizm v gody pervoi mirovoi voiny, 1914–1917*. Leningrad: Nauka, 1967.

———. *Samoderzhavie, burzhuaziia i dvorianstvo v 1907–1911 gg*. Leningrad: Nauka, 1978.

Dvorianov, V. N. *V sibirskoi dal'nei storone . . . (Ocherki istorii politicheskoi katorgi i ssylki, 60-e gody XVIII v.—1917 g.)*. 2nd rev. ed. Ed. A. F. Khatskevich. Minsk: Nauka i tekhnika, 1985.

Elwood, R. Carter. "The Malinovskii Affair: 'A Very Fishy Business.'" *Revolutionary Russia* 11 (June 1998): 1–16.

———. *Roman Malinovskii: A Life without a Cause*. Newtonville, Mass.: Oriental Research Partners, 1977.

———. *Russian Social Democracy in the Underground: A Study of the RSDRP in the Ukraine, 1907–1914*. Assen, the Netherlands: Van Gorcum & Co., 1974.

Emmons, Terence. *The Formation of Political Parties and the First National Elections in Russia*. Cambridge, Mass.: Harvard University Press, 1983.

"Evno Azef: Istoriia ego predatel'stva." *Byloe* 2 (1917): 195.

Figes, Orlando. *A People's Tragedy: The Russian Revolution, 1891–1924*. New York: Penguin, 1998.

Figes, Orlando, and Boris Kolonitskii. *Interpreting the Russian Revolution: The Language and Symbols of 1917*. New Haven: Yale University Press, 1999.

Florinskii, M. F. *Krizis gosudarstvennogo upravleniia v Rossii v gody pervoi mirovoi voiny: Sovet ministrov v 1914–1917 gg*. Leningrad: Izd. LGU, 1988.

Fricke, Dieter. *Bismarcks Prätorianer: Die Berliner politische Polizei im Kampf gegen die deutsche Arbeiterbewegung (1871–1898)*. Berlin: Rütten & Loening, 1962.

Fuller, William C. *Civil-Military Conflict in Imperial Russia, 1881–1914*. Princeton, N.J.: Princeton University Press, 1985.

Galvazin, Sergei. *Okhrannye struktury Rossiiskoi imperii: Formirovanie apparata, analiz operativnoi praktiki*. Moscow: Sovershenno sekretno, 2001.

Ganelin, R. Sh. "24 Fevralia 1917 g." *Klio* 2 (1998): 75–82.

———. "Diskussiia." In *Rabochie i intelligentsiia Rossii v epokhu reform i revoliutsii, 1861–fevral' 1917 g*. St. Petersburg: Blits, 1997.

Gatrell, Peter. "'Constitutional Russia': A Response." *Revolutionary Russia* 9 (June 1996): 82–94.

Geifman, Anna. *Entangled in Terror: The Azef Affair and the Russian Revolution*. Wilmington, Del.: Scholarly Resources, 2000.

————. *Thou Shalt Kill: Revolutionary Terrorism in Russia, 1894–1917*. Princeton, N.J.: Princeton University Press, 1993.

Glazunov, M. M., and B. A. Mitrofanov. "Sudebnyi protsess nad pervym Peterburgskim Sovetom rabochikh deputatov." *Sovetskoe gosudarstvo i pravo*, no. 12 (1975): 13–20.

Golinkov, D. L. *Krushenie antisovetskogo podpol'ia v SSSR*. 2 vols. Moscow: Politicheskaia literatura, 1978.

Golubeva. O. D. *V. D. Bonch-Bruevich—Izdatel'*. Moscow: Kniga, 1972.

Gorelov, I. E. *Bol'sheviki i legal'nye organizatsii rabochego klassa*. Moscow: Vysshaia shkola, 1980.

Gorodnitskii, R. A. *Boevaia organizatsiia partii sotsialistov-revoliutsionerov v 1901–1911 gg*. Moscow: Rosspen, 1998.

Grekov, N. V. *Russkaia kontrrazvedka v 1905–1915 gg.: Shpionomaniia i real'nye problemy*. Moscow: Moskovskii obshchestvennyi nauchnyi fond, 2000.

Haimson, Leopold H. "'The Problem of Political and Social Stability in Urban Russia on the Eve of War and Revolution' Revisited." *Slavic Review* 59 (Winter 2000): 848–75.

————. "The Problem of Social Stability in Urban Russia, 1905–1917." In *The Structure of Russian History: Interpretative Essays*, ed. M. Cherniavsky. New York: Random House, 1970.

Hasegawa, Tsuyoshi. "Crime, Police, and Mob Justice in Petrograd during the Russian Revolutions of 1917." In *Religious and Secular Forces in Late Tsarist Russia: Essays in Honor of Donald W. Treadgold*, ed. Charles E. Timberlake. Seattle: University of Washington Press, 1992.

————. *The February Revolution: Petrograd, 1917*. Seattle: University of Washington Press, 1981.

Hildermeier, Manfred. *Die Sozialrevolutionäre Partei Russlands. Agrarsozialismus und Modernisierung im Zarenreich (1900–1914)*. Cologne: Böhlau Verlag, 1978.

Hughes, Michael. "'Revolution Was in the Air': British Officials in Russia during the First World War." *Journal of Contemporary History* 31 (1996): 75–97.

Iakovlev, L. S. "Kontrrazvedka Rossii nakanune i v gody pervoi mirovoi voiny." In *Istoricheskie chteniia na Lubianke, 1997 god: Rossiiskie spetssluzhby: Istoriia i sovremennost'*, ed. A. A. Zdanovich, M. N. Petrov, and V. N. Khaustov. Moscow: Velikii Novgorod, 1999.

Izmozik, V. S. "Pervye sovetskie instruktsii po perliustratsii." *Minuvshee* 21 (1997): 155–74.

————. "Rossiiskie chinovniki 'Chernykh kabinetov' v nachale XX v." In *Rossiia v XIX–XX vv.: Sbornik statei k 70-letiiu so dnia rozhdeniia Rafaila Sholomovicha Ganelina*, ed. A. A. Furenko. St. Petersburg: Dmitrii Bulanin, 1998.

Izmozik, V. S., and B. M. Vitenberg. "Kto Vy, gospodin Krivosh?" *Iz glubiny vremen*, no. 11 (1999): 161–72.

Kalmykov, A. Iu. "K voprosu o roli 'chernykh kabinetov' v sisteme politicheskogo syska v nachale XX veka." In *Politicheskii sysk v Rossii: Istoriia i sovremennost'*. St. Petersburg: Izd. Sankt-Peterburgskogo universiteta ekonomiki i finansov, 1997.

Kaptelov, B. I., and Z. I. Peregudova. "Byl li Stalin agentom okhranki?" *Voprosy istorii KPSS*, no. 4 (1989): 91–98.

Karpeev, I. V. "Kontrrazvedyvatel'noe otdelenie." In *Gosudarstvennost' Rossii: Slovar' Spravochnik*. 4 vols. to date. Moscow: Nauka, 1996–2001.

Khasegava, Ts. "Fevral'skaia revoliutsiia: Konsensus issledovatalei?" In *1917 god v sud'bakh Rossii i mira: Fevral'skaia revoliutsiia ot novykh istochnikov k novomu osmysleniiu*, ed. P. V. Volobuev et al. Moscow: Institut rossiiskoi istorii RAN, 1997.

Khaziakhmetov, E. Sh. "Organizatsiia pobegov politicheskikh ssyl'nykh iz Sibiri v 1906–1917 godakh." *Ssylka i obshchestvenno-politicheskaia zhizn' (XVIII–XX v.)*, ed. L. M. Goriushkin. Novosibirsk: Nauka, 1978.

———. "Polozhenie politicheskikh ssyl'nykh Sibiri mezhdu revoliutsiiami 1905 i fevralia 1917 gg." *Ssyl'nye revoliutsionery v Sibiri (XIX v.–fevral' 1917 g.)*. Vol. 2. Irkutsk: Irkutskii gos. universitet, 1974.

Kimerling, Elise. "Civil Rights and Social Policy in Soviet Russia, 1918–1936." *Russian Review* 41 (January 1982): 24–46.

Kir'ianov, Iu. I. "Pravye partii v Rossii nakanune i v fevral'sko-martovskie dni 1917: Prichiny krizisa i khrakha." In *1917 god v sud'bakh Rossii i mira: Fevral'skaia revoliutsiia ot novykh istochnikov k novomu osmysleniiu*, ed. P. V. Volobuev et al. Moscow: Institut rossiiskoi istorii RAN, 1997.

Koehler, John O. *Stasi: The Untold Story of the East German Secret Police*. Boulder, Colo.: Westview, 1999.

Kolonitskii, B. I. "Politicheskaia pornografiia' i desakralizatsiia vlasti v gody pervoi mirovoi voiny: Slukhi i massovaia kul'tura." In *1917 god v sud'bakh Rossii i mira: Oktiabr'skaia revoliutsiia: Ot novykh istochnikov k novomu osmysleniiu*, ed. S. V. Tiutiukin et al. Moscow: Institut rossiiskoi istorii RAN, 1998.

Kornev, V. V. "II Gosudarstvennaia duma: Sotsial-demokratiia i krakh kadetskogo konstitutsionalizma." *Voprosy istorii KPSS*, no. 4 (1991): 139–54.

Kozlova, K. V., and V. I. Startsev. "Nikolai Vissarionovich Nekrasov—radikal'nyi politik, 1905–1917 gg." *Iz glubiny vremen* 7 (1996): 79–100.

Koznov, A. P. "A fakty govoriat ob odnom." *Voprosy istorii KPSS*, no. 2 (1991): 151–55.

———. "Bor'ba bol'shevikov s podryvnymyi aktsiiami tsarskoi okhranki v 1910–1914 gg." *Voprosy istorii KPSS*, no. 9 (1988): 59–74.

———. "Metamorfozy politicheskogo detektiva: Komu sluzhil L. P. Men'shchikov." *Kentavr*, no. 4 (1993): 115–28.

Krivoshein, K. A. *A. V. Krivoshein (1857–1921 g.): Ego znachenie v istorii Rossii nachala XX veka*. Paris: n.p., 1973.

Krupina, T. D. "Politicheskii krizis 1915 g. i sozdanie Osobogo soveshchaniia po oborone." *Istoricheskie zapiski* 83 (1969): 58–75.

Kulikov, S. V. "Vysshaia tsarskaia biurokratiia i Imperatorskii dvor nakanune padeniia monarkhii." *Iz glubiny vremen* 11 (1999): 21–108.

Lambroza, Shlomo. "The Pogroms of 1903–1906." In *Pogroms: Anti-Jewish Violence in Modern Russian History*, ed. John D. Klier and Shlomo Lambroza. Cambridge: Cambridge University Press, 1992.

Laporte, Maurice. *Histoire de l'okhrana: La police secrete des tsars, 1880–1917*. Paris: Payot, 1935.

Lauchlan, Iain. *Russian Hide-and-Seek: The Tsarist Secret Police in St. Petersburg, 1906–1914*. Helsinki: Finnish Literature Society, 2002.

Laverychev, V. Ia. *Tsarizm i rabochii vopros v Rossii (1861–1917 gg.)*. Moscow: Mysl', 1972.

Leggett, George. *The Cheka: Lenin's Political Police*. Oxford: Clarendon, 1981.

Leiberov, I. P. "V. I. Lenin i Petrogradskaia organizatsiia bol'shevikov v period mirovoi voiny (1914–1916 gg.)." *Voprosy istorii KPSS*, no. 5 (1960): 65–79.

Leonov, M. I. *Partiia sotsialistov-revoliutsionerov v 1905–1907 gg.* Moscow: Rosspen, 1997.

Levin, Alfred. "Petr Arkad'evich Stolypin: A Political Appraisal." *The Journal of Modern History* 37 (1965): 445–63.

———. "Russian Bureaucratic Opinion in the Wake of the 1905 Revolution." *Jahrbücher für Geschichte Osteuropas* 11 (1963): 1–12.

———. *The Second Duma: A Study of the Social-Democratic Party and the Russian Constitutional Experiment.* 2nd ed. Hamden, Conn.: Archon, 1966.

———. "The Shornikova Affair." *The Slavonic and East European Review*, American series 2, vol. 21 (November 1943): 1–18.

Lieven, Dominic. "Bureaucratic Authoritarianism in Late Imperial Russia: The Personality, Career, and Opinions of P. N. Durnovo." *The Historical Journal* 26 (1983): 391–402.

Likhomanov, A. V. *Bor'ba samoderzhaviia za obshchestvennoe mnenie v 1905–1907 godakh.* St. Petersburg: Rossiiskaia natsional'naia biblioteka, 1997.

Lin'kov, I. I., V. A. Nikitin, and O. A. Khodenkov, eds. *Gosudarstvennye deiateli Rossii XIX–nachala XX v.: Biograficheskii spravochnik.* Moscow: Izd. MGU, 1995.

Loginov, V. T. "Lenin i 'Pravda.'" In *Bol'shevistskaia pechat' i rabochii klass Rossii v gody revoliutsionnogo pod"ema, 1910–1914.* Moscow: Nauka, 1965.

Lur'e, F. M. "Azef i Lopukhin." *Neva*, no. 9 (1990): 164–76.

———. *Politseiskie i provokatory.* St. Petersburg: Chas Pik, 1992.

Lur'e, F. M., and Z. I. Peregudova. "Tsarskaia okhranka i provokatsiia." *Iz glubiny vremen* 1 (1992): 51–83.

McDaniel, Tim. *Autocracy, Capitalism, and the Revolution in Russia.* Berkeley: University of California Press, 1988.

McKean, Robert B. "The Bureaucracy and the Labour Problem, June 1907–February 1917." In *New Perspectives in Modern Russian History*, ed. Robert B. McKean. New York: St. Martin's, 1992.

———. "Constitutional Russia." *Revolutionary Russia* 9 (June 1996): 33–42.

———. *St. Petersburg between the Revolutions: Workers and Revolutionaries, June 1907–February 1917.* New Haven: Yale University Press, 1990.

McReynolds, Louise. *The News under Russia's Old Regime: The Development of a Mass-Circulation Press.* Princeton, N.J.: Princeton University Press, 1991.

Melancon, Michael. "'Marching Together!': Left Bloc Activities in the Russian Revolutionary Movement, 1900 to February 1917." *Slavic Review* 49 (Summer 1990): 239–52.

———. "The Ninth Circle: The Lena Goldfield Workers and the Massacre of 4 April 1912." *Slavic Review* 53 (Fall 1994): 766–95.

Mikhailov, N. V. *Sovet bezrabotnykh i rabochie Peterburga v 1906–1907 gg.* Moscow: Rossiiskaia akademiia nauk, 1998.

———. "V. S. Voitinskii i peterburgskie rabochie v gody Pervoi rossiiskoi revoliutsii." In *Intelligentsiia i rossiiskoe obshchestvo v nachale XX veka.* St. Petersburg: Sankt-Peterburgskii filial Instituta rossiiskoi istorii, 1996.

Mints, I. I. "Revoliutsionnaia bor'ba proletariata Rossii v 1914–1916 godakh." *Voprosy istorii*, no. 11 (1959): 59–61.

Miroliubov, A. A. "Dokumenty po istorii Departamenta politsii perioda pervoi mirovoi voiny." *Sovetskie arkhivy*, no. 3 (1988): 80–83.

Mironenko, S. V. , and Gregory L. Freeze, eds. *Putevoditel'.* Vol. 1: *Fondy Gosudarstvennogo arkhiva Rossiiskoi Federatsii po istorii Rossii XIX–nachala XX vv.* Moscow: Blagovest, 1994.

Morozov, K. N. *Partiia sotsialistov-revoliutsionerov v 1907–1914 gg.* Moscow: Rosspen, 1998.

Mulukaev, R. S. *Politsiia v Rossii (IX v.–nach XX v.)* Nizhnii Novgorod, 1993.

Narbutov, R. B. "Proekt razvitiia politseiskikh organov Rossii 1907 goda." *Sovetskoe gosudarstvo i pravo,* no. 11 (1990): 125–33.

Narskii, I. V. "Paradoks avtoritarnoi povsednevnosti: Vzaimootnosheniia levoradikal'noi oppozitsii i vlasti v Rossii nachala XIX v. na lokal'nom urovne: Po ural'skim materialam." *Istoricheskie nauki—Vestnik cheliabinskogo gosudarstvennogo pedagogicheskogo instituta* 1 (1995): 50–62.

Nelipovich, S. "V poiskakh 'vnutrennego vraga': Deportatsionnaia politika Rossii, 1914–1917. In vol. 1 of *Pervaia mirovaia voina i uchastie v nei Rossii (1914–1918): Materialy nauchnoi konferentsii.* 2 vols. Moscow: Voennaia byl', 1994.

Neuberger, Joan. *Hooliganism: Crime, Culture, and Power in St. Petersburg, 1900–1914.* Berkeley: University of California Press, 1993.

Nikolaev, P. N., et al., eds. *Russkie pisateli, 1800–1917: Biograficheskii slovar'.* 4 vols. to date. Moscow: Sovetskaia entsiklopediia, 1989–1999.

Novikova, N. "Velikoe kniazhestvo Finliandskoe v imperskoi politike Rossii." In *Imperskii stroi Rossii v regional'nom izmerenii (XIX–nachalo XX veka): Sbornik nauchnykh statei,* ed. P. I. Savel'ev. Moscow: Moskovskii obshchestvennyi nauchnyi fond, 1997.

Ostroumov, S. S. "Repressii tsarskogo pravitel'stva protiv revoliutsionnogo dvizhenia v Rossii v period imperializma: Ugolovno-statisticheskoe issledovanie." *Vestnik moskovskogo universiteta. Pravo,* series 12, no. 3 (1976): 35–42.

Ostrovskii, A. V. "Ostorozhno, Masony." *Iz glubiny vremen* 6 (1996): 163–73.

Otechestvennaia istoriia: Istoriia Rossii s drevneishikh vremen do 1917 goda: Entsiklopediia. Moscow: Bol'shaia Rossiiskaia entsiklopediia, 1994.

Papadatos, Pierre A. *Le délit politique: Contribution à l'étude des crimes contre l'État.* Preface by Jean Graven. Geneva: Librairie E. Droz, 1954.

Pavlov, D. B. *Esery-maksimalisty v pervoi rossiiskoi revoliutsii.* Moscow: Izd. Vsesoiuznogo zaochnogo politekhnicheskogo instituta, 1989.

Payne, Howard C. *The Police State of Louis Napoleon Bonaparte, 1851–1860.* Seattle: University of Washington Press, 1966.

Peregudova, Z. I. "Biblioteka revoliutsionnykh izdanii Departamenta politsii." In *Gosudarstvennye uchrezhdeniia i obshchestvennye organizatsii SSSR: Istoriia i sovremennost': Mezhvuzovskii sbornik.* Moscow: Moskovskii gosudarstvennyi istoriko-arkhivnyi institut, 1985.

———. "Deiatel'nost' komissii Vremennogo pravitel'stva i sovetskikh arkhivov po raskrytiiu sekretnoi agentury tsarskoi okhranki." *Otechestvennye arkhivy,* no. 5 (1998): 10–22.

———. *Nesostoiavshaiasia reforma politsii: Po materialam Komissii senatora A. A. Makarova.* Vol. 14. Moscow: Glavnyi informatsionnyi tsentr MVD Rossii, 1992.

———. *Politicheskii sysk Rossii, 1880–1917.* Moscow: Rosspen, 2000.

———. "Prizhiznennye izdaniia V. I. Lenina v kollektsii nelegal'nykh izdanii Ts-GAOR." In *Politicheskaia ssylka i revoliutsionnoe dvizhenie v Rossii: Konets XIX–nachalo XX v.: Sbornik nauchnykh trudov,* ed. L. M. Goriushkin. Novosibirsk: Nauka, Sibirskoe otdelenie, 1988.

————. "Sluzhba naruzhnogo nabliudeniia v russkoi politsii." In *Gosudar', Gosudarstvo, Gosudarstvennaia sluzhba.* Vol. 1 of *Reka vremen.* Moscow: Ellis Lak/Reka Vremen, 1995.

————. "Vazhnyi istochnik po istorii revoliutsionnogo dvizheniia: Kollektsiia perliustratsii GARF SSSR." In *Istoricheskii opyt Velikogo Oktiabria: K 90–letiiu akademika I. I. Mintsa.* Moscow: Nauka, 1986.

Pipes, Richard. *Russia under the Old Regime.* New York: Charles Scribner's Sons, 1974.

————. *The Russian Revolution.* New York: Vintage, 1990.

Platonov, Oleg. *Ternovyi venets Rossii: Tainaia istoriia masonstva, 1731–2000.* 3rd ed. Moscow: Russkii Vestnik, 2000.

Polianskii, N. N. *Tsarskie voennye sudy v bor'be s revoliutsiei, 1905–1907 gg.* Moscow: Izd. Moskovskogo universiteta, 1958.

Politicheskie partii Rossii, konets XIX–pervaia tret' XX veka: Entsiklopediia. Moscow: Rosspen, 1996.

Ponomarev, B.N., ed. *Partiia bol'shevikov v bor'be za sverzhenie tsarizma, 1904–fevral' 1917 goda.* Vol. 2 of *Istoriia kommunisticheskoi partii Sovetskogo soiuza v shesti tomakh.* 6 vols. Ed. P. N. Pospelov. Moscow: Izd. politicheskoi literatury, 1966.

Porter, Bernard. *The Origins of the Vigilant State: The London Metropolitan Police Special Branch before the First World War.* London: Weidenfeld and Nicolson, 1987.

Praisman, L. G. *Terroristy i revoliutsionery, okhranniki i provokatory.* Moscow: Rosspen, 2001.

Pravilova, E. A. "Administrativnaia iustitsiia v poreformennoi Rossii." *Angliiskaia naberezhnaia 4: Ezhegodnik* (1997): 177–94.

Pushkareva, I. M. *Rabochee dvizhenie v Rossii v period reaktsii, 1907–1912 gg.* Moscow: Nauka, 1989.

————. "Rossiiskoe obshchestvo nachala XX v. i individual'nyi politicheskii terror." In *Individual'nyi politicheskii terror v Rossii, XIX–Nachalo XX v.: Materialy konferentsii,* ed. K. N. Morozov et al. Moscow: Memorial, 1996.

————. *Zheleznodorozhniki Rossii v burzhuazno-demokraticheskikh revoliutsiiakh.* Moscow: Nauka, 1975.

Rabe, Volker. *Der Widerspruch von Rechtsstaatlichkeit und strafender Verwaltung in Russland, 1881–1917: Motive, Handhabung und Auswirkungen der administrativen Verbannung von Revolutionären.* Wissenschaftliche Beiträge Karlsruhe. No. 14. Karlsruhe: Verlag M. Wahl, 1985.

Raskin, D. I., et al., eds. *Vysshie i tsentral'nye gosudarstvennye uchrezhdeniia Rossii, 1801–1917.* 4 vols (2 vols. to date). St. Petersburg: Nauka, 1998–2001.

Raskol'nikov, F., ed. "Volneniia vo flote v 1915 godu." *Krasnyi arkhiv* 9 (1925): 94–103.

Rawson, Donald C. "The Death Penalty in Late Tsarist Russia: An Investigation of Judicial Procedures." *Russian History* 11 (Spring 1984): 29–52.

————. *Russian Rightists and the Revolution of 1905.* Cambridge, U.K.: Cambridge University Press, 1995.

Riha, Thomas. "Constitutional Developments in Russia." In *Russia under the Last Tsar,* ed. Theofanis George Stavrou. Minneapolis: University of Minnesota Press, 1969.

Robbins, Richard G. "Vladimir Dzhunkovskii: Witness for the Defense." *Kritika* 2 (Summer 2001): 635–54.

Rogger, Hans. "Russia in 1914." *Journal of Contemporary History* 1 (October 1966): 95–119.

Romanov, V. V. *Na strazhe Rossiiskoi monarkhii: Politicheskaia politsiia Povolzh'ia v 1905–1907 gg.* Ul'ianovsk: Ul'ianovskii gos. universitet, 1999.

Romanov, V. V., and G. B. Romanova. *Zakat politicheskoi politsii rossiiskoi imperii: Likvidatsiia podrazdelenii Otdel'nogo korpusa zhandarmov v Simbirskoi gubernii v 1917–kontse 20–x gg. XX v.* Ul'ianovsk: Ul'ianovskii gos. universitet, 2000.

Roosa, Ruth Amende. *Russian Industrialists in an Era of Revolution: The Association of Industry and Trade, 1906–1917,* ed. Thomas C. Owen. Armonk, N.Y.: M. E. Sharpe, 1997.

Rozental', I. S. "Stranitsy zhizni generala Dzhunkovskogo." *Kentavr,* no. 1 (1994): 90–103.

Ruud, Charles A. *Russian Entrepreneur: Publisher Ivan Sytin of Moscow, 1851–1934.* Montreal: McGill-Queens University Press, 1992.

Ruud, Charles A., and Sergei A. Stepanov. *Fontanka, 16: The Tsars' Secret Police.* Montreal: McGill-Queens University Press, 1999.

Schapiro, Leonard. *The Communist Party of the Soviet Union.* New York: Random House, 1959.

Schleifman, Nurit. *Undercover Agents in the Russian Revolutionary Movement: The SR Party, 1902–1914.* London: Macmillan, 1988.

Shatsillo, K. F. "Lenskii rasstrel i tsarskoe pravitel'stvo: Po materialam Chrezvychainoi sledstvennoi komissii Vremennogo pravitel'stva." In *Bol'shevistskaia pechat' i rabochii klass Rossii v gody revoliutsionnogo pod"ema, 1910–1914.* Moscow: Nauka, 1965.

Shcherbakov, N. N. "Chislennost' i sostav politicheskikh ssyl'nykh v Sibiri, 1907–1917 gg." *Ssyl'nye revoliutsionery v Sibiri (XIX v.–fevral' 1917 g.).* Vol. 1. Irkutsk: Irkutskii gos. universitet, 1973.

———. "Iz istorii suda i vysylki v Sibir' rukovoditelei vooruzhennkh vosstanii i chlenov voenno-boevykh organizatsii RSDRP." *Ssyl'nye revoliutsionery v Sibiri (XIX v.–fevral' 1917 g.).* Vol. 2. Irkutsk: Irkutskii gos. universitet, 1974.

Shilov, D. N., ed. *Gosudarstvennye deiateli Rossiiskoi imperii, 1802–1917: Biobibliograficheskii spravochnik.* St. Petersburg: Dmitrii Bulanin, 2001.

Shishkin, Oleg. *Ubit' Rasputina.* Moscow: OLMS-PRESS, 2000.

Shub, David. *Lenin: A Biography.* 1948. Reprint, New York: Pelican, 1966.

Sidorova, Maria Viktorovna. "Istoriki s Fontanki, 16." *Otechestvennye arkhivy,* no. 4 (1993): 40–47.

Solodkov, T. *Bol'shevistskaia gazeta "Pravda" v Belorussii (1912–1917 gg.).* 2nd ed. Minsk: Belarus', 1972.

Startsev, V. I. *Russkoe politicheskoe masonstvo nachala XX veka.* St. Petersburg: Tret'ia Rossiia, 1996.

Stepanov, S. A. *Chernaia sotnia v Rossii (1905–1914 gg.).* Moscow: Rosvuznauka, 1992.

———. *Zagadki ubiistva Stolypina.* Moscow: Progress-Akademiia, 1995.

Stepanskii, A. D. *Samoderzhavie i obshchestvennye organizatsii Rossii na rubezhe XIX–XX vv. Uchebnoe posobie po spetskursu.* Ed. N. P. Eroshkin. Moscow: Tip. Glavarkhiva SSSR, 1980.

Svatikov, S. G. "Sozdanie 'Sionskikh protokolov' po dannym ofitsial'nogo sledstviia." In *Evrei i russkaia revoliutsiia: Materialy i issledovaniia,* ed. O. V. Budnitskii. Moscow: Gesharim, 1999.

Swain, Geoffrey R. "Freedom of Association and the Trade Unions, 1906–14." In *Civil Rights in Imperial Russia,* ed. Olga Crisp and Linda Edmondson. Oxford: Clarendon, 1989.

————. *Russian Social Democracy and the Legal Labour Movement, 1906–14*. London: Macmillan, 1983.

Sypchenko, A. V. *Narodno-sotsialisticheskaia partiia v 1907–1917 gg.* Moscow: Rosspen, 1999.

Thurston, Robert W. *Liberal City, Conservative State: Moscow and Russia's Urban Crisis, 1906–1914*. New York: Oxford University Press, 1987.

Tiutiukin, S. V. *G. V. Plekhanov: Sud'ba russkogo marksista*. Moscow: Rosspen, 1997.

————. *Iul'skii politicheskii krizis 1906 g. v Rossii*. Moscow: Nauka, 1991.

Usherovich, Saul [S.]. *Smertnye kazni v tsarskoi Rossii: K istorii kaznei po politicheskim protsessam s 1824 po 1917 god*. 2nd ed. Khar'kov: Izd. Politkatorzhan, 1933.

Vishnevskii, Edvard. *Liberal'naia oppozitsiia v Rossii nakanune pervoi mirovoi voiny*. Moscow: Rossiia molodaia, 1994.

Vlasov, V. V. "Sozdanie, deiatel'nost' i slom MVD Vremennogo pravitel'stva." *Sovetskie arkhivy*, no. 5 (1983): 45–49.

Volkogonov, Dmitrii. *Stalin: Triumph and Tragedy*. Ed. Harold Shukman. New York: Grove Weidenfeld, 1991.

————. *Trotskii: Politicheskii portret*. 2 vols. Moscow: Novosti, 1992.

Waldron, Peter. "States of Emergency: Autocracy and Extraordinary Legislation, 1881–1917." *Revolutionary Russia* 8 (June 1995): 1–25.

Weissman, Neil B. *Reform in Tsarist Russia: The State Bureaucracy and Local Government, 1900–1914*. New Brunswick, N.J.: Rutgers University Press, 1981.

Wheatcroft, Stephen G. "The Crisis of the Late Tsarist Penal System." In *Challenging Traditional Views of Russian History*, ed. Stephen G. Wheatcroft. Houndsmills, Basingstroke, Hampshire: Palgrave Macmillan, 2002.

Williams, Robert. *The Other Bolsheviks: Lenin and His Critics, 1904–1914*. Bloomington: Indiana University Press, 1986.

Wortman, Richard S. *Scenarios of Power: Myth and Ceremony in Russian Monarchy*. Vol. 2: *From Alexander II to the Abdication of Nicholas II*. Princeton, N.J.: Princeton University Press, 2000.

Zdanovich, A. A. "Organizatsiia i stanovlenie spetssluzhb Rossiiskogo flota." In *Istoricheskie chteniia na Lubianke, 1997 god: Rossiiskie spetssluzhby: Istoriia i sovremennost'*, ed. A. A. Zdanovich, M. N, Petrov, and V. N. Khaustov. Moscow: Velikii Novgorod, 1999.

Zuckerman, Frederic S. *The Tsarist Secret Police in Russian Society, 1880–1917*. New York: New York University Press, 1996.

Zuev, G. I. "Politicheskii rozysk okhrannogo otdeleniia v rossiiskom flote." *Klio* 2 (1998): 181–85.

Zyrianov, P. N. *Petr Stolypin: Politicheskii portret*. Moscow: Vysshaia shkola, 1992.

INDEX

Italicized page numbers refer to photographs.

Abrosimov, V. M., 211, 215
Academic Club of Moscow, 180
Administrative banishment, 43–44
Administrative binding orders, 68
Administrative exile, 3–4, 22, 41; challenges to, 30; decline of, 147; effects of, 23; incidence of, 72, 147; by military authorities, 162; from Poland, 44; release from, 139; restricting use of, 44, 63, 112, 139; unpopularity of, 222
Administrative officials: and civic activism, 154; and control over trade unions, 26; efforts to limit abuses of, 62–63, 77, 112; increased powers of, during World War I, 160, 214; and interference in Duma elections, 60–61, 73; maintenance of order by, 34, 68; material conditions of, 184; and periodical publications, 25; and regulation of public organizations, 179; and right-wing violence, 39–40; and Ukrainian nationalism 157. See also Officials; Senior officials
Administrative punishments, 3; abolition of, 208; in borderlands, 6; increased case load of, 41; number of, 43, 72; proposed abolition of,

150; restrictions on, 13.
Adrianov, A. A., 169–70
Agafonov, V. K., 210; and number of informants, 213
Agentura. See Informants
Akimov, M. G., 16
Aleksandr Mikhailovich, Grand Duke, 199
Alekseev, B. K., 120
Alekseev, M. V., 199; alleged plot by, 195; and proposal to create military dictatorship, 187; proposed to head government, 204
Alexander Lycée, 19, 176
Alexander II, 3; monument to, 11, 124
Alexander III, 4
Alexander III Historical Museum, 112, 209
Alexandra Fedorovna (empress), 193, 201; alleged attempt on life of, 198; and appointment of A. D. Protopopov, 189; and audience granted to A. T. Vasil'ev, 191; on V. F. Dzhunkovskii, 174; interference of, in government affairs, 191, 194; on A. N. Khvostov, 175, 183; on P. G. Kurlov, 82; and murder of G. E. Rasputin, 196; and Rasputin, 121, 189, 194; and rumors of treason, 184, 195; on N. B. Shcherbatov, 175; unpopularity of, 197
All-Russian Railroad Union, 26. See also Trade unions
Amfiteatrov, A. V., 198
Amnesty: demands for, 30; of political prisoners, 97, 139, 208, 211

Anarchist Party, 59
Anarchists, 125; informants among, 129; and Special Section, 58
Andreev, V. I., 100
Andrei Vladimirovich, Grand Duke, 195
Andronnikov, M. M., 177–78
Anglo-American historians, 221
Anti-German agitation, 168–71
Anti-German pogrom, 168
Anti-Jewish agitation, 170
Anti-Semitism, 123; and Beilis affair, 155–56; within police apparatus, 211
Apartments, secret police, 9, 18, 70, 98, 108, 161
Apteka Island, 174; explosion on, 35, 42; memorial to victims of explosion at, 64
Arbitration chambers for labor disputes, 149
Archives, Russian, xii, 136, 209
Ardov, T., 188
Argunov, A. A., 85, 88, 91
Arkhangel'sk, 54, 165
Armand, I. F., 132
Armenian nationalist movement, 116
Arrests, xi; number of, 41
Article 87 of the Fundamental Laws, 42, 46
Ascher, Abraham: and assessment of Stolypin, 28; and right-wing violence, 64
Austria, 78, 169
Auxiliary agents. *See* Informants
Avksent'ev, N. D., 214, 219
Avrekh, A. Ia.: and dismissal of V. N. Kokovtsov, 156; on